# Setting the Agenda

*Responsible Party Government in the U.S. House of Representatives*

Scholars of the U.S. House of Representatives disagree over the importance of political parties in organizing the legislative process. On the one hand, nonpartisan theories stress how congressional organization serves members' nonpartisan goals. On the other hand, partisan theories argue that the House is organized to serve the collective interests of the majority party. This book advances our partisan theory and presents a series of empirical tests of that theory's predictions (pitted against others). It considers why procedural cartels form, arguing that agenda power is naturally subject to cartelization in busy legislatures. It argues that the majority party has cartelized agenda power in the U.S. House since the adoption of Reed's rules in 1890. The evidence demonstrates that the majority party seizes agenda control at nearly every stage of the legislative process in order to prevent bills that the party dislikes from reaching the floor. Given our empirical evidence, we question the validity of theories that do not take into account the substantial influence of political parties.

Gary W. Cox is a professor of political science at the University of California, San Diego. In addition to numerous articles in the areas of legislative and electoral politics, he is author of *The Efficient Secret* (winner of the Samuel H. Beer dissertation prize in 1983), coauthor of *Legislative Leviathan* (winner of the Richard F. Fenno Prize in 1994), and author of *Making Votes Count: Strategic Coordination in the World's Electoral Systems* (1997), which received the American Political Science Association's awards for the best book in political science (Woodrow Wilson Foundation Award), the best book in comparative politics (Gregory Luebbert Prize), and the best book in political economy. His latest book, *Elbridge Gerry's Salamander,* analyzes the political consequences of the reapportionment revolution in the United States. Cox is a former Guggenheim Fellow and was elected to the American Academy of Arts and Sciences in 1996 and to the National Academy of Sciences in 2005.

Mathew D. McCubbins is the Chancellor's Associates Chair VIII in the Department of Political Science at the University of California, San Diego. He is the coauthor of four other books: *The Logic of Delegation* (1991), winner of the American Political Science Association's 1992 Gladys M. Kammerer Award; *Legislative Leviathan* (1993), winner of the American Political Science Association Legislative Studies Section's 1994 Richard F. Fenno Prize; *The Democratic Dilemma* (Cambridge University Press, 1998); and *Stealing the Initiative* (2000). He is also editor or coeditor of eight additional books and has authored more than seventy-five scientific articles, with one winning the Congressional Quarterly Prize for best article on legislative politics. Professor McCubbins was a Fellow at the Center for Advanced Study in the Behavioral Sciences in 1994–5. He served as a coeditor of the *Journal of Law, Economics & Organization.* He has a B.A. from the University of California, Irvine, and an M.S. and Ph.D. from the California Institute of Technology. Professor McCubbins is a Fellow of the American Academy of Arts and Sciences.

T0370653

# Setting the Agenda

*Responsible Party Government in the U.S. House of Representatives*

GARY W. COX
MATHEW D. McCUBBINS
*University of California, San Diego*

CAMBRIDGE
UNIVERSITY PRESS

CAMBRIDGE UNIVERSITY PRESS
Cambridge, New York, Melbourne, Madrid, Cape Town, Singapore,
São Paulo, Delhi, Dubai, Tokyo, Mexico City

Cambridge University Press
The Edinburgh Building, Cambridge CB2 8RU, UK

Published in the United States of America by Cambridge University Press, New York

www.cambridge.org
Information on this title: www.cambridge.org/9780521619967

First published 2005
Reprinted 2007

*A catalogue record for this publication is available from the British Library*

*Library of Congress Cataloguing in Publication Data*

Cox, Gary W.
Setting the agenda : responsible party government in the U.S.
House of Representatives / Gary W. Cox, Mathew D. McCubbins.
   p. cm.
Includes bibliographical references and index.
ISBN-13: 978-0-521-85379-8 (hardback)
ISBN-10: 0-521-85379-6 (hardback)
ISBN-13: 978-0-521-61996-7 (pbk.)
ISBN-10: 0-521-61996-3 (pbk.)
1. United States. Congress. House. 2. United States. Congress.
House – Committees. 3. United States. Congress. House – Rules and
practice. 4. Political parties – United States. I. McCubbins,
Mathew D. (Mathew Daniel), 1956– II. Title.
JK1410.C695 2005
328.73'072–dc22     2005001319

ISBN 978-0-521-85379-8 Hardback
ISBN 978-0-521-61996-7 Paperback

*To Karen Cox and Sue McCubbins*

# Contents

# Figures and Tables

# Acknowledgments

*Setting the Agenda* is the product of our interest in the role the majority party plays in the U.S. House of Representatives. Throughout the book, we analyze how the majority party seizes agenda control at nearly every stage of the legislative process, in the process arguing that a version of responsible party government can and does exist in our polity. The results, arguments, and conclusions contained within represent countless hours of analyzing data, crafting arguments, and drafting chapters, but, fortunately for us, we were not alone in this process.

We first want to acknowledge the financial support that made this book possible. The National Science Foundation, grant numbers SBR-9422831 and SES-9905224, and the Public Policy Research Project at University of California, San Diego, generously contributed to our data collection and research efforts, and the University of California, San Diego, Committee on Research supported us with various grants throughout the early stages of our research. We owe a debt of gratitude to each of these institutions.

We also acknowledge those colleagues and friends who graciously shared their data. David Rohde's and Keith Poole's datasets were invaluable to our research, and we also benefited tremendously from the data that Garrison Nelson, Howard Rosenthal, Robert Hennig, and Greg Wawro made available to us. Such contributions and generosity made possible many of the results that we present throughout this book.

We presented portions of this book at many conferences and seminars, where we received comments for which we are also grateful. Two seminars in particular – the legislative politics seminar at Washington University, led by Steven Smith, Randy Calvert, and Gary Miller, and a week-long seminar at the Center for Behavioral Research in the Social Sciences at Harvard – were particularly helpful to us in revising and improving upon an earlier manuscript of the book. We owe special thanks to Jim Alt for hosting the latter seminar and for providing us with an invaluable opportunity to present our work, and we are also grateful for the feedback of the seminar participants who trudged through the snow and record-low temperatures to attend our presentations: Jim Alt, Ken Shepsle, Rebecca Morton, Thomas Romer, Jim Snyder, Greg Wawro, Eric Schickler, Keith Poole, John Londregan, and Walter Mebane.

We also received comments and suggestions from many people at our home institution, University of California, San Diego, and we owe a great deal to our dedicated research assistants: Scott Basinger, Adriana Bejan, Cheryl Boudreau, Andrea Campbell, Chris Den Hartog, Joel Johnson, Nathan Monroe, and Nick Weller.

**Setting the Agenda**

*Responsible Party Government in the U.S. House of Representatives*

# 1

# Introduction

Modern democracy is unthinkable save in terms of the parties.

– Schattschneider 1942

The party system that is needed must be democratic, responsible and effective – a system that is accountable to the public, respects and expresses differences of opinion, and is able to cope with the great problems of modern government.

– American Political Science Association 1950

Thus, if the parties were in trouble, so too was democracy.

– White 1992

## I.I. INTRODUCTION

For democracy in a large republic to succeed, many believe that responsible party government is needed, with each party offering voters a clear alternative vision regarding how the polity should be governed and then, if it wins the election, exerting sufficient discipline over its elected members to implement its vision (cf. Ranney 1951; American Political Science Association 1950). America was once thought to have disciplined and responsible parties. Indeed, students of nineteenth-century American politics saw parties as the principal means by which a continental nation had been brought together: "There is a sense in which our parties may be said to have been our real body politic. Not the authority of Congress, not the leadership of the President, but the discipline and zest of parties has held us together, has made it possible for us to form and to carry out national programs" (Wilson 1908: 218, 221; cf. Bryce 1921: 119).

Since early in the twentieth century, however, critics of American politics have often argued that congressional parties are largely moribund. Some contend that they have become nothing more than labels for like-minded politicians who act together when they agree but otherwise pursue their own agendas and careers (Mayhew 1974). A chorus of critics depict members of Congress as dedicated to the pursuit of graft, campaign contributions, and the emoluments of office and as captured by interest groups who seek to turn public policy into private favors (McConnell 1966; Fiorina 1977a; Weingast, Shepsle, and Johnson 1981; Buchanan 1968; Becker 1983; Stigler 1971; Lowi 1969; Schattschneider 1960; for surveys see Cox and McCubbins 1993, Chapter 1, and Munger and Mitchell 1991).

Even though Congress does suffer from many infirmities, we will argue that a hitherto unrecognized form of responsible party government has characterized U.S. politics since the late nineteenth century. As in the traditional view of responsible party government, our theory depicts congressional parties as electorally accountable and legislatively responsible, at least to an important degree. We differ from the traditional view, however, in at least two ways.

First, whereas traditional theories stress the majority party's ability to marshal a cohesive voting bloc as the source of its legislative power, our theory stresses the majority party's ability to set the agenda as the key to its success. The importance of this distinction can be suggested by recalling that the most prominent line of criticism of partisan theories focuses directly on the issue of voting cohesion.

Many prominent scholars, including Schattschneider (1942: 131–2), Mayhew (1974), and Kalt and Zupan (1990), view legislators' votes as driven primarily by their constituents' and their own opinions, with partisan considerations playing a distinctly secondary role. Building on such views, Krehbiel (1993, 1998) argues that the two parties' attempts to influence votes either are negligible or cancel each other out.

If, as these theories suggest, party pressures cancel out, however, then the majority party cannot marshal its troops effectively, as required by traditional theorists of responsible party governance. Instead of being driven toward the platform promises of the majority party by the force of its discipline, policies in Congress will be driven to the center of congressional opinion by the logic of the famous median voter theorem.

If one accepts the traditional view that parties are strong only to the extent that they can affect their members' behavior on substantive votes, and if one views congressional votes as positioning policy along a single left-right continuum, then Krehbiel's argument is persuasive. In particular, given these two assumptions, majority parties matter only if they can secure nonmedian policy outcomes, and, in order to do this, they must engage in the unenviable and unlikely-to-succeed task of regularly pressuring their centrist members to vote against their constituents' and/or their own opinions.

Our emphasis on agenda control deflects this canonical criticism of partisan theories in the following way. We do not model voting in Congress as if there were a single vote on a single dimension (per the standard unidimensional spatial model); rather, we envision a series of votes on different issues. This opens up the possibility that, even if the majority party were unable to secure a nonmedian outcome on any given issue considered in isolation – a debatable premise – it might nonetheless greatly affect the overall legislative outcome if it prevents some issues from being voted on at all.

FIGURE 1.1. Illustration of leftward and rightward policy moves

To see how agenda-setting power can affect legislative outcomes, imagine a newly elected Congress and the set of existing government policies – label them $q_1, \ldots, q_n$ – that it faces. Each of these policies could in principle be adjusted, sliding them further to the left or right (e.g., less stringent or more stringent regulation of abortion). The newly elected members of the House have opinions regarding how each of the $n$ policies should ideally be positioned along their respective left–right dimensions. Denote the center of congressional opinion (the median ideal position) regarding each policy by $F_1, \ldots, F_n$ for the $n$ policies.

Note that one can divide the existing government policies into two main categories, depending on the relationship between the legislative median, $F_j$, and the status quo, $q_j$. In one category are policies that lie to the left of the current center of congressional opinion, $q_j < F_j$. If the House votes on a bill to change such a policy from the status quo (e.g., $q_j^L$ in Figure 1.1) to the floor median, $F_j$, the result will be a *rightward* policy move. In the second main category are policies that lie to the right of the current center of congressional opinion, $q_j > F_j$. If the House votes on a bill to change such a policy from the status quo (e.g., $q_j^R$ in Figure 1.1) to the floor median, $F_j$, the result will be a *leftward* policy move.

Now suppose in this simple example that Democratic majorities can block bills that propose rightward policy moves from reaching votes on the floor, thereby killing them without the necessity of a clear floor vote on the bill itself. The Democrats' blocking actions might take many forms, such as a chair refusing to schedule hearings, a committee voting not to report, the Rules Committee refusing to report a special rule, or the speaker delaying a particular bill. Each of these actions might in principle be appealed to the floor and reversed via a series of floor votes. It is a maintained assumption of our approach that the transaction costs involved in such appeals are typically so high (see Chapter 4) that the majority's delaying tactics are effective in killing (or forcing changes in) the bills they target.[1] To the extent that they are successful, the Democrats will produce a legislative agenda on which *every bill actually considered on the*

---

[1] We view "remote majoritarian" arguments (e.g., the argument that the discharge procedure guarantees that any floor majority wishing to extract a particular bill from committee can do so) as establishing interesting theoretical benchmarks, not as empirically defensible models. In our view, such arguments are somewhat similar to the Coase theorem (another argument that explicitly relies on an assumption of zero transaction costs).

*floor proposes to move policy leftward.* As a natural consequence, a majority of Democrats will support every bill.

This example, we hasten to add, overstates what our theory actually predicts (e.g., there are rightward policy moves that even the Democrats would like to make and, similarly, leftward policy moves that even the Republicans would support, when the status quo is extreme enough). Nonetheless, the discussion so far suffices to illustrate the potential power of a minimal form of agenda control (just the power to block) and makes clear that our theory sidesteps critiques that focus on the debility of party influence over floor votes (such as Krehbiel's). We can deny both the notion that parties must secure nonmedian outcomes issue by issue in order to matter and the notion that parties must exert discipline over how their members vote on bills in order to matter.[2] Agenda control alone suffices – if it can be attained – to exert a tremendous influence over policy outcomes.

In sum, traditional theories of responsible party government see a Democratic (or Republican) majority as mattering because the majority can marshal its troops *on a given issue* and thereby attain policy outcomes that differ from those preferred by the median legislator *on that issue.* Aldrich and Rohde's theory of conditional party government shares this perspective: "most partisan theories would yield the expectation that the majority party would have sufficient influence...to skew outcomes away from the center of the whole floor and toward the policy center of [majority] party members" (Aldrich and Rohde 1995: 7). Such theories are vulnerable to Krehbiel's critique and its predecessors. In contrast, our theory sees a Democratic (respectively, Republican) majority as mattering because the majority can prevent reconsideration of status quo policies lying to the left (respectively, to the right) of the current median legislator on a given policy dimension – thereby filling the agenda mostly with bills proposing leftward (respectively, rightward) policy moves.

We should add that we do not view American parties as incapable of disciplining their troops. Indeed, we believe they regularly seek additional support on close votes, employing both carrots and sticks in the process. Such efforts can even lead to nonmedian outcomes on particular issues (typically via procedural maneuvers, such as closed rules, rather than by outvoting the opposition on the merits). However, the majority party's efforts on the floor are designed to *complement* whatever degree of agenda manipulation has already occurred by corralling a few votes on the margin, not to coerce moderate members to cast risky votes in order to maximize party cohesion. Picking which bills will be

---

[2] In the example just given, we can assume that every bill actually considered simply moves policy to the legislative median and that the parties exert nil influence on their members' votes on final passage. Even with these assumptions, the conclusion remains – in the example – that a Democratic House will only be allowed to consider leftward policy moves. Thus, all policy changes actually made will be leftward – a very important policy effect achieved without securing nonmedian outcomes on any given dimension and without party influence over members' votes on bills. Our theory does require that the majority party is able to control the outcomes of key procedural votes, and this may entail influencing their members' behavior on such votes.

voted on at all – that is, which status quo policies will be at risk of change – is the primary technique; garnering enough votes to eke out a victory is important but secondary.

A second way in which our theory differs from traditional notions of responsible party government is that the latter stress the enactment of new policies – as promised in the party platforms – as the main normative criterion by which one should judge whether party government is operating successfully. In contrast, our theory stresses the avoidance of party-splitting issues, hence the preservation of some existing policies, as the key to the political survival of majority parties (whatever its normative merits).

We do not claim that parties cannot or do not compile positive records of accomplishment and are restricted merely to the preservation of portions of the status quo. Even the most heterogeneous majorities in congressional history, such as the Democrats of the 1950s, were able to agree on a number of new legislative goals and accomplish them. Thus, we have argued previously (Cox and McCubbins 1993), and will argue again in Chapter 10, that control of the legislative agenda can also be translated into the enactment of some or all of the majority party's platform. However, as we explain in Chapter 10, the majority's success in changing policies, unlike its success in preserving policies, depends on its internal homogeneity.

Another way to frame this second difference is to say that we envision two stories in the edifice of party government, not just one. The first, or bedrock, story involves securing a super-proportional share of offices for the party's senior members, imposing a minimal (primarily negative) fiduciary standard on those senior officeholders, and thereby ensuring that the party collectively is able to prevent items from appearing on the floor agenda. The second, or super-structural, story consists of enhancing the ability of the party's officeholders to push (as opposed to preventing) bills, imposing a more demanding fiduciary standard upon them (one requiring that they use their new powers for the collective benefit) and thereby enhancing the party's collective ability to push items onto the floor agenda.

By shifting the terms of debate from the majority party's ability to marshal its troops on a given issue to the majority party's ability to decide which issues are voted on to begin with, and from the majority party's ability to change policies to its ability to preserve policies, we seek to provide a new theoretical grounding for partisan theories of congressional organization – and to defend it empirically. In what follows, we will show that our theory explains important features of the postbellum history of the U.S. House of Representatives extremely well. To set the stage for that demonstration, in this chapter we provide a précis of our theory and outline the remaining chapters.

## I.2. A PRÉCIS OF PROCEDURAL CARTEL THEORY

There are two main approaches in the literature on congressional organization. One view stresses how well congressional organization serves members' nonpartisan goals. For example, the House is declared well organized to (1) promote the reelection of its members (Mayhew 1974, 1991; Shepsle and Weingast 1984c), (2) make gains from legislative trade possible (Weingast and Marshall 1988), (3) make specialization and the efficient generation of information possible (Gilligan and Krehbiel 1989, 1990), and (4) aid in bargaining with the other chamber or other branches of government (Diermeier and Myerson 1999; Epstein and O'Halloran 1999). Political parties are explicitly denied a consequential role in these theories.

On the other hand, a new generation of partisan theories argues that the House is well organized to serve the collective interests of the majority party (Cooper 1970; Cooper and Brady 1981; Sinclair 1983, 1995; Stewart 1989; Kiewiet and McCubbins 1991; Cox and McCubbins 1993; Maltzman and Smith 1994; Binder 1997; Evans and Oleszek 2002; Gamm and Smith 2002). One variant of partisan theory, known as the *conditional party government* model (Rohde 1991; Aldrich 1995; Aldrich and Rohde 2001), focuses on how the majority party leadership's powers expand as the members they lead become more alike in political preference (and more different from the opposition) – leading ultimately to greater voting discipline and thus to greater success in legislating for the majority. Another variant, while accepting a version of the conditional party government thesis, focuses on an array of procedural advantages enjoyed by the majority party that are not conditional on its internal homogeneity. We call this variant "procedural cartel theory" (Cox and McCubbins 1993, 1994, 2002), the key aspect of which is the majority party's use of agenda control to achieve its desired outcomes.[3]

While we develop procedural cartel theory at length in Chapter 2 and in *Legislative Leviathan* (1993), here we can briefly note four key claims that distinguish our approach. First, legislative parties arise, we believe, primarily to manage electoral externalities involved in running campaigns in mass electorates. Second, legislative parties are best analogized, we believe, to legal or accountancy partnerships, with various gradations of junior and senior partners. Third, legislative parties – especially in systems where floor voting discipline is costly to secure, as in the United States – specialize in controlling the agenda, rather than in controlling votes. That is, they seek to determine what is voted on to begin with, rather than to dictate their members' votes issue by issue (although they do regularly seek votes on the margin). Fourth, a legislative majority party allocates both negative (delay or veto) rights and positive (accelerating or proposal) rights among its senior partners (and groups thereof), but the mix of such rights changes with the degree of preference homogeneity among the party's members.

To explain the last point, note that there is a trade-off between increasing veto power (and suffering higher negotiation costs in order to do anything) and

---

[3] We provide an extensive survey of the literature on the organization of legislatures with a comparison of the models and analogies they each employ in Cox and McCubbins (2004). One can find this literature review on our web site at *www.settingtheagenda.com*.

increasing proposal power (and suffering higher externalities from the decisions made by those with such power).[4] The more *heterogeneous* the preferences within a given coalition, the more that coalition's partners will wish to limit the proposal rights of other partners, which necessarily entails strengthening their own and others' veto rights. The value of the coalition then comes more and more in keeping certain issues off the agenda and stabilizing the associated status quo policies. The more *homogeneous* the preferences within a given coalition, the more that coalition's partners will agree to expand each other's proposal rights, which necessarily entails weakening their own and others' veto rights. The value of the coalition then comes more and more in pushing certain issues onto the agenda with the hope of changing the associated status quo policies. Regardless of the coalition's homogeneity or lack thereof, regardless of whether its value stems more from stabilizing status quo policies or more from changing status quo policies, it will continue to seize the vast bulk of offices endowed with special agenda-setting rights and thus to cartelize agenda power. In this sense, *party government is not conditional* on the level of agreement within the party; rather, the nature of party government simply changes, from a more progressive vision (implicitly taken to be the only party government worth having in most of the previous literature) to a more conservative vision.[5]

Having stated our inclinations on four important distinctions within the family of partisan theories, we can now diagram the elements of our theory (see Figure 1.2). Reading up from the bottom of the figure, we start with "majority party's control of delegated agenda powers," that is, with its control of the powers inherent in the various offices of the House endowed with such powers (e.g., the speakership and committee chairs). The better the majority party's control of such powers is, the more able will it be to fashion a favorable record of legislative accomplishment, although certainly other factors enter into this as well (such as the party of the president).[6] The more favorable is the majority party's record of legislative accomplishment, the better its reputation or brand name will be, although again there are other factors that affect this, too (such as the president's actions). The better the majority party's brand name, the better will be the prospects for (re)election of its various candidates and the better will be the prospects for (re)attainment of majority status. The senior partners of the majority party care in particular about the latter because their ability to retain their chairs, speakerships, and other offices depends crucially on their party retaining its majority.

---

[4] Such a trade-off was noted long ago, in connection with the question of how large a majority (bare, three fifths, two thirds, etc.) would be optimal, by Buchanan and Tullock (1962).

[5] Our purpose is neither to extol conservatism nor to denigrate progressivism on normative grounds. Rather, we simply wish to point out that preserving the existing status quo can be immensely politically valuable to two or more coalition partners, either when the partners all agree that the status quo is better than available alternatives or when they disagree strongly over how to change that status quo.

[6] Note that a "favorable record" may include both positive achievements (enacting new laws) and negative achievements (protecting old laws).

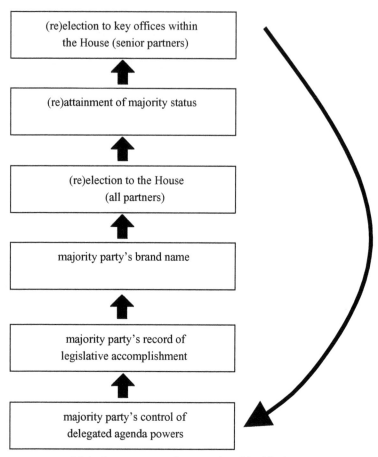

FIGURE I.2. Majority-party agenda control and legislative success

Reading the diagram top-down, instead of bottom-up, one starts with individual members of Congress assumed to care both about (re)election to the House and (re)election to offices within the House. They recognize that (re)election (especially to internal posts) depends crucially on majority status, which in turn depends on maintaining a favorable brand name for the party. Maintaining a favorable brand name, in turn, depends on the party's record of legislative accomplishment, hence on its ability to solve the various cooperation and coordination problems that arise within the legislative process. The party solves these problems primarily by delegating agenda power to its senior partners.

Because the element in this theory that we most wish to stress concerns agenda power, we turn now to a more extended consideration – albeit still abbreviated – of the cartel thesis. The next chapter provides a fuller elaboration of our theory.

## 1.3. THE PROCEDURAL CARTEL THESIS

The broadest thesis of this book, which resonates in many legislatures world-wide, is that *agenda power in busy legislatures is almost always cartelized.* To put it another way, even though voting power in democratic legislatures is everywhere equal, proposal and veto power are everywhere unequal.

What do we mean by agenda power being cartelized in the specific case of the U.S. House? We provide a fuller explanation in the next chapter but for now suffice it to say that the agenda is cartelized when (1) special agenda-setting powers are formally delegated to various offices, such as committee chairs, the speakership, and the Rules Committee; (2) the majority party's members secure most of these offices, so that "agenda-setting services" can be procured only from members of the procedural cartel, just as certain kinds of economic services or goods can be procured only from the relevant economic cartel; and (3) the majority party's "senior partners," who hold these agenda-setting offices, act according to a minimal fiduciary standard – namely, that they do not use their official powers to push legislation that would pass on the floor against the wishes of most in their party.

Note that the features we have just listed also characterize most parliamentary governments (cf. Döring 1995): (1) Special agenda-setting powers are formally delegated to cabinet ministers, presiding officers, and directing boards (the analogs of the U.S. chairs, speaker, majority leader, and Rules Committee, respectively); (2) the governing coalition's members secure most, if not all of these offices (cf. Carroll, Cox, and Pachón 2004); and (3) the governing coalition's "senior partners," who hold these agenda-setting offices, respect a norm according to which no bills are pushed that would split the governing coalition (Tsebelis 2002). It is often true that many parliamentary procedural cartels expect an even greater level of cooperation between their senior partners than would have been expected of U.S. committee chairs during the uneasy alliance of Northern and Southern Democrats in 1937–60. Nonetheless, the structural design of the most basic form of party government is similar across a wide range of systems: break the theoretical equality of legislators by creating a class of agenda-setting offices, ensure that the governing coalition's senior partners secure these offices, and deal with the consequent problems of agency loss and floor discipline, as best the local conditions permit.

The basic design of party government within legislatures admits a trade-off between two costly methods of maintaining the power and advantages of these agenda-setting offices: procedural agenda control and voting discipline. Designing and maintaining rules that establish agenda control is costly; ensuring that members of the majority party vote with the party is also costly. Different legislatures, depending on their circumstances, choose different mixtures of these two costly mechanisms.

The question remains, why should agenda power be cartelized according to this basic recipe, in so many legislatures? Let us sketch out an answer to this question, based on our continuing research in comparative legislative studies

(Amorim Neto, Cox, and McCubbins 2003; Cox, Masuyama, and McCubbins 2000; Carroll et al. 2004; Campbell, Cox, and McCubbins 2002; Den Hartog 2004). We plan to articulate this argument more fully in future work.

Although the details of legislative procedure differ widely across the world's democratic legislatures, one generalization holds universally: Important bills can only pass pursuant to motions formally stated and voted upon in the plenary session.[7] The necessity of acting pursuant to formally stated motions means that every bill must consume at least some plenary time, if it is to have a chance at enactment. Simply put, plenary time is the sine qua non of legislation.

If all legislators have equal access to plenary time, then plenary time is a common pool resource, and rising demand for such time leads to various problems in the legislative process (cf. Cox 1987; Den Hartog 2004; Weingast and Marshall 1988). Can a coalition restrict access to plenary time, enhancing its own members' abilities to propose and block, while diminishing those of the opposition? At a very general level, models such as those of Duggan and Banks (2000), Calvert and Fox (2000), and Diermeier and Feddersen (1998) illustrate how stable restrictions on access to plenary time should be possible, as part of a repeat-game equilibrium. In these models, a majority of members benefit from better access, at the expense of the minority suffering worse access, to plenary time. The majority is held together by the threat that failure to abide by certain norms of behavior (stipulated in equilibrium play) will bring down the coalition, and with it each majority member's superior access to plenary time.

We suggest a somewhat more detailed and concrete recipe by which access to plenary time is restricted. A procedural cartel endows (or inherits) offices with agenda-setting powers, secures those offices for its senior partners, and ensures minimally fiduciary behavior by those senior partners.

How is it that such cartels stick together? In addition to the threat that the whole arrangement can come crashing down, depriving senior members of their offices or stripping those offices of their powers, we would add two additional reasons why access-hogging majorities, once formed, are stable. First, individual nonpivotal legislators in the majority have reason to fear punishment – such as lack of promotion, lack of aid for pet bills, demotion and, ultimately, expulsion from the majority – should they violate crucial norms of behavior (we elaborate such an argument in Cox and McCubbins 1993, 1994). Second, building up a mechanism by which to regulate access to plenary time (creating offices endowed with various special veto and proposal powers and ensuring that one's members secure those offices) entails large fixed costs and very low marginal costs on any particular policy or decision. The large fixed costs arise in creating and maintaining (1) the party's brand name and (2) the rules, procedure, precedent, and interpretation that establish and clarify the powers of agenda-setting offices (on the latter, cf. Chapter 4). To the extent that the parties

---

[7] In Italy, *leggine* (little laws) can be passed directly by committees, without consideration in the plenary session. However, *leggine* and their ilk exist only because the plenary session has delegated authority, and the plenary retains the ability to rescind the authority to emit them.

succeed in establishing themselves as the only viable route to the top offices, they can become very stable indeed.

Assuming that agenda-setting offices exist and that procedural cartels take most of them (but not all, see Chapter 2), why are senior partners subject to the minimal fiduciary standard we suggest, wherein they cannot use their official powers in such a way as to split their party? Note that, if this minimal standard is not imposed, one has a model similar to the committee government model in the United States (cf. Cox and McCubbins 1993, Chapter 1, for a review of the literature) or the ministerial government model in comparative politics (Laver and Shepsle 1996). Agenda power is delegated to offices, and the governing coalition takes most of these offices; however, the occupants of those offices are then free to act as they please. The result is that, if negotiations between chairs/ministers do not suffice to clinch a policy program supported by all, then the logical possibility exists that different chairs/ministers may push bills that a majority of their coalition would unsuccessfully oppose on the floor. We argue that, to avoid such events, the handiwork of chairs/ministers is subject to central screening – by the Rules Committee and majority floor leaders in the United States, and by the cabinet, directing board, and majority in the typical parliamentary system. The central screen helps ensure that chairs/ministers routinely foresee very low chances of success from using their official powers to push bills that would be (a) supported on the floor by most of the opposition and a swing group of the governing coalition and (b) opposed by a majority of their own party.

In our model, chairs/ministers remain free to use their official powers to *block* bills their partners wish to see passed. The only crime is using those powers to *push* bills that then pass despite the opposition of most of the governing coalition. If this crime of commission can be avoided, the majority coalition can determine which status quo policies will be preserved and which will run the risk of being overturned by bills allowed onto the floor.

## I.4. OUTLINE

In the rest of the book, we proceed as follows. Part I (Chapter 2) conveys the logic and intuition of partnerships that cartelize agenda control. In our view, U.S. legislators seek not just reelection but also advancement in the internal hierarchy of posts within the House, good public policy, and majority status for their parties. Their parties compete in mass elections, just as business firms compete in mass markets, by developing brand names. These brand names are public goods to the members of the party, and the value of the brand depends on the party's legislative record of accomplishment. Thus, a key problem for legislative parties is to manage the legislative process, securing the best possible record, hence the best possible brand name or reputation. We also explain how procedural cartels work: how various incentives to "cheat" on the cartel are managed so that the majority party's overall control of the agenda is rarely challenged.

In Part II (Chapters 3 through 9), we examine the consequences of different distributions of agenda power among legislators. We test our Cartel Agenda Model, in which only the majority party wields effective veto power, against two alternatives: a model in which both parties possess veto power (as in the pre–Reed's rules House) and a model in which neither party wields a veto (Floor Agenda Model).

In Chapter 3, we formalize the Cartel Agenda Model (a simplified view of the procedural cartel theory) and the Floor Agenda Model of legislative organization, with a particular focus on who controls the legislative agenda. In the Cartel Agenda Model, one can think of the agenda setter as the majority party leadership, whose reelection incentives ensure a centrist-within-the-majority-party stance. In the Floor Agenda Model, the agenda is determined as if by majority vote on the floor.

Chapter 4 argues that changes in the House rules during the 1880s, culminating in Reed's rules, greatly advantaged the majority party, and that subsequent changes in House rules and organization have not significantly altered that advantage. We show that, after Reed's rules became a permanent part of House organization, over 80 percent of the bills allowed to reach the final-passage stage in a typical Congress proposed to move policy toward the majority party median (as compared to only 57 percent in pre-Reed Congresses).

We examine negative agenda control empirically in Chapter 5. To measure such control, we examine the frequency of majority and minority final-passage *rolls*. Operationally, we say that the party has been *rolled* on a given final passage vote if a majority of its members vote against the bill, but the bill nonetheless passes. Think of a legislative train leaving the station and a party that has tried to stop it – but been run over. We find that the majority party's roll rate is much lower than the minority's roll rate. Moreover, variations in the two parties' roll rates conform to what one would expect under the Cartel Agenda Model, rather than the Floor Agenda Model.

In Chapter 6, we refine our theory by considering the costs the majority party bears when it blocks bills that a majority of the House prefers to the status quo. We note that it will not always be worthwhile to block legislation, particularly if the majority party believes the Senate or president will stop the legislation anyway. From this perspective, *inconsequential* rolls of the majority party (i.e., those that do not lead to enactments) are consistent with the majority controlling the main levers of agenda power. Consequential rolls, however, remain inconsistent with the theory. Empirically, we find that only about one half of all majority rolls were consequential.

The role the Committee on Rules plays in setting the legislative agenda is examined in Chapter 7. To test the majority party's control of the Rules Committee, we examine every vote held in the House on motions to adopt special rules from the 54th to the 105th Congress. We find that the majority party has a lower roll rate than the minority party on such votes, regardless of the particular arrangement of minority, majority, and floor medians.

In Chapter 8, we extend our argument that committee chairs act as agents of the majority party. We find that bills are virtually never reported from committee against the wishes of a majority of the committee's majority party members.

Chapter 9 investigates which direction bills that reach a final-passage vote propose to move policy: to the left or to the right. We show that the proportion of final-passage bills proposing to move policy leftward is significantly related to the location of the majority party median, regardless of which conception of the pivot structure of the House one adopts. This provides the single most compelling test of the various theories that we present in this book. The outcome clearly favors procedural cartel theory.

In Part III, we first examine positive agenda power in Chapter 10. In particular, we examine how varying the homogeneity of preferences within the majority party affects the majority party's ability to enact its agenda. In Chapter 11, we conclude with an overview of our findings and their implications.

# PART I

# WHY PARTY GOVERNMENT?

# 2

# Procedural Cartel Theory

> The job of speaker is not to expedite legislation that runs counter to the wishes of the majority of his majority.
>
> – Speaker Dennis Hastert (R-IL)[1]

In this chapter, we present and discuss the assumptions that undergird procedural cartel theory. To provide a context for comparison, however, we first briefly survey the literature on partisan legislative organization.

## 2.1. THEORIES OF PARTISAN LEGISLATIVE ORGANIZATION

Much of the literature on legislative organization focuses on why political parties are created within legislatures in the first place. We divide extant explanations into those that hinge primarily on the internal legislative payoffs to forming parties and those that hinge primarily on the external electoral payoffs. We then turn to survey the literature on how parties are organized and what parties do.

### 2.1.1. Why Are There Parties in Legislatures?

#### 2.1.1.1. Parties are Created to Solve Internal Collective Action Problems

One line of theorizing about why parties exist is similar to the distributive line of argument regarding committees. Absent any organization (other than a voting rule for floor decisions), legislators face a chaotic and unpredictable agenda. They cannot be sure that the legislature will not vote tomorrow to strip them of benefits conferred today. Nor is it clear how to ensure that the benefits are conferred to begin with, given a world where any legislator can move any amendment at any time.

---

[1] Quoted in Babington (2004).

In order to deal with the unpredictability – and unprofitability – of the unorganized legislature, legislators form political parties to bind themselves together in durable coalitions. Gains from legislative trade that could not be accrued without parties are thus accrued. Probably the clearest exponents of such a view of legislative parties are Schwartz (1977) and Aldrich (1995), but many others similarly stress the purely legislative payoffs to forming a party (e.g., Smith and Gamm 2001; Young 1956).

### 2.1.1.2. *Parties Are Created to Solve External Collective Action Problems*

An alternative theory views legislative parties as being formed primarily to accrue electoral gains. Modern political parties facing mass electorates, similar to modern corporations facing mass markets, have a strong incentive to fashion and maintain a brand name. Such brand names are, however, public goods to all politicians running under the party's label. Thus, parties arise in order to ensure that the usual problems of providing and maintaining public goods are overcome – and in particular to internalize electoral externalities that would otherwise arise. Probably the clearest exponents of this view of legislative parties are Cox and McCubbins (1993), but others (e.g., Kiewiet and McCubbins 1991; Cox 1987; Evans and Oleszek 2002; Strøm 1990) similarly stress how legislative actions can foster valuable collective reputations (brand names) and how politicians take legislative action with an eye to such payoffs.

### 2.1.2. How Are Parties Organized?

If parties exist to solve collective action problems, as seems the main tenet in the literature, then how do they organize to solve these problems? The literature has several suggestions, which we now survey.

### 2.1.2.1. *Parties as Firms*

Many scholars envision parties as being similar to the firms depicted in the literature on industrial organization (cf. Alchian and Demsetz 1972; Tirole 1988), in that they involve delegation to central agents (party leaders) in order to reduce transaction costs and ameliorate collective action problems (e.g., Cooper and Brady 1981; Sinclair 1983, 1995; Stewart 1989; Rohde 1991; Maltzman and Smith 1994; Binder 1997; Cox and McCubbins 1993; Döring 2001; Gamm and Smith 2002). Scholars in this tradition implicitly accept the industrial organization literature's focus on hierarchical firms with single chief executive officers.

### 2.1.2.2. *Parties as Partnerships*

In the case of the political party, we believe a more fruitful analogy is to partnerships, such as law or accountancy firms, in which various gradations of senior partners provide overall strategic and tactical direction to the firm. The "senior partners" in our story – at least as regards the majority party – will be committee and subcommittee chairs, majority party floor leaders, campaign finance committee chairs, and the like. Agenda-setting and other powers are distributed across the offices held by these senior partners rather than fully concentrated in the hands of the speaker, just as the right to recruit new clients and take on new jobs is distributed among the senior partners in a law or accountancy firm, rather than fully concentrated in the hands of the firm's president. Similarly, just as the job of ensuring that no senior partner's actions impinge too unfavorably on a law firm's overall reputation falls not just on the firm's president but also on the other senior partners collectively, so too the job of policing committee chairs falls partly to the speaker and partly to informal politics centered on the party caucus.

### 2.1.3. What Do Parties Do?

Once organized, what do parties do to mitigate the collective action problems that are assumed to be the reason for their existence?

#### 2.1.3.1. Parties as Floor Voting Coalitions

Some partisan theories view parties primarily as floor voting coalitions. In such theories, the central issue is the degree to which parties can discipline their members, ensuring a cohesive voting bloc on the floor, even when there are internal disagreements over policy.

The best-known model that seeks to explain variations in American parties' ability to discipline their members, and hence enact programs, is the conditional party government model of Aldrich (1995), Rohde (1991), and Aldrich and Rohde (2001). In this model, majority party backbenchers delegate more power to their party leaders, when preferences vary less within each party and more between the parties. Party government is thus conditional on a sufficient disagreement in preferences between the parties (relative to their internal disagreements) arising. When this condition is met, American parties act more in accord with the traditional model of responsible party government.

#### 2.1.3.2. Parties as Procedural Coalitions

Other partisan theories, including our own, view parties primarily as procedural coalitions. For such theories, the central issue is the majority party's ability to control the legislative agenda, defined as the set of bills considered and voted on the floor.

### 2.1.4. How do Majority Parties Control the Agenda?

Strict party discipline, at least on important votes, is one method for the majority party or coalition to control legislative outcomes. When party leaders have the means to impose discipline on their backbenchers, agenda control is attained by the extension of the will of the party leadership. But, where discipline is costly, other methods may be substituted. In considering these other methods, there is an important distinction to be made between positive and negative agenda power. Positive agenda power is the ability to push bills through the legislative process to a final-passage vote on the floor. Negative agenda power is the ability to block bills from reaching a final passage vote on the floor. Formal and informal models of legislative parties differ in whether they depict parties as controlling the agenda via the allocation of proposal rights (positive agenda power) or veto rights (negative agenda power).

### 2.1.4.1. *Parties as Allocating Proposal Rights*

Two examples of theories in which proposal rights are the key resource allocated by parties to their members are Laver and Shepsle's (1996) model of ministerial government and Diermeier and Feddersen's (1998) model of the vote of confidence. In a common interpretation of Laver and Shepsle's model, multiparty coalition governments allocate ministerial portfolios to their various member parties, with each minister then possessing both positive and negative agenda power in his respective jurisdiction. Thus, each minister can make proposals directly to the assembly, without needing cabinet clearance. In Diermeier and Feddersen's model, coalitions of legislators allocate increased "recognition probabilities" to their members, thereby increasing their ability to make proposals. Once recognized, a given member of a coalition again needs no preclearance by other members of the coalition for his proposals: They go straight to a final-passage vote in the plenary.

### 2.1.4.2. *Parties as Allocating Veto Rights*

An alternative view of parties is that they allocate negative agenda power, or veto rights, among their members. Tsebelis (2002) takes this view of parliamentary coalitions. Rather than view individual parties as possessing both negative and positive agenda power across a range of issues (those under the jurisdiction of the party's ministers), Tsebelis views parties as possessing a general veto over the entire range of issues the coalition must face – therefore no coalition partner possesses unilateral proposal power. Similarly, Cox and McCubbins (2002) view majority parties primarily as allocating veto (or delaying) power to various offices held by their senior partners, such as committee chairs and speakers, thus necessarily lessening the proposal power of any given party member or subset of members.

## 2.2. PROCEDURAL CARTEL THEORY

In this section, we list the assumptions and motivating principles of procedural cartel theory. Assumptions 1–5 are from our previous book, *Legislative Leviathan*, and are defended at length in the second edition of that volume. Assumption 6 is new to this book, and, accordingly, we expand on it here (in Section 2.3). After elaborating the assumptions of our theory, we sketch some of the intuitions that have steered our research (in Section 2.4) and conclude (in Section 2.5). In subsequent chapters, we will present and test simplified and formalized models consistent with the broader theory presented here.

> **Assumption 1:** Members of Congress seek reelection to the House, internal advancement within the House, good public policy, and majority status.

In our previous work (Cox and McCubbins 1993), our formal statement of members' goals included three of the motivations just discussed: reelection, internal advancement, and majority status.[2] Key to our approach was the assumption that majority status confers substantial benefits. In particular, advancement to committee chairs and other key posts in the House is possible only if one's party gains a majority, and advancement of one's legislative projects is greatly facilitated by majority status.[3] Thus, majority status is arguably an essential gateway to internal advancement and policy goals. The more substantial the benefits of majority status are, the more incentive they provide to the senior partners in a given party to pursue majority status – hence to undertake the sorts of agenda-setting actions that we describe in the remainder of the book.

> **Assumption 2:** The reputation (or brand name) of a member's party affects both the member's personal probability of reelection and, more substantially, the party's probability of securing a majority.

We have discussed this premise at length in our previous work (see Cox and McCubbins 1993, Chapter 5). To the extent that this assumption holds, a political party's reputation is a *public good* to all candidates sharing the party's label. More specifically, if a party's reputation improves or worsens, all members benefit or suffer together, regardless of whether they contributed to the improvement or worsening.

> **Assumption 3:** A party's reputation depends significantly on its record of legislative accomplishment.

The policies with which a particular party and its leaders are associated – both those it promotes and those it opposes – can significantly affect the party's

---

[2] We did not there formally incorporate the third of Fenno's (1973) famous trio of goals: the pursuit of good public policy. In this book, however, we adapt the standard spatial model of policy making for much of our argument, and this model is sufficiently abstract so that one can easily read personal policy goals into it. Thus, one can add the pursuit of policy as one of the goals that is consistent with the model we present here – although we do not insist on that interpretation.

[3] As an example of the importance of majority status for members' legislative projects, consider the statements that Representative Ralph Hall made as he switched from being a member of the Democratic minority to being a member of the Republican majority: "This is the first time, I've just been zeroed out [by the Appropriations Committee]. . . . I've always said that if being a Democrat hurt my district, I'd either resign, retire or switch parties. . . . And it hurt my district this time [because I was denied funds]" (Wolf 2004).

reputation. A recent example of this is the budget battle waged between Speaker of the House Newt Gingrich and President Bill Clinton in 1995. This battle led to the opening of the new fiscal year without a federal budget, causing the closure of nonessential government services. For present purposes, the important point about this budgetary stand-off is simply that it led to a sharp reduction in the popularity of congressional Republicans and their leaders, as measured by thermometer ratings in mass surveys (Jacobson 1996). In other words, in this instance a leader's legislative policy – that of refusing to compromise on the budget – led directly to a decline in the party's overall popularity.

We assume that this anecdote points to a more general phenomenon, in which legislative actions taken by various members of the party can affect the overall party's reputation on the margin. There is some disagreement about how much and how quickly party identification incorporates new events and evaluations (cf. Gerber and Green 2000). For our purposes, we need simply to assert a position similar to that adopted by V. O. Key (1966), in which parties' legislative actions *do* consequentially affect voters' behavior. Whether the path by which legislative actions influence votes is through party reputations (party identification) or through some shorter-term partisan pathways is less important.

> **Assumption 4:** Legislating – hence compiling favorable records of legislative accomplishment – is akin to team production and entails overcoming an array of cooperation and coordination problems.

Achieving their goals – reelection, internal advancement, and majority status – requires passage of legislation, yet legislators' ability to accomplish things on their own is quite limited. Legislation must be accepted by majorities in both houses of Congress and be signed by the president to become law.[4] To get through even one house, moreover, a bill needs to get scarce floor time and the support of a majority coalition, both of which are costly and difficult to achieve. Legislating thus requires that members somehow join forces, cooperate, and engage in "team production" (Alchian and Demsetz 1972).

Team production, however, means confronting and overcoming a variety of collective action and coordination problems. For example, all members would like to spend more money on their own districts than might be optimal from their party's perspective (Cox and McCubbins 1993); all members would like to have free access to floor time, but the result could be that nothing can get done reliably (Cox 1987); divergent national, regional, and partisan interests might lead members to pursue different policies in the absence of some coordinating mechanism (Calvert 1995). Most important for our theory, as noted above, the party label itself is a public good (for party members) that is subject to free-rider problems. Managing the party label is the primary collective action problem that members of a party must solve, and their collective goal of solving this and

---

[4] Alternatively, of course, a bill can be vetoed, and the veto can be overridden by two thirds of both houses.

other collective action problems is the sense in which they are members of a partnership.

> **Assumption 5:** The primary means by which a (majority) party regulates its members' actions, in order to overcome problems of team production in the legislative process, is by delegating to a central authority.

Though other solutions for collective action problems exist, the most common solution seems to be delegation to a central authority – an idea that appears in a wide variety of literatures (cf. Olson 1965; Alchian and Demsetz 1972; Salisbury 1969; Frohlich, Oppenheimer, and Young 1971; Frohlich and Oppenheimer 1978; see Kiewiet and McCubbins 1991 and Cox and McCubbins 1993, Chapter 4, for more detailed discussions).[5] Three common elements in all these works are that the central authority to whom power is delegated monitors individual behavior, controls carrots and sticks with which to reward and punish individuals, and is motivated to solve the collective action problem(s) faced by the group. Along these lines, the core point of our previous book (Cox and McCubbins 1993) is that majority party members delegate to party leaders the authority to manage legislative resources and the legislative process in order to solve the cooperation and coordination problems they face, including maintaining the value of the party label.[6]

How are party leaders motivated to use their delegated powers for collective, rather than purely personal, gain? We argue that members wishing to hold important offices in the House (such as the speakership and committee chairs) know that the only realistic route to getting these offices is for their party to attain a majority of seats and for them to be in sufficiently good standing with their caucus to be (re)nominated for such offices.[7] Thus, the more valuable are the top posts going to the majority party's senior members, the more motivated are those members to ensure the party's continued majority status (and their own good standing).

As noted in the previous chapter, we believe that political parties are more fruitfully analogized to legal or accountancy partnerships than to strictly hierarchical single-leader firms (or armies). Thus, when we speak of delegation to

---

[5] Among the other solutions suggested in the literature are preplay communication, repeated play, and property rights (Tirole 1988; Friedman 1971).

[6] Describing the authority associated with party leadership, Dennis Hastert stated, "So I have two functions. One is governmental, the other political. The governmental function is to run the House, move legislation through, make sure the chairmen and the committees are all operating smoothly.... The other function is political. I have to recruit the best possible candidates for Congress and make sure they have the financial and other resources they need to run or, if they're already in Congress, to make sure they have enough to stave off potential challengers" (Hastert 2004: 181–2).

[7] Speaker Dennis Hastert clearly recognized the importance of majority status and being in good standing with his party. He emphasized, "Stripped to its essentials, my job is to run the House and make sure we [Republicans] hold the House" (Hastert 2004: 181).

a central authority, we do not mean literally to a single person but instead to a group of "senior partners."

> **Assumption 6:** The key resource that majority parties delegate to their senior partners is the power to set the legislative agenda; the majority party forms a procedural cartel that collectively monopolizes agenda-setting power.

This is our key assumption, and our point of departure from most of the previous literature. A *procedural cartel* is a coalition of legislators who constitute a majority in the assembly, share a common label (at least in the United States), and cartelize the agenda via the following basic strategy. First, the cartel creates (or, more typically, inherits) a set of offices endowed with special agenda-setting powers. In the case of the U.S. House, the main agenda-setting offices are the committee chairs, slots on the Rules Committee, and the speakership.[8] Second, the cartel ensures that its members get all, or nearly all, of the agenda-setting offices.[9] Third, cartel members expect those appointed to agenda-setting offices to *always* obey "the first commandment of party leadership" – *Thou shalt not aid bills that will split thy party* – and to sometimes obey the second commandment – *Thou shalt aid bills that most in thy party like*. Fourth, cartel members expect rank-and-file members to support the agenda-setting decisions rendered by officeholders when those decisions are made in conformity to the expectations just noted. Fifth, the cartel's leadership takes action to maintain cooperation and coordination within the cartel.

We use the term "cartel" because procedural cartels, like economic cartels, seek to establish a collective monopoly on a particular resource (in this case, agenda-setting power), seek to restrict supply of products made with this resource (in this case, bills that are placed on the floor agenda), and face problems of free-riding (in this case, members reluctant to vote for a party measure when such a vote will not sell well back home, or members eager to use their delegated agenda powers for personal gain). We have also used the term "legislative leviathan" to describe party organizations within legislatures, in order to emphasize their sometimes considerable degree of centralized authority.[10]

---

[8] Although the speakership is a constitutional office, its agenda-setting powers, as well as those of the other offices mentioned, are stipulated in House rules and precedents. The cartel controls the allocation of agenda power to the various offices to the extent that it can control votes on the adoption of rules.

[9] In the United States, the cartel ensures a near-monopoly on agenda-setting offices to the extent that it can control the relevant votes on the floor (on election of the speaker and appointment of committees). To aid in controlling these floor votes, the cartel establishes an intracartel procedure to decide on the nominee for speaker and on a slate of committee appointments.

[10] The role of the majority party has also been analogized to former Soviet Congresses. Indeed, as Hastert (2004: 250) notes, "Representative David Obey ... compares the way the House is run today to 'the old Soviet Congresses – stamp of approval and ratify' rather than using your own judgment. Well, Obey was here when Democrats ran the place.... Talk about rubber stamps and domination by a party that had lots of votes and squish room. They were ruthless. They did

Indeed, even during their relatively decentralized periods, parties in the U.S. House have been more hierarchical and stable than the typical economic cartel. Even though neither term's connotations are fully satisfactory, in this book we will refer to party organizations as forming procedural cartels (and we will stress the analogy of a group of senior partners directing a law or accountancy firm rather than of a CEO running a corporation or a general commanding an army).

## 2.3. HOW DOES THE MAJORITY CARTELIZE THE AGENDA?

In this section, we reconsider the defining features of "procedural cartels," as mentioned in Assumption 6. At this point, we wish only to argue that these features *plausibly* characterize the modern (i.e., post-Reed) House of Representatives; we will return to them in greater detail later in the book.

### 2.3.1. The Structure of Agenda-Setting Offices

An initial question is whether there exist offices endowed with special agenda-setting powers in the House and whether these offices' powers were in some sense chosen by the majority party. By "special agenda-setting powers," or agenda power for short, we refer to any *special* ability to determine which bills are considered on the floor and under what procedures. Because any member can participate in an attempt to discharge a bill, we would not count "the ability to participate in a discharge attempt" as an "agenda power" in our sense. Such an ability is not special; it is general. In contrast, only members of the Rules Committee can participate in fashioning special rules,[11] and only chairs can delay bills merely by not scheduling them – to mention two examples of agenda power as we define it.

Given this definition, there obviously do exist offices in the House endowed with agenda power. As noted previously, the most important of these include the committee and subcommittee chairs, the seats on the Rules Committee, and the speakership.

Did the majority party in some sense choose the level of agenda power delegated to the various agenda-setting offices? Yes, in two senses.

First, the House adopts rules anew in each Congress. These rules are proposed by the majority party and are usually adopted on a straight party-line vote. Thus, among other things, the majority chooses (or reaffirms) the delegation of agenda power in those rules.

Second, the modern structure of agenda power in the House was erected in the period 1880–94 to enable the majority party to legislate, even against

---

things like the old Soviet Congresses, such as removing offenders from their hideaway offices, grabbing their office furniture, and taking their parking spots away."

[11] A "special rule" is a resolution reported by the Rules Committee that regulates the consideration of a bill or resolution.

the wishes of the minority. In Chapter 4, we will show that the House's rules have not, since 1894, changed so as to erase the majority party advantages accrued in this period. In particular, the minority party's ability to delay has not been restored, nor has the central position of the Rules Committee been significantly altered.[12] The powers of the speaker have waxed and waned, but when they have changed, they have simply been redistributed within the majority party, not allocated to any minority party members. In this sense, the majority party chose the structure of agenda power and the majority's overall advantage has remained largely constant since the 1890s (a claim we defend at length in Chapter 4).

### 2.3.2. Who Gets the Agenda-Setting Offices?

A second question is whether the majority party sets up a procedure for selecting the occupants of the agenda-setting offices that is likely to lead in principle, and does lead in practice, to its members winning most of the agenda-setting offices. The answer in practice is clear: the majority party secures all chairs, the speakership, and a super-proportional share of seats on the Rules Committee. It also secures super-proportional shares on the major committees that enjoy privileged access to the floor and on conference committees (which also exercise special agenda-setting powers) (Cox and McCubbins 1993).

As for the procedures regulating access to the House's agenda-setting posts, they all include an initial stage in which each party decides on nominees for the various posts, followed by a choice between, or ratification of, the parties' nominees in the House. The choice of a speaker is largely unregulated, as this is the first vote in each Congress and occurs before the adoption of rules. The choice of all other agenda-setting posts – committee positions of various sorts – is regulated. In particular, since 1917 the procedure has been as follows. First, the majority party informs the minority of how many seats each party will receive on each committee. Second, each party submits a slate specifying its nominees for its designated committee positions. Third, the two party slates are combined into a single resolution that is then voted up or down (since 1917 it has not been permissible to amend the slates on the floor). Given these procedures, it is not surprising that the majority party has never failed to secure a monopoly on chairs, the speakership, and a disproportionally large share of seats on the control and conference committees.[13]

---

[12] We are talking here about the powers of the Rules Committee, not its membership.

[13] Decrying this monopoly power of the majority party, Dennis Hastert stated, "The truth is that since the last time we had a majority in 1954 only one Republican, Missouri's Bill Emerson, had ever stood on the House Floor – and he stood there as a page. We [the Republicans] had been in the wilderness so long that nobody remembered anything about being in the leadership. We didn't even know where the special back rooms were; we didn't even know where the *keys* to those rooms were" (Hastert 2004: 118).

### 2.3.3. Fiduciary Behavior of Officeholders

A third question is whether party members expect that party officeholders will exercise their official powers partly for the benefit of the party, rather than purely to pursue personal goals, and whether officeholders who do not act as expected are sanctioned in some way. Since agenda cartelization entails delegation of authority from party backbenchers to party leaders, cartelization creates the possibility of mischief by party leaders (i.e., not serving the collective interests of the party). Much of the literature implicitly adopts a strict standard by which to judge when officeholders act in the interest of their party, according to which they must aid legislation favored by significant majorities of their party. For example, the well-known accounts of Judge Smith's tenure on the Rules Committee point out – quite accurately – that he frequently obstructed legislation desired by large portions of his own party, and they conclude from this that Smith was acting in pursuit of his own or his faction's interests, not his party's.

Delay or outright obstruction of bills that significant portions of one's party want to turn into "party issues" represents an agency loss, but it does not mean that the persons in question have utterly abandoned representing or serving their party. After all, the wets in Thatcher's government delayed and obstructed when they could, and many other examples of hard bargaining over tough issues in coalition governments involve such tactics. Are we to conclude from every instance of persistent obstruction by elements of the governing coalition that the coalition is entirely toothless?

We think that would be premature. There are less stringent standards that might serve as "lines in the sand" demarcating behavior that is minimally fiduciary from behavior that is treasonous. Here, we wish to characterize such a standard, one that we believe has been expected of officeholders in the House at least since the late nineteenth century. This standard focuses on crimes of commission – pushing legislation one's party mostly dislikes – not on crimes of omission – failing to aid (or actively blocking) legislation one's party mostly likes. Crimes of commission increase in seriousness (1) with the proportion of the party that dislikes it and (2) if the bill actually passes. As a specific benchmark, *we claim that officeholders are expected never to push bills that would pass despite the opposition of a majority of their party.* We call such an event – passage of a bill against the votes of a majority of a given party – a *roll* of that party. If the majority's officeholders are not held to even the minimal standard of not using their powers to roll their own party, then they do indeed look like nonpartisan figures willing (and able with impunity) to build shifting coalitions in support of their projects.

An example of a violator of our proposed standard is Representative Phil Gramm (D-TX) who, during the negotiations leading to the first Reagan budget, clearly used his position in a way intended to roll his own party. In this specific instance, Democratic party leaders branded Gramm's behavior as unconscionable after they discovered it and took quick actions to sanction him, including stripping him of the posts he had abused (Roberts 1983a).[14]

Other similar examples can be cited. In 1924, eight Republicans on the Rules Committee cooperated on the passage of a strengthened discharge procedure, which most majority party members opposed; six of them were removed from the committee in the next Congress (in which the offending rule was also eviscerated cf. Hasbrouck 1927: 163–4). In 1975, Chairman Richard Ichord of the Internal Security Committee, a longtime thorn in the side of liberal Democrats, found that the committee had essentially been disestablished, due largely to actions taken in the Democratic Caucus (Jacobs 1995). In all these cases, the majority party caucus essentially *denied renomination* to wayward officeholders. There was no House vote needed to ratify the majority's decision; moreover, it would have been difficult to reject those decisions in the House, given that each party's slate of committee nominations is unamendable under House rules. To the extent that threats to deny renomination are credible, they induce officeholders to abandon, or at least sweeten, bills that substantial portions of their party dislike.

Our position is that these anecdotes generalize. In any period of congressional history, an officeholder behaving as Gramm did would have met with comparable reactions. In any period, it would be common knowledge that the standard of "not conspiring, explicitly or implicitly, with the enemy to roll one's own party" would apply to officeholders and that violators of this standard could expect to lose their offices and/or face other sanctions.

Many in the congressional literature seem to believe that sanctions against officeholders, especially against committee chairs, were simply not feasible in the period from 1937 to 1960. If this were so, then one should expect that Southern Democrats in this period used their agenda powers with impunity to push bills that they and the Republicans agreed on. Such "conservative coalition" bills, moving policy rightward, would have provoked splits in committees chaired by Southerners – with Northern Democrats outvoted by a combination of Southern Democrats and Republicans. Moreover, such bills would easily have made it to the floor, with the help of a Rules Committee often seen as controlled by the conservative coalition in this period. Once on the floor, conservative coalition bills would have *both* split the majority party *and* passed. Passage would follow as long as the number of conservative Southern Democrats plus regular Republicans exceeded the number of Northern Democrats plus liberal Republicans. Put another way, as long as the policy being changed lay to the left

---

[14] A number of his coconspirators, the so-called Boll Weevils, were also punished by then-Speaker Tip O'Neill. For example, John Breaux of Louisiana and Roy Dyson of Maryland failed to win spots on the Budget and Appropriations committees, respectively (Roberts 1983a). In Breaux's place, the Democratic Party awarded the Budget Committee position to Martin Frost, a Texas Democrat who had "proven himself to be a national Democrat" (Roberts 1983b). Although G. V. Montgomery of Mississippi was reelected chairman of Veterans' Affairs, he lost 53 votes in the party caucus and remarked that conservatives would henceforth likely be more cooperative with their party leaders in Congress (Roberts 1983a).

of the House median, the conservative coalition would have outvoted a majority of the Democratic Party. We assess the impact of the conservative coalition in detail, and evaluate these predictions, in Chapter 7. For now, suffice it to say that we do not find significant evidence of Southern Democrats defecting from their party and joining with Republicans to successfully push an agenda unpalatable to Northern Democrats.

### 2.3.4. Loyalty from the Rank and File

A final question is: how does a procedural cartel ensure that its rank-and-file members support the agenda-setting decisions of its officeholders, even though at least some members' short-term interests would be better served by voting against those decisions? A key to the answer is that votes taken on procedural decisions (e.g., a vote to ratify a special rule proposed by the Rules Committee or to sustain a decision rendered by the speaker) are more obscure to constituents than are ordinary substantive votes (cf. Froman and Ripley 1965). If a member votes for a bill her constituents oppose on final passage, she runs a clear risk. If she supports a special rule filled with arcane boilerplate that helps ensure the bill's success, she runs a smaller risk.[15] Thus, party pressures can affect members' decisions on procedure more than their decisions on substance, even though all legislators know that procedural motions directly affect substantive outcomes.[16]

Another key point is that the cartel does not need the loyalty of every member on every vote. Often, it needs only enough votes to snatch victory from the jaws of defeat on close and important votes (cf. King and Zeckhauser 2003). This is a much more limited and manageable task than enforcing some minimum standard of cohesion across the board, which some mistakenly take to be what any "partisan" model must predict.

Is there evidence that cartels in the U.S. House do demand loyalty? Alexander (1970 [1916]: 210) notes that, soon after Reed's elevation of the Rules Committee to its modern status, members chafed under the expectation that "one must support whatever the Rules Committee brought forward or become irregular." More recently, Republican Whip Tom DeLay (R-TX) has made the party's expectations regarding behavior on procedural motions clear to his freshmen (Burger 1995).

To buttress such anecdotal evidence that majority parties do expect loyalty on key procedural votes, one can also point to more systematic evidence that the majority party's rank and file support their officeholders' agenda-setting

---

[15] In Arnold's (1990) terms, procedural votes are less "traceable."

[16] Nokken's (2004) analysis demonstrates that departing members of Congress in lame duck sessions increasingly vote with their party (as opposed to their constituency). The explanation for this phenomenon is that when constituency constraints are severed (as they are in this situation), members vote with their party in hopes that the party will reward them for their loyalty by aiding them in their future career moves.

decisions, while minority party members oppose them. First, after the packing of the Rules Committee in 1961 (and especially after the procedural reforms of 1973), members have voted with their parties significantly more than would be expected on the basis of their left–right position on a wide range of procedural and organizational votes (Cox and Poole 2002).[17] Second, in the postreform Congress, majority party members have been prone to support special rules, even when they then vote against the bill in question, while minority party members have exhibited the opposite tendency (Sinclair 2002a). Sinclair's interpretation of this evidence is that majority party members are supporting their leaders' agenda-setting decisions, even when they oppose the substance of the proposals aided by the special rule in question, while minority party members oppose the Rules Committee's resolutions, even when they support the measure being aided. Third, more evidence of parties' influence over their members' voting behavior is reviewed in Chapter 10.

In addition, party leaders reward party members' loyalty on key votes, and especially on "agenda votes" in which the leaders of the two parties take opposing positions.[18] More loyal members are more likely to be appointed to the most desirable committees and to have committee transfers granted than are less loyal party members (Cox and McCubbins 1993, Chapter 7).

In summary, majority party leaders make clear their expectations of loyalty on certain key procedural votes; there is evidence that party pressures are greater on such votes (Cox and Poole 2002; Sinclair 2002a); and there is evidence that more loyal members get better committee assignments (for the postwar period, see Cox and McCubbins 1993, Chapter 7; for the period following Reconstruction, see Nokken and Goodman 2003; see also Maltzman 1997). These findings are all consistent with a picture in which majority party leaders both *expect* and *get* "loyalty on the margin," enough to make the difference between winning and losing on close votes (King and Zeckhauser 2003).

Nevertheless, it is the very costliness of enforcing discipline in the U.S. House that helps to explain why U.S. parties principally rely on controlling the legislative agenda to achieve their legislative goals. In the model of responsible party government (American Political Science Association, 1950), parties ensure cohesive voting blocs through a combination of control over nominations and disciplining their members. U.S. parties, however, have relatively weak nominating powers. Similarly, discipline is weaker in the United States than in some other countries. This puts more emphasis on agenda control, or influencing the bills and motions on which members must vote, as the single most powerful mechanism by which legislative outcomes can be affected in the

---

[17] Quantitatively, Cox and Poole estimate about five to 10 votes switching on key procedural votes, which is consistent with qualitative evidence regarding vest pocket votes.

[18] Loyalty is always important in committee assignments, but during times of high homogeneity within the majority party, there may be an increased premium placed on legislative competence. High levels of intraparty homogeneity decrease the relative importance of high loyalty and increase the importance of competence (Wawro 2000, Crook and Hibbing 1985).

U.S. House. By using agenda control, the party can prevent votes on which its disciplinary abilities would be strained or broken.

### 2.3.5. What About Quitting the Party?

In the discussion of fiduciary behavior and loyalty in Sections 3.3 and 3.4, we did not address the issue of why members of a cartel do not quit their party, join the other side, and form a new cartel (with a better share of the spoils for themselves). In particular, one might wonder why centrist members cannot extract a better deal. Why are not all the committee chairs centrists, for example? Alternatively, why are not centrist chairs free to exercise agenda power in any way they see fit, subject only to majoritarian and not specifically partisan constraints?

There are three points we would urge in answer to this line of inquiry. First, it is rare for a single member to be pivotal (Senator James Jeffords in May 2001 being the most notable exception). Typically several members must simultaneously switch parties in order to bring down the current cartel. Potential defectors must thus *coordinate*, not just in the sense of jumping at the same time but also in the sense of negotiating, *before* actually defecting, with their prospective new partners over the division of the spoils.[19]

Second, and more important, it is ex ante costly to switch parties. The Grenvillite faction in late eighteenth-century English politics could pivot freely, little constrained by electoral considerations, because they literally owned their seats. In the modern U.S. House, however, elections are partisan, and party labels count for a lot. When a member switches party labels, can he communicate that fact – and at what cost – to his constituents? How many voters in his former party will continue out of habit or loyalty to support that party? How many voters in the new party will remember that he used to be in the other party and refuse to support him on that ground? Among those voters who do learn of the member's switch, how many will view it as purely opportunistic, making the representative seem unreliable? Can he combat such ideas at low cost? How many names on the member's donor list will stop contributing? Who has been planning to run for the other party and how will they react to the incumbent's switch? All these questions about electoral ramifications – and more besides – would have to be considered by prospective defectors, at least if they are prudent.

Third, it is ex post costly to switch parties. Grose and Yoshinaka (2003) report "that incumbent legislators who switch parties have poorer showings after their switch in both general and primary election contests." Moreover, if one regresses the number of terms remaining in a legislator's career in Congress

---

[19] The Jeffords case is informative here, as it demonstrates the costs of negotiating a defection. The Democrats gave Senator Jeffords the chairmanship of the Environment and Public Works Committee as an inducement to switch parties, which required Harry Reid to give up his status as the ranking Democrat on the committee (Lancaster 2001).

*t* on her seniority (i.e., the number of terms already served through Congress *t*) and a dummy variable equal to 1 if the member switched parties in Congress *t*, one finds the switched party dummy variable to have a statistically significant coefficient of roughly –3. In other words, by one crude estimate, the cost of switching parties is three fewer terms in the House than would otherwise be expected, given a member's current seniority.[20]

These various costs help explain why actual party switching has been rare in the House and Senate. To the extent that the exogenous electoral costs of switching are large, moreover, it would follow that the threat of switching parties would not be as effective as it would be in a pure spatial representation of politics, such as those described by Riker (1962) or Krehbiel (1998).

## 2.4. CONCLUSION

In this chapter, we have laid out the main assumptions underpinning our theory of legislative parties. In our view, U.S. legislators seek not just reelection but also advancement in the internal hierarchy of posts within the House, good public policy, and majority status for their parties. Their parties compete in mass elections, as business firms compete in mass markets, by developing brand names. The value of a party's brand name depends on its legislative record of accomplishment. Thus, a key problem for majority parties is to manage the legislative process, in order to secure the best possible record, hence contributing to the best possible reputation.

This much was already evident in our original exploration of congressional organization, *Legislative Leviathan*. In this book, we develop several additional themes.

First, we portray agenda control as the key to the majority party's influence over the legislative process. In the responsible party government model, the primary mechanisms by which a party overcomes collective action problems, so that it can enact a program, are screening candidates and disciplining

---

[20] The analysis covers only the 80th through 100th Congresses. It is a crude estimate for two main reasons. First, the (negative) correlation between whether a member switches parties and how long that member continues in the House may be only partly due to switching being bad per se. Perhaps members who switched had very poor electoral prospects, had they remained in their parties, and switched for this reason. So far as we know, however, there is no systematic evidence that party switchers did face greater electoral risks than the typical nonswitching member. Indeed, Ansolabehere, Snyder, and Stewart (2001) find qualitative evidence that discomfort with being ideological misfits accounts for legislators' switching; however, Castle and Fett (2000: 236–7) find that switching is more likely the more ideologically out of step a member is with his copartisans, controlling for a measure of primary electoral risk. Second, our data do not include the full number of terms served by members whose careers continue past the 100th Congress. For these members, the number of terms remaining is coded as zero. As there were no members who switched parties in the 100th Congress, this defect of the data biases our estimate of the cost of switching downward. In other words, if we knew the correct total terms remaining for all members whose careers reached the 100th Congress, the difference between switchers and nonswitchers would be even larger than we report here.

legislators. In the U.S. context, however, both screening and discipline are – although utilized to some extent – relatively costly. This raises the importance of a third technique to manage conflicts between collective and individual goals: controlling the agenda so that the sharpest conflicts are never even considered on the floor.

How does a legislative majority party work to control the agenda? The mechanism is similar to that portrayed in *Legislative Leviathan*. Certain members of the party – whom we have here dubbed the "senior partners" – are given valuable offices wielding substantial agenda-setting powers. In order to secure their party's (re)nomination for these offices, senior partners are expected to obey a minimal commandment of party loyalty – namely, not using their official powers in order to promote bills that will, if considered on the floor, lead to serious splits in the party (operationalized as *rolls* in the coming chapters). The rank and file, meanwhile, are also expected to obey a minimal commandment of party loyalty – namely, supporting their officeholders' agenda-setting decisions, especially on the more procedurally arcane (yet substantively critical) votes. Their incentive to support such procedural maneuvers is the prospect of better internal advancement and a greater chance of majority status for the party as a whole.

Analogizing parties to partnerships is our second main point of departure from *Legislative Leviathan*, where we more often focused on the speaker and the top few leaders rather than the entire set of party members holding agenda-setting offices. Law and accountancy partnerships are designed to allow their senior partners considerable autonomy. By stressing the analogy to a partnership and the importance of agenda power, our approach naturally raises the question of how specific agenda powers are distributed among senior partners.

There are many theoretical possibilities, such as allocating *all* agenda power to the top party leader, allocating proposal power(s) to various senior partners, or allocating veto power(s) to various senior partners. We have argued that, whatever the details of agenda-power allocation, all majority parties in the U.S. House since adoption of Reed's Rules have structured agenda power in such a way that it is very difficult to roll them.

Closely related to the issue of what powers are distributed to which senior partners is the question of what standards of behavior those partners are expected to uphold. At one theoretical extreme, senior partners may have no fiduciary responsibilities to their parties. This is the case, for example, in Laver and Shepsle's (1996) depiction of ministerial government and Dion and Huber's (1996) study of the U.S. Rules Committee. Agenda power is clearly allocated in these models but officeholders are then free to act in pursuit of their own interests, with neither formal checks (e.g., the necessity of securing their party's renomination) nor informal norms to constrain them. At the other theoretical extreme, senior partners may be expected completely to subordinate their personal goals to the party's. This is implicitly the case, for example, in Ranney's (1951) or the American Political Science Association's (1950) portrayal of responsible party government. Agenda power is not mentioned in such models, but officeholders are clearly enjoined to marshal their parties behind a coherent party platform.

We have opted for a theoretical middle ground of sorts, in which the norm to which senior partners are held depends on the internal homogeneity of the party. If the party is extremely heterogeneous (perhaps similar to a multiparty coalition government in other countries), then only a minimal standard can be realistically enforced: that of not using one's official powers to push legislation that will roll the party. As the party becomes more homogeneous, its senior partners are held to a higher standard, in which they must also use their official posts to help push legislation that most in the party support. Thus, for example, Jamie Whitten (D-MI) continued as chair of the powerful Appropriations Committee in the 1970s because he considerably increased his willingness to cooperate with the party leadership in pushing through Democratic priorities, even those he personally found distasteful (Crook and Hibbing 1985).

Why does the fiduciary standard become higher for more homogeneous parties? This prediction is entailed by our theory because procedural cartels, as we describe them, primarily distribute veto power among the senior partners of the party. Distributing veto power necessarily interferes with pushing through an ambitious program of legislation, as each senior partner with a veto in a particular policy area has to be brought on board. Thus, the ability of a procedural cartel to legislate necessarily depends on how similar their senior partners' preferences are. (We return to this point, and discuss the theory of conditional party government, in Chapter 10.)

Even when a majority's senior partners disagree on a wide range of issues, however, it becomes no easier to roll the majority party (i.e., pass bills that most majority party members dislike) because some senior partner or partners with relevant veto power will derail the bill. Thus, even internally divided majority parties do not surrender their *negative* agenda-setting power. They simply avoid bills that cannot be passed and move on to bills that can be passed, which tend to be less ideological and more porcine. The minority benefits from the internal divisions of the majority, in the sense that the bills the senior partners can agree on are less likely to have a clear ideological bite to them, hence less likely to roll the minority. But the minority is no more successful in dismantling the majority's previous accomplishments than before. Nor does it benefit by receiving a larger share of chairs, of staff, or of pork.

Because negative agenda power is the bedrock and "first story" of party government, in our view, most of this book considers the consequences of such power. We return to the "second story" of party government, and discuss when a majority party might wish to build up such a story by readjusting the mix of positive and negative agenda power, in Chapter 10.

PART II

NEGATIVE AGENDA POWER

# 3

# Modeling Agenda Power

I believe it to be the duty of the Speaker ... standing squarely on the platform of his party, to assist in so far as he properly can the enactment of legislation in accordance with the declared principles and policies of his party and by the same token to resist the enactment of legislation in violation thereof.[1]

– Speaker Nicholas Longworth (R-OH), 1925

My fifth principle is to please the majority of the majority. On occasion, a particular issue might excite a majority made up mostly of the minority.... The job of Speaker is not to expedite legislation that runs counter to the wishes of the majority of his majority.... On each piece of legislation, I actively seek to bring our party together. I do not feel comfortable scheduling any controversial legislation unless I know we have the votes on our side first.[2]

– Speaker Dennis Hastert (R-IL), 2003

## 3.1. INTRODUCTION

In this chapter, we begin modeling agenda power – the ability to influence what gets voted on, when, and how. We argue that the majority party routinely uses its near-monopoly of formal agenda power in order to keep bills off the floor agenda that would, if passed, displease majorities of its membership.[3] This negative agenda power is *unconditional*, in the sense that its exercise does

---

[1] Excerpt from Galloway (1968: 144), citing Speaker Longworth in 1925.

[2] Excerpt from Speaker Dennis Hastert's (R-IL) November 12 address at the Library of Congress titled "Reflections on the Role of the Speaker in the Modern Day House of Representatives," reprinted in *Roll Call*, November 17, 2003, p. 4.

[3] Barney Frank, a longtime member of the House of Representatives, shares the same opinion, claiming that the job of the majority-party leadership is to protect its members from having to vote on issues on which they do not want to vote. He made this observation while speaking before a class at the University of California, San Diego (personal communication from Gary Jacobson).

not vary with the similarity of the party's members' (constituency-induced or personal) ideas of good public policy.

The formal basis for our conclusions is a standard spatial model of legislative procedure in which legislators and policy proposals are arrayed from left to right along a number of ideological or issue dimensions. Two variants of this model embody starkly different assumptions about who controls the floor agenda. In one model, the floor agenda is determined by a majority vote on the floor, hence implicitly by the median legislator in the House (on each dimension). We call this the *Floor Agenda Model*. In a second model, the floor agenda is determined by the senior partners of the majority party – such as the committee chairs and top floor leaders – whom we assume act with an eye to the interests of their party. More specifically, we assume that the senior partners will block bills opposed by a majority of the majority party from reaching the floor agenda. We call this the *Cartel Agenda Model* (Cox and McCubbins 1993, 1994, 2002).

We view the Cartel Agenda Model as a formal variant of the procedural cartel theory that structures this book. The Floor Agenda Model is a similarly simplified version of the nonpartisan theories of legislative organization that we surveyed in Chapter 1. In Chapter 5, we test hypotheses derived from these two formalized models. In later chapters, we bring in other formal variants to this idealized model, while preserving the central contrast in assumptions about who controls the agenda.

## 3.2. MODELING THE FLOOR AGENDA

### 3.2.1. Background Assumptions

In path-breaking research, Shepsle (1979) and Shepsle and Weingast (1981, 1987) modeled the House agenda process and examined the consequences of agenda power. They relied on a spatial analogy wherein policy choices correspond to points in a multidimensional Euclidean space (cf. Downs 1957; Black 1958; Kramer 1977). For simplicity and ease of exposition, we will adapt their well-known model to our purposes.[4]

In particular, we use the following six assumptions to model agenda setting in the House:

- **Dimensions of policy choice.** First, there are $n$ policy instruments that can be adjusted by the legislature. For example, the minimum wage can be increased or decreased; the criteria to qualify for welfare payments can be loosened

---

[4] These models are idealized representations of legislative politics that focus on only a few aspects of behavior. Just as in a regression equation, these models necessarily omit some variables and considerations. If the models capture the more important elements, and ignore the less important, then they may provide useful predictions – but certainly one does not expect them to be errorless. To probe the robustness of our models, we relax some (but of course not all) of the auxiliary assumptions in future chapters, while preserving the core distinction between agendas set on the floor and agendas set in the councils of the majority party.

or tightened; and so forth. There is a commonly known status quo point for each instrument. For example, the status quo minimum wage might be $5.25; the status quo qualifying criteria might require an annual income less than $14,000; and so forth. Both status quo policies and policy proposals (bills) are represented as points in $n$-dimensional Euclidean space. We refer in what follows to policy instruments, dimensions, and issues synonymously.

- **Legislators.** Second, there are $K$ members in the legislature, whose preferences over the policy dimensions are additively separable and who vote strategically. Specifically, on any given dimension $j$, legislator $k$ has a unique ideal point on that dimension, $x_j^k$, which is common knowledge. The utility that legislator $k$ derives from a given policy vector, $z = (z_1, \ldots, z_n)$, declines with the sum of the distances between $x_j^k$ and $z_j$: $u_k(z) = -\sum_j |x_j^k - z_j|$. We assume that members seek to maximize the utility that they derive from the final policy choice of the House (i.e., to minimize the summed distances between their ideal points and the final choices on each dimension).[5] A consequence of this assumption is that the model of policy choice is, in essence, reduced to a series of independent unidimensional choices.

- **Bill introduction.** Third, any member of the House may introduce a bill dealing with any single issue dimension. Such bills may or may not be allowed onto the floor, depending on the actions taken at the agenda-setting stage.

- **Agenda setters.** Fourth, there exist agenda-setting agents who have the right to block bills from reaching the floor within their (fixed) jurisdictions.

- **Legislative sequence.** Fifth, the legislative sequence consists of only four stages: (1) Members introduce bills; (2) some agent selects (or some agents select) the bills that the floor will consider (more specifically, the agents veto the bills they wish to veto and the remainder are thereby selected for floor consideration); (3) the floor then considers the bills presented to it, one by one, amending them as it sees fit; (4) the floor then votes on final passage of each bill (as amended if amended). In later chapters, we unpack the agenda-setting stage into substages corresponding to consideration in the relevant substantive committee and in the Rules Committee.

- **Open rules.** Sixth, we focus on the special case in which all bills are considered under open rules, subject only to a germaneness restriction, as this is the simplest case to exposit. We also briefly digress to consider the case of closed rules, showing that our main predictions remain unaltered.

Shepsle (1979: 350) suggests that there are three possible agenda-setting agents in the House: the Committee of the Whole, legislative parties, and

---

[5] With these assumptions about members' preferences, the model is slightly more general than the standard unidimensional spatial model – indeed, if $n = 1$, that model emerges as a special case. Although more general, the model is just about as easy to deal with analytically: one can consider each dimension in isolation and use ordinary unidimensional results, such as the median voter theorem (Black 1958). The "additively separable" utility assumption is not necessary for our results. Much the same results could be derived by assuming strictly quasi-concave utilities, although in this case germaneness restrictions would play a crucial role. See Cox (1999).

committees. The third possibility, wherein autonomous and independent committees set the floor agenda, is the topic of Shepsle and Weingast's (1981, 1987) classic analyses. Our focus is on the agenda-setting powers of the first two agents listed: the floor as a whole and the parties – in particular, the majority party.

In one of the models to follow, parties are not appropriate "analytic units" (cf. Mayhew 1974), and the floor agenda is determined as if by majority vote on the floor (in the spirit of Krehbiel 1998). Another way to put it is that the sole veto agent on any given dimension is the median legislator on that dimension. In our second model, one can think of the agenda setters as the majority party's senior partners, who have a fiduciary responsibility to block bills that would roll their party. Thus, it is as if bills are blocked whenever a majority in the majority party's caucus wishes.[6]

For ease of exposition, and without loss of generality, we also incorporate in these models an assumption that members of the majority party are generally to the left of members of the minority party (we are thinking of the long period of Democratic dominance from the early 1930s to the mid 1990s). More formally, let $m_j$ denote the location of the median member of the minority party on dimension $j$. Let $M_j$ denote the location of the median member of the majority party on dimension $j$. Finally, let $F_j$ denote the location of the median member of the House on dimension $j$. We assume that $M_j < F_j < m_j$ for all $j$.[7] Note that the assumption allows some Democrats to be to the right of some Republicans, or even to the right of a majority of them, on some (even all) dimensions. Similarly, some Republicans may be to the left of some Democrats, or even a majority, on some (even all) dimensions. Note also that no assumption is made that the same member of Congress is the median on all dimensions, although this is possible within our model.

We assume that the location of the status quo on any given dimension, which we also assume is the reversion, may vary. The world deals out "shocks" that upset the best-laid plans of previous legislatures, so that the status quo outcome

---

[6] Aldrich (1995) proposes a model very similar to ours. His is a variant, like ours, of Shepsle (1979). He assumes that agents of the majority party have the sole ability to put bills on or keep bills off the floor. He also assumes, as we do, that the agenda-setting agents only allow bills onto the floor if their passage "will make at least a majority of the majority party better off than the status quo" (p. 180).

Our models differ primarily in the uses to which they are put. Aldrich is primarily interested in (1) the conditions under which an equilibrium exists in the single-shot version of his model and (2) the conditions under which an equilibrium exists in a repeat-play version of his model. In contrast, we are not much interested in existence issues; indeed, we deflect attention from such matters by assuming additively separable preferences, which makes existence easy to prove. The bulk of our effort is devoted to deriving conclusions from the model about (1) the majority-party roll rate, (2) the minority-party roll rate, and (3) the typical direction of proposed policy movement of bills reaching a final-passage vote.

[7] Formally, $m_j$ is the median of the $\{x_j^k : k$ is a member of the minority party$\}$, with similar definitions for $M_j$ and $F_j$. For convenience, we shall assume that each median is always a unique point, rather than an interval.

on any given dimension may have drifted over a number of years (e.g., a once generous minimum wage erodes with inflation) or experienced a sudden shift (e.g., various foreign policy dimensions look quite different after the fall of the Berlin Wall). Formally, we assume that the status quo on dimension $j$ at time $t$, denoted $SQ_{jt}$, is such that $SQ_{jt} = SQ_{j,t-1} + \varepsilon_{jt}$, where $SQ_{j,t-1}$ is the status quo as it was at the end of the previous legislature and $\varepsilon_{jt}$ is the shock (thought of as arriving at the beginning of Congress $t$) dealt out by Nature.[8]

The model is simplest if one assumes that the policy shocks chosen by Nature become common knowledge at the beginning of the game. With this assumption, the location of the status quo on each dimension is also common knowledge.

All told, the sequence of moves in the model is as follows. First, Nature chooses the policy shock $\varepsilon_{jt}$ for each dimension $j$, which then becomes common knowledge. Second, members introduce bills. Third, the agenda-setting agent(s) decide(s) to block some of the introduced bills from reaching the floor agenda. Fourth, the floor considers all bills reported, amending them as the members see fit. Fifth, the floor then either passes or rejects the amended bill by majority vote.

### 3.2.2. Voting on the Floor

Regardless of how the floor agenda is set, the following observations hold. At final passage, some bill $b_j$ (possibly an amended version of the bill originally reported to the floor) will be pitted against the status quo $SQ_j$ on dimension $j$. Because the vote at this stage is binary, a member with ideal point $x$ will vote for the bill if and only if $b_j$ is closer to $x$ than is $SQ_j$.[9]

### 3.2.3. The Cartel Agenda Model

In the Cartel Agenda Model, we assume that the senior partners of the majority party (e.g., committee chairs) and groups of senior partners (e.g., the majority contingent on the Rules Committee) can block bills dealing with issues in their respective jurisdictions from reaching the floor agenda. Each senior partner may exercise his veto to block bills that he personally opposes, even if a majority of his party would prefer to see the bills pass. For example, conservative committee chairs in a Democratic House may block bills that the progressive wing of their party embraces. The model can thus accommodate conventional accounts

---

[8] The legislators' ideal points on each dimension might also be time-indexed (although we do not keep track of that notationally here): the legislator from a given district may be new, or may have undergone an ideological conversion. Thus, even if there is no shock to the status quo on a particular dimension, it may be nonmedian owing to changes in the location of the median legislator.

[9] Our model ignores the complexities that arise from bicameralism and presidential vetoes, though it could be adapted to include these. For example, in Chapter 9, we deal with a version of Krehbiel's model of pivotal politics (Krehbiel 1998).

of the Congress during the North–South split in the Democratic Party, which record considerable progressive frustration with the delaying tactics of Southern Democrats (cf. Rohde 1991).

Two real-world features of the way the majority party distributes vetoes make it very unlikely that bills that would roll the majority party can make it to the floor. The first feature is redundancy. Bills typically must pass a series of veto points. After they are introduced, the typical (important) bill must be considered and reported by a standing committee, considered and granted a special rule by the Rules Committee, and scheduled for floor consideration by the speaker. At each of these stages, senior partners in the majority party are well positioned to delay or kill them. As long as the senior partners controlling at least one of the veto gates through which the bill must pass are representative of the majority party as a whole, they will have personal incentives to veto the bill and thus protect the majority from a roll.

The second feature is that officeholders know they have a fiduciary responsibility to block bills that would result in policy changes that a majority of the majority party opposes, in accord with the quoted remarks of Speakers Longworth and Hastert at the beginning of the chapter. Ignoring this responsibility entails, among other things, a risk that they will not be renominated for their post(s).[10]

In our model, we idealize the considerations just noted – the creation of multiple vetoes and the imposition of a minimal normative restraint on senior officeholders' behavior – by assuming that they suffice to ensure that, whenever a majority of the majority party would like to see a bill blocked, some senior partners will in fact block it, either because they share the majority's views or because they feel a fiduciary obligation to do so. Two consequences of this assumption are:

> **Result C1:** No dimension $j$ on which the status quo $(SQ_j)$ is preferred to the floor median $(F_j)$ by a majority of the majority party is ever scheduled for floor consideration.
>
> **Proof:** The senior partners of the majority party can anticipate that, if they put a bill dealing with dimension $j$ on the floor agenda, this bill will be amended to the floor median (and then passed). The partners will therefore schedule for floor consideration only those dimensions on which the median majority party legislator prefers $F_j$ to $SQ_j$. But this implies never scheduling a dimension on which $SQ_j$ is preferred to $F_j$ by a majority of the majority party.[11]

---

[10] As an example, consider Jones' (1968) discussion of Speaker Joseph Cannon and Chairman of the Committee on Rules Howard Smith. Both of these leaders were exceptionally powerful but demonstrated only limited accountability to party membership. As a result of such limited accountability (or "excessive leadership" as Jones calls it), both leaders ultimately lost their majorities.

[11] We should note that the formal model does not incorporate a Senate or president. Thus, the notion that the House majority might log-roll with the president – allowing itself to be rolled on

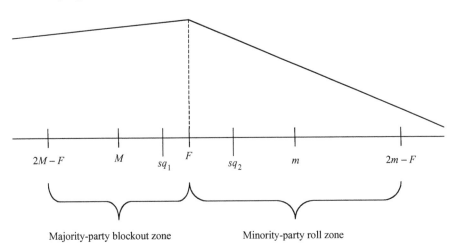

FIGURE 3.1. The idealized Cartel Agenda Model

**Result C2:** No bill opposed by a majority of the majority party's members ever passes.

**Proof:** From Result C1, the majority party's senior partners will report to the floor only bills concerning dimensions on which a majority of the majority party prefers $F_j$ to $SQ_j$. Any bill reported to the floor will, if it does not already propose to move policy to $F_j$, be amended to do so (as we assume open rules). Thus, *all* bills reported to the floor will, on the final-passage vote, pass with a majority of the majority party voting in favor.

Figure 3.1 helps to illustrate these results. As noted previously, $M$, $F$, and $m$ denote the location of the median legislator in the majority party, the whole House, and the minority party, respectively. If the status quo lies closer to $M$ than does $F$ (i.e., lies in the "majority party blockout zone" extending from $2M - F$ to $F$), then a majority of the majority party will oppose putting the issue on the floor agenda. Hence, per Result C1, dimensions with status quo points in the majority party blockout zone will never be scheduled for floor consideration. Thus, for example, a bill to change $sq_1$ will *not* be reported to the floor (as $sq_1$ is preferred by $M$ to $F$), whereas a bill to change $sq_2$ *may* be reported to the floor (as $F$ is preferred by $M$ to $sq_2$).

one bill in return for the president's signature on another – does not yet arise. We do consider such possibilities in our case-by-case discussion of majority-party rolls (Chapter 6) and in our discussion of the validity of rolls as indicators of veto power (Appendix: Construct Validity and External Validity).

### 3.2.4. The Floor Agenda Model

In the Floor Agenda Model, we assume that the bills to be considered on the floor are determined by majority vote on the floor. It is simplest to imagine that the median legislative agent, for each dimension $j$, moves that a bill implementing $F_j$ be put onto the floor agenda. (If some other bill is put on the agenda, it will be amended to $F_j$ before passage.)

Under this agenda structure, *all* dimensions $j$ with $SQ_j$ not equal to $F_j$ are considered on the floor. (Recall that there are no opportunity, proposal, or consideration costs in the standard unidimensional spatial model on which we are building.) If $SQ_j$ is to the left of $F_j$, then the median and all to her right will vote to consider a bill and then to pass it (as amended if amended). If $SQ_j$ is to the right of $F_j$, then the median and all to her left will vote to consider a bill and then to pass it (as amended if amended). Thus, contrary to the Cartel Agenda Model, both $sq_1$ and $sq_2$ in Figure 3.1 would be altered. Will a majority of majority party agents ever vote against the placement of a bill on the floor agenda in this model. Will they ever oppose a bill on final passage? The following results give the answers:

> **Result F1:** A majority of the majority party will vote against putting a particular dimension $j$ on the floor agenda (but will lose) if and only if the status quo ($SQ_j$) is closer to the majority party median ($M_j$) than is the floor median ($F_j$).

> **Corollary F1:** The probability with which a majority of the majority party unsuccessfully opposes placing an issue $j$ on the floor agenda is a function of (1) how large the interval between $M_j$ and $F_j$ is and (2) the distribution of $SQ_j$.

> **Result F2:** A majority of the majority party will vote against a bill pertaining to dimension $j$ on final passage (but will lose) if and only if the status quo ($SQ_j$) is closer to the majority party median ($M_j$) than is the floor median ($F_j$).

> **Corollary F2:** The probability with which a majority of the majority party unsuccessfully opposes a bill on final passage is a function of (1) how large the interval between $M_j$ and $F_j$ is and (2) the distribution of $SQ_j$.

Note that similar results hold for the minority party. Just substitute "minority party" for "majority party" and "$m_j$" for "$M_j$" in the preceding claims.

### 3.3. PROPOSAL RIGHTS AND REGIMES OF EXCEPTION

In the Cartel Agenda Model, the senior partners of the majority party receive only veto rights. It is thus possible that "too many" status quo policies may be protected, from the majority party's perspective.

One way to combat the problem of gridlock engendered by distributing vetoes is to create *exceptions* to the veto regime. The House majority party has adopted such a strategy repeatedly. For example, the Rules Committee has the right to "extract" bills from other committees in certain circumstances, while the speaker has the right to recognize members seeking to suspend the rules. Both extraction and suspension of the rules can override a committee's veto and bring a bill to the floor. Similarly, granting privilege to a particular committee (i.e., the right to report bills directly to the floor) is a way to avoid the Rules Committee's veto.

It is, of course, possible that the majority party might err in allocating exceptional proposal rights. For example, it might give privilege to a particular committee only to find that the committee then reports bills that will roll the majority. In order to avoid this outcome, the majority takes several precautions. As we have shown previously (Cox and McCubbins 1993), committees that have both privileged access to the floor and important jurisdictions also (1) have more majority party members than would be warranted by the party's share of seats in the House alone, (2) have contingents that are consistently representative of the majority party as a whole, and (3) are held to a higher fiduciary standard (e.g., members of Ways and Means were clearly expected to act with an eye to the party's broader interests).[12] We can also point out that "privilege" does not entail automatic waiver of points of order. Thus, the Appropriations Committee rarely uses its privilege, as its bills now all require points of order to be waived and thus all require special rules (Kiewiet and McCubbins 1991). In practice, then, the "veto overrides" that the House has instituted do not pose much threat to the prediction we articulated in Section 2.3.

Theoretically, of course, we again idealize matters by assuming that the majority party is careful enough in delegating special proposal powers, so that they cannot be used to advance bills that would roll the majority party. With this assumption, our previous theoretical results (C1 and C2) – predicting that the majority party will never be rolled – are preserved.

It is of course possible that our first-order approximation of the lay of the agenda-setting land is too crude, or even wildly off base (as it would be if the Floor Agenda Model holds). Fortunately, our rather stringent prediction is susceptible to empirical falsification. One can, and we will, examine the voting record of the House to see if the majority party has been rolled. As will be seen, the simple Cartel Agenda Model comes remarkably close to fitting the empirical record.

### 3.4. CHOOSING BETWEEN AGENDA STRUCTURES

The reader may also wonder why the structure of agenda power posited in the Cartel Agenda Model could arise, given that the House as a whole must approve its own rules. To explore this issue, imagine that there is an initial vote

---

[12] We can also note that changes in membership never make the majority-party contingents on these committees less representative of the majority party as a whole (0 of 48 instances for Democrats) and usually make the contingents more representative (6 of 9 instances for Democrats) (Cox and McCubbins 1993: 224–8).

at which the House is faced with a binary choice between rules that cartelize the agenda and rules that let the floor decide the agenda. If the House chooses to cartelize the agenda, it then operates according to the Cartel Agenda Model outlined earlier. If, on the other hand, the House chooses not to cartelize the agenda, it then operates according to the Floor Agenda Model. The question is, under what conditions will the House choose to cartelize the agenda?

The quick answer is that all members of the majority party will favor cartelizing the agenda, to the extent that this conveys office and distributive benefits to them. By "office benefits," we mean that holding high office carries with it a flow of *nonpolicy benefits*, in addition to any influence over policy it may confer. Being chair, for example, brings in campaign contributions, confers prestige, affords the opportunity to hire and direct staff, and so on. By "distributive benefits," we mean a larger share of the pie in any distributive issues that the House decides.[13] The only downside to cartelizing is that consistently centrist members may suffer a net policy loss from the majority's veto. This loss must be counterbalanced by office and distributive benefits in order to secure the centrists' support.

The payoff to a given majority party legislator from adopting rules that cartelize the agenda, rather than leaving the agenda to the floor, can be written:

> Payoff to adopting cartel rather than floor agenda rules
> = Policy gain − Policy loss + Office benefits + Distributive benefits

The legislator may enjoy policy gains from the majority party veto on some dimensions (Policy gain), may suffer losses due to the veto on other dimensions (Policy loss), and may – regardless of these policy gains and losses – accrue some nonpolicy office and distributive benefits.[14] The larger are the latter benefits,

---

[13] The real-world Congress faces a variety of issues. Some of these issues can be formally represented as spatial or left–right policy dimensions of the kind that our model envisions – and for which it is meaningful to talk of a median legislator. Others, however, are closer to the purely distributive issues envisioned, for example, in Baron and Ferejohn (1989) – in which Congress must decide how to divide the federal budget pie among members' districts, and *there simply is no median legislator*. We might have based our model on the Baron–Ferejohn framework, by adding an agenda-setting stage in which the majority party's senior partners could veto proposals. Had we done so, we would still have found that such agenda power conferred a clear advantage on the majority party's members. Indeed, if any proposal that did not command the support of a majority of the majority party would be vetoed, then the central prediction of our spatial model would transfer to the distributive setting: the majority party would never be rolled. Yet, in a distributive setting, there would be no puzzle as to why the majority party's members would vote for rules to sustain a cartel because all members would be strategically symmetric. There would be no median legislator who had to sacrifice his strategic advantages for the sake of the party. Thus, as the ratio of distributive to spatial issues increases, the median legislator's preferences pose an increasingly small constraint on policy outcomes (cf. Jackson and Moselle 2002).

[14] More formally, for legislator $k$, Policy gain$_k = \sum_{i \in G_k} |F_i - x_i^k| - |q_i - x_i^k|$, where $G_k = \{i: x_i^k$ is closer to $q_i$ than to $F_i$, and $M_i$ is closer to $q_i$ than to $F_i\}$. The cartel blocks consideration of bills dealing with the dimensions in $G_k$, and this benefits $k$ as he prefers the status quo to the floor median on such dimensions. In contrast, Policy loss$_k = \sum_{i \in L_k} |q_i - x_i^k| - |F_i - x_i^k|$,

and the more widely distributed they are among the majority party's members, the more likely it is that every majority-party member will vote to cartelize the agenda (if the only other alternative is to leave the agenda up to the floor).

Would centrists – those at or near the floor median on most dimensions – really benefit from a cartel, by the preceding calculus? They suffer mostly policy losses, in the sense that particular bills that they would support are blocked from reaching the floor by the cartel, whereas such bills would not be blocked if the floor controlled the agenda. To see why this net policy loss will not typically carry the day, we note three points.

First, the "policy loss" that the consistently centrist members suffer is not overt. These members are asked to forego the opportunity to change policy on some dimensions. They are never asked to vote straightforwardly for the status quo against a bill moving policy to the legislative median. Rather, they are simply asked not to lift a finger in forcing one of the banned bills onto the floor. If their constituents come to complain, their only complaint can be about lack of effort (hard to prove), not about voting the wrong way. If things go well, the bill will never make it out of committee, and so most majority-party members will not be forced to vote even on a procedural motion involving the bill, much less on a final-passage motion. From this perspective, the electoral costs to centrist members of cartelizing the agenda are minimized.

Second, we believe that the office and distributive benefits noted previously are very substantial. We defend this notion at length in the second edition of *Legislative Leviathan* but can review the argument briefly here. First, the majority party's senior partners get all committee and subcommittee chairs, super-proportional shares of seats on the most important standing committees and on virtually all conference committees, and the speakership. Second, the majority party's leaders also take the lion's share of staff allocations in the House. Third, the majority party's members enjoy a significant fund-raising advantage, estimated at $36,000 per member per electoral cycle in the House (Cox and Magar 1999; Ansolabehere and Snyder 2000). Fourth, the majority party's members never receive a smaller share and sometimes receive a larger share of pork-barrel projects. Fifth, districts served by senior members of the majority party exhibit higher economic growth rates (Levitt and Poterba 1999). Thus, we believe that the payoff to cartelizing the agenda (as opposed to letting the floor decide its own agenda) is positive for all majority party members.

Third, consistently centrist members can in principle be given larger office and distributive benefits to counterbalance their policy losses. This line of argument suggests that consistently centrist members should receive more office and distributive benefits than other members of the party. We are not aware of any systematic evidence that centrists do receive greater office and distributive benefits, but we can point out that the conventional wisdom regarding Southern

where $L_k = \{i: x_i^k$ is closer to $F_i$ than to $q_i$, and $M_i$ is closer to $q_i$ than to $F_i\}$. The cartel blocks consideration of bills dealing with the dimensions in $L_k$, and this harms $k$, who prefers the floor median to the status quo on such dimensions.

Democrats during the North–South split, especially after the election of 1948, is that (a) a disproportionate share of their members chaired committees and (b) a disproportionate share of pork-barrel benefits went to their districts.

The argument thus far focuses on a binary choice between a floor agenda structure and a majority party procedural cartel. One might ask what happens if the minority party can seek to lure centrist defectors from the current majority. This question brings us back to the issue of stability – why one particular cartel can stay in business – which we mentioned briefly in Chapter 1. As we noted in Chapter 1, any group of defectors would wish to coordinate their defection (lest they end up being nonpivotal) and to negotiate the division of spoils in advance – all of which is costly. Moreover, each incumbent member of the House got there by choosing, at some early point in her career, to affiliate with one of the major parties. That affiliation forms an important part of each legislator's political reputation. Defection opens the legislator to questions about judgment (why did you choose that party in the first place?) and credibility (if you will flip-flop on which party you affiliate with, why should anyone believe your specific policy commitments?). These questions can potentially be answered, but it is costly to do so, especially if one's next opponent is well funded. Thus, in essence, legislators in a given party have posted a bond, corresponding to the electoral value of their current partisan affiliation, which they necessarily forfeit if they defect (Cox and McCubbins 1994). These bonds, in turn, make coalitions stable by making changes costly, even in multidimensional settings (cf. Sloss 1973; Lupia and Strøm 1995).

We can close by reconsidering what is at stake in this digression. Our analytical strategy in this book is to posit a model and see if the world comports with its predictions. As the rest of the book will demonstrate, the model does well, empirically speaking. The potential criticism we have discussed in this section assumes an alternative model, one in which there is a single legislator – the median – who holds all the strategic cards, and which asks how such a person would ever consent to the creation of the rules we posit. Our response boils down to saying that the alternative model omits most of the reasons that make a procedural cartel attractive – the office benefits, the distributive benefits, the heterogeneity of strategic position across issues. After one brings these features into analytical view, it is not hard to see why a party would wish to cartelize the agenda (i.e., take the lion's share of the office and distributive benefits for its members and agree on a delegation of vetoes that ensures that majority party rolls are not feasible).

If we are wrong about why cartels form or about why they might be stable, that is certainly a defect in our overall thinking. It will not change the empirical findings we present, however. These findings are not at all what one would expect on the assumption that cartels are unattractive relative to floor agenda setting, or on the argument that no cartel could possibly be stable. Each of these alternatives leads one down a very different theoretical path. They are also inconsistent with the data we marshal.

## 3.5. CONCLUSION

We have presented two idealized models of agenda control and derived hypotheses from each about the behavior of actors in the legislative process. The models are idealized in the sense that we have abstracted away factors that would confound our results, trading off descriptive realism for theoretical clarity. In the next two chapters, we interpret and test the hypotheses derived here.

Our initial analytical goal is to convince the reader that there is a substantial empirical payoff to separating the agenda-setting and voting stages of the legislative process. In many models, these two stages operate by the same logic. In both stages, it is simply a matter of mustering voting strength in floor votes, and whoever can do this can first decide what proposals to allow onto the floor and then vote them up or down (perhaps after amendment). Such models lead to the dominance of the median legislator, sometimes modified by constitutional constraints (such as Senate filibusters and presidential vetoes). In our model, the agenda-setting stage is greatly influenced by special powers delegated disproportionately to senior members of the majority party, whose decisions are difficult to overturn by appeal to floor majorities. The floor stages of those bills that are considered at all, however, proceed as in the older models. In the next several chapters, we show that the Cartel Agenda Model performs well empirically – and outperforms the rival assumption that delegated agenda powers have negligible effect, so that any floor majority can get any bill it wishes to the floor.

## APPENDIX 3.A

Let $R_j(x) = 2x - b_j$ denote the point that is equally far from $x$ as is $b_j$ but on the opposite side of $x$ from $b_j$. If $x < b_j$, then $R_j(x)$ is just as far to the left of $x$ as $b_j$ is to the right of $x$. If $x > b_j$, then $R_j(x)$ is just as far to the right of $x$ as $b_j$ is to the left of $x$. In either case, $R_j(x)$ is utility-equivalent to $b_j$ for the member with ideal point $x$. Then:

> **Lemma 1:** Consider a member with ideal point $x$ on dimension $j$ voting on final passage of bill $b_j$.
>
> (a) If $x < b_j$, the member votes in favor of $b_j$ if and only if $SQ_j \notin [R_j(x), b_j]$;
> (b) If $x > b_j$, the member votes in favor of $b_j$ if and only if $SQ_j \notin [b_j, R_j(x)]$.
>
> **Proof:** Omitted.

4

# The Primacy of Reed's Rules in House Organization

Our government is founded on the doctrine that if 100 citizens think one way and 101 think the other, the 101 are right. It is the old doctrine that the majority must govern. Indeed, you have no choice. If the majority does not govern, the minority will; and if the tyranny of the majority is hard, the tyranny of the minority is simply unendurable. The rules, then, ought to be so arranged as to facilitate the action of the majority.

– Thomas Brackett Reed 1887

Besides giving the chair the power to count a quorum and to refuse to entertain motions it regarded as dilatory, the rules provided that the Rules Committee should write for each bill a special rule that would determine the conditions under which the bill would be considered. Since Reed was the dominant member of the Rules Committee, this last measure increased his power still further. The Democrats had warned darkly that "the Speaker, instead of being as for the past one hundred years the servant of the House, shall be its master."

– Cheney and Cheney 1983

## 4.1. INTRODUCTION

In this chapter, we examine the rules and organization of the post-Reconstruction House of Representatives. We begin by systematically describing changes in House rules and organization in the period 1880–1988 (the 46th to 100th Congresses). We then make three main points: First, the modern structure of agenda power in the House – in which access to the floor is regulated by the Rules Committee and the delegation of privilege to selected committees – was erected primarily in the period 1880–94, especially with the implementation of "Reed's rules"; second, and more importantly, this structure of agenda power greatly advantages the majority party; and third, subsequent changes in House rules and organization have not greatly altered the structure erected in the 1880s.

In order to test our main points – that the Reed rules permanently and significantly changed voting behavior and policy outcomes in the House and that subsequent rule changes have not undone these changes – we employ a dataset of House final-passage votes that we will use repeatedly throughout the book.[1] This set of bills, which we shall henceforth refer to as our *Post-Reconstruction data*, consists of observations on all House final-passage votes on bills in the H.R. series, for Congresses 45–105 (1877–1998).[2] For each final-passage vote, we ascertain whether the bill in question proposed to move policy left, right, or neither. (The basis for such assessments is simply whether one can predict support for the bill on each vote in terms of each member's left–right ideology, as measured by Poole–Rosenthal DW-NOMINATE scores.) We find that the proportion of proposed policy moves that favored the majority party (i.e., left for Democratic majorities, right for Republican majorities) increases abruptly, substantially, and permanently with the adoption and later readoption of Reed's rules. Indeed, as we will show, after Reed's rules became a permanent part of House organization, over 80 percent of the bills allowed to reach the final passage stage in the typical Congress proposed to move policy toward the median voter in the majority party.

## 4.2. HOUSE RULES

### 4.2.1. Defining the Universe of Rule and Organizational Changes

In this section, we discuss changes in House rules and organization. We begin by considering two databases of rule changes, constructed by Binder (1997) and Schickler (2000). Binder (1997) focuses on the creation and suppression of "minority rights," while Schickler (2000: 271) includes "any alterations in rules that were intended either to advance or to undermine the majority party and its leaders in their efforts to shape the House agenda." Both employ a similar methodology, which consists of carefully culling through the standard sources on House procedural history and recording the rule changes noted therein.[3]

---

[1] In order to identify final passage votes – as opposed to votes on amendments and the like – we conducted a systematic search through the Inter-University Consortium for Political and Social Research (ICPSR) roll call codebooks. ICPSR has collected information on roll calls for every Congress from 1789 to the present. The codebooks contain a one-paragraph description of every motion that received a roll call vote in the House. The one-paragraph descriptions for most final-passage votes contain the words "to pass"; however, because not every final-passage vote was described with these words, we also selected votes described with the word "passage" for our analysis. Our dataset of final-passage votes that we used can be found at *www.settingtheagenda.com*.

[2] To be precise, our Post-Reconstruction data does not include absolutely *all* final-passage votes on H.R.'s; rather, it includes only votes that require a majority for passage. It therefore excludes votes to suspend the rules and pass a bill and votes to override a veto. It also does not include votes on conference reports.

[3] Schickler and Binder rely on widely used historical works such as McConachie (1974) [1898], Alexander (1970) [1916], Hasbrouck (1927), and Galloway and Wise (1976), as well as House Precedents compiled by Hinds (1907), Cannon (1936), and Deschler (1976). In addition, they

We employ an alternative method for finding rule and organizational changes: looking through standard online databases for all recorded votes pertinent to rule and organizational changes.[4] Our method yields a larger number of rule changes than is included in either previous study.

Before we can say *how many* more rule changes we have found, it will help to consider the unit of accounting. There are three ways that one might count rule changes. First, one might ask of each Congress whether any rule changes (satisfying stipulated criteria) occurred or not. This is the approach that both Binder and Schickler take. They accordingly code each *House* as having made changes relevant for their purposes or not. A second approach is to take as the unit of accounting, not an entire Congress, but instead each separate *final-passage vote* that effected one or more rule changes. The unit of observation here would be a vote to change the rules, and there might be several in a given Congress. As a third option, one might count each individually identifiable change in the rules, in which case the unit of observation would be each individual provision to change a rule, several of which might be included in a single rule-changing resolution.

Although it might seem that counting individual rule changes is the best approach, to do so comprehensively would be a gargantuan and intractable task.[5] Our approach accordingly is to count each resolution (or amendment to a resolution) that changed House rules or organization and got one or more roll call votes (we present a detailed list of our set of resolutions in Appendix 4.A). We exclude some resolutions because they were in effect for less than six months. We exclude others because they had no discernible partisan consequences (i.e., they did not affect the agenda control structure in the House). This leaves us with a total of 124 resolutions with rule or organizational changes in the period 1880–1988 that had nontrivial partisan effects.[6]

Binder and Schickler, who focus on rule changes only, mention 36 of our 124 resolutions. The 88 resolutions that neither Binder nor Schickler mentions fall into three categories: (1) 56 resolutions that affect House organization, by which we mean the funding and staffing of committees; (2) 25 resolutions that affect the establishment or jurisdiction of committees – an activity that we argue

---

use a variety of other sources. See Appendix 1 of Binder (1997) and Appendix A of Schickler (2000) for details.

[4] We use Voteview 2.9. The software is available at Keith Poole's web site, currently at: *voteview. ucsd.edu/default.htm*. See Poole and Rosenthal (1997) for further discussion.

[5] The problem can be illustrated by considering the great reform of the rules adopted in 1880. Alexander (1970 [1916]: 194) notes that what this reform "did was to retain twelve rules entirely, drop thirty-two because obsolete or unnecessary, and condense one hundred and twenty-five into thirty-two, making a total of forty-four, each subdivided into clauses." It would be very difficult to decide what a "rule" was (since each House rule is itself subdivided into clauses that are logically separable, and each clause often contains many potentially independent stipulations), hence to count all the rules abolished or adopted even in this single action by the House.

[6] We include all the resolutions identified by either Binder or Schickler in our overall dataset, although a few would have been excluded by one of our two selection criteria (too short a lifespan or not partisan enough in effect).

should be considered rule-making; and (3) 7 changes to the standing rules (or precedents) of the House. Let's consider each of these categories in turn.

### 4.2.2. Organizational Changes

A class of decisions that are frequently pushed to a recorded vote in the House concern committee staffing and funding. We include all House decisions (pursuant to a recorded vote) to fund or staff one or more committees as *organizational* changes, rather than *rule* changes.[7] They are important because they materially affect what committees, their chairs, and their minority party members can do.

Binder includes, as affecting minority rights, guarantees of a minimum proportion of minority staff in 1970 and 1974 and the abolition of those guarantees in 1971 and 1975. Schickler also includes these cases (except the guarantee extended in 1974, on the grounds that it was never actually implemented). We include all four of these changes, too, classifying them as rule changes (thus they are not counted in the total of 56 resolutions changing House organization).

In addition to these *general* guarantees of staffing, which do rise to the status of rules in the colloquial sense, there are also a number of orders affecting the funding and staffing of *particular* committees, often with regard to particular investigations. We include these under the rubric of organizational changes. Thus, for example, we include no fewer than 38 decisions that were pushed to a roll call vote in the 96th Congress (part of a general Republican protest against the injustice of Democratic rule). Additionally, we include 18 other funding and staffing imbroglios scattered across the years, such as the battle over funds for the Judiciary Committee's conduct of the impeachment hearings against President Richard M. Nixon. All told, there are 56 *organizational* changes. None of these changes are included in either Binder or Schickler's datasets – not surprisingly, as these scholars explicitly focus on more traditionally defined *rule* changes.

### 4.2.3. The Establishment and Jurisdiction of Committees

Rule X of the House stipulates which committees are to exist and what their jurisdictions are to be. Thus, we include all creations or abolitions of committees, and all alterations in their jurisdictions, as "rule changes," as does the House itself, provided that we can find an explicit vote of the House that effects the change in question. Binder, given her focus on minority rights, includes no

---

[7] One can even make a case for considering these funding and staffing actions as "rules." Orders directing committees of the House to undertake certain investigations have been in Rules' jurisdiction since the first decade of the twentieth century (See *Hinds' Precedents* 4: 4322; *Cannon's Precedents* 7: 2048). Thus, the House has, in essence, put such orders under the heading of "rules," as the committee's official jurisdiction remains "rules, joint rules and the order of business." However, ordering a particular investigation logically entails staffing and funding it – and thus these matters too have the character of "rules."

such actions in her dataset. Schickler includes only three in his dataset: the creation and abolition of the House Un-American Activities Committee and the abolition (but not the creation) of the Joint Committee on Atomic Energy. These actions were indeed famous and partisan. However, there were many other less famous cases of the creation or abolition of a committee in which the action was pushed to a roll call vote. Indeed, we find 23 such rule changes and an additional two changes that altered the jurisdictions of committees.

### 4.2.4. Other Rule Changes

Putting organizational changes aside, separate actions taken by the House to alter the House committee structure account for the bulk of the rule changes that we include, but that Binder and Schickler do not. The remainder of the difference is due to seven miscellaneous items that we have uncovered by systematically searching through House roll call votes. Some of these items are votes to sustain a speaker's decision, thereby establishing precedents. Others are votes to amend the standing orders. We list these items in Appendix 4.A.4 to show that they are sometimes important and partisan actions.[8]

### 4.2.5. The Partisan Nature of Rule Changes

In their studies of rule changes, Binder and Schickler were both primarily interested in how often rule changes advantaged either the majority or the minority party. We will explore this shortly. With our newly constructed dataset on House rule changes, we can first address another of Binder and Schickler's questions: How many of the rule changes were majority party victories, and how many were minority party victories? Deciding whether a given resolution benefits the majority or minority is not always straightforward, especially if there are multiple changes within one resolution. We have accepted the judgments of Binder and Schickler on the rule changes that they identify.[9] For other rule changes, we rely principally on the partisan divisions on the adoption vote and secondarily on supplemental information (when available).

Given our classifications of each rule change as favoring the majority or minority, we find that *most changes benefit the majority*. Of the 56 organizational changes in the dataset, 98 percent were majority party victories. Of the 27 committee adjustments in the dataset, 74 percent were majority party victories. Of the 41 other rule changes, 73 percent were majority party victories. Thus,

---

[8] In one case, Binder and Schickler do mention a rule-change resolution, but they do not seem to believe it to be relevant. A vote in the 93rd Congress increased the number of suspension days, as both Binder and Schickler note. The same vote also changed House rules to allow "the Speaker to adjust the meeting time of the House with the approval of a majority, eliminating the previous requirement that he obtain unanimous consent. Republicans claimed that this removed an important element of minority rights" (cf. *Congressional Quarterly Almanac* 1973: 30).

[9] Binder and Schickler do not often disagree in their judgments about rule changes. Of course, identifying rule changes is subjective and there is room to debate whether particular events should or should not be included, but we do not debate these judgments here.

on a simple bean-counting basis, the majority party wins much more often than it loses on rule and organizational changes.

In fact, we think this bean counting vastly understates the advantage that the majority derives from rule changes in the House. If one considers the *importance* of different rule changes, the majority party's dominance appears even greater.

### 4.2.6. How Level Is the Playing Field?

Our view is that the rules of the legislative game have been heavily stacked in the majority party's favor since the readoption of Reed's rules in 1894. Reed set out at the beginning of the 1880s to change the House's rules, to enable the majority party to enact its agenda. He succeeded. Rule changes since then have not returned the House to anything like the playing field it had prior to Reed's reforms.

Having stated our thesis baldly, we now proceed to elaborate it (and even add some shading). Our first point of elaboration will be to describe the set of changes that Reed (and others) brought about and how these changes tilted the field to the majority party's advantage. In this task, we rely extensively on Den Hartog (2004). Our second point will be to show that rule changes subsequent to 1894 did not alter the fundamentals of the system that Reed established. Some changes had important political effects, but they did not restore to the minority any abilities that it had enjoyed prior to the Reed revolution.

#### 4.2.6.1. *Reed's Revolution: Moving from a Dual Veto System to a Procedural Cartel*

The majority party was at a local nadir of relative agenda power after Reconstruction. The reason for this was twofold. First, the number of bills introduced in the House continued to increase – especially with the return to the House of the Southern members, the rapid growth of the nation, and the introduction of new states. Second, all these bills piled up on the calendars, from whence they were to be taken off in the order introduced. The only techniques the House had to alter this regular order were unanimous consent and suspension of the rules, the latter requiring a two-thirds vote. Third, the rule book was still rife with opportunities for dilatory tactics and motions, such as the infamous disappearing quorum,[10] and these procedures led to such obstruction and delay that the House became an object of public ridicule (Galloway 1968: 132).[11]

---

[10] The minority would demand a call of the House to verify the presence of a quorum when the majority did not have all its troops in the chamber. Minority members would then *not* answer when their names were called. Thus, because a quorum could not be attained with *only* majority members answering the call, the House could not conduct further business.

[11] Indeed, a *Washington Post* editorial at the time emphasized that "The system of rules is the prime cause of the wonderful inertia of this unwieldy and self-shackled body....In stalling legislation and keeping everybody else from doing anything a few members are all powerful, but when it comes to passing laws little can be done except by what is practically unanimous

Putting all this together, the minority party had a natural and effective strategy. To prevent the majority party from passing its agenda in a timely fashion, it had merely to insist that bills be taken in the regular order, then delay each bill so taken as much as possible. In this way, it could extract concessions from the majority for agreeing to suspend the rules and proceed with the bills the majority preferred. In sum, the procedure of the 1870s allowed the minority to frustrate the majority, in essence granting the minority party an agenda veto.[12] This established a situation where both parties held agenda vetoes (the dual veto system we alluded to earlier), as the majority party had a veto by the same means as the minority party. Thus, although neither party may have held absolute, unchallengeable vetoes, they could muster the force necessary to delay or reject many policy changes under the House rules at the time.

Thomas Brackett Reed emerged, soon after his entry into the House, as a major player in remaking the old rules. He stated his views on party government succinctly in 1880: "The best system is to have one party govern and the other party watch; and on general principles I think it would be better for us to govern and for the Democrats to watch" (*Congressional Record*, April 22, 1880, p. 2661).[13] The end result of the two parties' maneuvers over the decade of the 1880s was to guarantee that the role of "watching" was the minority's only option. Through a series of moves, the House created the modern system of agenda control – under which virtually all important legislation gets to the floor via (1) privilege, (2) special rules granted by the Rules Committee, or (3) suspension of the rules.

In addressing the majority party's procedural problems, Reed (and other rule-makers) did not seek to meddle with the free introduction of bills by members and committees. Rather, he sought – most famously – to break the minority's power to delay and – less well known but no less important – to ensure the majority's ability to take bills flexibly from the calendars, in any order it chose.

4.2.6.1.1. CURBING DILATORY MOTIONS. The adoption of Reed's rules in 1890 is routinely noted as an epochal event in House procedural history. Most of Reed's innovations at this time were calculated to break the minority party's power to delay. In particular, he introduced: (1) a rule giving the speaker the

---

consent" (*Washington Post* 1888, "Slowly Doing Nothing," quoted in Galloway 1968: 132). Later editorials also denounced the system of rules that was then in place, arguing that the "un-Democratic, un-Republican, and un-American rules of the House of Representatives...have submitted that body to a petty committee of debaters" (Galloway 1968: 132).

[12] Depending on how clogged the calendar was and the minority party's willingness to pay the costs of exercising these rights, this agenda veto held by the minority party and its members could be closer to a suspensory veto, meant to slow down (and thus make more expensive) the passage of the majority's program, or closer to an absolute veto, over which the majority could not appeal.

[13] Even though his preferences on party government were clear, Reed was opportunistic when it came to House rules, decrying the use by Democrats of ploys, when they were in the majority, that he later used himself when the Republicans had a majority.

power to refuse to recognize members seeking to make dilatory motions, (2) a rule allowing the speaker to count all members physically present in the chamber during quorum calls, even if those members chose not to answer when their names were called, (3) a rule lowering the quorum in Committee of the Whole and permitting closure of debate by majority vote on any part of a bill being considered, and (4) a rule allowing the speaker to refer House bills, Senate bills, and messages from the president to appropriate committees (including conference committees) without debate. Of these changes, the most famous by far is the second, which disabled the "disappearing quorum" tactic that had so frustrated majority parties. It was this change above all that led to the minority party's members storming into the well of the House in outrage and that has assured Reed's rules a place in the history books.[14]

4.2.6.1.2. ENSURING THE MAJORITY'S ABILITY TO SELECT BILLS. Another, and no less important, pillar of Reed's reform was to ensure the majority party's ability to choose flexibly, from among all the bills on the calendars, those it would put on the floor next. To accomplish this goal, Reed's primary tactic was to bolster the powers of the Rules Committee.

Rules had already been made a standing committee by the general reforms of 1880; it was already chaired (since 1858) and appointed by the speaker; and it had already secured the right to report, at any time, privileged resolutions concerning the House's rules. In 1882, Reed exploited a contested election case to establish that Rules' reports had precedence over motions to recess in particular and over dilatory motions in general. In 1883, Reed crafted the first modern special rule – which allowed the House to suspend the rules by simple majority vote, rather than a two-thirds vote – in order to send a hotly partisan tariff bill to conference with the Senate in the waning weeks of a lame duck Congress (with a Democratic majority coming in).[15] The Democrats raised a point of order against the report, "on the ground that 'it does not constitute and is not a rule' because the special order addresses only a 'separate, distinct, specific measure' and not the general system of House rules" (Oleszek 1998: 10). In other words, the Democrats were complaining that the Republicans were changing the rules just for this one bill and what was the point of having rules if they could be changed at any time to suit each bill? The Republican speaker, however, ruled against the point of order and was sustained on appeal. In 1887, it was the Democrats' turn to add to the powers of the Rules Committee, when Speaker Carlisle effectively expanded Rules' jurisdiction from "rules and joint rules" to "rules, joint rules and the order of business," thereby increasing the panel's ability to regulate traffic to the floor. This expansion in jurisdiction was

---

14  For analyses of the adoption of Reed's rules, see Galloway and Wise (1976), Alexander (1970) [1916], and Binder (1997).

15  As Roberts and Smith (2003) report, the Rules Committee's role in setting the agenda was still very limited for several Congresses after the first special rule was adopted. After the 47th Congress, there were no special rules adopted and only seven special orders adopted through the end of the 50th Congress.

formally recognized and established in Reed's rules, passed in 1890 (Oleszek 1998).[16]

Thus by 1890, Rules had been transformed from a committee entitled only to propose *general* rules to a committee entitled to propose *special* rules that would govern the order in which bills would be taken from the calendars (or sent to conference) and that could be adopted by simple majority vote.[17] Rules' resolutions, moreover, were privileged and could not be blocked by dilatory motions. Finally, because Rules was chaired and appointed by the speaker, the majority party's control of its actions was virtually assured,[18] and majority party members quickly found that support for those actions on the floor was a litmus test of party loyalty.[19] In this way, Reed and other innovators had created a viable system by which the majority party could flexibly alter the regular order of bills on the calendars.

The usefulness of this system in protecting the majority from votes that it did not want to face was recognized immediately. As early as the 51st Congress, "the power of special rules to restrict policy alternatives and provide political cover for the majority party" (Roberts and Smith 2003: 6) was pointed out by a minority party member, Representative Blount (D-GA), in the following terms:

[I]f it was permissible for me to state what occurred in the Republican caucus last night, I could show an infinite amount of division; I could show just such a division on the other side of the House as makes it necessary to put the whip of this order upon them to save them from such a record as would be terrible to them.... Your Republican platform declared for silver coinage. In your secret councils many of you have recognized the importance of some sort of coinage of silver, yet here is an order changing the rules of this House to escape that issue in the Congress of the United States.

(*Congressional Record*, June 5, 1890, p. 5646)

---

[16] Beginning in the 51st Congress, the Rules Committee's new role as the House agenda setter became evident as the number of special orders and special rules adopted on the floor increased dramatically. As Roberts and Smith (2003) report, the 51st Congress saw five special orders and seven special rules adopted, as compared to the seven special orders and no special rules that were adopted in the previous four Congresses. By the 53rd Congress, there were eight special orders and 24 special rules adopted.

[17] We acknowledge that the full potential of special rules took slightly longer to be realized – per Bach (1990) and Roberts and Smith (2003).

[18] As Oleszek (1998: 11) puts it, "Needless to say, Reed dominated the Rules Committee. According to one account, the Speaker would inform the two Democrats on the [five-person] panel that [we] 'have decided to perpetrate the following outrage.' Then he would read and give the two Democrats 'a copy of whatever special order had been adopted by the majority of the committee.'"

[19] Alexander (1970 [1916]: 210) refers to members being disturbed by "the feeling, created by the tyranny of alleged party necessity, that one must support whatever the Rules Committee brought forward or become irregular. In fact, nothing better illustrates the extraordinary power that the desire to be regular wields in the House than the dumb fidelity with which the great majority of members yield to this shibboleth."

### 4.2.6.2. The Permanence of Reed's System of Agenda Control: Dilatory Motions

After Reed's system of agenda control had been constructed, with its decisive advantage for the majority party, subsequent rule changes never pushed the playing field in the House back to anything close to what it had been in the 1870s. To show this, we first review changes that affected the minority's power to delay (in this section), then changes that affected the Rules Committee (in the next section). Although there were political changes of great importance that affected how the system operated, the fundamentals of the system – structural majority party advantages in regulating the flow of bills from the calendars to the floor and weak minority party ability to delay – did not change.

The main threat to our claim that the majority party's procedural advantage continued largely undisturbed from 1894 (when Reed's rules were readopted) to the present is, of course, the famous revolt against Speaker Cannon in 1910. As is well known, a coalition of Progressive Republicans and Democrats combined at that time to force important changes in House procedure. As Forgette (1997: 391) has noted, however, the revolt against Cannon in 1910 "did not undo all of Reed's [r]ules." Forgette notes in particular that the speaker retained the power to reject dilatory motions and to count a quorum, the two main antidelaying innovations that Reed had introduced. The House also retained the reduced quorum in Committee of the Whole and the automatic referral of bills and items "on the Speaker's table" – two additional blows against minority obstruction. Indeed, the revolt against Cannon hardly affected Reed's system as far as dilatory tactics were concerned.[20]

If dilatory motions and tactics were not restored (or created anew) in the revolt against Cannon, were they in subsequent years? In our dataset of rule changes, there are six that *further erode* the minority's ability to delay.[21] As against these six, there is one that (slightly) improves the minority's ability to delay: the Legislative Reorganization Act of 1970 guaranteed some minimal debate time for the opposition on amendments, on motions to recommit, and on conference reports. All told, then, the particular dilatory measures that the minority used prior to Reed's rules have not been restored, nor have functional equivalents been invented.

---

[20] Of the rule changes effected in the revolt against Cannon, the only one that might be viewed as increasing the minority's power of delay was the guarantee that an opponent of each bill would be given the opportunity to offer a motion to recommit, if the previous question had been employed by the bill's proponents. In practice, however, the motion to recommit has not been effective as a dilatory tactic.

[21] In 1965, the right to demand a vote on engrossing bills was abolished. In 1970, reading of the Journal was dispensed with. In 1973, restrictions on obstruction were introduced. In 1976, Rules was allowed to report resolutions waiving the requirement that conference reports be available two hours before their consideration. In 1977, quorum calls were prohibited during debate. In 1979, the threshold required for forcing a recorded vote was increased (and various procedures were streamlined).

### 4.2.6.3. *The Permanence of Reed's System of Agenda*
### *Control: The Rules Committee*

In this subsection, we consider three central powers that the Rules Committee had acquired by 1890: (1) the right to report to the floor at any time, (2) the right to have its reports immediately considered (protection against dilatory motions), and (3) the right to report "special rules" regulating the order in which bills are taken off the House calendars and setting the order of business. Our main point is simply that these powers of the Rules Committee have not changed significantly since their institutionalization in 1890–4. Indeed, subsequent actions have sometimes clarified or strengthened Rules' power. For example, in 1933 the House amended its rules to provide that special rules reported by the Rules Committee not be divisible.

If the core capacities of the Rules Committee have remained intact, have new rules undermined the practical consequences of these core capacities? The only real possibilities along these lines that the extant literature raises are two: a series of rule changes intended to make it easier for bills to bypass Rules and a series of rule changes that affected the membership of Rules.

4.2.6.3.1. BYPASSING RULES. The House and Union calendars continued to be crowded with bills after Reed's system of agenda control was put in place. Thus, the real logjam for unprivileged bills continued to be at the stage of getting from the calendars to the floor (at least for those unable to command the two-thirds majority needed for suspension of the rules). To navigate this logjam at the calendar-to-floor stage, members had two basic options. First, they could petition Rules for a special rule. However, Rules could delay action on or refuse requests for special rules. Thus, members sought methods to force Rules to take action on "their" special rules. Second, if Rules could not be made to budge, a member might seek some novel procedural route to the floor that bypassed Rules entirely.

Thus, procedural fights in the House that Reed built have tended to focus on Rules' ability to delay or block legislation – an ability inherent in, indeed inseparable from, the system of agenda power that he constructed. Three of the best-known procedural innovations of the first half of the twentieth century – Calendar Wednesday, the discharge procedure, and the 21-day rule – were all attempts by various elements of the House to bypass the tyranny of Rules. We shall consider each in turn, but it is best to state our conclusion at the outset: although each of these innovations lessened the power of Rules to delay or block legislation, none of them put the majority party anywhere near its pre-Reed predicament of having to process all the bills on the calendars in order and in the teeth of effective minority delay. After discussing these three failures to bypass Rules, we briefly consider the one permanent and effective means of bypassing Rules: the system of privilege.

4.2.6.3.2. CALENDAR WEDNESDAY. By the closing weeks of the 60th Congress, Speaker Joseph Cannon had so angered the moderate wing of his party that many Progressives sought, in combination with the Democrats, to change the House's rules. In order to forestall an even worse outcome, the regular Republicans offered a resolution to institute a Calendar Wednesday. Under this procedure, each Wednesday would be reserved for a call of the committees and each committee, when called, would have the opportunity to bring up unprivileged bills that had not been granted special rules by the Rules Committee. As Binder (1997: 133) notes:

Although [Calendar Wednesday] did not exclusively empower a political or partisan *minority*, supporters of the new rule intended to weaken majority leaders' control of the agenda and to ensure action on bills preferred by Democratic minorities and/or Republican Progressives. With an agenda otherwise structured by a partisan rules committee, circumventing the regular and privileged order of business was deemed necessary to weakening majority leaders' control of the floor.[22]

Although Calendar Wednesday was viewed at the time of its creation as "perhaps the most vital of the reforms that the progressives won under Cannonism" (Galloway and Wise 1976: 140), in practice only two bills as of 1984 had ever successfully been pushed through the procedure (cf. Oleszek 1984: 120). Oleszek (1984: 120) explains its ineffectiveness as stemming from four considerations:

(1) Only two hours of debate are permitted, one for proponents and one for opponents. This may not be enough to debate complex bills. (2) A committee far down in the alphabet may have to wait weeks before its turn is reached. (3) A bill that is not completed on one Wednesday is not in order the following Wednesday, unless two-thirds of the members agree. (4) The procedure is subject to dilatory tactics precisely because the House must complete action on the same day.

Given the ease with which a determined minority of the House could block action on a bill brought up via Calendar Wednesday, it has been useless as a vehicle for truly circumventing Rules. It might be serviceable for *uncontroversial* measures, but such measures have better options via the Consent Calendar (now the Corrections Calendar) in any event. Thus, as Galloway and Wise (1976: 140–1) note, the procedure is almost always dispensed with.

4.2.6.3.3. DISCHARGE. Another of the major innovations introduced by the Progressive–Democratic alliance in 1910 was the discharge procedure. Although Krehbiel (1995) has suggested that this procedure provides the means to bypass majority party agenda control,[23] we emphasize that with the possible exceptions of the 68th and 72nd Congresses, the discharge procedure has

---

[22] The actual vote on adoption of Calendar Wednesday saw 86 percent of the Republicans obeying their party leaders' instructions and voting in favor, with 99 percent of the Democrats voting against, presumably on the calculation – motivating the regular Republicans' action in the first place – that this would render more radical reform less likely.

[23] Some scholars also suggest that the Democrats were able to make the discharge procedure more workable. In our view, the procedure has always been cumbersome and costly enough that it can be used to apply pressure effectively only on issues that are highly salient. See Appendix 4.B for further discussion.

never allowed the minority to push its bills effectively against majority party opposition. Indeed, in the early forms of the discharge rule, the most that discharge might have done was put a bill on a calendar, where it could die just as easily as in committee – especially if Rules was opposed to it. It was not until 1924 that the possibility of discharging the Rules Committee itself (of special rules) was introduced. Even after this possibility was reintroduced in the modern version of the discharge procedure, however, discharge remained an unwieldy and difficult procedure (cf. Beth 1998). As detailed defenses of these points will take some time, we present them in Appendix 4.B.

4.2.6.3.4. THE 21-DAY RULE. In 1949, in the 81st Congress, a special procedure for discharging the Rules Committee, known as the 21-day rule, was instituted for the first time. The rule gave *committee chairs* the right (on specified days) to bring certain special rules to the floor – namely, those that their committee had submitted to the Rules Committee and that Rules had not favorably reported to the floor within 21 days. This rule was repealed in the next Congress by a coalition of Southern Democrats and Republicans following Republican gains in the congressional elections of 1950 (Robinson 1959). A similar rule was adopted in 1965, in the 89th Congress, although in this version the speaker had complete discretion in recognizing members seeking to make motions under this rule, and any member of a committee, designated by that committee, might make the motion.[24]

Schickler (2000) views the 21-day rule as a majority party gain, presumably because liberal Democrats seeking to end-run the conservative blockade in the Rules Committee were the force behind its introduction. Galloway (1976, pp. 68–9), in contrast, asserts that "those who believed that the party in power should control legislative action" opposed the rule, while "those who believed in the principle of majority rule by the whole House" favored the rule. In other words, by Galloway's account, the 21-day rule was a majority party loss. Finally, Binder (1997) does not view the rule as enhancing minority rights, given that majority party members (chairs in the 1949 version, the speaker in the 1965 version) are explicitly empowered under it.

We would side with Binder on this matter. The 21-day rule was only adopted in two Congresses with large Democratic majorities. It did not transfer formal agenda power between the majority and the minority parties. Rather, it took power away from a body (the Rules Committee) on which the majority had a more-than-proportional share of seats and gave it to other members of the majority party: committee chairs in the 1949 version and the speaker in the 1965 version. In other words, *the 21-day rule simply redistributed formal agenda power within the majority party*. Had it been effective, it would have granted the power to bypass the Rules Committee to other agents of the majority party.

4.2.6.3.5. PRIVILEGE. There is one way to partly get around the blocking power of the Rules Committee: to grant privileged access to the floor to certain

---

[24] See *Deschler's Precedents*, Chapter 17, section 52, p. 3037.

committees for certain bills. The House has indeed made such grants since the nineteenth century. The main point we would stress is that the most important grants of privilege have always been made to committees on which the majority party has given itself super-proportional representation – in particular, Ways and Means, Appropriations, and Budget. Thus, grants of privilege have always been consistent with majority-party control of the agenda, in the sense that they merely transfer control over access to the floor from one "stacked" committee to another. Privilege, like the 21-day rule, has thus mostly affected the distribution of agenda power within the majority party, not the partisan balance of agenda power.

4.2.6.3.6. BYPASSING RULES BY AMENDING SPECIAL RULES. If a complete end-run of the Rules Committee has never been engineered (with the partial exception of the system of privilege), what about amending Rules' recommendations? If the committee simply reports resolutions to the House, why not amend those resolutions on the floor to secure whatever the majority du jour wishes?

The key to avoiding agenda control by shifting floor majorities is the routine practice of moving the previous question on special rules (cf. Finocchiaro and Rohde 2002). If the previous question is carried, then the House proceeds immediately to an up-or-down vote on the special rule. Accepting the rule typically gives the majority what it wants. Defeating the rule puts the ball back into Rules' court: they can try again. Only if the previous question is defeated does control of the agenda pass to the floor (as, after defeat, the special rule itself can be amended and then adopted).

The practice of moving the previous question before voting on special rules allows majority party members whose constituents disapprove of the underlying bill the maximum amount of "cover" in supporting their party. They are not asked to vote directly for the objectionable bill, nor even for the special rule that will regulate debate and amendment on that bill. They (seemingly) are only asked to vote for a motion to bring the special rule to a quick vote. The majority party has made clear that support for the previous question is a key test of party regularity, even more important than supporting the Rules Committee's proposed rules (see Burger 1995). As a consequence, one finds a certain number of cases (56 in the postwar House) in which the House defeats a proposed rule and yet does not defeat the previous question (Finocchiaro and Rohde 2002: 13). Dissidents in the majority party can thus express serious disgruntlement without ceding agenda control to the floor.

4.2.6.3.7. THE MEMBERSHIP OF RULES. Reed's system of agenda control required *both* that the Rules Committee have ample powers *and* that the majority party be able to control its members. When Reed first constructed his system, he himself as speaker chaired the Committee on Rules and appointed all the other members. Thus, he had created not only a powerful and flexible tool, the special rule, but he had also ensured that the majority party leadership would control its usage. In the 1910 revolt against Cannon, however, the speaker was removed from the Committee on Rules and the committee itself was to be elected by the House rather than appointed by the speaker. Did this new system of appointing Rules mean that the majority no longer had a structural advantage in controlling it?

We say no, for two main reasons. First, and most important, the majority party gave itself a more-than-proportional share of the seats on the Rules Committee, starting in 1910. Moreover, the majority's bonus in seats has been larger when its share of House seats is smaller (Aldrich and Rohde 2000: 43–5). Second, starting in the first decade of the twentieth century, each party has proposed a slate of committee appointments for its own members, and starting in 1917, the House resolution proposing committee appointments has been unamendable. Thus, each party has had substantial control over which of its members will get onto which committees.

These structural advantages of the majority party have remained constant from the 1910s to the present. What has changed is the majority's practical ability to control its members on Rules. Pursuant to a series of unlucky or imprudent appointments in the 1930s (cf. Schickler 2001: 163–8), when the party had very large majorities and perhaps thought it could afford a more diverse membership on Rules, the Democrats lost effective control of the committee. The damage, moreover, could not easily be undone because the North–South split within the party made seniority violations almost prohibitively costly to the party. Thus, the party had to endure a period from 1937 to 1960, during which the conservative coalition could effectively block many liberal policy initiatives.

We wish to stress two points, however. First, although the Democrats could no longer rely on Rules as an effective means of pushing through liberal legislation, they could, for the most part, continue to rely on Rules not to push through conservative legislation. This much is clear from the pattern of voting on rule adoption (Chapter 7) and final-passage votes (Chapter 5). Second, the loss of Rules as an instrument of partisan achievement was a Democratic malady, not a general feature of congressional governance.[25] Respect for seniority did not prevent the Republicans from purging several members of their contingent on Rules in the 1920s. Nor did it prevent them from using Rules for partisan purposes in the 80th and 83rd Congresses (Bolling 1965). This reflects our main point: the rules governing appointment to the Rules Committee had not changed. A sufficiently united majority party could still use the appointment procedure effectively to ensure adequate control of the committee, and hence use special rules for partisan purposes. A divided party, however, might well find that, lacking consensus on policies within its caucus as a whole, it would also lack firm control of its contingent on Rules when it came to prosecuting a partisan legislative agenda. To put the point another way, what did not change

---

[25] Indeed, "between the two World Wars the party caucus disintegrated, party discipline declined, and party government was replaced by loose coalitions of voting blocs with shifting leadership. Attempts to bind the party membership to vote for measures designed to carry out platform pledges were rarely made by House Democrats and never by the Republicans" (Galloway 1968: 141–2).

was the rules governing Rules; what did change was the political composition of the majority party and hence of its contingent on the Rules Committee.

## 4.3. TESTING THE PRIMACY OF REED'S RULES

Thus far in this chapter, we have argued that the adoption of Reed's rules is the primary watershed in postbellum House organizational history. Before Reed's rules were adopted, postbellum majority parties had little better agenda-setting powers than their oppositions did. Afterwards, majority parties had significant advantages that fluctuated relatively little. In particular, the majority gained a flexible method of getting bills from the calendars to the floor (via the Rules Committee), while the minority continued to labor under the old and increasingly unworkable default procedures (i.e., via "regular order"). The minority's ability to delay was also curbed, while the majority's ability to delay was relatively unimpaired.[26]

We think the simplest way to conceptualize the effect of these changes is to say that, prior to Reed's rules, both the majority and minority party wielded effective powers of delay, tantamount to vetoes. After Reed's rules, in contrast, only the majority party could block bills effectively; the minority could still voice its dissent, but it could no longer so delay legislation that its views had to be accommodated in the final bills passed.[27]

In this section, we test the proposition that Reed's rules abruptly diminished the minority party's ability to delay legislation, by looking at the proportion of bills reaching a final-passage vote that proposed to move policy toward the majority party (left if the Democrats were in the majority, right if the Republicans were in the majority). We need first show that an abrupt diminishment of the minority's powers of delay should theoretically affect the proportion of bills proposing to move policy toward the majority.

To see why this is so, recall the model presented in the previous chapter. The House faces a number of separate issues. On each issue $j$, there is a status quo policy, $q_j$, and the median Democrat, $M_j$, is to the left of the median legislator, $F_j$, who in turn is to the left of the median Republican, $m_j$. Figure 4.1 shows an example issue dimension (dropping the subscript $j$'s).

Suppose first that both parties effectively have a veto over the consideration of issues on the floor. In this case, the majority party will veto any issue for which

---

[26] The majority could delay bills either by bottling them up in committee (with the help of the relevant chair), leaving them to languish on the calendars (with the help of the Rules Committee), or delaying their appearance on the floor (with the help of the majority leader and speaker). Neither the ranking minority members, the minority contingent on Rules, nor the minority leader wielded comparable powers, which is why the minority had had recourse to the "disappearing quorum" and dilatory motions, both curbed by Reed's rules.

[27] To put the point more precisely, we view Reed's rules as moving the House significantly along a continuum, ranging from "both parties have a veto" to "only the majority has a veto." How close to the former pole the pre-Reed House came is not in our scope of investigation; see Den Hartog (2004).

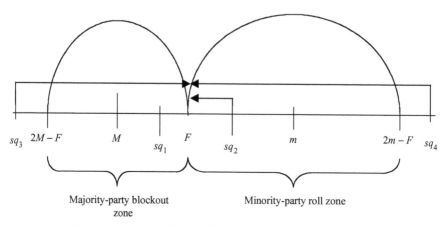

FIGURE 4.1. Status quos that will and will not be put on the agenda and amended to $F$

the status quo policy lies in the "majority party blockout zone" designated in the figure. To see why, consider the status quo labeled $sq_1$. Were the majority to allow the floor to reconsider policy on this issue, the floor would change the policy from $sq_1$ to $F$, thereby moving policy rightward, away from the majority's median, $M$. Anticipating this, the majority will block consideration of the issue. Similarly, the minority party will veto any issue for which the status quo policy lies in the "minority-party roll zone" designated in the figure. To see why, consider the status quo labeled $sq_2$. Were the minority to allow the floor to reconsider policy on this issue, the floor would change the policy from $sq_2$ to $F$, thereby moving policy leftward, away from the minority's median, $m$. Anticipating this, the minority will block consideration of the issue.

Thus, when both parties effectively wield vetoes, the only status quo policies that will be reconsidered on the floor are those in the far left, such as $sq_3$, and those in the far right, such as $sq_4$. The proportion of bills that propose to move policy toward the majority party – left, in this example, as we assume the Democrats are in the majority – is thus equal to $R/(R + L)$, where $R$ is the number of status quo points lying in the far right and $L$ is the number of status quo points lying in the far left.

Now suppose that the minority's ability to block issues is removed. All the issues with status quo points lying in the minority-party roll zone can now be considered on the floor. Denoting the number of such issues by $r$, the proportion of bills that propose to move policy toward the majority party (left, in this case) is $(r + R)/(r + R + L)$. Note that this proportion exceeds the proportion calculated in the case of dual vetoes, $R/(R + L)$. Thus, holding constant legislators' preferences (their left–right scale positions) and the distribution of status quo policies, diminishing the minority's power to delay legislation should lead to an increase in the proportion of final-passage bills that propose to move policy toward the majority party.

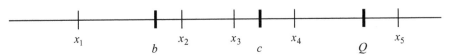

FIGURE 4.2. Identifying the direction of policy change

Hence, we test the following two hypotheses:

$H_1$: Adoption of Reed's rules significantly increased the proportion of final passage bills proposing to move policy toward the majority party.

$H_2$: Changes in House rules subsequent to adoption of Reed's rules have not restored the minority's power to delay and hence have not significantly reduced the proportion of final-passage bills proposing to move policy toward the majority party.

To test these hypotheses, we use our Post-Reconstruction roll call data.

An initial issue is operational: how does one determine whether a particular bill proposes to move policy leftward or rightward? Figure 4.2 illustrates the intuition of our answer. For any bill $b$ that proposes to change policy from $Q$ to $b$, there will be a cutpoint $c = (Q + b)/2$ that divides legislators into those voting yes and those voting no. Those on the same side of the cutpoint as $b$ will vote for the bill, while those on the same side as $Q$ will vote against the bill. So, if we find that legislators with ideal points $x_1$, $x_2$, and $x_3$ all vote yes and that legislators with ideal points at $x_4$ and $x_5$ all vote no, then we can infer that the cutpoint is between $x_3$ and $x_4$, and that the bill moves policy to the left.

More generally, we can determine whether a bill is significantly to the left of the status quo, significantly to the right of the status quo, or neither, by examining each final-passage vote statistically, to see if further-left members were more likely to support the bill (indicating a bill left of the status quo), further-right members were more likely to support the bill (indicating a bill right of the status quo), or neither. Technically, we ran a probit regression for each final-passage vote in which the dependent variable is coded 1 if the member voted for the bill and the independent variables are a constant term and each member's ideological location (first dimension DW-NOMINATE score):

$$Y_{ik} = \alpha_k + \beta_k DW_i + \varepsilon_{ik} \tag{4.1}$$

where, for a given Congress, $Y_{ik}$ is member $i$'s vote on issue $k$, $\alpha_k$ and $\beta_k$ are probit coefficients, $DW_i$ is member $i$'s DW-NOMINATE score, and $\varepsilon_{ik}$ is a stochastic error term. Leftward policy moves are indicated by $\beta_k < 0$, whereas rightward moves are indicated by $\beta_k > 0$.

Insignificant coefficients, $\beta_k$, can theoretically arise when the status quo is extreme enough to produce a nearly or actually unanimous vote. They also arise on votes that simply do not "scale" in one dimension. In our analysis, we use only those votes on which the coefficient for ideology, $\beta_k$, was significant. Thus, both votes that do not scale and votes that are nearly or actually unanimous are dropped.[28]

Aggregating across the significant roll calls within each Congress, we can then compute the proportion of bills reaching final passage that seek to move policy "toward the majority party" (leftward in the case of the Democrats, rightward for the Republicans). We call this proportion $P_{Maj}$.[29]

### 4.3.1. Reed's Rules and Policy Moves "Toward the Majority"

To test whether Reed's rules were indeed the watershed we claim them to have been, we measure $P_{Maj}$ before and after their adoption. We employ a control series regression discontinuity research design, in which the introduction of Reed's rules is the treatment. We have pretest (i.e., pre–Reed's rules) and post-test (i.e., post–Reed's rules) measures on our dependent variable, $P_{Maj}$, for both our treatment group, the House, and a control group where Reed's rules were not applied, the Senate. Inferences drawn from a perfect control series regression discontinuity research design can be comparable in internal validity to conclusions drawn from a randomized experiment (Trochim 2001: 222).

We cannot claim that our particular research design is a perfect specimen of its type, primarily because senators may have adjusted their behavior in some way, in reaction to the procedural changes within the House. To the extent that the Senate did so, its usefulness as a control group is lessened (in the same way that a medical control group's usefulness is lessened if they know that the treatment group has been treated and adopt healthier habits as a consequence). Even if the Senate did react to the House's change, however, it remains true that (1) its procedure was not *directly* affected by the adoption of Reed's rules and (2) it faced the identical distribution of status quo policies as the House. The Senate is thus particularly useful in ruling out alternative explanations of any changes in $P_{Maj}$ that we find that are of the form "Well, a variable X changed, coincidentally at the same time as the adoption of Reed's rules, and altered the distribution of status quo policies in a way that produced more policy moves toward the majority party."[30]

---

[28] For the Post–Reconstruction period, there were 3,668 total votes in our dataset. We excluded 713, making the percentage of votes that we excluded 19 percent.

[29] More precisely, when the Democrats (Republicans) hold the majority, $P_{Maj}$ is the number of bills in the H.R. series for which the final-passage vote is scalable ($\beta_k$ is significant) and shows a significant leftward (rightward) policy movement, divided by the total number of bills in the H.R. series for which the final-passage vote is scalable and shows a significant leftward or rightward policy movement.

[30] In other words, by comparing the House to the Senate, we can alleviate one of the major threats to the validity of any regression discontinuity test: the possibility of a spurious discontinuity in the pre–post relationship on $P_{Maj}$ that happens to coincide exactly with the introduction of Reed's rules. The most obvious possibility under the heading of a spurious discontinuity would arise if, exactly coinciding with the introduction of Reed's rules (but not caused by it), the distribution of status quo points shifted dramatically toward the minority party. Comparison

We further address the possibility of a spurious discontinuity by including a trend variable in our estimation of $P_{Maj}$ (*Trend$_t$*, which takes the value zero in the 45th Congress and increases by one for each subsequent Congress). This helps us counter criticisms of the form: "Yes, there were more policy moves toward the majority party after Reed's rules, but the proportion of such moves had been trending upward steadily for reasons unrelated to the adoption of Reed's rules."

The validity of our test (indeed, any regression discontinuity test) is also dependent on the degree to which we can control for the other factors that influence $P_{Maj}$, other than the postulated change in the balance of blocking power between the two parties. To address this potential threat to validity, we include a variable measuring the size of the majority party (*Majority margin$_t$*, which is the difference between the percentage of seats held by the majority party and 50 percent, in each Congress) and a variable indicating Congresses between the revolt against "czar rule" in 1910 and the packing of the Rules Committee in 1960 (*Revolt$_t$*, which takes the value one for the 62nd through 86th Congresses and zero otherwise). These two variables help model variations in $P_{Maj}$ within each of the pre- and post-Reed eras.

Our main independent variable is *Reed$_t$*, which takes the value one for Congresses operating under Reed's rules, and zero otherwise.[31] We expect the coefficient on *Reed* to be positive and significant.

We estimated the following regression using the extended beta binomial method[32] recommended by King (1989) and Palmquist (1999) for cases such as ours, in which the dependent variable is an aggregation of individual binary choices that are likely not independent of one another:

$$P_{Maj,t} = \alpha + \beta_1 Reed_t + \beta_2 Trend_t + \beta_3 Revolt_t$$
$$+ \beta_4 Majority\ margin_t + \varepsilon_t$$

where $\alpha$, $\beta_1$, $\beta_2$, $\beta_3$, and $\beta_4$ are estimated coefficients, $\varepsilon_t$ is an error term, and $t$ denotes Congresses from the 45th through the 105th.[33] We estimate a similar regression for the Senate for the same time period.

Our results, displayed in Table 4.1, can be summarized as follows: first, there is no significant trend in $P_{Maj}$, but it does tend to be larger when the majority party holds a larger share of seats. Our analysis suggests that $P_{Maj}$

with the Senate largely removes this as a plausible objection, even if the Senate is reacting in some fashion to the House's change.

[31] We code *Reed* as zero in Congresses 45–50 and 52; we code it as one in all other Congresses, 51 and 53–105.

[32] Extended beta binomial (EBB) is an estimation technique used originally in toxicology studies in which there are both individual and litter effects of a treatment. In studies of Congress we believe EBB is an appropriate technique because there are both individual and Congress-level factors that influence the probability of being rolled (for more on EBB see Haseman and Kupper 1979; Kupper and Haseman 1978; Williams 1975).

[33] We have no reason to expect, nor did we find (when including lags of the dependent variable), any evidence of autoregressive structure in the data.

TABLE 4.1. *The Effects of Rule Changes on the Proportion of Final-Passage Bills That Move Policy Toward the Majority, Congresses 45–105*

| Independent Variables | Model 1 | Model 2 | Model 3 | Model 4 | Model 5 |
|---|---|---|---|---|---|
| Reed | 1.210** | 1.345*** | 1.229** | 1.212*** | 1.239*** |
| | (0.405) | (0.263) | (0.405) | (0.250) | (0.248) |
| Majority Margin | 0.027 | 0.027 | 0.028 | 0.017 | 0.017 |
| | (0.015) | (0.015) | (0.015) | (0.016) | (0.016) |
| Revolt | −0.314 | −0.363 | −0.310 | | |
| | (0.215) | (0.186) | (0.197) | | |
| Trend | 0.003 | | | | |
| | (0.007) | | | | |
| SchickRC | | | | 0.251 | |
| | | | | (0.145) | |
| Schickplus | | | | | 0.273** |
| | | | | | (0.132) |
| CalWed | | | 0.081 | | |
| | | | (0.203) | | |
| Discharge | | | −0.208 | | |
| | | | (0.226) | | |
| TwentyOne | | | 0.162 | | |
| | | | (0.454) | | |
| Holman | | | 0.167 | | |
| | | | (0.191) | | |
| Constant | 0.063 | 0.073 | −0.064 | 0.085 | 0.032 |
| | (0.247) | (0.247) | (0.285) | (0.250) | (0.247) |
| $\gamma$ | 0.039*** | 0.040*** | 0.034** | 0.042*** | 0.040*** |
| | (0.014) | (0.015) | (0.014) | (0.015) | (0.014) |
| Log likelihood | −1336.385 | −1336.477 | −1335.5 | −1336.808 | −1336.244 |
| Pseudo $R^2$ | 0.040 | 0.040 | 0.040 | 0.040 | 0.040 |
| N = | 61 | 61 | 61 | 61 | 61 |

Standard errors in parentheses; ** indicates $p < .05$; *** indicates $p < .01$.
Our estimation technique is extended beta binomial regression. The dependent variable is the proportion of bills that move policy toward the majority party.

would increase by about half a percentage point for every percentage point increase in the majority party's margin of control in the House. Increasing from the smallest observed majority margin (0.1) to the average margin (9.2) would increase the proportion of final-passage bills moving policy toward the majority by about 4.2 percentage points. This effect is statistically significant in a one-tailed test ($p = .03$).

Second, and more important for our purposes, $P_{Maj}$ is substantially larger in Houses operating under Reed's rules than in those operating without them. The estimated proportion of bills moving policy toward the majority party was about 57 percent, in non-Reed Congresses but about 81 percent in Reed Congresses.[34] The difference of 24 percentage points is statistically significant at conventional levels ($p = .003$).

Third, $P_{Maj}$ declines by about 5 percentage points after the revolt against Cannon. However, this decline is statistically insignificant and substantively small relative to the estimated increase due to Reed's rules (24 percentage points). When we drop the insignificant *Trend* variable (see Model 2), we find a slightly larger and statistically significant decline in the postrevolt period of about 5.5 percentage points.[35]

All told, the results in Table 4.1 suggest that the adoption of Reed's rules abruptly increased the majority party's ability to control the agenda, with only marginal or second-order change thereafter.[36]

When we estimate a similar regression for the Senate (our control group), we find that Reed's rules had no discernable effect.[37] Specifically, the treatment variable for Reed's rules was *not* significant in the Senate regression on $P_{Maj}$, although $P_{Maj}$ does increase in the Senate both as majority margin increases (*Majority Margin*) and over time (*Trend*). There was also a significant decline in $P_{Maj}$ in the Senate following the Progressive revolt.[38] Taken together, the results in Table 4.1 and the results of our Senate regression complete our control series regression discontinuity test.

Figure 4.3 reinforces our results by displaying the proportion of final-passage bills that seek to move policy toward the majority party in both the House and Senate for the 45th to 105th Congresses. As can be seen, Reed's rules, which were permanently adopted in the House during the 53rd Congress, had a significant effect on $P_{Maj}$ in the House, but they had no real effect in the

---

[34] In the Senate, the proportion of Senate-originated bills moving policy toward the majority party averages 75 percent in the post-Reconstruction period (weighted average is approximately 80 percent).

[35] Our results remain much the same if one controls for the heterogeneity of preferences within the majority party (via the standard deviation of first dimension DW-NOMINATE scores within the majority party).

[36] Note also that each of the gamma coefficients in Table 4.1 is significant. Because we estimated these regressions using the extended beta binomial distribution, gamma tests for "overdispersion." The positive and significant coefficients that we obtain suggest that the probability of a majority-party vote is not constant across observations (King 1989; Palmquist 1999).

[37] Specifically, we estimated an extended beta binomial regression and obtained the following results for the Senate:

$$P_{Maj,t} = \alpha(0.860; \text{se} = 0.319) + \beta_1(-0.128; \text{se} = 0.584)Reed_t$$
$$+ \beta_2(0.034; \text{se} = 0.012)Trend_t + \beta_3(-1.617; \text{se} = 0.643)Revolt_t$$
$$+ \beta_4(0.047; \text{se} = 0.013)Majority\ margin_t + \varepsilon_t$$

[38] The Progressive revolt in the Senate occurred one Congress later than in the House (62nd Congress in the Senate, as opposed to the 61st Congress in the House). Accordingly, for the Senate regression, we code the Revolt variable equal to 1 from the 62nd Congress onward, and for the House regression, we code the Revolt variable equal to 1 from the 61st Congress onward.

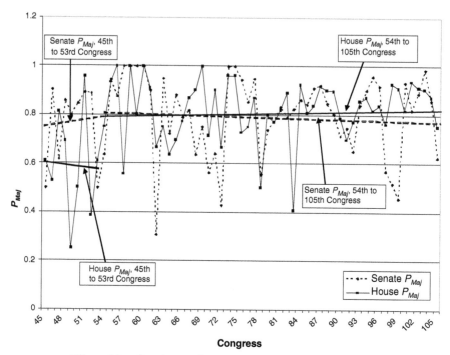

FIGURE 4.3. Effect of Reed's rules on the proportion of bills moving policy toward the majority party

Senate. Furthermore, the House regression lines vary without trend before the adoption of Reed's rules, increase abruptly when those rules were adopted, and then again vary without trend (albeit at a much higher level).

Moreover, one can see some of the finer details of the data in this figure. Look in particular at the House figures in the 50th to 53rd Congresses. The 50th was the last pre-Reed Congress, and only 50 percent of the bills reaching final passage proposed to move policy toward the majority. The 51st was the Congress in which Reed adopted his famous rules, and $P_{maj}$ shoots up to 96 percent. In the 52nd Congress, the Democrats took over the House and repealed Reed's rules: $P_{maj}$ declines to 38 percent. In the 53rd Congress, the Democrats restored part, but not all, of Reed's rules, and $P_{maj}$ increased to 61 percent. Finally, in the 54th and succeeding Congresses, Reed's rules have remained fully in force, and, as one can see, the data fluctuate without trend around the post-Reed mean of about 81 percent.

The abrupt and permanent change in $P_{Maj}$ in the House is difficult to understand within any of the prominent "partyless" views of congressional organization. Scholars such as Mayhew (1974) and Krehbiel (1997) doubt that the majority party has had any significant procedural advantage over the minority in the postwar era. Presumably, these scholars would expect Reed's rules to have had either little effect to begin with or an effect that was reversed by later rule changes. Yet the data are inconsistent with both expectations. We investigate in Chapter 9 whether one can explain variations in the proportion of final-passage bills proposing leftward or rightward moves in terms of the preference distribution of the House (and the location of the pivots), finding that one cannot.

### 4.3.2. Other Rule Changes and Policy Moves "Toward the Majority"

Our results also address a small debate between us (Cox and McCubbins 1997) and Schickler and Rich (1997). Schickler and Rich argue that rule changes in the House can best be predicted by what House centrists want, rather than by what the majority party wants – casting doubt on our (1993) claim that the majority party derives substantial benefits from the rules. We respond by arguing that most of the rule changes examined by Schickler and Rich are "marginal" and leave the "base" of the rules (which we view as heavily biased in favor of the majority party) intact. Thus, it does not matter much what predicts rule changes of the sort examined by Schickler and Rich, at least when it comes to assessing the size of the majority party's procedural advantage.

We can now directly test Schickler and Rich's hypotheses, by adapting the design just used to assess the effects of Reed's rules. If Schickler and Rich are correct, then we should find that these other rule changes had systematic effects comparable in size to the adoption of Reed's rules. If we are correct, then we should find that these other rule changes had substantially smaller effects than that of Reed's rules.

One way to approach the issue is to examine the introduction of individual rules over time. We focus on five major rule changes in particular: the Holman rule, the 21-day rule, and stipulations regarding the size of the Rules Committee, Calendar Wednesday, and the discharge petition. Each of these rules was revisited several times by the House. Each is associated with sometimes-famous organizational battles (see the discussions above and in Schickler 2001). We have coded each systematically (in line with coding by Schickler (2000), among others, where relevant) so that we can keep track of when each rule was introduced, repealed, strengthened, or weakened. The Holman rule and the 21-day rule are particularly straightforward: each is either "on" or "off" for each Congress, so simple dummy variables suffice to keep track of them:

> $Holman_t$ is a dummy variable coded one for Congresses in which the Holman rule was in effect.
>
> $TwentyOne_t$ is a dummy variable coded one for Congresses in which the 21-day rule was in effect.

To keep track of majority-hostile changes in the size of the Rules Committee, we use the $Revolt_t$ variable already introduced (the Committee was expanded in the 61st Congress, to the majority party's apparent detriment, and then again in the 87th, to its benefit). Both Calendar Wednesday and the discharge procedure were changed several times. In these cases, we simply follow Schickler's (2000) method and code each change as making it easier or harder to use the given procedure.[39] From this, we create two variables that capture changes in these procedures, each of which ranges in value between $-3$ and $0$ in our dataset:

> $CalWed_t$, a running sum that codes the cumulative number of rule changes, as of Congress $t$ (inclusive), that make it easier or harder for members to use the Calendar Wednesday procedure (for Congresses prior to the procedure's creation, the variable is coded zero; for Congresses in which there was a rule change that made it easier to use the Calendar Wednesday procedure, we subtract 1 from the running tally; and, for Congresses in which there was a rule change that made it harder to use the Calendar Wednesday procedure, we add 1 to the running tally).
>
> $Discharge_t$, a running sum that codes the cumulative number of rule changes, as of Congress $t$ (inclusive), that make it easier or harder for members to use the discharge procedure (for Congresses prior to the procedure's creation, the variable is coded zero; for Congresses in which there was a rule change that made it easier to use the discharge procedure, we subtract 1 from the running tally; and, for Congresses in which there was a rule change that made it harder to use the discharge procedure, we add 1 to the running tally).

All the variables are coded so that a positive coefficient is expected by Schickler, except for $Revolt_t$ (where a negative is expected).

Model 3 in Table 4.1 displays the results of our extended beta binomial analysis when we add to Model 2 four additional variables – $Holman_t$, $TwentyOne_t$, $CalWed_t$, and $Discharge_t$. As can be seen, none of the newly included variables exert a significant effect on the proportion of bills that propose to move policy toward the majority, while estimates of the impact of the previously included variables are only slightly affected.[40] Thus, Reed's rules and the majority party's margin of control remain significant factors; the revolt against Cannon has about the same estimated impact but is no longer statistically significant.

Another approach to studying the impact of rules would be to cumulate the various rule changes into some sort of summary measure. We have tried two – a variable coded by Schickler (2000) that tracks pro- and antimajority changes in each Congress (*SchickRC*) and a slightly modified version of that variable, where we add in the seven "other" rule changes identified in our sweep but missed by Schickler (*Schickplus*). In both cases, a Congress is scored $+1$ if there was at least one promajority change and no antimajority changes, $-1$ if there

---

[39] Where our coding is cumulative, however, Schickler's is not. Schickler's coding is directed at constructing a Congress-by-Congress measure of all partisan rule changes; thus, it takes on the value, 1, $-1$, or 0 for each Congress, depending only on the instance of changes within that Congress. In constructing *CalWed* and *Discharge*, our aim was to track the relative majority–minority party advantage in a single type of rule over a number of Congresses. Thus, we borrow the $-1/+1$ coding scheme from Schickler but construct it as a cumulative variable, where the value of a change in a given Congress is added to or subtracted from the value in the previous Congress.

[40] The newly included variables are jointly insignificant, as well.

was at least one antimajority change and no promajority changes, and 0 if there were either no changes or both pro- and antimajority changes. In both models, we also include *Reed* and *Majority Margin*. The dependent variable is $P_{Maj}$.

Models 4 and 5 of Table 4.1 display the results of these other extended beta binomial analyses. Schickler's rule change variable (Model 4) is significant at only the .08 level, with a coefficient about one fifth the size of the *Reed* coefficient. This relative magnitude remains essentially unchanged when we add in our seven other changes (Model 5), but the level of significance increases.[41] Even though the rule changes identified by Schickler (and the additional changes identified by us) do seem to have some systematic effect on the ability of the two parties to pursue their agendas, their magnitude is small compared to the advantage bestowed upon the majority party by Reed's rules.

All told, we believe the evidence we have presented strongly supports the main thesis of this chapter: that when it comes to rule changes affecting the majority party's control of the agenda, the adoption of Reed's rules stands out from all others in importance – so much so that congressional history can be simply divided into pre-Reed (small advantage) and post-Reed (large advantage) (Hinds 1907; McConachie 1974 [1898]; Alexander 1970 [1916]; Galloway and Wise 1976). The main caveat we would register to this conclusion is that the time period we examine here begins with the 45th Congress in 1877 and so we have nothing here to say about the Civil War Congresses and their prebellum predecessors. On these earlier Congresses and the majority's varying ability to control the agenda, see Den Hartog (2004).

## 4.4. CONCLUSION

In this chapter, we have argued three main points: that the modern structure of agenda power in the House was erected in the period 1880–94, that this structure of agenda power greatly advantages the majority party, and that subsequent changes in House rules have not moved it significantly away from the structure erected in 1880–94. Of these three points, the first two have ample precedents in the previous literature, even if we present the case somewhat differently. It is really the last that constitutes a controversial position, and so we review it more extensively here.

What we call the modern structure of agenda power differed from its predecessor in two main ways. First, the minority party (and other minorities) had substantially reduced powers to delay legislation. Second, the majority party (through its floor and committee leaders) had substantially enhanced powers to set the House agenda.

The first point to make is that the minority's powers of delay were neither restored to their pre-Reed levels, nor pushed back significantly in that direction,

---

[41] We also tried a cumulative version of Schickler's variable and a version where we added in organizational changes and committee adjustments (from Appendix 4.A). Neither variable is quite significant, and their coefficients remain at about one fifth of the coefficient of *Reed*.

by any subsequent rule changes. The first pillar of the House that Reed built has remained fully intact.

The second point is more complex but of a similar flavor. The majority party's ability to set the House agenda depends on two devices: special rules emitted from the Rules Committee and privileged bills reported from a few "privileged" committees. In order for this system of agenda control to work in the majority party's favor, it is necessary that privilege and special rules be the *only* viable pathways to the floor for controversial bills, and it is also necessary that the majority party has rule-based advantages in controlling the relevant committees. Both conditions were fully met in the system as originally constructed. Moreover, we believe that both have continued to be met ever since.

The Rules Committee's power to determine which bills from the calendars are considered, and in what order, has been seriously challenged on only a few brief occasions in House history. The only real and permanent loophole in its ability to block bills is the system of allocating privilege to selected committees. Thus, since 1890–4, it has almost always been true that controversial bills had a chance of experiencing life on the floor only if they were either reported from a privileged committee or given a special rule by the Rules Committee.

It has also been true, since 1890–4, that the majority party has an advantage in controlling the "control" committees – Rules, plus the major committees with privileged access to the floor. Prior to the early twentieth century, the speaker appointed all the committees. After the revolt against Cannon, the majority party has consistently given itself more than a proportional share of seats on the key committees. We will expand upon this topic in Chapter 7, by examining in detail the extent to which the Rules Committee acts as a faithful agent of the majority party.

Here, we have provided evidence of the importance of Reed's rules in bolstering the majority party's agenda power by analyzing the proportion of bills reaching the final-passage stage that propose to move policy toward the majority party. Looking at Post-Reconstruction Congresses operating without Reed's rules (45th–50th and 52nd Congresses), one finds that this proportion is about 57 percent on average. In contrast, the analogous figure is 81 percent in Post-Reconstruction Congresses operating with Reed's rules (51st and 53rd–105th Congresses).[42] Evidently, when the majority party broke the minority's ability to delay and established a method by which it could flexibly select which bills the floor would consider next, it was able to increase greatly the proportion of final-passage bills that proposed to move policy toward its median. No other rule changes in the Post-Reconstruction House come close to matching the impact of Reed's rules.

[42] The contrast between 82 percent and 52 percent is one simple indication of the impact of Reed's rules. Earlier in the chapter, in Table 4.1, we examined the difference controlling for various other considerations, finding a still-large contrast (81 percent versus 57 percent).

## APPENDIX 4.A.1. PROCEDURES USED IN COMPILING THE DATASET

Our dataset of rule changes was compiled by systematically searching a database of roll call votes in the House. We used special roll call software – Voteview 2.9 for Windows – to narrow our search to votes dealing with "internal organization" (by the Peltzman coding). We then looked at the summary provided for each such roll call, to determine whether or not it pertained to a change in House organization or rules.

We first identified all roll call votes that pertained to organizational or rule changes. We then grouped together any set of organizational/rule changes that was adopted via one or more related roll call votes and treated this as a single resolution. So, for example, if three distinct rule changes were adopted on a series of roll calls that included two amendment votes and one final-passage vote, those three rule changes would all be lumped together as a single resolution. Similarly, if several rule changes were adopted on an amendment vote, these changes would be lumped together as a single resolution. In an instance like the last example, where the final-passage vote was not a roll call vote, we verified that the rule resolution passed by going to the *Congressional Record*.

Of course, there are likely to be some rule changes that we have missed using this method. For example, we miss any instances where the speaker makes a ruling that changes the rules of the House but that is never challenged in a roll call vote. Similarly, we miss instances where rules change as a result of a proposal that is adopted without a roll call vote at *any* stage of its consideration. Despite these potential omissions, we are satisfied that our method captured all the major rule changes in the House over the time period that we investigate; neither Schickler nor Binder, nor any of the other standard secondary sources, report any rule changes that we miss.

In compiling our final dataset, we excluded any rule changes that (1) were in effect less than six months or (2) did not have significant partisan consequences. We considered rule change resolutions as having partisan consequences if at least one of the roll call votes on the resolution was a party vote (pitting over 50 percent of Democrats against over 50 percent of Republicans). In a few cases, however, we included rule-change resolutions that did not have a partisan roll call but that were coded by either Schickler (2000) or Binder (1997) as having had partisan consequences. In all, we excluded 41 rule-change resolutions because they were positively known to have been in effect less than six months, 59 resolutions because they did not have partisan consequences, and 19 resolutions that failed on both counts.

On the following pages is a list of all the resolutions included in our dataset, separated into four categories: organizational changes, creation or abolition of committees or changes in their jurisdictions, miscellaneous changes, and resolutions that include rule changes identified by Schickler and/or Binder. We highlight in bold font those changes regarding the Reed rules, the Holman rule, Calendar Wednesday, the discharge procedure, the 21-day rule, or the Rules Committee's powers.

APPENDIX 4.A.2. LIST OF ORGANIZATIONAL AND RULE CHANGES

| Congress (Year) | Summary |
| --- | --- |
| **56 Organizational Changes** | |
| 50 (1888) | Employed a clerk for five committees |
| 53 (1893) | Provided an assistant clerk for the Committee on Naval Affairs |
| 61 (1909) | Provided for clerks for three committees |
| 65 (1918) | **Provided an assistant clerk for Committee on Rules** |
| 67 (1921) | Funded the joint committee on the executive branch reorganization |
| 84 (1955) | Funded investigations of the Small Business Committee |
| 92 (1971) | Increased allowances for certain committees |
| 93 (1973) | Funded the Judiciary Committee for impeachment duties |
| 95 (1977) | Funded the Committee on the JFK and MLK Assassinations |
| 95 (1977) | Funded the Committee on Congressional Operations |
| 96 (1979) | Funded the Committee on Veterans Affairs |
| 96 (1979) | Funded the Committee on Small Business |
| 96 (1979) | Funded the Committee on Armed Services |
| 96 (1979) | Funded the Committee on Banking, Finance, and Urban Affairs |
| 96 (1979) | Funded the Committee on House Administration |
| 96 (1979) | Funded the Committee on Ways and Means |
| 96 (1979) | Funded the Committee on Public Works |
| 96 (1979) | Funded the Committee on Education and Labor |
| 96 (1979) | Funded the permanent select Committee on Intelligence |
| 96 (1979) | Funded the Committee on Foreign Affairs |
| 96 (1979) | **Funded the Committee on Rules** |
| 96 (1979) | Funded the Committee on the District of Columbia |
| 96 (1979) | Funded the Judiciary Committee |
| 96 (1979) | Funded the Committee on Science and Technology |
| 96 (1979) | Funded the Committee on Interior and Insular Affairs |
| 96 (1979) | Funded the Committee on Government Operations |
| 96 (1979) | Funded the Committee on the Post Office and Civil Service |
| 96 (1979) | Funded the Committee on Committees |
| 96 (1980) | **Funded the Committee on Rules** |
| 96 (1980) | Funded the Committee on Agriculture |
| 96 (1980) | Funded the Committee on Science and Technology |
| 96 (1980) | Funded the Committee on Merchant Marine and Fisheries |
| 96 (1980) | Funded the Committee on Ways and Means |
| 96 (1980) | Funded the Committee on Government Operations |
| 96 (1980) | Funded the Committee on Banking, Finance, and Urban Affairs |
| 96 (1980) | Funded the Committee on Interior and Insular Affairs |
| 96 (1980) | Funded the Committee on Foreign Affairs |
| 96 (1980) | Funded the Committee on the Post Office and Civil Service |
| 96 (1980) | Funded the Committee on Public Works |
| 96 (1980) | Funded the Committee on Aging |
| 96 (1980) | **Funded the Committee on Rules** |
| 96 (1980) | Funded the Committee on House Administration |
| 96 (1980) | Funded the Committee on Education and Labor |

| Congress (Year) | Summary |
| --- | --- |
| 96 (1980) | Funded the Judiciary Committee |
| 96 (1980) | Funded the Committee on Committees |
| 96 (1980) | Funded the Committee on Narcotics Abuse and Control |
| 96 (1980) | Funded the Committee on Interstate and Foreign Commerce |
| 96 (1980) | Funded the Committee on House Administration |
| 97 (1981) | Package of funding for House Committees |
| 97 (1982) | Package of funding for House Committees (2nd Session) |
| 98 (1983) | Package of funding for House Committees |
| 98 (1984) | Package of funding for House Committees (2nd Session) |
| 98 (1984) | Funded the Committee on Hunger |
| 99 (1985) | 4.45 percent funding increase for House Committees |
| 100 (1987) | Package of funding for House Committees |
| 100 (1988) | Package of funding for House Committees (2nd Session) |

### 25 Committee Jurisdiction or Establishment Changes

| | |
| --- | --- |
| 48 (1883) | Created the Committee on Liquor Traffic |
| 51 (1890) | Created the World's Fair Committee, to be appointed by the speaker |
| 57 (1901) | Made the Committee on the Census a standing committee; created the select committee on Industrial Arts and Expositions; abolished select Committee on Examination and Disposition of Documents |
| 58 (1903) | Made the Committee on Industrial Arts and Expositions a standing committee |
| 60 (1908) | Created a speaker-appointed committee to investigate wood prices |
| 61 (1910) | Created a committee to investigate the Interior Department |
| 62 (1911) | Created a committee to investigate antitrust |
| 66 (1919) | Created a speaker-appointed committee to investigate the War Department. |
| 83 (1954) | Created a joint committee to study postal reclassification |
| 84 (1955) | Created a committee to investigate Indiana bridge tolls |
| 91 (1970) | Created a committee to study events in Southeast Asia |
| 93 (1973) | Created a committee to study committee procedures |
| 94 (1975) | Created a committee on intelligence |
| 95 (1977) | Renewed the Committee on the JFK and MLK Assassinations |
| 95 (1977) | Created the Committee on Ethics |
| 95 (1977) | Created the Committee on Congressional Operations |
| 95 (1977) | Created a "permanent" select Committee on Intelligence |
| 95 (1977) | Transferred control of the House Beauty Shop |
| 95 (1978) | Renewed the Committee on the JFK and MLK Assassinations |
| 96 (1979) | Established the Committee on Committees |
| 96 (1979) | Created a committee on the outer continental shelf |
| 96 (1980) | Transferred Energy Committee jurisdiction to the Committee on Interstate and Foreign Commerce |
| 98 (1984) | Created Committee on Hunger |
| 99 (1985) | Renewed Committee on Hunger |

(*continued*)

APPENDIX 4.A.2 *(continued)*

| Congress (Year) | Summary |
| --- | --- |
| 100 (1987) | Renewed Committee on Hunger |

### 7 Miscellaneous Rule Changes

| | |
| --- | --- |
| 46 (1879) | Gave privilege to three committees |
| 47 (1882) | Prohibited minority committee from offering substitutes or resolutions |
| 67 (1922) | **Gave the chair of Rules more discretion over when to report bills** |
| 88 (1963) | **Permanently expanded the Rules Committee to 15 members** |
| 95 (1977) | Provided additional funds for the majority and minority leadership offices |
| 99 (1985) | Upheld the chair's ruling: motion to correct CR (Committee Rule) is not privileged |
| 100 (1987) | **Waived the two-thirds rule for consideration of Rules reports** |

### 36 Rule Changes Noted by Schickler and/or Binder

| | |
| --- | --- |
| 46 (1880) | Clerk prohibited from calling house to order without the speaker; expanded appropriations jurisdictions for the Agriculture Committee; prohibited amendments to general appropriations bills; required debate on Suspension of the Rules and Previous Question; suspension motions restricted to first and third Mondays; reinstated seconding of suspension motions |
| 47 (1882) | Only one motion to adjourn allowed before and after previous question is ordered |
| 47 (1883) | Suspension votes reduced from two thirds to a simple majority for some bills; **Rules Committee granted power to report bill-specific rules** |
| 51 (1890) | **Reed's rules adopted** |
| 52 (1892) | **Reed's rules repealed** |
| 53 (1894) | **Readopted Reed's disappearing quorum rule** |
| 54 (1896) | **Readopted remainder of Reed's rules** |
| 60 (1909) | **Established Calendar Wednesday** |
| 61 (1909) | Created Consent Calendar; **strengthened Calendar Wednesday;** motion to recommit secured for the minority |
| 61 (1910) | **Changed Rules Committee size and makeup; removed speaker** |
| 61 (1910) | **Created discharge procedure** |
| 62 (1911) | **Tightened discharge petition requirements;** tightened germaneness requirement on revenue bills; **restored the Holman rule** |
| 62 (1912) | **Discharge Calendar delayed in the order of business** |
| 64 (1916) | **Made Calendar Wednesday process more workable** |
| 68 (1924) | Loosened germaneness rule on revenue bills; **loosened discharge signature requirement; Rules Committee pocket veto banned** |
| 68 (1924) | Two-thirds vote required to waive layover rules |
| 69 (1925) | **Discharge petition rule tightened** |
| 72 (1931) | **Discharge signatures reduced to 145; loosened speaker control over discharging conferees** |
| 73 (1933) | **Special orders reported by Rules Committee made nondivisible** |

| Congress (Year) | Summary |
|---|---|
| 74 (1935) | **Discharge signatures increased from 145 to 218** |
| 79 (1945) | Established House Un-American Activities Committee |
| 81 (1949) | **21-day rule adopted, making it easier to bypass Rules** |
| 82 (1951) | **21-day rule repealed** |
| 87 (1961) | **Expanded Rules Committee to 15 (+2 Democrats, +1 Republican)** |
| 89 (1965) | **21-day rule adopted, making it easier to bypass Rules**; demanding engrossed bills prohibited |
| 90 (1967) | **21-day rule repealed** |
| 90 (1967) | Created Committee on Ethics, with equal majority/minority representation |
| 91 (1970) | Dispensed with Journal reading unless ordered by a majority; minority right to call witnesses guaranteed; minority party staff increased; minority party guaranteed one-third investigatory funds; printing of minority views to be included in committee reports; minority guaranteed debate time |
| 92 (1971) | Minority party guarantee of committee staff funds eliminated |
| 93 (1973) | Number of suspension days increased; speaker allowed to change meeting time of the House with a majority vote |
| 93 (1974) | Guaranteed vote on any nongermane Senate amendment; quorum calls severely limited; cluster voting on suspensions allowed |
| 94 (1975) | Proxy voting ban in committee eliminated |
| 94 (1976) | Conference reports available 2 hours before consideration |
| 95 (1977) | Increased the number of days for suspensions |
| 96 (1979) | Increased threshold for demanding a recorded vote; no quorum necessary prior to approving the Journal; only one vote allowed on approving the Journal; eliminated seconding of suspension motions |
| 98 (1983) | Limited riders to appropriations bills |

## APPENDIX 4.A.3. A NOTE ON OUR CODING OF THE HOLMAN RULE

The Holman rule is a device intended to allow a majority party in the House to deal on better strategic terms with a president of the opposite party. Specifically, it allows the Appropriations Committee to attach legislative riders to its bills as long as the changes in existing law serve to reduce expenditures. It was first adopted in the 44th Congress (1876) when a Democratic House majority faced a Republican president, dropped in the 49th Congress (1885) when a Democratic House faced an incoming Democratic president, readopted in the 52nd Congress (1891) when a Democratic House faced a Republican president, dropped again in the 54th Congress (1895) when a Republican House faced a Republican president, readopted in the 62nd Congress (1911) when a Democratic House faced a Republican president, and then refurbished substantially in the 98th Congress (1983) when a Democratic House faced a Republican president.

The rule allows the Appropriations Committee to insert legislation into general appropriations bills. The majority party can thus insert some of its legislative priorities – those the president would veto if submitted separately – in the safe confines of a general appropriations bill that must be passed. The logic is similar to that governing the use of omnibus continuing resolutions (Kiewiet and McCubbins 1991) and omnibus bills (Krutz 2001), both of which are used more intensively under divided government in order to present the president with unvetoable or veto-proof packages.

We count every adoption of the Holman rule as an important victory for the majority party. Thus, we include in our database the adoptions in 1891 and 1911, as does Schickler. Binder includes neither, as the rule does not explicitly address minority rights.

What about removals of the Holman rule? We do not count these as minority victories or majority losses. The rule is removed in 1885 and 1895, when the majority party enjoys a president of the same party and thus does not need the additional ability to create omnibus vehicles.

APPENDIX 4.A.4. SEVEN RULE CHANGES THAT WE INCLUDE BUT THAT PREVIOUS SCHOLARS DO NOT

Item 1: In the 46th Congress, the House conferred privileged access to the floor on three financial committees (Ways and Means; Banking and Currency; Coinage, Weights, and Measures). The vote to do so was highly partisan, with 92 percent of the majority Democrats supporting the change and 96 percent of the minority Republicans opposing it (see the 10th vote in the Congress).

Item 2: In the 47th Congress, during debate on a resolution relating to the land grants of the Northern Pacific Railroad Company, the speaker ruled that the minority of a committee had no power to append substitutes or resolutions proposing legislation to its reports, and that such power is reserved for the majority of a committee. On a motion to table an appeal of the chair's ruling, the House upheld the speaker, with 98.9 percent of the majority Republicans voting to support, and 98.5 percent of the minority Democrats voting to overturn (see the 230th vote in the Congress).[43]

Item 3: In the 67th Congress, the Speaker rendered a decision on a point of order that enhanced the Rules Committee's power to determine the time at which special rules would be brought up to the floor, at the expense of ordinary members. In particular, the speaker held that the chair of Rules could "report a bill within any reasonable time as fixed by the Committee [on Rules]" and that

---

[43] We include this event from 1882 in our dataset on the following grounds. Either the minority had previously exercised the right of appending matter to committee reports, or it had not. If it had exercised such a right, then the speaker's decision ended this right. If it had not exercised such a right, then evidently the minority was trying to assert such a right in the 47th Congress – with the speaker rebuffing their claim and in the process clarifying an ambiguity in the existing rules. Either a clear or a potential minority right was eradicated.

the member who had introduced the bill in question had no right to call up the bill (or the special rule governing its consideration) as a question of privilege. In the 227th roll call of the 67th Congress, the House voted to table an appeal from the speaker's decision, thereby ratifying it (with 99 percent of the minority party voting against the motion to table and 86 percent of the majority party voting in favor). Had the original point of order been sustained, the Rules Committee's ability to control the flow of legislation to the floor would have been lessened, with the original sponsors of bills correspondingly empowered.

Item 4: In the 88th Congress, the House permanently expanded the Rules Committee from 12 to 15 members (see the 3rd vote in the Congress). Binder and Schickler are well aware of this change but choose not to include it, viewing it as simply a continuation of the action in the previous Congress. We include it as a separate item because there was a separate vote.

Item 5: In the 95th Congress, the House agreed to H.R. 393, authorizing additional funds for office personnel and equipment for the party leaders and whips (with the lion's share going to the majority). On final passage, 93 percent of the majority party (Democrats) voted in favor of the resolution, while 73 percent of the minority party (Republicans) voted against (see the 96th vote).

Item 6: In the 99th Congress, the speaker ruled that a motion to make a correction in the *Congressional Record* did not raise a question of privilege. The minority Republicans challenged the speaker's decision, but their challenge was rebuffed on a straight party-line vote (see the 67th vote).

Item 7: In the 100th Congress, fewer than five months after the start of the first session, the House adopted H.R. 157, which waived the requirement for a two-thirds vote to consider a special rule on the same day that it was reported. The vote on the rule change was almost strictly along party lines, as 99 percent of the majority party (Democrats) voted to waive the requirement, while 95 percent of the minority party (Republicans) voted against the change (see the 86th vote).

## APPENDIX 4.B. THE DISCHARGE PROCEDURE

In its original form, the discharge procedure was not a threat to the majority party's control of the agenda. First, motions to discharge were limited to public bills and joint resolutions. Thus, the Rules Committee could not be discharged of a special rule, as these took the form of simple resolutions. Second, motions to discharge could pass only with "an affirmative vote of a majority of the membership of the House." As Hasbrouck (1927: 142) noted, attendance rates in the House at that time were sufficiently low that requiring approval by a majority of the whole membership was often tantamount to requiring nearly unanimous approval of those present and voting. Third, the majority party leadership did not find it difficult to hamstring the rule, making it completely unworkable and inducing the House to agree in dispensing with the Discharge Calendar on most days. The main tactic was to introduce a fake discharge motion and then insist on reading the bill to be discharged in its entirety until the time allotted for discharges had been exhausted (see Hasbrouck 1927: 142–4).

When the Democrats came into power, they changed the discharge rule (on April 5, 1911), putatively to make it more workable. As Binder (1997: 140) notes, however, "their solution in practice *constrained* members' rights to initiate a committee discharge" (italics added). Moreover, the Democratic leadership used adjournment motions to avoid sitting on Mondays (the only day discharge motions were in order) and, when the House finally did sit on a Monday, the leadership used a special rule from Rules to skip over all discharge motions. It was not until the next session of the House, in January 1912, that any discharge motions were considered. And then it transpired that the minority leadership had filed motions to discharge some of the majority party's key bills before they were ready, with the result that some had to be abandoned (Hasbrouck 1927: 146–7). The Democrats responded on February 3, 1912, by relegating the Discharge Calendar to third place on Mondays, behind both the Unanimous Consent Calendar and motions to suspend the rules. In the next year, as further protection, "the discharge rule was suspended on June 3, 1913, for the duration of the special session" (Hasbrouck 1927: 147). As Hasbrouck (1927: 147) notes, "the discharge rule remained for ten years a 'dead letter.'"

It was not until 1924 that the rules governing discharge were again revisited, in an attempt to make the procedure workable. Having realized that discharge was unworkable, a group of Progressives led by Charles Crisp (D-GA) set out to reform the rule. The circumstances were similar to those in 1910, with a Progressive-Democratic alliance pressuring a Republican majority. The important changes in the discharge procedure were as follows. (1) Under the old rule, a motion to discharge had to be seconded by a majority of those present with voting by tellers. Under the new rule, a motion to discharge was put at the clerk's desk and required 150 signatures (about the size of a typical majority of those present at the time) to be seconded. This allowed the committee subject to discharge to negotiate with those signing or threatening to sign the petition. (2) Discharge motions were moved to first place in the order of business on the first and third Mondays of each month (instead of third place as formerly). (3) The vote to discharge required only an ordinary majority of a quorum, instead of a majority of the whole membership of the House. (4) "Any signer of the discharge petition could move immediate consideration of the bill. Formerly, it had merely gone to its appropriate calendar, where it was little better off than in committee" (Hasbrouck 1927: 152–3). (5) "The new rule applied to resolutions as well as to bills. Thus a proposal to change the rules, to adopt a special order, or to undertake an investigation, if held up in the Committee on Rules, could be brought out by a discharge motion" (Hasbrouck 1927: 152–3).

The 1924 version of the discharge procedure was in fact used to push a bill regulating railroad labor disputes several steps through the legislative process, in the teeth of a determined filibuster. It thus did seem to be a workable procedure and one that had the potential to disrupt the majority party's control of the agenda. However, in the end, the bill did not pass. Moreover, when the Republican majority increased in the 69th Congress, they promptly removed from the Rules Committee all but two of the eight Republican members of the last House, who had agreed to report the new procedure from Rules. The new Rules Committee then brought in a new procedure designed to be unworkable.[44] As a Democratic leader noted, the Republicans knew "that they have proposed a rule which hermetically seals the door against any bill ever coming out of a committee" against their leaders' wishes (Hasbrouck 1927: 164). Nonetheless, the new rule was adopted.

The discharge procedure was liberalized in the 72nd Congress (1931–2) due once again to a push by Crisp and the Progressives. Motions to discharge no longer had to be seconded and had to be signed by only 145 members (down from 218) to be put on the Discharge Calendar. Once on the calendar, motions could be brought up on the second and fourth Mondays of each month (rather than on just the third). Approval of discharge required a simple majority of those voting, rather than a majority of the whole House. Whereas the old rule had merely placed the discharged bill on the appropriate calendar, the new rule allowed the House to choose between this course and the immediate consideration of the bill "under the general rules of the House." Although the new rule clearly made discharge more workable than did the old, we would note that any coalition using the discharge procedure to push legislation anathema to the Rules Committee still faced a tougher parliamentary row to hoe than would an equally sized coalition with Rules' backing. If the coalition chose to place the bill on the appropriate calendar, they would then need to mount a second discharge petition in order to force the Rules Committee to report a special rule for the bill (something that was allowed under the new procedure). If instead they chose to consider the bill immediately, they would have to do so under the general rules of the House, which means that all points of order against the bill would be admissible, that all amendments would be in order, and that the full array of dilatory tactics could be employed. (The majority party could choose to consider its bills under the general rules of the House. In practice, however, it *never* does because these rules make it very difficult to legislate effectively, especially for a controversial or complex bill.)

The Democrats again weakened the discharge motion in the 74th House (1935), increasing the signature requirement once again to 218. Binder (1997: 153) opines that the reform of discharge in 1935 ended any challenge to Rules' agenda power. Beth (1998) describes discharge as difficult by design, providing comprehensive statistics on how infrequently it has been used.

---

[44] Among other things, the motion to discharge (1) had to be seconded by 218 members voting by tellers, (2) had to be signed by 218 members, (3) had to be approved by 218 members, (4) was in order only on the third Monday of each month, and (5) only had the effect of removing the bill from committee and placing it on the appropriate calendar, rather than bringing it to the floor (Hasbrouck 1927: 163–4).

For most of the Congresses after 1894, the discharge procedure did not seriously challenge the Rules Committee's ability to control the legislative agenda. Even in the 68th and the 72nd–73rd Congresses, when the discharge procedure was at its most workable, it took a disciplined, committed, and patient majority to push bills through the procedure if the majority party leaders were opposed.

To the extent that the discharge procedure was an effective tool, it was used as an instrument of the majority party leadership against the blockade of the Rules Committee. The most famous instance of a successful discharge petition came in 1938, when the Rules Committee was holding up consideration of the Fair Labor Standards Act.[45] At the urging of President Roosevelt, the majority party leadership championed the effort to discharge the Rules Committee. The discharge was successful, but after floor consideration the bill was recommitted unexpectedly; however, the bill was reported again and blocked by the Rules committee. Thus, the majority party leadership once again successfully spearheaded the effort to discharge Rules. This time the bill passed the House and was signed into law.

Thus, in response to those who argue that the discharge procedure undermines the ability of the majority party to control the agenda, we emphasize that the discharge petition is not a major (or even minor) thoroughfare of legislation and, therefore, does not undo majority party agenda control. As the preceding discussion demonstrates, discharge petitions are extremely difficult to use successfully,[46] and as a result are almost never undertaken (See Beth 1999, 2001; Oleszek 2004).[47] Furthermore, even where there have been attempts to strengthen and simplify the discharge petition, the actual procedure has been difficult, particularly if it is used against a similarly sized coalition that has the backing of the Rules Committee or majority leadership and seeks to keep the bill off the agenda. Indeed, using the discharge procedure to get around committees does not do members any good if they lack the backing of the Rules Committee or the majority-party leadership.

---

[45] For an excellent account of the legislative history of this bill, see Douglas and Hackman (1938).

[46] Indeed, Oleszek (2004) emphasizes that the discharge procedure is difficult to use partly because majority-party leaders often urge their members not to sign discharge petitions.

[47] From 1931 to 2002, 513 discharge petitions were filed in the House, but only 47 attracted the required number of signatures, and only 19 bills were actually discharged and passed by the House (Oleszek 2004).

# 5

# Final-Passage Votes

Certainly since early in their history, the House of Representatives and the Senate have relied on parties and committees to provide the structure that enables them to get their work done. Parties organize the chambers and provide coordination; committees do most of the substantive work on legislation.

– Sinclair 2002b

## 5.1. INTRODUCTION

The Republican majority dominated the agenda of the Ways and Means Committee in the 108th Congress. Of the 64 bills reported by the committee, 61 were sponsored by Republicans. Only three bills sponsored by Democrats made it out of committee and only two of these passed the House. Both successful Democratic bills were sponsored by Tom Lantos (D-CA), both involved relations with Burma, and both passed under suspension of the rules – pursuant to motions made by Republicans – with only two dissenting votes.

In contrast to the broad support that the two Democratic bills garnered on a minor matter, many of the 61 Republican bills reported by Ways and Means were hotly partisan and involved major matters. Perhaps the hottest of all bills reported by Ways and Means concerned pension reform.

In what the Democratic minority dubbed "an egregious abuse of power and a pointless provocation," House Republicans on Ways and Means used every tactic available to them to push legislation (H.R. 1776) that would reform employer pension plans (Ota, Higa, and Hughes 2003). It all began when Chairman Bill Thomas (R-CA) changed the original version of the bill, brought it up for consideration at an 11:00 P.M. meeting of the committee, and then insisted that all members be ready to vote on it the next morning. Needless to say, the Democrats, who had only ten hours to consider the bill, were outraged. Staging a procedural protest, the Democrats demanded a line-by-line reading of the measure and then retreated to a library next door to study the measure. They left only one member – Representative Fortney Stark (D-CA) – in the hearing room to watch over the proceedings and to make sure that Republicans did not shortcut the reading of the bill (Ota et al. 2003; Hastert 2004).

However, as soon as the Democrats left the room, Thomas ordered that the reading of the measure be stopped (a move that normally requires unanimous approval of all members present), and he then banged his gavel before Stark could object – or so Thomas claims. Indeed, following this maneuver by the Republican majority, Stark argued that he had in fact objected, but that Thomas incorrectly said that his objection was untimely (Ota et al. 2003). Offering yet another explanation for what happened that morning, Speaker Dennis Hastert (R-IL) insisted that "Stark wasn't paying attention, so when the reading stopped, Thomas moved the bill – bang, bang, bang – just like that . . . we were lucky, too, that Stark blew it" (Hastert 2004: 248).

For reasons that also remain a matter of dispute, Thomas summoned the Capitol Police sometime during this incident. According to House Democrats, Thomas called the police in order to eject them from the library where they were discussing the details of the bill (Ota et al. 2003). Republicans argue that Thomas called the police because Stark, after failing to stop Thomas from moving the bill, physically threatened Representative Scott McInnis (R-CO). Despite the conflicting interpretations of the pandemonium surrounding the markup of the pension bill, three facts are undisputed: (1) After the squabble over the reading of the bill, a furious Stark stormed out of the room; (2) with all of the Democrats elsewhere, the Republicans passed the bill by a voice vote; and (3) the Democrats' effort to lodge an official protest in the form of a resolution (offered by Minority Leader Nancy Pelosi) to void the committee's actions and to reprimand Thomas was tabled, 170–143, on a party-line vote (Ota et al. 2003). Thus, despite the Democrats' protests and objections, the Republican majority was able to roll past the Democrats and emerge victorious.

Majority parties do not run roughshod over minority opposition every day in the House. Neither, however, are partisan bills rare or confined to the recent past.[1] More important for present purposes, events in which committee chairs treat a majority of their own party with similar roughness, on behalf of legislation supported by the minority and centrist defectors from the majority, are vanishingly rare. This suggests – in conformity with our theory – that committee chairs and other officeholders are constrained from using their agenda-setting

---

[1] For example, as the Democratic majority won nearly every battle during the Great Society, Representative William Cramer (R-FL) complained that "'it looks like we now have the great stampede instead of the Great Society'" (Hunter 1965, quoting Cramer). Similarly, Representative Peter Frelinghuysen Jr. (R-NJ) claimed that "'we [the Republicans] have been blackjacked, gagged, threatened and bulldozed to accept something that we know is not good'" (CQ Almanac 1964, quoting Frelinghuysen Jr.). During the passage of the Contract with America, however, it was the Democrats' turn to complain as the Republican majority continued "to roll untrammeled through the components of the Contract with America" (Rosenbaum 1995). As minority member Representative Melvin Watt (D-NC) exclaimed, "'I've been banging my head against the wall all day'" (Seelye 1995, quoting Watt).

powers to advance bills that would roll the majority party but are free to use their powers to advance bills that would roll the minority party. In this chapter, we provide systematic evidence pertinent to judging whether this claim is valid.

In particular, we generate testable hypotheses that put the Cartel Agenda Model and the Floor Agenda Model head to head. Using roll call voting data from the 45th to 105th Congresses (1877 to 1998), we then test our hypotheses and find substantial evidence supporting the Cartel Agenda Model. We also show that negative agenda control is an advantage of majority status that is not conditional on changes in the internal homogeneity of the majority party.

## 5.2. COMPARING THE FLOOR AGENDA AND CARTEL AGENDA MODELS: PREDICTED ROLLS

Hypotheses C1 and C2 from Chapter 3 both have testable implications that can be stated in terms of the concept of a *roll*. We say that a party is rolled at the agenda-setting stage when a majority of the party unsuccessfully opposes the placement of a particular bill on the floor agenda. A party is rolled at final passage when a majority of its members unsuccessfully oppose a particular bill's final passage. In terms of rolls, Result C1 says the majority party is never rolled at the agenda-setting stage, while Result C2 says it is never rolled at final passage.

We should hasten to note that these "the majority party never gets rolled" predictions are similar in analytic status to other predictions drawn from complete information models, such as "there is never any war" or "there are never any vetoes" (cf. Cameron 2000). These sorts of results should be viewed as baselines illustrating the extreme case of zero uncertainty and no costs to acting. Add a little uncertainty into these models, and it is well known that one begins to get "mistakes" – in the present context, mistakes in which the agenda setter schedules a bill that a majority of the majority party dislikes (because, for example, the status quo point turns out not to be where it was most likely to be). We explore a model with costly action in Chapter 6 and one with incomplete information in Chapters 8 and 9, showing that the main results derived here are largely preserved.

Our second result, C2, can be restated in terms of roll call "cutpoints." In a unidimensional spatial model, the cutpoint of a roll call pitting a bill, $b_j$, against a status quo, $SQ_j$, is simply the point midway between the two: $c_j = (b_j + SQ_j)/2$. It is called a cutpoint because it splits the legislators into two homogeneous behavioral classes: All those to the left of the cutpoint vote for the leftmost alternative, while all those to the right of the cutpoint vote for the rightmost alternative. Our result C2 is equivalent to the following proposition: no bill generating a cutpoint between $M_j$ and $F_j$ ever passes.[2]

---

[2] Note that the majority party will be rolled on a roll call if and only if the cutpoint lies between $M_j$ and $F_j$.

Now consider what happens when closed rules are allowed but are controlled by the majority party (i.e., as if by a majority vote in the party caucus). In this case, the majority-party median on a given dimension is strictly more powerful than in the open-rule case and can make take-it-or-leave-it offers to the floor median, as in the classic "setter" model of Romer and Rosenthal (cf. Rosenthal 1990). The following points can be easily verified.

First, even though it remains true that no status quo point lying between $M$ and $F$ will be targeted by a bill that reaches the floor (because the majority party median can only lose by allowing such bills onto the floor), under a closed rule it is possible that status quo points lying between $2M - F$ and $M$ will be targeted. Under an open rule, the majority-party median anticipates that any such status quo point will be shifted to the floor median; to avoid this outcome, no bill is allowed on the floor. Under a majority-controlled closed rule, in contrast, status quo points in the region $(2M - F, M)$ can be shifted to the majority-party median and passed without amendment. Thus, our result C1 changes somewhat.[3]

Second, our result C2 – and its cutpoint version – remain the same. The majority, fortified with the additional power of setting closed rules, still blocks all bills that would roll it, and this is still equivalent to blocking all bills that yield cutpoints between $M$ and $F$. In what follows, we focus on testing C2, a prediction that follows both from the "weaker" version of majority-party agenda control (in which the party must live with open rules) and from the "stronger" version (in which it can fashion closed rules).[4]

Now consider Hypotheses F1 and F2 from Chapter 3. First, it should be understood that under the Floor Agenda Model there is no reason to expect the majority party to have a low roll rate merely because it has a majority. To illustrate this point, consider a *leftist* majority party (i.e., a majority party most of whose members' ideal points lie to the left of the median legislator's ideal point). Suppose that a bill moving a status quo $SQ$ to $F$ is proposed, where $M < SQ < F$ (i.e., the status quo lies between the majority party and floor medians). Under the Floor Agenda Model, the bill will pass even though a majority of

---

[3] The original statement of C1 is "No dimension $j$ on which the status quo $(SQ_j)$ is preferred to the floor median $(F_j)$ by a majority of the majority party is ever scheduled for floor consideration." This is equivalent to preserving all status quo points such that $SQ_j \in [2M_j - F_j, F_j]$. With majority-controlled closed rules, the only status quo points that will be preserved will be such that $SQ_j \in [M_j, F_j]$. That is, the majority party will change status quo points in the interval $[2M_j - F_j, M_j]$, when it can control the amount by which those status quo policies are changed (via a closed rule).

[4] We make two further observations about these results. First, something of the same results survives into multidimensional models in which legislators have spherical indifference contours. In particular: if the agenda is set as if by majority vote in the majority caucus, then the only bills that are scheduled move policy closer to the majority-party yolk (the smallest hypersphere that intersects all majority-party median hyperplanes). In the unidimensional model, the yolk collapses to the median, and so it is the median that acts as the "policy attractor." Second, the standard unidimensional spatial model assumes that there are no opportunity, consideration, or proposal costs. Changing any of these zero-cost assumptions slightly would not centrally affect the majority party's negative agenda-setting success.

the majority party will vote against it. In other words, *the mere fact that the majority party has a majority, even a big one, does not protect it from being rolled.*

The frequency of majority-party rolls depends on how many status quo points there are in the interval between $2M - F$ and $F$ (see Figure 3.1), relative to the total number of status quo points altered in the session – not on the majority's size.[5] Theoretically, it is hard to say much about where the status quo points are, but we use two principles to help pin them down. First, if the House median shifts to the left (right) between $t$ and $t + 1$, then the status quo points at $t + 1$ should tend to be to the right (left) of the new median. Second, if status quo policies are subject to stochastic shocks, then they should be distributed relatively widely and symmetrically around the lagged House median.[6]

To explore the Cartel Agenda Model's predictions, we first analyze all joint resolutions[7] reaching a final-passage vote[8] in the House between the 83rd and 105th Congresses (inclusive).[9] We henceforth call this our Postwar dataset – thus, the difference between our Post-Reconstruction and Postwar datasets is that the former (i.e., final-passage votes on H.R. bills for Congresses 45 through 105) is a longer time series but covers only H.R. bills; the latter is a shorter time series but covers a broader swath of bills.[10]

We coded each final-passage vote as either ordinary (only a majority required for passage) or extraordinary (a super-majority of two thirds required for passage), excluding the latter from analysis.[11] We identify rolls by examining how

---

[5] Assuming the distribution of status quo points has no areas of zero density, a necessary and sufficient condition for the majority party to have a zero probability of losing under the Floor Agenda Model is $M_j = F_j$ for all $j$. This might happen, for example, if the majority party consisted of a single unitary party (which successfully imposed a single ideal point on its members). But it should be a rare event in cases where parties cannot be taken as "analytic units."

[6] Results in later chapters will enable us to say more about the distribution of status quo points. Suffice it to say for now that *either* there are very few "bad" issue dimensions (i.e., those with status quo points nearer to the median of the majority party than is the floor median), *or* any "bad" issues are not brought to the floor for consideration (they are blocked), *or* any "bad" issues are packaged together with others in such a way that a majority of the majority party can support the omnibus bill. Our preferred interpretation, for which evidence will be adduced as the book progresses, is that there are plenty of "bad" issues.

[7] Joint resolutions require the approval of both the Senate and the president and become public laws, if approved by all branches (or if a presidential veto is overridden). They are put by the House into four classes or series: H.R., S., H. J. Res., and S. J. Res.

[8] We include votes to approve conference reports as "final-passage votes" here.

[9] Our analysis is based on a House roll call dataset compiled by David Rohde and maintained by the Political Institutions and Public Choice Program at Michigan State University. To obtain a copy of the data, contact David Rohde at rohde@msu.edu.

[10] In addition, we used different methods to identify final-passage votes on joint resolutions in the two datasets. For the Post-Reconstruction data, we used the method described in footnote 40 of Chapter 4. For the Postwar data, this information is coded in Rohde's data (available at *www.settingtheagenda.com*).

[11] We exclude bills requiring a super-majority to pass because it is not surprising that the majority party can avoid being rolled on super-majority votes.

TABLE 5.1. *House Rolls on Final-Passage Votes for Majority and Minority Parties, by Congresses 45–105*

| Congress | Majority Rolls | Minority Rolls | Total Final-Passage Votes | Majority Party |
|---|---|---|---|---|
| 45 | 5 | 7 | 21 | Democrats |
| 46 | 5 | 19 | 55 | Democrats |
| 47 | 5 | 15 | 45 | Republicans |
| 48 | 1 | 8 | 46 | Democrats |
| 49 | 6 | 4 | 27 | Democrats |
| 50 | 3 | 3 | 10 | Democrats |
| 51 | 1 | 17 | 25 | Republicans |
| 52 | 1 | 4 | 18 | Democrats |
| 53 | 1 | 11 | 25 | Democrats |
| 54 | 0 | 8 | 12 | Republicans |
| 55 | 1 | 12 | 18 | Republicans |
| 56 | 0 | 6 | 7 | Republicans |
| 57 | 3 | 4 | 13 | Republicans |
| 58 | 0 | 3 | 4 | Republicans |
| 59 | 1 | 5 | 11 | Republicans |
| 60 | 0 | 3 | 5 | Republicans |
| 61 | 1 | 10 | 11 | Republicans |
| 62 | 0 | 10 | 24 | Republicans |
| 63 | 1 | 10 | 23 | Democrats |
| 64 | 2 | 7 | 27 | Democrats |
| 65 | 0 | 6 | 37 | Democrats |
| 66 | 1 | 11 | 38 | Republicans |
| 67 | 0 | 16 | 34 | Republicans |
| 68 | 1 | 7 | 22 | Republicans |
| 69 | 0 | 6 | 20 | Republicans |
| 70 | 0 | 2 | 10 | Republicans |
| 71 | 0 | 5 | 10 | Republicans |
| 72 | 1 | 8 | 16 | Democrats |
| 73 | 0 | 13 | 27 | Democrats |
| 74 | 2 | 12 | 31 | Democrats |
| 75 | 0 | 10 | 22 | Democrats |
| 76 | 2 | 10 | 32 | Democrats |
| 77 | 0 | 9 | 38 | Democrats |
| 78 | 4 | 1 | 29 | Democrats |
| 79 | 2 | 5 | 41 | Democrats |
| 80 | 0 | 7 | 35 | Republicans |
| 81 | 2 | 14 | 41 | Democrats |
| 82 | 0 | 7 | 23 | Democrats |
| 83 | 0 | 8 | 38 | Republicans |
| 84 | 2 | 3 | 43 | Democrats |
| 85 | 2 | 5 | 43 | Democrats |
| 86 | 2 | 16 | 49 | Democrats |
| 87 | 1 | 19 | 56 | Democrats |

| Congress | Majority Rolls | Minority Rolls | Total Final-Passage Votes | Majority Party |
|---|---|---|---|---|
| 88 | 2 | 29 | 81 | Democrats |
| 89 | 0 | 34 | 114 | Democrats |
| 90 | 1 | 16 | 121 | Democrats |
| 91 | 4 | 12 | 150 | Democrats |
| 92 | 4 | 7 | 150 | Democrats |
| 93 | 1 | 30 | 236 | Democrats |
| 94 | 3 | 57 | 227 | Democrats |
| 95 | 2 | 44 | 187 | Democrats |
| 96 | 0 | 31 | 157 | Democrats |
| 97 | 2 | 24 | 96 | Democrats |
| 98 | 3 | 44 | 103 | Democrats |
| 99 | 1 | 35 | 89 | Democrats |
| 100 | 2 | 40 | 116 | Democrats |
| 101 | 1 | 39 | 108 | Democrats |
| 102 | 0 | 39 | 142 | Democrats |
| 103 | 1 | 56 | 160 | Democrats |
| 104 | 1 | 63 | 136 | Republicans |
| 105 | 3 | 51 | 133 | Republicans |

the membership of each party voted on each final-passage vote. If the "nay" votes exceeded the "aye" votes for one party, but the measure passed nonetheless, then we code that party as having been rolled on that vote.

The House majority party was rolled on 1.7 percent (54 times out of 3,134) of all ordinary final-passage votes on joint resolutions in the Postwar dataset. This is an average of 2.1 majority rolls per Congress in the 83rd–105th Congresses. The analogous figures for the minority party were an overall roll rate of 25.9 percent (811 rolls out of 3,134 votes) and 35.3 rolls per Congress.[12]

To explore the Cartel Agenda Model's predictions further, we analyze the votes in our Post-Reconstruction data. Table 5.1 displays the number of rolls on bills in the Post-Reconstruction data for both the majority and minority parties in each Congress. The average number of times the majority party was rolled in a Congress is 1.5, and the median number is 1. By contrast, the average number of rolls of the minority party is 16 with a median of 10. All told, the majority was rolled 90 times out of 3,668 votes, compared to 1,017 times for the minority.

Figures 5.1 and 5.2 present the House and Senate roll rates for both the majority and minority parties. First, it is immediately obvious from these figures that the majority party almost always has a considerably lower roll rate than the minority party. Second, the Senate and House roll rates appear to move

---

[12] In addition, we have examined the possibility that the majority party is infrequently rolled on final-passage votes on bills but is more frequently rolled on subsequent votes to adopt conference reports. We find that the majority party is rolled on conference adoption at rates similar to its roll rates on final passage of bills.

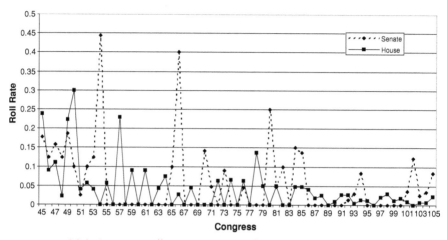

FIGURE 5.1. Majority-party roll rate in House and Senate, Congresses 45–105

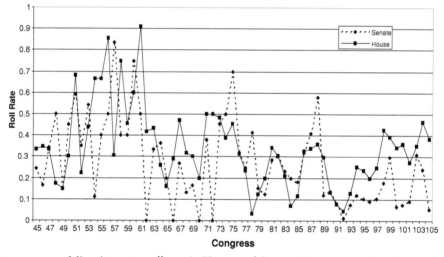

FIGURE 5.2. Minority-party roll rate in House and Senate, Congresses 45–105

together. The Senate appears to have a few large spikes in the majority roll rate, but some of these are caused by a dearth of final passage votes, so that only one or two rolls cause a high roll rate.

## 5.3. A DIGRESSION ON THE U.S. SENATE

In the Senate, the majority party's roll rate is a bit less than 6 percent, while the minority party's roll rate is greater than 28 percent (using Post-Reconstruction data). Thus, the Senate majority party's roll rate is over twice that of the House majority party (6 percent versus $90/3,668 = 2.5$ percent) but, in both chambers, the minority party suffers a much greater roll rate than does the majority. We can also note that the Senate majority party's roll rate is more variable across time than is the House majority party's.

Although it is beyond the scope of the present volume to develop a theory of agenda control for the Senate, we can offer some observations as preliminary steps toward such a theory.

First, the Senate majority party's larger and more variable roll rate may be related to the Senate's inability to fully control its own agenda. For example, the president controls nominations, which the Senate must approve or reject; while the House initiates budget legislation, which again the Senate must approve or reject. When the president and Senate are from different parties, the president may make some nominations that the Senate majority would prefer not to consider on the floor but feels constrained by public pressure to consider. Similarly, when the House and Senate are of different parties, the House may raise issues that the Senate majority would prefer not to consider but feels constrained to.

Second, under unified partisan control, the Senate may benefit from the House's greater agenda control by strategically using conference committees. Indeed, Van Houweling (2003) argues that the Senate and House may collude in their use of conference committees.

Third, when the President and Senate are unified Senators may face pressure from the President to pass the party's legislation (King 1983, Edwards 1989, Bond and Fleisher 1990, Beckman 2004). Beckmann, in particular, argues that the President will place intensive pressure on pivotal members of the Senate, which may give the party the advantage it needs to pass policies preferred by the majority party.

Fourth, the Senate may make greater use of indirect agenda control techniques because it has less ability to directly control the agenda. For instance, one tool the majority party may use is to "fill the agenda tree," which determines the items that actually receive floor time.

Fifth, in the modern era the Senate also seems to utilize giant omnibus budget legislation, which cannot be filibustered, to enact a wide range of policies. For example, Senate Republicans attached a provision to the 2006 budget to allow oil drilling in the Arctic National Wildlife Refuge, which was a highly contentious issue (Stolberg 2005).

Sixth, contrary to popular (and some scholarly) belief, the majority party in the Senate may exercise agenda control through its substantial power to interpret its standing rules and precedent. Perhaps the clearest example of such a rule is the one that requires 60 votes to invoke cloture and end a filibuster. Although various scholars have considered the cloture requirement to be an exogenous rule that the majority party cannot alter (the reason being that any attempt to alter the cloture requirement or eliminate the filibuster would, in turn, be filibustered by the minority party), recent research has demonstrated that the majority party in the Senate is able to alter the cloture requirement and has done so in the past without requiring a super-majority (Schickler and Wawro 2004). Furthermore, recent discussions of the "nuclear option" – a procedure whereby the chair can reinterpret precedent to reduce or eliminate the cloture requirement and then deflect any objections by putting them to a majority vote on the floor – suggest yet another weapon that the majority party might use to control the agenda (Dart 2003; Hulse 2003). Thus, at the end of the day, the rules in the Senate, as in the House, are determined by the majority party.

The combination of methods of agenda control we have reviewed – piggybacking on the House's agenda powers, filling the amendment tree, and threatening to use the "nuclear option" in response to filibusters – may help explain why the Senate majority party does as well as it does. Although the Senate majority does not appear to be as effective as the House majority in achieving its legislative goals, we present evidence throughout this book that it is nonetheless able to substantially affect legislative outcomes.

## 5.4. AGENDA CONTROL IN THE HOUSE: RESULTS

For now we will concentrate on the House of Representatives. The idealized Cartel Agenda Model provides a very close approximation to the observed behavior of members of the majority and minority parties in the House. The majority was rolled 1.7 percent of the time in the Postwar data, and 2.5 percent of the time in the Post-Reconstruction data. Moreover, as shown in Table 5.1, in 45 of the 47 Congresses from our Post-Reconstruction data in which the majority party was the same as in the previous Congress, the minority roll rate exceeded the majority roll rate, often by a factor of ten. The prediction errors here are few, numbering only 90 in the Post-Reconstruction data and 54 in the Postwar data. Also, as we will show in Chapter 6, these errors arise almost entirely as the result of factors that are explainable outside of our model, but that we can control for in our analysis.

In contrast, the Floor Agenda Model does not seem to provide as close an approximation to the data on roll rates. If we make reasonable assumptions about the distribution of status quo points prior to a Congress,[13] then we would expect the majority-party roll rate in most Congresses to equal or exceed the minority-party roll rate (when the current majority party was also the majority in the preceding Congress). As we noted, this happened only twice in the 47 post-Reconstruction Congresses in which the majority party was the same as in the preceding Congress (see Table 5.1).

## 5.5. COMPARING THE FLOOR AGENDA AND CARTEL AGENDA
##        MODELS: COMPARATIVE STATICS

The principal way to test the Cartel and Floor Agenda Models is to study the hypothesized relationships between variables in the models. In research design terms, this is commonly known as a dose–response study, in which changing the dose level of some treatment is hypothesized to have an effect on outcomes

---

[13] "Reasonable" means symmetric or, if not symmetric, skewed toward the prior Congress's major-ity party median.

TABLE 5.2. *Predicted and Estimated Effects of Distance on Roll Rates, Majority and Minority Parties, Congresses 45–105*

|  | Majority $\hat{\beta}$ | Minority $\hat{\beta}$ |
|---|---|---|
| Cartel Agenda Model Predicted $\hat{\beta}$ | 0 | + |
| Floor Agenda Model Predicted | + | + |
| Effect of $Distance_{ct}$ on $Rollrate_{ct}$, | 1.488 | 2.597* |
| estimated via EBB[a] | (2.233) | (0.393) |

* Indicates $p < .05$.

[a] For the majority equation, the estimated constant term is $-3.584$ (with a standard error of 0.478); the estimated gamma is 0.034 (0.014); $N = 61$; Log likelihood = $-406.778$; pseudo $R^2 = 0.0374$. For the minority equation, the estimated constant term is $-1.983$ (0.199); the estimated gamma is 0.044 (0.013); $N = 61$; Log likelihood = $-2052.353$; pseudo $R^2 = 0.0522$.

within a certain range.[14] In economics and physics, these sorts of relationships are known as comparative statics. Basically, the model leads to predictions about how one or more variables should change in response to changes in other variables.

Under the Floor Agenda Model, the probability that the majority party is rolled on a final-passage vote increases with the distance between $M_j$ and $F_j$ for all $j$, while the probability that the minority is rolled on a final-passage vote increases with the distance between $m_j$ and $F_j$ for all $j$. Under the Cartel Agenda Model, the second of these comparative statics expectations holds – the opposition should lose more often as its median member is more distant from the floor median – but the first does not – the majority party should never lose and thus its roll rate should be unrelated to the distance between the majority party and floor medians. More specifically, we test the following hypotheses (which are summarized in the first two rows of Table 5.2):[15]

$H_{cartel}$: $Rollrate_{maj,t}$ is not related to $Distance_{maj,t}$, c.p.
$H_{floor}$: $Rollrate_{maj,t}$ is positively related to $Distance_{maj,t}$, c.p.
$H_{both}$: $Rollrate_{min,t}$ is positively related to $Distance_{min,t}$, c.p.

where

$Rollrate_{maj,t}$ is the majority party's roll rate in Congress $t$
$Rollrate_{min,t}$ is the minority party's roll rate in Congress $t$

[14] This is another quasi-experimental, nonequivalent group, post-test-only design in which we measure the effects of a treatment on one of two groups, with one group getting the treatment (i.e., majority status), and the other group not getting it.

[15] Note that we cannot observe the distance between party medians and the floor median on a dimension-by-dimension basis. But we can use multidimensional scaling results, such as the NOMINATE scale produced by Poole and Rosenthal (see Poole and Rosenthal 1997), to estimate the average location of the party and floor medians across all dimensions in a Congress.

*Distance*$_{maj,t}$ is the absolute difference between the majority party and floor
medians on the first dimension of DW-NOMINATE in Congress $t$

*Distance*$_{min,t}$ is the absolute difference between the minority party and floor
medians on the first dimension of DW-NOMINATE in Congress $t$

To test these hypotheses, we estimated the model

$$Rollrate_{ct} = \alpha_c + \beta_c Distance_{ct} + \varepsilon_{ct}$$

using the extended beta binomial method, for reasons explained in Chapter 4.
We have also rerun this model using robust ordinary least squares (OLS) and
minimum logit chi-squared (MLCS) methods, with the same substantive results.
See Appendix 5.B for details of our estimations.

The third row of Table 5.2 shows the results of our EBB estimations. We find
that there is no significant relationship between how far the majority party's
median is from the House median in a given Congress and its roll rate in
that Congress ($\beta = 1.488$; standard error $= 2.233$). In contrast, the minority
party's roll rate tends to be significantly higher when its median member is
further from the House median ($\beta = 2.597$; standard error $= 0.393$).[16] These
findings conform to the Cartel Agenda Model.[17] We cannot say that the data
*refute* the Floor Agenda Model, however, because the power of the test is only
about 70%.[18] That is, our test gave us only a seven out of 10 chance of finding
evidence in support of the Floor Agenda Model, whereas the standard is an
80 percent chance. Thus, even though the data and relationships between the
variables do not support the Floor Agenda Model, we cannot, on the basis of
this test, reject that model.

The comparative statics evidence just described tells no more strongly against
the floor model than did the point estimates adduced earlier, as it is possible to
explain both results on the hypothesis that the distribution of status quo points

---

[16] Note that we estimated similar EBB regressions for our control group, the Senate. Indeed, the
only difference between our House and Senate estimations is that, in our Senate estimations,
we included only those Congresses with more than 10 final-passage votes to control for those
Congresses that had very few roll call votes. Specifically, we obtained the following results
for the majority party in the Senate: $Rollrate_{ct} = \alpha_c(-4.364; se = 1.152) + \beta_c(7.464; se = 4.489) Distance_{ct} + \varepsilon_{ct}$. We also estimated the corresponding regression for the Senate minority party: $Rollrate_{ct} = \alpha_c(-3.167; se = 0.596) + \beta_c(2.585; se = 0.974) Distance_{ct} + \varepsilon_{ct}$. Thus,
as in the House, *Distance* does not significantly affect the majority party's roll rate, but it does
significantly increase the minority party's roll rate.

[17] We have also rerun these models with various lag structures to control for autocorrelation. This
did not affect our results.

[18] Normally, we worry mostly about Type I errors – that is, finding that an effect is significant
when it actually is not significant. Hence, we usually insist that the probability of Type I error
is no greater than 5%; that is, we expect confidence levels of at least 95% as a standard for
claiming that a relationship exists. In contrast, the usual standard for Type II errors – that is,
finding that an effect is not significant when it actually is significant – is a probability of no more
than 20 percent that Type II error is being committed (Trochim 2001: 262–5). In the case of our
test of the Floor Agenda Model, the probability of Type II error is 20–30 percent. The power of
a test is 1 minus the probability of Type II error, so the power of our Floor Agenda Model test
is only a little over 70 percent.

is very thin in the interval between $2M - F$ and $F$. Put another way, the Floor Agenda Model is consistent with any nonnegative slope if one can freely choose the distribution of status quo points.

The comparative statics results do provide a stronger test of the Cartel Agenda Model, however. Although it is possible to explain away a "small" roll rate for the majority by explicitly modeling the costs of acting, uncertainty, and errors, it would not be similarly possible to explain away a significant relationship between the majority-party roll rate and the majority's distance from the House median (as any uncertainty should produce errors that are uncorrelated with this distance). As it turns out, however, there is no such relationship to explain away.

In other work, a similar result has been found in the U.S. Senate. Campbell et al. (2002) perform a nearly identical test of how roll rates vary with the interaction of distance from the floor median and majority- and minority-party status (the model is the same, but the estimation technique differs). They find that the distance between the majority-party median and the floor median is not significantly related to the majority party's roll rate, whereas for the minority party the distance between majority-party median and the floor median has a significant effect on roll rates.

## 5.6. PREFERENCE SHIFTS

Let us turn now to consider some differing predictions that the Cartel Agenda Model and Krehbiel's (1998) pivot model make regarding how party roll rates should react when congressional preferences shift. Suppose that bills are passed at $t - 1$ in accordance with the pivot model and that these bills establish the status quo on each dimension at the end of period $t - 1$ (call this $Q_{j,t-1}$). Suppose also that Nature adds a "policy shock" to each dimension ($\varepsilon_{j,t}$) at the beginning of period $t$. The status quo at the beginning of period $t$ is then $SQ_{jt} = Q_{j,t-1} + \varepsilon_{j,t}$. The distribution of $SQ_{jt}$ thus depends on (1) what Congress did at $t - 1$ and (2) the distribution of $\varepsilon_{j,t}$. We can make similar assumptions about the Cartel Agenda Model, with the $Q_{j,t-1}$ values established in accord with that model and then perturbed by Nature.

With these assumptions about how status quo points are generated, what can we say about the two models' comparative statics predictions? We relegate the technical details to Appendix 5.A; however, the basic predictions are as follows. The pivot model predicts that both the majority party's and the minority party's roll rates should be sensitive to congressional preference shifts. The majority party, for example, should be rolled more often after preferences shift away from it (to the right, in our case) but be rolled less often after preferences shift toward it (to the left). In contrast, the Cartel Agenda Model agrees that preference shifts will affect the *minority* party's roll rate but claims that such shifts will have no effect on the *majority* party's roll rate.

In order to test these competing comparative statics, we, again, analyzed final-passage roll rates for both the minority and majority parties on the House floor. The unit of analysis is thus a party-Congress, and we estimate separate regressions for the majority and minority parties. Our dependent variable is, again, *Rollrate$_{ct}$*.

The main independent variable is *PrefShift$_{ct}$*, a variable capturing the preference shift *away from* party *c* between Congress *t* and *t* − 1 (so rightward shifts are positive if *c* is the Democratic Party, whereas leftward shifts are positive if *c* is the Republican Party).[19] We also include, as a control in our analysis, a measure of conservative coalition activity. This variable, *CC_SCORE*, gives the percent of all votes in each Congress on which a majority of Southern Democrats and Republicans opposed a majority of Northern Democrats. It is included because conventional accounts would suggest that conservative coalition activity should produce rolls on final-passage votes.

The Cartel Agenda Model predicts that (1) the constant term will be positive and significant in the minority-party regression (the minority party should be rolled significantly more often, and preference shift and conservative coalition activity should be held constant) but insignificant in the majority party regression, and (2) the coefficient on *PrefShift$_{ct}$* will be insignificantly different from zero in the majority-party regression but positive and significant in the minority-party regression.

The pivot model predicts the constant term in both the majority and minority regressions will be insignificantly different from zero: if *PrefShift$_{ct}$* is zero, then there should be no status quo points outside the gridlock zone, and hence no rolls of either party. It also predicts that the coefficient on *PrefShift$_{ct}$* will be positive and significant for both parties. Thus, the pivot model agrees with the Cartel Agenda Model regarding the constant term in the majority-party regression (it should be zero) and the slope term in the minority-regression (it should be positive). But the two models disagree regarding the slope term in the majority-regression and the constant term in the minority regression.

The results of OLS and MLCS regression

$$Rollrate_{ct} = \chi_c + \beta_c PrefShift_t + \gamma_c CC\_SCORE_t + G_t \qquad (5.1)$$

are reported in Table 5.3. The results conform closely to the predictions of the Cartel Agenda Model and not so closely to the predictions of the pivot model. In particular, even though $\hat{\beta}_c$ is positive and significant in the regression for the minority party, we cannot reject the null hypothesis that it is zero for the majority party.[20] Interestingly, the analysis also shows that the greater the activity of the conservative coalition in a Congress, the greater are roll rates for both parties. These results give us added confidence that the Cartel Agenda Model captures, at least partly, some of the underlying principles of legislative organization.

---

[19] More precisely, let $S_t = F_t - F_{t-1}$, where $F_t$ denotes the median D-NOMINATE score in Congress *t*. Then *PrefShift$_{ct}$* = $S_t$ if *c* = Democrats and *PrefShift$_{ct}$* = $-S_t$ if *c* = Republicans.

[20] Estimating the model using a block logit technique produces qualitatively similar results.

TABLE 5.3. *Effect of Preference Shifts on Roll Rates*

|  | Majority $\hat{\beta}$ | Minority $\hat{\beta}$ |
| --- | --- | --- |
| Estimated OLS coefficients[a] | | |
| *Rollrate* for House final-passage votes | 0.08 | 0.33 |
|  | (0.09) | (0.16) |
| Estimated MLCS coefficients[b] | | |
| *Rollrate* for House final-passage votes | 1.53 | 1.90 |
|  | (0.84) | (0.58) |

[a] $N = 53$ (for both regressions), $F(4, 48) = 2$ (majority) and 6.98 (minority), Adjusted $R^2 = -0.12$ (majority) and 0.42 (minority), $CC\_SCORE$ (majority) $= 0.02(0.01)^*$ and $CC\_SCORE$ (minority) $= .03(.02)^*$ where $^* = p > .05$.

[b] $N = 53$ (for both regressions), $F(4, 48) = 14.36$ (majority) and 10.49 (minority), Adjusted $R^2 = 0.54$ (majority) and 0.42 (minority), $CC\_SCORE$ (majority) $= 0.60$ $(0.12)^*$ and $CC\_SCORE$ (minority) $= 0.11 (0.60)$ where $^* = p > .05$.

## 5.7. CONDITIONAL VERSUS UNCONDITIONAL PARTY GOVERNMENT

Our research shows that the majority party rarely unsuccessfully opposes a bill on final passage (about 1–3 percent of the time in our samples). We also find no systematic relationship between (a) the distance between the majority-party median and the House median and (b) the party's roll rate on final-passage votes.

These results support the Cartel Agenda Model and the simple view of negative agenda control captured therein. As our analysis spans more than a century of congressional history, our results suggest that the majority party's negative agenda power has been a constant feature of congressional organization during that time. In terms of the notion of conditional party government (see, e.g., Rohde 1991; Aldrich and Rohde 1997, 1998), *the majority party's negative agenda control is not conditional*; in other words, it does not vary with the party's heterogeneity.

To verify this point, we regressed the majority-party roll rate (for each Congress from the 73rd through the 99th) on the party's

> *Heterogeneity*$_{ct}$, the standard deviation of majority-party members' first-dimension DW-NOMINATE scores) for Congress $t$

We found that heterogeneity had no effect on the majority party's roll rates.[21] However, positive agenda control (the ability to get items on the agenda), which is the focus of the conditional party government model (see Cooper and Brady 1981; Rohde 1991; Aldrich and Rohde 1998, 2000), may well be conditional, in

[21] Using OLS, we regressed the majority-party roll rate on a constant and our operationalization of heterogeneity, which yielded the following estimate: *Rollrate*$_{ct}$ = $0.041 - 0.076 *$ *Heterogeneity*$_{ct}$, with a standard error of 0.100 on *Heterogeneity*$_{ct}$ ($p$-value of roughly .45 in a two-tailed test); $R^2 = 0.0227$; $N = 27$).

that the size of the positive agenda does vary with majority party heterogeneity (as we demonstrate elsewhere).

## 5.8. CONCLUSION

We began this chapter with an example of the majority party's power to push its agenda through the legislative process, and we then tested our Cartel Agenda Model and the Floor Agenda Model, subjecting both to refutation. The tests clearly do not refute the Cartel Agenda Model. Instead, the data appear quite supportive of that model. In contrast, the data are not so supportive of the Floor Agenda Model. In chapters that follow, we present more powerful tests and evidence that allow us to claim that the Floor Agenda Model lacks conclusion validity.

Two additional points are worth noting before we move on to the next chapter. First, we wish to emphasize that our conclusion does not depend on the unidimensional nature of the Cartel and Floor Agenda Models. If multidimensional bills were possible, one could certainly find such bills that would roll the majority party. The empirical absence of majority-party rolls thus implies definite restrictions on the agenda, even in multidimensional policy spaces.

Note finally that what we have done in this chapter is to provide evidence that a procedural cartel has existed in the House for the period we have investigated. Our approach has been to *assume* the existence of a procedural cartel and then to look for the consequences that should follow on this assumption. This chapter has not addressed the issue of why procedural cartels arise or persist once established.

## APPENDIX 5.A

Consider nine cases, depending on whether the policy shocks tend to push things left, right, or neither; and whether preferences, as measured by the floor median's ideal point at time $t$, $F_{jt}$, shift left, right, or neither. Formally, the policy shock tendency can be captured by the expected value of $\varepsilon_{j,t}$. If $E(\varepsilon_{j,t}) < 0$, then Nature tends to push the status quo leftward. If $E(\varepsilon_{j,t}) > 0$, then Nature tends to push the status quo rightward. Finally, if $E(\varepsilon_{j,t}) = 0$, then Nature pushes neither left nor right. As regards preference shifts, the simplest case to consider is one in which the entire distribution of ideal points shifts left or right, by a fixed amount, $\delta_{jt}$ (so that $\delta_{jt} = F_{jt} - F_{j,t-1}$). Preferences shift left, right, or neither as $\delta_{jt}$ is less than, greater than, or equal to zero.

To explain the pivot model's predictions regarding the majority party, recall that the probability (before Nature's policy shock is realized) that the majority party will be rolled on dimension $j$ can be expressed as $P = \Pr[SQ_{jt} \in (2M_{jt} - F_{jt}, f_{jt})]$. Because $SQ_{jt} = Q_{j,t-1} + \varepsilon_{jt}, M_{jt} = M_{j,t-1} + \delta_{jt}, F_{jt} = F_{j,t-1} + \delta_{jt}$, and $f_{jt} = f_{j,t-1} + \delta_{jt}, P$ can be rephrased as $P = \Pr[Q_{j,t-1} + \varepsilon_{jt} \in (2M_{j,t-1} - F_{j,t-1} + \delta_{jt}, f_{j,t-1} + \delta_{jt})]$. Subtracting $Q_{j,t-1}$ throughout, one gets $P = \Pr[\varepsilon_{jt} \in (2M_{j,t-1} - F_{j,t-1} + \delta_{jt} - Q_{j,t-1}, f_{j,t-1} + \delta_{jt} - Q_{j,t-1})]$. If we denote the cumulative distribution function of $\varepsilon_{jt}$ by $G$, then $P = G(f_{j,t-1} + \delta_{jt} - Q_{j,t-1}) - G(2M_{j,t-1} - F_{j,t-1} + \delta_{jt} - Q_{j,t-1})$.

Differentiating $P$ with respect to $\delta$ yields $\partial P/\partial \delta(\delta) = g(f_{j,t-1} + \delta_{jt} - Q_{j,t-1}) - g(2M_{j,t-1} - F_{j,t-1} + \delta_{jt} - Q_{j,t-1})$, where $g$ is the probability density function associated with $G$. We know that $Q_{j,t-1} \in [f_{j,t-1}, v_{j,t-1}]$ because Congress will have altered any status quo points lying outside the $t-1$ gridlock zone. Thus, $\partial P/\partial \delta(0) = g(f) - g(f-d)$, where $f = f_{j,t-1} - Q_{j,t-1} \leq 0$ and $d = f_{j,t-1} - (2M_{j,t-1} - F_{j,t-1}) > 0$ so that $f - d < f$. If $g$ is single-peaked about zero, then $f - d < f \leq 0$ implies $g(f) - g(f-d) > 0$, hence $\partial P/\partial \delta(0) > 0$. Since $\partial P/\partial \delta(\delta)$ is a continuous function of $\delta$, this suffices to show that $\partial P/\partial \delta(0) > 0$ for all $\delta$ in an interval $I$ around zero. (It can be shown that $I = (-\infty, -f + 0.5d)$.) In words, the probability $P$ of a majority party roll increases as preferences in Congress shift more to the right (i.e., away from the majority, which is presumed to be leftist).[22]

Thus, the pivot model's prediction – $\partial P/\partial \delta > 0$ – is in stark contrast to the Cartel Agenda Model 's prediction that $\partial P/\partial \delta = 0$. It can be shown, however, that both models predict $\partial P/\partial \delta(\delta) < 0$ for all $\delta$ in an interval including zero; that is, the minority party's roll rate decreases with larger rightward shifts in congressional preferences.[23]

### APPENDIX 5.B

In this appendix, we describe three different analyses of the relationship between a party's roll rate and its distance from the floor median (OLS, MLCS, and EBB). Denote party $c$'s estimated median in Congress $t$ by $P_{ct}$, the estimated floor median by $F_t$, and the distance between these two by $Distance_{ct} = |P_{ct} - F_t|$. $Distance_{ct}$ will be the main independent variable in what follows, with party roll rates the dependent variable.

One approach is to estimate the relationship via ordinary least squares:

$$Rollrate_{ct} = \chi_c + \beta_c Distance_{ct} + \varepsilon_{ct} \tag{5.2}$$

where $Rollrate_{ct}$ is the roll rate for party $c$ in Congress $t$. Equation (5.2) can be estimated by OLS because the number of observations that make up the denominator in the proportion, $Rollrate_{ct}$, averages more than 50. Thus, $Rollrate_{ct}$ should be approximately normally distributed. We expect, however, that Equation (5.2) will suffer from heteroscedasticity (the number of votes per Congress varies by two orders of magnitude) and serial correlation. To correct for heteroscedasticity, we used the Huber–White sandwich estimator of variance.

---

[22] However, sufficiently large rightward preference shifts eventually decrease $P$ (if congressional preferences shift far enough right, then the only status quo points that remain will tend to be so far left of the new congressional preference distribution that even the majority-party median wishes to change them; thus, although there will be change on these dimensions, the majority-party will not be rolled on them).

[23] A caveat similar to that registered in the previous footnote is in order. For sufficiently large leftward preference shifts, even the minority party may favor changing the status quo.

TABLE 5.A.1. *OLS, MLCS, and EBB Estimates of Effects of Distance on Roll Rates, Majority and Minority Parties, Congresses 45–105*

|  | Majority $\hat{\beta}$ | Minority $\hat{\beta}$ |
|---|---|---|
| a. Effect of *Distance$_{ct}$* on | 0.044 | 0.532* |
| *Rollrate$_{ct}$*, estimated via robust OLS[a] | (0.096) | (0.042) |
| b. Effect of *Distance$_{ct}$* on | 0.0160 | 2.214* |
| *Rollrate$_{ct}$*, estimated via MLCS[b] | (2.026) | (0.393) |
| c. Effect of *Distance$_{ct}$* on | 2.13 | 2.24* |
| *Rollrate$_{ct}$*, estimated via EBB[c] | (2.39) | (.397) |

* Indicates $p < .05$.

[a] The estimated constant terms are 0.027 (majority) and 0.042 (minority). The estimated coefficients for the autoregressive terms are $\gamma_1 = -0.009$ (majority) and 0.221 (minority) for the first lag of the dependent variable and $\gamma_2 = 0.029$ (majority) and $-0.053$ (minority) for the second lag of the dependent variable. A joint test of the null hypothesis that $\gamma_1 + \gamma_2 = 0$ can be rejected in both cases. $N = 59$, $F(3, 55) = 0.29$ (majority) and 14.62 (minority), Prob $> F = 0.8331$ (majority) and 0.000 (minority), $R^2 = 0.0084$ (majority) and 0.4735 (minority).

[b] The estimated constant terms are $-2.059$ (majority) and $-1.752$ (minority). The estimated coefficients for the autoregressive terms are $\gamma_1 = 0.154$ (majority) and 0.132 (minority) for the first lag of the dependent variable and $\gamma_2 = 0.185$ (majority) and $-0.099$ (minority) for the second lag of the dependent variable. A joint test of the null hypothesis that $\gamma_1 + \gamma_2 = 0$ can be rejected in both cases. $N = 59$, $F(3, 55) = 4.29$ (majority) and 15.67 (minority), Prob $> F = 0.0086$ (majority) and 0.0000 (minority), $R^2 = 0.1895$ (majority) and 0.4608 (minority).

[c] The estimated constant terms are $-4.02$ (majority) and $-1.99$ (minority). The estimated coefficients for the autoregressive terms are $\gamma_1 = .038$ (majority) and 1.44 (minority) for the first lag of the dependent variable and $\gamma_2 = 1.15$ (majority) and $-0.841$ (minority) for the second lag of the dependent variable. Prob $> \text{chi}^2 = 0.0000$ (majority) and 0.0002 (minority), $R^2 = 0.0558$ (majority) and 0.0286 (minority).

To correct for autocorrelation, we included one- and two-term lags of the dependent variables as right-hand-side variables. Further diagnostics of our regression suggested no other problems for our estimation.

Maddala (1983: 18–30) suggests the minimum logit chi-squared technique of Berkson (1953) as an alternative method to estimate Equation (5.1). In this technique, the dependent variable is the smoothed logit of the roll rate:

$$\log\left[(Rollrate_{ct} + (2^*Totalfpv_t)^{-1})/(1 - Rollrate_{ct} + (2^*Totalfpv_t)^{-1})\right]$$

where *Totalfpv$_t$* is the total number of final passage votes for Congress *t*. One estimates the model using weighted least squares with weights $Totalfpv_t \times (Rollrate_{ct} + (2^*Totalfpv_t)^{-1}) \times (1 - Rollrate_{ct} + (2^*Totalfpv_t) - 1)$. This technique should approximate a logit regression on *Roll$_{cjt}$* (i.e., a dummy for whether party *c* is rolled on vote *j* in Congress *t*) without exaggerating our number of observations and biasing our tests. A third method of estimation, and the one most appropriate given our data, is extended beta binomial. On this method, see for example, King (1989).

The results from an OLS estimation of $Rollrate_{ct}$ for final-passage floor votes are reported in Table 5.A.1, row a. As the Cartel Agenda Model predicts, the estimated coefficient $\hat{\beta}_c$ for the majority party is statistically indistinguishable from zero, while the estimated coefficient for the minority party is positive and highly significant ($p < .001$, two-tailed test). This suggests that the likelihood of rolling the majority party on the floor is not significantly related to the distance between the majority party and floor medians, but the likelihood of rolling the minority increases as its median member is more distant from the floor median.

The MLCS estimates for final-passage floor votes are reported in Table 5.A.1, row b. The results are quite similar to the Huber–White OLS estimates: We cannot reject the null hypothesis that $\hat{\beta}_c$ for the majority party is equal to zero; however, we can reject the null hypothesis that $\hat{\beta}_c = 0$ for the minority party.

The EBB estimates for final-passage floor votes are reported in Table 5.A.1, row c. The results are quite similar to the OLS and MCLS estimates. We are not able to reject the null hypothesis that $\hat{\beta}_c$ for the majority party is equal to zero, while we can reject the null hypothesis that $\hat{\beta}_c = 0$ for the minority party.

# 6

# The Costs of Agenda Control

## 6.1. MOVING BEYOND THE IDEALIZED MODEL

The idealized agenda control model that we developed in Chapter 3 assumes that the majority party can *costlessly* control the legislative agenda. *Given* costless control – and other simplifications – the model predicts that the majority party should *never* be rolled.

Controlling the agenda, however, is not perfectly costless, even in a well-functioning cartel. Consider, for example, bills that are pushed by an opposition-party president. For such bills, the majority party in the House may face intense public pressure to put the bill on the floor. The cost of blocking the president's proposal may increase to such an extent that it is no longer worth blocking the bill. The result might be either some sort of interbranch deal, or an outright victory for the president. In either case, the blocking agents for the majority party may be forced to allow such bills onto the agenda and will, as a result, be rolled.

To accommodate this sort of possibility, we assume in this chapter that it may be costly for the majority party to block bills. In particular, there is an exogenous cost, $c_j$, that the majority must pay in order to block bills on dimension $j$, with $c_j \geq 0$. Although we take this cost as given when the majority must decide whether to block or not, we imagine – as the previous example suggests – that the cost reflects public interest in the issue at hand, which of course can be drummed up by presidents, minority parties, interest groups, and other actors.

With costly blocking, the agents of the majority party will block a bill on dimension $j$ if and only if the value of blocking it (i.e., the value of preventing a policy change from the status quo $q_j$) exceeds the cost of blocking it, $c_j$. Thus, with costly blocking, a positive majority party roll rate may arise, when the benefit of blocking on one or more bills is too low to justify the cost.

It is important to distinguish majority-party rolls that arise because the cost of blocking is particularly high and those that arise because the benefit is particularly low. On the one hand, rolls that occur because the cost of blocking is too high (e.g., because the minority party has succeeded in raising the public profile of a particular issue so much that the majority is forced to allow a bill onto the floor, despite the undesirable consequences that then follow) are inconsistent with our emphasis on the majority's agenda power. In the extreme, if the minority party could secure floor consideration of any issue it wished, merely by alerting the media, then there would be almost nothing left of the posited majority-party advantage in controlling the agenda.

On the other hand, majority-party rolls that occur because the benefit of blocking is *nil* are not inconsistent with our general approach. Consider, for example, a bill *b* that everyone knows the Senate or President will reject. The majority party in the House can allow *b* to be passed by the House, without suffering any actual policy change. Thus, even though the majority will suffer a roll on *b*, the roll will be *inconsequential* in the sense that the bill – despite passing the House – will not be enacted and, hence, policy will remain at the status quo.

We examine the frequency of inconsequential and consequential rolls in this chapter. We show that roughly half of the already-small number of majority-party rolls are in fact inconsequential and thus not inconsistent with our theory. We also show that most consequential majority-party rolls are the result of opposition-party presidents and Senates seizing the agenda from the House majority party.

Costly agenda control also raises the possibility that the majority may sometimes bend but not break. Instead of blocking a bill outright, the majority may either bring an unwanted bill to the floor on procedurally unfavorable terms, hoping for its demise, or package the bitter pill in a larger and sweeter omnibus vehicle. We introduce the concept of a *quasi-roll* to cover such cases, in which the majority is unable to avoid floor consideration of a particular issue but does not suffer a roll as a consequence of dealing with it (much less an actual change in policy).

## 6.2. THE COSTS AND BENEFITS OF BLOCKING

In this chapter, we suppose that the majority party must pay a cost, $c_j$, to block a bill dealing with dimension $j$. If $c_j = 0$ for all $j$, the model reduces to our idealized Cartel Agenda Model. On the other hand, if $c_j$ is always so large as to deter the majority from using its blocking power – another way of saying it has no such power – then the model reduces to the idealized Floor Agenda Model. Thus, the model with the additional parameters $\{c_j\}$ provides a natural bridge between our polar models, both of which emerge as special cases.[1]

---

[1] The comparative statics of the general model are also intermediate between the cartel and floor models. If the $c_j$'s are small enough, then one expects that the majority roll rate will be insensitive to the distance between the majority and floor medians, as in the Cartel Agenda Model. If the $c_j$'s are large enough, then one expects that the majority roll rate will be systematically related to this distance, as in the Floor Agenda Model.

Recognizing that blocking may be costly motivates a closer look at the benefits of blocking because the majority will block only if the benefits exceed the costs. Let's assume that the majority party cares about policy outcomes (i.e., about actual enactments), not merely the passage of a bill through the House. In this case, when the party dislikes a particular bill (that would pass the House if scheduled for consideration), it may reason as follows. If the bill will go on to pass the Senate and be signed by the president, then there is some benefit to blocking it in the House, as this blocking is essential to preventing the bill from being enacted. If, on the other hand, the bill will be rejected in the Senate or vetoed (without hope of override) by the president, then there is no benefit to blocking the bill: The status quo will be preserved regardless of whether the bill is blocked in the House or not. Thus, the benefit of blocking a bill in the House that would be stopped later in the legislative process is nil to members who care only about policy outcomes.

A more general statement of the model is this. Suppose that, if the majority party allows the House to consider a bill $b_j$ on a dimension $j$ with status quo $q_j$, then the ultimate policy outcome – after bargaining with the Senate and president – will be $A_j$. More formally, let $\theta_j:(q_j, b_j) \to A_j$ be the function that maps a (status quo, House bill) pair into an ultimate enactment, $A_j$. For example, $\theta_j$ could be the mapping that Krehbiel (1998) advances in his pivotal politics model (in which the ultimate outcome depends only on the location of the veto pivots and the status quo; see Chapter 10).[2] If $A_j = \theta_j(q_j, b_j)$ is worse than $q_j$ (for the majority party median), then there is some benefit to blocking it in the House because this blocking is necessary to prevent an unwanted policy change.

Let's further assume that the majority party in the House faces very small costs of blocking. Now consider a bill $b_j$ that would roll the majority party, if scheduled for a final-passage vote in the House. If the bill will (after passage) lead to an ultimate outcome $\theta_j(q_j, b_j)$ that the majority dislikes, then the majority blocks it from reaching a vote in the House.[3] On the other hand, if the bill will not lead to an enactment, even if passed by the House, then the majority can schedule the bill and allow it to pass, suffering what we call an *inconsequential* roll (i.e., a roll that does not lead to an actual change in policy).[4] Our main prediction thus changes from "the majority party will never unsuccessfully

---

[2] If no bill is ultimately enacted, then $A_j = q_j$ (the status quo policy remains in force). If some bill, possibly $b_j$ but possibly some amended version thereof, is ultimately enacted, then $A_j$ represents that bill.

[3] The assumption here is that the benefit of preserving the status quo always exceeds the very small costs of blocking. Indeed, this condition defines what we mean by "very small." Essentially, we assume lexicographic preferences – first, get the best policy outcome possible; second, if policy is held constant, save the costs of blocking.

[4] A consideration that we do not incorporate in the model but that may certainly be important in some cases is that allowing a bill to be considered and passed on the House floor will take up scarce time in the plenary session and provide publicity for issues the majority may not wish to publicize.

oppose the passage of a bill" to "the majority party will never unsuccessfully oppose the passage of a bill that is ultimately enacted." Put in terms of rolls, our main prediction changes, from the majority party will never be rolled, to *the majority party will never be consequentially rolled*.

How might we adapt this simple benefit–cost model of agenda setting to make it less idealized and perhaps more realistic? Two ways seem straight-forward. First, if for some bill the probability of enactment, conditional on passage by the House, is positive but less than unity, then the majority party may sometimes accept a calculated risk – let an unwanted bill pass the House, hoping for its demise later – and end up on the wrong side of the risk. Thus, imprecise knowledge of bills' fates may generate consequential rolls. Second, the majority party may sometimes be consequentially rolled simply because the costs of blocking exceed the benefits. This sort of consequential roll would be more likely to arise on minor bills (where the benefit of blocking is lower) or on bills supported by a popular president (where the cost of blocking may be higher).

In what follows, we begin with the most extreme and simple model, in which the majority always knows whether a bill it passes will succeed or fail later in the process and faces small costs to blocking. This model retains the most powerful majority party, is closest to our previous ideal model, and therefore runs the greatest risk of empirical falsification. We will test it by considering the number and nature of both inconsequential and consequential rolls.

## 6.3. INCONSEQUENTIAL AND CONSEQUENTIAL ROLLS

In this section, we begin with an example of an inconsequential roll and then present some statistics on the frequency of both inconsequential and conse-quential rolls from the 83rd to the 105th Congress (for which we usually have excellent historical accounts of legislative activity). We next consider a subset of landmark and major bills (as identified by Howell et al. 2000), showing that the gap between the two parties' consequential roll rates on such bills is substan-tially larger than in the overall dataset. Finally, we consider how the frequency of consequential rolls changed after adoption of Reed's rules in 1891.

### 6.3.1. An Inconsequential Roll: Campaign Finance Reform Under Gingrich

An example of an inconsequential roll occurred in Newt Gingrich's second term as speaker. The GOP leadership wished to prevent campaign finance reform, especially that embodied in the Shays–Meehan bill (a companion to the Senate's better-known McCain–Feingold measure), from being considered. The Repub-lican leaders' first strategy, in response to public pressure, was to bring another campaign finance reform bill to the floor (H.R. 3581). This bill's demise was certain because it was carefully laden with provisions distasteful to members on both sides of the aisle; no amendments could be offered, and a two-thirds majority was required for passage.

Even some Republicans grumbled about the leadership's tactics, and Shays–Meehan proponents responded by filing a discharge petition. After the signatories to the petition topped 200 (mostly from Democrats but increasingly from Republican reform advocates), the Republican leadership agreed to bring Shays–Meehan to the floor. They did so, however, on terms *very* unfavorable to passage. The special rule crafted for consideration of campaign finance made another bill the underlying bill; it allowed Shays–Meehan and ten other bills as substitute amendments, with the proviso that only the substitute attracting the largest majority (if any did attract a majority) could replace the underlying bill; and they allowed amendments to each of the substitutes. After a protracted debate to which the leadership allowed many scheduling interruptions, the GOP leaders held their party on a second special rule, one that allowed at least 258 more amendments to the substitute proposals. As the *Congressional Quarterly Almanac* noted (1998: 18–14), "the challenge for Shays and Meehan [is] to steer their proposal through a gauntlet of GOP-backed amendments that, if adopted, would make it all but impossible for Democrats to support the final product." Surprisingly, the bill survived its ordeal more or less intact. By the time it did so, however, the end of the term was nearing, and it had become clear that the Senate would not pass McCain–Feingold. Perhaps secure in this knowledge, the House leaders put no further obstacles in the way of passage and, on August 8, 1998, the House voted 252–179 to pass the Shays–Meehan bill. All but 15 Democrats voted for passage, with 61 Republicans joining them. The Republicans were thus rolled as a result but, as universally expected, the Senate failed to act, and the bill died.

### 6.3.2. The Number of Inconsequential and Consequential Rolls

In this section, we consider the number of inconsequential and consequential rolls in our Postwar dataset. We restrict our analysis to this era because we can easily trace each majority- and minority-party roll using such sources as *Congressional Quarterly Weekly Reports*. For this period, moreover, Rohde has identified the type of each vote held in the House (e.g., vote on amendment, on motion to table, on final passage). Using Rohde's dataset (and legislative histories where needed), one can identify each final-passage vote for each joint resolution and determine whether the majority party was rolled or not, as well as whether the joint resolution in question was enacted or not.[5]

---

[5] We include votes on conference reports as "final-passage" votes. However, if a particular bill rolled the majority both on final passage and on the conference report, we count this in some analyses as one roll of the majority, not two. A joint resolution includes all resolutions in the H.R., S., H.J.Res., and S.J.Res. series. These require approval by both the Senate and president and become public laws if approved by all three branches.

As noted in the previous chapter, in our Postwar data there were a total of 49 majority party rolls on final-passage votes for joint resolutions (out of 3,134 recorded final-passage votes). Of these, 24 (49 percent) led to enactments, while 25 – like the campaign finance reform bill under Gingrich – did not. Thus, slightly more than half of all rolls may be explained simply by the majority party's incentive to economize on blocking resources when it realizes that a particular bill will fail later in the legislative process anyway. Empirically, we cannot verify that the majority party's leaders *actually* calculated the probability of the bill failing later in each of the 25 cases of a majority-party roll that went nowhere. We can, however, point out that leaders of the majority party are well placed to calculate such probabilities.

How does the prediction that there should be *no* consequential rolls for the majority party fare? It holds in nine of the 23 Congresses we examined (or 39.1 percent). On average, however, there was slightly more than one public law enacted against the wishes of the House majority party per Congress (or 0.8 percent of all recorded final-passage votes on joint resolutions over this time).

For the minority party, however, we see a larger number of consequential rolls. Analyzing data for even-numbered Congresses 84–98, we find that there were 92 consequential minority rolls out of 931 final-passage votes, giving us a consequential minority roll rate of approximately 9.9 percent.[6] When we analyze the majority party's consequential rolls for these same Congresses, we find that they suffered only four consequential rolls (a consequential majority roll rate of approximately 0.43 percent). Thus, the minority party is over 20 times more likely than the majority party to be consequentially rolled in this time period.

### 6.3.3. Consequential Rolls on Important Enactments

Since Mayhew's (1991) pathbreaking work, a number of scholars have compiled lists of important enactments. In this section, we combine one such list (Howell et al. 2000) with detailed legislative histories we possess for evennumbered Congresses from the 84th to 98th Congresses. Of the 147 enactments in the top two categories of importance during these Congresses ("landmark" and "major"),[7] we found that the majority party was rolled on three (for a roll rate of 2.0 percent), while the minority party was rolled on 36 (for a roll rate of 21.1 percent). Note that the majority's roll rate increases on these most important legislative battles – from the 0.43 percent reported earlier to

---

[6] When calculating the minority party's consequential roll rate, we coded all minority rolls that were "passed in lieu" as nonconsequential, thereby erring on the side of underestimating the minority party's consequential roll rate.

[7] Howell et al. (2000) have two top categories, A and B. Group A comprises "landmark enactments," similar to Mayhew's Sweep 1 data. Group B consists of "major enactments" that are mentioned in either the *New York Times* or *Washington Post* end-of-session review or that receive six or more pages of coverage in the *Congressional Quarterly Almanac*.

TABLE 6.1. *Extended Beta Binomial Estimate of the Effects of Distance and Important Rule Changes on Minority-Party Roll Rates, Congresses 45–105*

| Independent Variables | Coefficient Estimates | Standard Errors |
|---|---|---|
| *Distance* | 2.884* | 0.489 |
| *Reed* | 0.883* | 0.331 |
| *Post-Revolt* | −0.285 | 0.335 |
| *Post-Reform* | 0.224 | 0.153 |
| *Constant* | −2.732* | 0.368 |
| Number of observations = 61 | | |
| Log likelihood = −2045.9543 | | |
| Pseudo $R^2$ = 0.0552 | | |

* Significant at 95 percent or greater level.

2.0 percent here. This increase, we believe, reflects the increased public salience of these landmark bills – which salience makes it more costly for the majority to exert agenda control. Note also that the minority's roll rate increases even more – from the 9.9 percent reported earlier to 21.1 percent here. This shows that the gap in the two parties' legislative success (as measured by the difference in their roll rates) is even larger, if one looks at the most important bills.

### 6.3.4. Party Rolls and Reed's Rules

We can use the notion of consequential rolls to further test the effect of Reed's rules. In particular, a second hypothesis is that the adoption of Reed's rules (which we view as changing the House from a dual-veto to a single-veto system) should have caused a decline in consequential majority party rolls.

If we look at Congresses before and after the adoption of Reed's rules, we find the following as regards consequential rolls on bills in the Post-Reconstruction dataset.[8] Of the 36 consequential majority-party rolls in this series, 14 occurred in the six pre-Reed Congresses (45th–50th) – or over two per year. In contrast, 21 consequential rolls occurred in the 55 post-Reed Congresses (51st–105th) – or 0.4 per year. The consequential roll rate (among H.R. final-passage votes only) was 6.9 percent prior to, and 1.0 percent after, the initial adoption of Reed's rules – a statistically significant decline.

Den Hartog (2004) explores a third prediction that follows from viewing Reed's rules as replacing a dual-veto system with one in which the minority no longer had a veto. In particular, such a change should have increased the roll rate for the minority party. Den Hartog shows that this indeed happened.

We provide our own version of the evidence in Table 6.1, which displays a regression of the minority party's roll rate on *Distance* (the distance between the

---

[8] For this larger time period, we have not systematically collected data on rolls in the S., H.J.Res., or S.J.Res. series, although we can say that roll rates across these series are similar to those in the H.R. series in the period for which we have data on all (the 83rd–105th Congresses).

minority party's median and the floor median first dimension DW-NOMINATE score) and three dummy variables indicating the most important rule changes in House history: the adoption of Reed's rules, the revolt against Cannon, and the adoption of reforms in the 93rd Congress. As we already noted in Chapter 5, both the Floor and Cartel Agenda Models predict that the minority party's roll rate should increase as its median diverges more from the floor median, and this is what we find. More important for present purposes, the minority-party roll rate increased substantially after adoption of Reed's rules, declined after the revolt against Cannon, and increased again after the reforms of the 93rd Congress. Given our characterization of the relative importance of the respective reforms, these responses are as expected. In particular, the impact of Reed's rules is clear (and significantly larger than either of the later reforms).

By testing three distinct hypotheses (one regarding the movement of policy, tested in Chapter 4; one regarding the majority party's consequential roll rate; one regarding the minority party's roll rate), we provide a strong test of our model of Reed's rules. Such tests are known as nonequivalent dependent-variable designs or pattern-matching designs and are accorded high marks for internal validity (Trochim 2001). Although the number of pre-Reed Congresses that we can include in our analysis is limited (as the party system changes radically if one moves much further back than the 45th Congress), such a limit should work against finding significant differences, not in favor of it. Yet, three distinct patterns predicted by our model all come in statistically significant.

## 6.4. THE COST OF BLOCKING, PUBLIC SALIENCE, AND DIVIDED GOVERNMENT

We are still left with 24 unexplained prediction errors in the Postwar period. We can further extend our model by considering the costs of blocking legislation under divided government and the costs to House members of blocking an opposition president's agenda.

We have assumed that the blocking cost, $c_j$, varies from issue to issue, depending on the issue's salience to the public. Thus, the majority party should be more likely to block issues that are cheaper to block, which is to say they are more likely to block less salient issues.

Can we assess the salience of issues? We suggest first that issues championed by the president should be more salient because the president can command press and public attention (Kernell 1986). Thus, we predict that $c_j$ is higher for issues on the president's agenda. This does not matter much unless the House majority disagrees with the president. Under what conditions will such disagreements arise? The most obvious predictor of disagreement is divided government (a House and president of opposite parties).[9] Thus, we predict that *the*

---

[9] See Cox and Kernell (1991), Mayhew (1991), and Fiorina (1992) for more on the causes and consequences of divided government.

*majority-party roll rate will be higher under divided government.* More-over, *rolls under divided government should occur on bills supported by the president.*

### 6.4.1. Does Divided Government Increase the Majority Roll Rate?

Investigating the incidence of majority-party rolls under divided and unified government during the 83rd–105th Congresses provides evidence favoring the first proposition just stated. Of the 24 unexplained consequential rolls in our Postwar data, 21 occurred under divided government (or 1.4 per Congress in the 15 Congresses when there was divided government), while 3 occurred under unified government (or 0.4 per Congress under unified government). Thus, if we accept the premise that blocking agenda items is on net more costly under divided government, then we are left with only three unexplained rolls of the majority party in these 26 Congresses. Using OLS, we regress the number of consequential rolls per Congress on a dummy variable indicating divided or unified government, and the results show a significant positive relationship, with about 1 more consequential roll per Congress under divided government.

### 6.4.2. Do Opposition Presidents Produce Majority-Party Rolls?

In this section, we explore whether the incidence of majority-party rolls under divided government relates, as expected, to the president's legislative priorities. To illustrate the possible effects of divided government on legislative agenda control, imagine that the Democrats control the House and face a Republican president. The president seeks legislation on a particular issue that the House Democrats would prefer to leave alone. Going public, the president succeeds in generating such public support for the legislation that the House Democrats feel compelled to schedule it for consideration in committee and then on the floor, whereupon they are rolled (Kernell 1986).

Does this scenario play out often enough to leave a systematic pattern of evidence? To investigate, we focus on the postwar period of Democratic hegemony in the House, the 84th–103rd Congresses. The unit of analysis is a bill. The dependent variable is

> *Roll$_{jt}$*, a dichotomous variable equal to one if the Democrats were rolled on final passage of the bill in question, zero otherwise.

We therefore employ probit in our analysis to estimate changes in the probability that the Democrats were rolled on a particular bill. We employ a multifactor regression design. The independent variables include three main effects:

> *Republican President$_t$*, a dichotomous variable equal to one if the president is Republican in Congress *t*.
> *Republican Senate$_t$*, a dichotomous variable equal to one if the Republicans are the Senate majority party in Congress *t*.

*President Yes$_{jt}$*, a dichotomous variable equal to one if the president urges a "yes" vote on final passage on vote $j$ in Congress $t$. The president's position on each bill is coded from the *Congressional Quarterly*'s accounting (provided by Rohde).

In addition to these three main effects, there are also two interactive effects:

*Republican President–Yes$_{jt}$*, a dummy coded 1 if there is a Republican president urging a "yes" vote on final passage, equal to the product of *Republican President$_t$* and *President Yes$_{jt}$*.

*Republican Senate–Yes$_{jt}$*, a dummy coded 1 if both the president and the Senate are Republican and the president urges a "yes" vote on final passage, equal to the product of *President Yes$_{jt}$* and *Republican Senate$_t$*.

To explain the definitions of these variables, consider first the indicator of whether the president urges passage of the bill. We expect that, when a Democratic president urges a "yes" vote on final passage, the Democratic majority in the House will also favor passage; thus, the probability of a roll may be depressed (although the Democrats, when they have a majority, favor passage of virtually every bill that reaches the final-passage stage, and so the effect may not be large). Things are much different when a Republican president urges passage of a bill. Some of these cases may correspond to bills that the president has succeeded in forcing onto the House agenda. Thus, the probability of a roll on such bills should be higher and the interaction term *Republican President–Yes* should have a positive coefficient. The second interaction term, *Republican Senate–Yes*, should reinforce the effect – adding to the president's agenda power the Senate's abilities to force items onto the congressional agenda. The exact model we estimate, using probit analysis, is

$$Roll_{jt} = \alpha + \beta_1 Republican\ President_t + \beta_2 Republican\ Senate_t$$
$$+ \beta_3 President\ Yes_{jt} + \beta_4 Republican President–Yes_{jt}$$
$$+ \beta_5 Republican\ Senate–Yes_{jt} + \varepsilon_{jt}$$

Our results, given in Table 6.2, suggest that the president and Senate do have some ability to affect the House agenda. Neither facing a Republican president nor facing a Republican Senate significantly affects the House Democrats' probability of being rolled, in and of itself; so the simplest conception of divided government seems not to affect the House agenda. The divided-government interaction effects, however, are significant. Bills that a Republican president supports are more likely to roll the House Democrats, especially if the Senate is also Republican.[10]

---

[10] Note that we also estimated the effects of divided government on majority- and minority-party roll rates in the Senate. We find that for the 84th–103rd Democratic Congresses:

   1. Senate majority (Democratic) roll rates are not affected by *Distance* but are significantly increased by Republican presidents (and significantly decreased by Democratic presidents). House party control is perfectly collinear with the other variables; thus, we do not estimate

TABLE 6.2. *Probit Estimate of the Effect of Republican Presidents and
Senates on Democratic Majority Rolls in the House, Congresses 84–103*

| Independent Variables | Coefficient Estimates | Standard Errors |
|---|---|---|
| *Republican President*$_t$ | −0.052 | 0.173 |
| *Republican Senate*$_t$ | −0.192 | 0.272 |
| *President Yes*$_{jt}$ | −0.557 | 0.348 |
| *Republican President–Yes*$_{jt}$ | 1.368* | 0.386 |
| *Republican Senate–Yes*$_{jt}$ | 0.897* | 0.370 |
| *Constant* | −2.257* | 0.135 |

Number of observations = 2,820
Log likelihood = −209.5855
Pseudo $R^2$ = 0.1379

* Significant at 95 percent or greater level.

To give some idea of the size of these effects, consider the following estimates derived from our probit analysis. The probability of a Democratic roll when there is a Democratic president or a Republican president who does not urge passage of the bill in question is the same – 0.01. The probability increases to 0.07 if there is a Republican president with a Democratic Senate, and the president supports passage. Finally, if there is a Republican president and Senate and the president supports passage, the probability of a roll triples, to 0.21.

These probabilities cannot be taken to reflect straightforward causal impacts. That is, Ronald Reagan could not have produced a 21 percent roll rate during

its effect. Specifically, we estimated the following regression (note that *Republican President* is coded as Republican President = −1, Democratic President = 0):

$$Rollrate = \alpha(-5600; se = 1.708)$$
$$+ \beta_1(1.193; se = 7.286)$$
$$Distance + \beta_2(1.505; se = 6.553)$$
$$Lag\ Rollrate + \beta_3(7.332; se = 4.615)$$
$$Lag\ 2\ Rollrate - \beta_4(1.975; se = 1.123)$$
$$Republican\ President + \varepsilon$$

2. Senate minority (Republican) roll rates are a positive and significant function of both *Distance* and Democratic presidents; that is, Republicans in the Senate get rolled more frequently when they are in the minority and when the president is a Democrat. They also get rolled significantly less often when the president is a Republican. House party control for this period is, again, collinear with the other variables, and thus so is the interaction term in Table 6.2. Specifically, we estimated the following regression:

$$Rollrate = \alpha(-4.139; se = 1.191)$$
$$+ \beta_1(7.478; se = 2.594)$$
$$Distance + \beta_2(-0.136; se = 2.189)$$
$$Lag\ Rollrate + \beta_3(3.705; se = 2.852)$$
$$Lag\ 2\ Rollrate - \beta_4(2.282; se = 0.720)$$
$$Republican\ President + \varepsilon$$

Taken together, these findings demonstrate that divided government has very similar effects in both the House and Senate.

his presidency simply by supporting all the bills that arrived at a final-passage vote in the House. Nonetheless, the patterns are consistent with the hypothesis that it is costly to block salient proposals (i.e. ones that are part of an opposition president's legislative agenda); were the president or Senate able occasionally to force bills onto the House agenda, one would expect the findings we reported.

Having seen that the priorities of opposition presidents do seem related to majority-party rolls in the House, we return now to examine some of these majority-party rolls in more detail. We begin with the single most important roll in our dataset – the Gramm–Latta budget reconciliation bill of 1981. This is a case, rare in our dataset, in which the president routs the House majority and, together with the Republicans in the Senate and conservative "blue dog" Democrats in the House, seizes control of the agenda process from the majority-party leadership.

We then turn to examine cases of what are in essence rolls by arrangement: The president and the House majority bargain and agree on a bill, but the House majority does not want to provide the bulk of the votes to pass all parts of the bill and so a majority party roll occurs in the process of implementing the deal.

### 6.4.3. Routs versus Deals

Thus far, we have provided evidence that suggests opposition presidents can, on occasion, roll the House majority party, both consequentially and inconsequentially. Our reading of the politics involved in majority-party rolls under divided government suggests two basic types: routs and deals. Rout-rolls are those on which the president wins outright and the House majority gets little of what it wanted. Deal-rolls are those on which a bargain is struck, with part of the agreement stipulating that the House minority party provides the bulk of the votes to pass one of the bills in the logroll. We consider several consequential rolls under divided government in greater detail, to illustrate these ideal types, and then provide a broader summary of our findings.

### 6.4.4. A Roll That Stemmed from Public Pressure Orchestrated by the President: Gramm–Latta

An example of a genuinely partisan majority roll, in which the bulk of the majority party was defeated by the bulk of the minority in combination with centrist defectors, is H.R. 3982, the Gramm–Latta budget reconciliation bill of 1981. In this case, Reagan and Senate Republicans faced off against House Democrats over spending and tax cuts. Even as the House Budget Committee pieced together the Democrats' version of the reconciliation bill, the Senate passed Reagan's version. When the Budget Committee reported, the administration and House Republicans declared it unacceptable and pushed an alternative version, known as Gramm–Latta II. They received crucial support from then-Democrat Phil Gramm and other conservative "Boll Weevil" Democrats.

The Rules Committee reported a rule designed to kill Gramm–Latta by forcing the House to decide sequentially on individual elements of the proposal. This would have amounted to a series of difficult votes to slash spending on programs such as Medicare and Social Security, knowing that the Democrat-favored reconciliation bill, which imposed smaller cuts on those programs and did so in a single omnibus bill, was also an option. In addition, the rule precluded some of the Gramm–Latta side payments aimed at garnering support from marginal members. This rule triggered a backlash from the Boll Weevils. After a strident debate in which Democratic leaders Tip O'Neill, Jim Wright, and Richard Bolling (Rules Committee chairman) unequivocally supported the rule, the Boll Weevils nonetheless defected from the party line, joining with Republicans to defeat it. The House then narrowly approved a rule that allowed an up-or-down floor vote on Gramm–Latta II.

On the floor, the House approved the Gramm–Latta amendment, 217–211. As on the vote on the rule the previous day, 29 Boll Weevils defected to vote with the GOP administration. The bill then passed the House on a 232–193 vote, with some additional Democrats voting in favor in order to be part of the conference process. After the conference, which produced a bill close to Reagan's original proposal, Bolling again threatened to block floor consideration. However, the threat was not carried out, and the bill soon passed the House. The Democrats' only silver lining was the opportunity, which they certainly seized for many years afterward, to blame cuts in services and increasing deficits on Reagan and the Republican Party (see, e.g., Tip O'Neill's comments as reported by Martin Tolchin in the *New York Times*, August 16, 1981).

### 6.4.5. A Roll That Stemmed from Bargaining with the President: Foreign Aid for El Salvador

When bargaining with a president of the opposite party, the majority leadership may actually want a given bill to pass as part of a deal with the president but prefer that the minority party provide most of the votes needed to pass it. An example of a majority roll of this sort is H.R. 5119, passed May 10, 1984. This was a foreign aid bill featuring, among its various spending authorizations, a controversial expansion of support to El Salvador (*Congressional Quarterly* 1984: 71–2, 82–4). President Reagan strongly supported aid to El Salvador as an anti-Communist measure, while liberal Democrats opposed it on human rights grounds. Meanwhile, many more conservative Democrats, notably Majority Leader Jim Wright (D-TX), supported the bill.

In both the Foreign Affairs Subcommittee on Western Hemisphere Affairs and the Foreign Affairs Committee itself, liberals prevailed and imposed sharp restrictions on aid to El Salvador, amending the bill in ways that Reagan strongly opposed. However, the Rules Committee sent the bill to the House under a special rule that stipulated a choice from among three alternatives: a Democratic version of the bill, the version reported from the Foreign Affairs Committee, and a Republican version. The rule stipulated that, after a series of up-or-down votes on the alternatives, the one with the most votes would be adopted. On the floor, Wright lined up his party's members and counted out the number he needed to ensure passage of the Republican substitute (which largely restored Reagan's proposal).[11] In return for the passage of his foreign aid bill, Reagan supported an expansion of welfare and urban spending that he had previously opposed (and which was enacted swiftly).

### 6.4.6. A Roll that Stemmed from Bargaining with the Senate: Expanding the Debt Ceiling

Another example of a majority roll involving divided government also comes from 1984: H.R. 5953, a bill to increase the debt ceiling (*Congressional Quarterly* 1984, 165). Both parties wanted to increase the debt ceiling – the Democrats in order to facilitate increased social spending, the Republicans in order to facilitate increased defense spending. Neither party wished to be clearly identified as the party that increased the debt ceiling, however, and each wanted to hold the other's spending priorities down. The House Democrats attempted to hold the debt ceiling bill hostage in order to force the Republican Senate to compromise on military spending. Twice, the Democrats soundly defeated the bill in the House to signal how serious their opposition to increased military spending was. However, Senate Republicans refused to yield, and the end of the session loomed. In the end, House Democrats blinked first, and enough Democrats switched their positions to pass the debt ceiling increase.

### 6.4.7. Routs and Deals: Summary

Plausibly, presidents can focus public attention on issues of their own choosing (Kernell 1986), thereby pressuring an otherwise reluctant House majority to take action. The House majority may be able to drag out hearings and otherwise talk the bill to death before it reaches the floor, or they may be able to set up floor consideration in such a way as to guarantee failure, or they may package the president's issue with others of their own choosing, producing an acceptable compromise. Failing these sorts of tactics, however, the majority may sometimes be forced into a more or less straightforward final-passage vote on an issue not of their choosing and be rolled as a consequence.

In this section, we have shown that majority-party rolls are more likely under divided government and especially on bills that the president pushes (under divided government). We have also examined the most important majority rolls under divided government and found that they can be divided roughly into two

---

[11] The House adopted the substitute on a 212–208 vote, with Democrats opposing it 56–200 and Republicans supporting it 156–8. It then passed the House, again supported by Republicans and Southern Democrats, and was opposed by liberal Democrats. *Congressional Quarterly* (1984: 83) noted that this was "a shift from normal practice on foreign aid bills, . . . [inasmuch as] a majority of Democrats voted against the bill, and a majority of Republicans voted for it."

groups: those where the majority loses outright (the prime examples being the Lockheed bailout and Gramm–Latta) and those where the majority essentially allowed itself to be rolled, as part of a deal with the president (you sign bill A; in return, we let a vote occur on bill B, but you have to provide most of the votes for passage).

After accounting for inconsequential rolls and rolls of the majority party during divided government, we are left with *three* unexplained majority-party rolls in the 26 Congresses in the postwar period (1953–98).[12] All three occurred under unified government and were consequential.[13] We now turn to building an explanation for these cases.

## 6.5. ROLLS THAT OCCUR UNDER UNIFIED GOVERNMENT

In considering rolls that occur under unified government, we will return to our Post-Reconstruction dataset, as there are only three in the Postwar dataset. Even in the larger dataset, we find only eleven consequential majority-party rolls occurring under unified government.[14] In the 34 Congresses organized under unified government between 1877 and 1997, the average number of consequential rolls (on bills in the H.R. series) per Congress was 0.3 (11/34), and there were no such rolls in 25 cases (74 percent).

Suppose now that we subtract from our list of 11 consequential majority-party rolls those that were *not* partisan battles (i.e., that did not involve large majorities on each side of the aisle voting against each other). Operationally, we define a vote as partisan if it pitted at least 75 percent of the majority party against at least 75 percent of the minority party.[15] How many consequential majority-party rolls on bills in the H.R. series were also partisan (from the 45th

---

[12] The minority-party consequential roll rate (based on even-numbered Congresses from the 84th to the 98th), though lower than its overall roll rate, is still substantial, averaging 9.9 percent, and ranging from 1.3 percent in the 92nd Congress to 17.5 percent in the 98th Congress. These rolls move policy toward the majority party 98 percent of the time and include major partisan platform items, such as the legislation enacted during the first four years of the New Deal, under Johnson and the Great Society, and under the Contract with America. Each was strenuously opposed by the minority. It would be hard to argue that these minority rolls were not, in fact, what they appeared to be, the exercise of agenda power by the majority in the teeth of minority opposition. A list of consequential minority rolls (which mainly include appropriations, tax, budgetary, and Social Security legislation) can be found in the addendum to this book and at *www.settingtheagenda.com*. Further, as we have shown, divided government – either with respect to the Senate, the president, or both – *reduces* the minority party's roll rate in the House, as would be expected by our model.

[13] In the eight Congresses organized under unified government between 1953 and 1998, the average number of consequential rolls per Congress was 0.4 (3/8), and there were no such rolls in five cases.

[14] Note that this analysis includes two of the three consequential majority rolls that occurred under unified government in the postwar period. The third consequential roll of this type was an H.J.Res. and, therefore, is not included in this analysis.

[15] Others have used similar definitions, especially the 50 versus 50 threshold. See Cooper, Brady, and Hurley (1977) for details.

to 105th Congresses)? The answer is two. One such roll occurred in 1883, on a bill refunding to the state of Georgia certain money it had expended for the common defense in 1777. The other such roll occurred in 1903, on a bill concerning a claim of the legal representatives of John L. Young. In other words, if one looks for the sort of majority-party roll that *least* fits our general approach – the minority party is strongly pushing the bill and the majority strongly opposing it (it is partisan); the bill leads to an enactment (it is consequential); and the roll occurs under unified government – one finds only two examples, one concerning a hundred-year-old war debt and one concerning a private claim. Neither seems to be a serious counterexample to our hypothesis.

What of the consequential majority-party rolls that were not partisan by our standard? There were nine. Of these, we have no hesitation in classifying five as *very minor*, as they concerned: a bill to waive extant rules and appoint D. T. Kirby to a captaincy in the army (1882), a bill for the relief of the book agents of the Methodist Episcopal Church South (1898), a bill providing for the extension of irrigation to the state of Texas (1906), a bill to establish an Army and Navy medal of honor roll (1916), and a bill providing pensions for the survivors of certain Indian wars in the period 1865–91 (1916).

This leaves four somewhat more important bills that did produce majority-party rolls under unified government and were ultimately enacted. Two of these saw both parties badly split on final passage.[16] Another bill, H.R. 1780 of the 78th Congress, did roll the majority party when it first passed the House. However, the bill was amended in conference to make it palatable to the majority, whereupon it passed the House with substantial majority-party support.

The single most important bill in the category of "consequential rolls under unified government" is clearly the North American Free Trade Agreement (NAFTA) of 1993. NAFTA began as an initiative of a Republican president, George Bush, in the face of Democratic majorities in the House and Senate, and continued its life after Bush's defeat as a priority of the incoming Democratic president, Bill Clinton. Clinton's strategy was to secure the necessary *procedural* support of the majority Democrats but actually pass the bill with mostly Republican votes – a pattern similar to other bills passed under wholly divided government. Let's consider each prong of Clinton's strategy in turn.

First, although Clinton certainly courted House Democrats' votes, the focus of his effort was directed at House Republicans. Clinton knew that organized labor was opposed to NAFTA and that, consequently, many Democrats would find supporting the measure very costly. He thus doggedly pressed Minority Whip Newt Gingrich to deliver more than half of the votes needed to pass NAFTA (*Congressional Quarterly Weekly* 1993: 3179).

The second part of Clinton's strategy was, evidently, to insist that the House Democrats not exert their agenda powers to block the bill's progress. Thus,

---

[16] One of these bills, H.R. 8555 of the 74th Congress, concerned replacing implicit with explicit subsidies for the merchant marine in the run-up to World War II. Another concerned an amendment to the Overseas Private Investment Act in 1978 (H.R. 9179 of the 95th Congress).

although NAFTA was referred to multiple committees, it rapidly made its way onto the Union Calendar, through the Rules Committee, and onto the floor with a favorable rule. On the key procedural vote – adopting the rule for consideration of NAFTA – only 52 of 254 Democrats (20 percent) voted against the rule. At final passage, in contrast, over 60 percent of House Democrats voted against the bill. Because the extent of Democratic opposition to the bill was well known, the majority party in the House seems to have given Clinton a clear path to a vote on final passage that would forseeably be a majority-party roll. All told, then, NAFTA seems to be another roll generated primarily by presidential strategy. This same pattern – of rolls being produced as a by-product of bargaining with the president – appears even more frequently under divided government.

## 6.6. CONCLUSION

In this chapter, we have modified our idealized Cartel Agenda Model by recognizing that the House majority party may face costs when it wishes to block an issue from being considered on the floor. We have also noted that in some cases there may be no benefit to blocking, in terms of preventing policy change, because the Senate or president will block any bill(s) in question. In the end, we are left with only one majority-party roll, the vote on NAFTA, that cannot be explained by simple extensions to our model or by simple analysis of the facts of the case.

With costs and benefits brought into view, the majority's agenda control appears more nuanced than in the idealized model. In the ideal model, the majority simply strangles unwanted bills at birth. In the model with costs and benefits more fully in view, the majority bends with the winds in various ways: It reluctantly puts hot issues on the floor but contrives their demise; or it accepts unwanted policy changes but manages to package them with those it desires. These quasi-rolls are instances in which the majority has not been able to block fully consideration of troublesome issues.

In addition to adding some realism to our depiction of agenda control, bringing costs and benefits into view also alters our main prediction. It is no longer rational for the majority leadership in the House to block bills that it knows will die in the Senate or on the president's desk: The status quo policy will be preserved whether they block or not, and blocking is costly. The central prediction of our theory thus changes from the majority will never unsuccessfully oppose a bill that passes the House to the majority will never unsuccessfully oppose a bill that is enacted. As we have seen, almost half of all majority-party rolls do not, in fact, lead to an enactment. Thus, the overall roll rate is 1.5 percent in the Postwar dataset, but the consequential roll rate is about .8 percent.

Finally, bringing costs and benefits into the model also generates new predictions. In particular, we argue that opposition presidents can on occasion force issues onto the House agenda and either rout the majority (e.g., Gramm–Latta) or, more frequently, trade one bill (the president would otherwise veto) for another (on which the majority is rolled). We find some evidence for these sorts of outcomes both in quantitative and qualitative assessment of the data.

It is perhaps worth emphasizing again that when we talk of the majority party, we are using a figure of speech. The models we present are most easily presented as if the majority caucus or the top party leadership or the majority party median takes the important actions. However, our point is not so much about the internal distribution of agenda power within the majority as about the share of such power the party's members collectively wield. Whether chairs, caucuses, or top leadership groups are more powerful, the best cards in the agenda-setting game are all held by members of the majority party. Given either that chairs and leaders are broadly representative of the rank and file, or that they are responsive to rank-and-file interests, it is very difficult to push bills through the legislative process that a majority of the majority party dislikes. More to the point, it is far more difficult to push such bills through than it would be were the House agenda constructed as if by a series of floor votes, as in the floor and pivot models.

# 7

# The Textbook Congress and the Committee on Rules

In Congresses of the late twentieth century, the Rules Committee consisted of thirteen members, nine from the majority party, four from the minority party. This heavy majority party ratio of 2 to 1 plus 1 reflected the committee's status since the mid 1970s as an "arm of the leadership" and "legislative gatekeeper." The committee of the 1990s served principally to assist the majority leadership in scheduling bills for floor action. Bills were scheduled by means of special rules that gave them priority status for consideration in the House and established procedures for their debate and amendment.

— U.S. House of Representatives, Committee on Rules, 2004

## 7.1. INTRODUCTION

In the 106th Congress, the Republican majority sought to pass legislation that would ensure increased accountability for juvenile offenders. After reneging on its promise to consider the bill under regular order, the majority party succeeded in having the matter referred to the Rules Committee. In the Democrats' view of events, Rules began by giving conflicting instructions to the minority party about how amendments should be drafted. In response to such instructions, Representative John Conyers (D-MI) exclaimed:

We ought to be honest about what really appears to be happening – a rule is being structured, in my judgment, so that the Republican leadership can isolate and kill the Senate passed gun violence amendments while still being able to point to what will be largely meaningless juvenile justice provisions.          (Letter to Henry Hyde 1999)

Conyers went on to accuse the Republican majority of purposely adding a series of "confusing and overlapping" amendments to the legislation so that the Rules Committee would have the discretion to sort everything out. In addition to these alleged tactics, what is not in dispute is that the Republican-led Rules Committee held a post-midnight meeting when adopting the rule for floor debate. Representative Conyers complained about this as well: "There can be no reason for the Rules Committee to craft a rule in the wee hours of the evening which cuts off debate and amendments on an issue that will affect so many of our children's lives" (Letter to Henry Hyde 1999). The Republican majority apparently found a reason.

This example from the 106th Congress is not at all atypical of how the minority party has viewed the Committee on Rules since the mid-1980s. However, many scholars view its role as being significantly different in earlier Congresses, and some even doubt that it serves as an agent of the majority party in recent Congresses. As our theory depends on the Rules Committee being at least a minimal agent of the majority party, we consider the role that the Rules Committee plays in setting the House agenda at length in this chapter.

Partly depending on the time period considered, one can find three main opinions expressed about the Rules Committee: (1) The committee is a faithful agent of the majority party; (2) the committee is an agent of an alternative majority, the conservative coalition; and (3) the committee is a "free agent," its members acting in pursuit of their own interests largely unfettered by party or coalitional ties. As the Rules Committee's history is usually written, these three roles have varied over time, as follows.

The committee began life firmly under the thumb of the speaker and clearly an agent of the majority party. When the speaker was expelled from the committee in the famous revolt of 1910 (cf. Jones 1968), the committee moved incrementally toward "free agency" but remained primarily an agent of the majority.[1] In 1937, pursuant to changes in membership (cf. Schickler 2001), the committee became an agent of the conservative coalition of Southern Democrats and Republicans, in opposition to the putative majority party (the Democrats).[2] In 1960, the committee was packed by the majority party and moved slightly back toward its role as an agent of the majority party, but the vast bulk of this transition occurred only after a series of reforms in the 1970s (cf. Jones 1968; Fox and Clapp 1970; Matsunaga and Chen 1976; Oppenheimer 1977, 1983).

In this chapter, we argue that throughout its history the Rules Committee has operated primarily as an agent of the majority party. Through its ability to structure the rules governing how legislation is considered, the Rules Committee

---

[1] Galloway (1968: 146) emphasizes that the Rules Committee was an agent of the majority party during the first Roosevelt administration. He notes that the committee used its broad powers to serve the interests of the Democratic leadership in the House, and he emphasizes that "the Rules Committee in the Seventy-third Congress [1933–1934] operated very definitely as an arm of the leadership and the House generally approved that kind of working relationship" (Galloway 1968: 146, quoting Lewis Lapham).

[2] Galloway (1968) also argues that the Rules Committee was an agent of the conservative coalition during this period. He notes that "instead of acting in the traditional manner as the responsible agent of the majority party and its leadership, the Rules Committee came under the control of a bipartisan coalition of Southern Democrats and North Central Republicans who used its power to block measures favored by the majority party and the Administration" (p. 147).

plays a major role in determining which legislation is passed and which is not. Before turning to more systematic evidence of this phenomenon, we present anecdotes from the 107th and 108th Congresses that demonstrate the majority party's ability to use rules to stifle minority-party obstruction.

After President Bush took office in 2001, the Republicans in the House and Senate made reform of the nation's energy policy a key goal. To that end, in 2003 energy legislation worked its way through the House and Senate, and eventually to a conference report that the Senate was unable to pass.[3] Energy legislation was again a priority in 2004, and the House Republicans introduced a bill that was identical to the 2003 conference report, as well as the U.S. Refinery Revitalization Act of 2004, which aimed to provide incentives for increasing refinery capacity. The Rules Committee then granted a joint rule to these two pieces of legislation that greatly stacked the deck in favor of the majority party. Indeed, the legislation received a closed rule that provided only one hour of debate for each bill. Not surprisingly, the rule-adoption vote was nearly along party lines – 225 yeas and 193 nays – with 218 Republicans and seven Democrats voting for the bill and 188 Democrats, four Republicans, and one independent voting against the bill.

As a result of this biased rule, Representative Edward J. Markey (D-MA) testified on the floor of Congress that

[Republicans] bring it [energy legislation] out here to the floor and what do they say to the Democratic Party, and, yes, to the American people? There are no amendments that can be made to this bill. We have conceived it in secret and we are going to pass it without amendment or without discussion, and that is the height of political arrogance because it leaves out the American people from the discussion.          (Markey 2004)

Sure enough, just as Markey suggested, the Republicans successfully passed both pieces of legislation, and rolled the minority party at the final vote on each of the bills. The Democrats' outrage and the strongly partisan nature of these votes suggest that the Rules Committee played an important role in the House's passage of energy legislation.

As a further illustration of how the Rules Committee is a weapon of the majority party, consider the events surrounding the House's passage of the Partial Birth Abortion Ban Act of 2002. Rolling over the minority party's objections, the Republican majority passed legislation banning late-term abortions (except when necessary to save the life of the mother) on a near-party-line vote of 274–151 (Hulse 2002). Most important for our purposes here, however, is the majority party's ability to use the Rules Committee to block the amendments that the Democratic minority so desperately wanted to add. Indeed, Republicans made sure that the bill was considered under a closed rule that banned amendments, thereby preventing six Democratic amendments from being added

---

[3] Interestingly, the Senate actually passed an energy bill from 2002 so that it could get to conference where Republicans could craft a conference report in secret (Goldreich 2003).

to the bill (Dlouhy 2002a, 2002b; House Report 107–608).[4] They also ensured that the rule waived all points of order and that it waived the requirement of a three-day layover of the committee report. As a result of such waivers, the Republican majority was able to bring the bill up for consideration just one day after the Judiciary Committee produced its report (House Report 107–608).

Needless to say, the Democrats were outraged. After trying in vain to add exceptions to the bill, the Democrats complained that Republicans were being unfair and that the unamended version of the bill was unconstitutional (Dlouhy 2002a; Fagan 2002a). As Representative John Conyers Jr. (D-MI) emphasized, "There has got to be a health exception.... Even if the bill passed the House and the Senate, the Supreme Court would again hold it unconstitutional.... If you don't understand this, we're in bad shape" (Fagan 2002b). Similarly, Representative Jerrold Nadler (D-NY) argued, "Whether you like it or not, you have to put it [the health exception] in the bill for the bill to be constitutional" (Fagan 2002a). Despite the Democrats' objections, the Republican majority, through its use of the Rules Committee, was able to prevail in the House.

To complement these anecdotes, we now systematically analyze how landmark changes in Rules' membership affected two of its central outputs – special rules and authorizations for committee investigations. We examine every vote held in the House on rule adoption from the 54th to the 105th Congress, identifying those that rolled the majority and those that rolled the minority party.[5] We also examine every vote held in the House on the authorization of committee investigations and funding (pursuant to resolutions proposed by Rules), again identifying party rolls. We thus provide a sort of statistical history of Rules' outputs and how they changed at each landmark (and in between, as well). The results provide new evidence bearing on the varying fidelity of the Rules Committee as an agent of the majority party over the twentieth century.

## 7.2. HOW SHOULD RULES' OUTPUTS CHANGE WHEN ITS MEMBERSHIP CHANGES?

Whereas legislative committees report various types of *joint* resolutions to the House (which, if approved by the Senate and signed by the president, become public laws), the Committee on Rules reports *simple* resolutions. Simple, or House, resolutions are no one's business but the House's. Neither the Senate nor the president has any say in whether they are adopted. Of the House resolutions reported by Rules, the best known are the so-called special rules, which (1) transfer bills from the House calendars to the plenary session and

---

[4] One of these amendments would have added a health exception to the bill, but it was rejected by a vote of 10–18. A similar amendment (in the form of a substitute) was rejected by voice vote (Fagan 2002b).

[5] The starting point here – the 54th Congress – is chosen because that is when Reed's rules were fully restored, after a brief hiatus. As we argued in Chapter 4, the central architectural features of the House that Reed built have remained largely unaltered since.

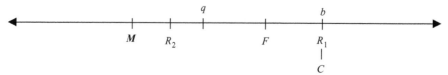

FIGURE 7.1. The Rules Committee as an agenda setter

(2) regulate their consideration (e.g., how long they can be debated, whether they are subject to points of order, and which amendments are in order). These special rules can make the difference between life and death for unprivileged controversial bills.

Whose interests do the members of Rules serve in writing special rules? On the one hand, members may act essentially as political independents, pursuing their own (and their constituents') favored policies, with negligible regard for their party's broader interests. On the other hand, members may act essentially as agents of their parties, greatly restraining their pursuit of their own (and their constituents') interests. Or, of course, the truth could lie anywhere in between.[6]

Let's first consider how Rules might act in response to membership changes, when its members are independent actors (not agents of their parties). A model of this case has been offered by Dion and Huber (1996). We present a simplified example consistent with their approach in order to illustrate a central point: When its members are independent, changes in Rules' membership should affect *both* parties' roll rates. To see why, consider a one-dimensional spatial model of a House with a Democratic majority and a conservative Rules Committee. Denote the Democratic median by $M$, the status quo policy by $q$, the floor median by $F$, and Rules' median by $R$. Assume that the left-to-right order of these points is as just given and displayed in Figure 7.1. The figure has one more ideal point, $C$, that of a hypothetical substantive policy committee chaired by a Southern Democrat and with a conservative majority similar to that reigning on Rules during the 1937–60 period.

Here is the story that goes with this figure. Both the relevant substantive committee and Rules favor legislation to move the status quo policy rightward. Given the particular constellation of ideal points, Rules would grant the committee a closed rule, allowing the committee to propose its ideal point, which coincides with Rules'. The floor median would approve the change, as the proposed bill is closer to $F$ than is the status quo. This observation resonates with the main point that Dion and Huber make in their analysis (which focuses on when Rules will grant closed rules). For our purposes, a more important observation is that the bill – with or without a closed rule – will roll the majority party on final passage.

---

[6] Later in the chapter, we return to the third possibility mentioned in the introduction to this chapter, that members of Rules may serve the conservative coalition.

Now imagine that the Rules Committee's median ideal point moves leftward, all else equal. Eventually, when $R$ is far enough left (specifically, when $R \leq q$), Rules will no longer be willing to grant any rule to a bill seeking to change $q$. This illustrates a more general result: The further right is Rules' median ideal point, the higher is the Democratic roll rate, and the lower is the Republican roll rate.

How would this result change if Rules' members were agents of their respective parties, in the "limited" sense that we introduced in Chapter 2 (i.e., they avoid rolling their own party on the floor)? Members of the majority party, if obedient to this tenet of party leadership, would be in a position to do something about it, as they constitute a super-majority on the committee. In particular, they could, if they wished, refuse to report any rule that would roll their party (even if their own constituents favored the underlying bill in question). Members of the minority party, in contrast, would not necessarily be able to protect their party from rolls. Thus, *the Cartel Agenda Model as applied to the Rules Committee implies that changes in Rules' median should affect the minority party's roll rate but not the majority's.*

Note that members of the majority on Rules are free, in this view, to deny rules to bills that their party colleagues like. The cardinal sin is to push bills they dislike onto the floor.

Thus, we have two distinct predictions. If one views members of the Rules Committee as independent actors, then the majority party's roll rate should respond to changes in the committee's median. By contrast, if one views members of the Rules Committee as obedient to the first commandment of party leadership, then the majority party's roll rate should be invariant with respect to changes in Rules' median, and the minority party's roll rate should change in a manner corresponding to changes in the Rules Committee. In the next sections, we investigate which of these predictions better fit the data.

## 7.3. THE CONVENTIONAL WISDOM ON RULES FROM 1937 TO 1960: THE TEXTBOOK CONGRESS

A debate regarding one period in the Rules Committee's history serves to illustrate the two views just articulated.[7] Some congressional observers view the Rules Committee in the period 1937–60 as blocking legislation that the bulk of majority-party members favored but either ignore or discount the possibility that Rules also pushed bills that the majority disliked. Other scholars see the Rules Committee as both blocking and pushing against the majority party's wishes. If the second camp is correct, then one should see a response in the majority party's roll rate after 1937. If the first camp is correct, then the response should be negligible. In the rest of this section, we further explain the positions involved in this debate.

[7] See Shepsle and Weingast (1995) for the defining features of the textbook Congress.

### 7.3.1. 1937

The year 1937 is conventionally cited as that in which the liberal–conservative split within the Democratic Party sharply worsened, leading to a generation in which the "conservative coalition" of Southern Democrats and Republicans wielded great influence on House affairs (Bolling 1965: 200, 201; MacKaye 1963: 5; Rohde 1991: 45). The Rules Committee was at the center of the new conservative coalition. Schickler (2001: 164) views "a series of soon-regretted committee assignments" as the proximal cause of the Democrats' loss of control of Rules. He notes that three Southern Democratic members of Rules – Cox, Smith, and Dies – had each looked considerably more loyal to Democratic policies when first appointed. Indeed, at the time of their appointments, Cox was "slightly to the *left* of the average House Democrat" (Schickler 2001: 164); Smith appeared to be a New Deal supporter, slightly to the right of the average Democrat and a follower of Rayburn; and Dies ranked as one of the more liberal Democrats. Each of these three members, however, shifted sharply to the right after their appointment, so that by 1937 the majority party found that the number of conservative Democrats on Rules was large enough, in combination with the Republicans, to control decisions. Under the leadership of its conservative members, Rules abandoned "its traditional role as party agent; it was embarking instead on a thirty-year period as an agent of opposition" (Dierenfield 1987: 59).

### 7.3.2. 1937–1960

In what sense was Rules an "agent of opposition" during the years of peak conservative control? The most frequently encountered view is that Rules acted to *block* liberal legislation. As most liberal bills were proposed by members of the majority party and as many of these were supported by its leadership, blocking liberal bills entailed frustrating the plans of the majority-party leadership. There are many accounts of how Rules did this, and we do not dispute them (see, e.g., Lapham 1954; Robinson 1963; Bolling 1965; Oppenheimer 1977).

A quite different claim, more rarely encountered, is that Rules *actively pushed* bills that the majority-party leadership opposed. Such a view is consistent with general claims that the conservative coalition "controlled" the House during the 1937–60 period (e.g., Shelley 1983) or that policy during this period was mostly conservative (e.g., Mayhew 2000). The most explicit supporter of this view, however, is Schickler, who claims that "the Rules Committee did not simply block legislation; it also actively promoted conservative priorities" (2001: 166). He cites two pieces of evidence for his view. First, he notes that "Lapham (1954, 125) counts 'about a dozen occasions' in just the 78th Congress of 1943–44 when the Rules Committee reported a rule that 'was unwanted or deficient in some respect from the point of view of [Chairman] Sabath and presumably the majority leadership.'" Second, he notes that Rules promoted a number of investigations "that undermined the electoral interests of non-Southern Democrats" (p. 167).

Let us first consider Lapham's discussion of special rules in the 78th Congress.[8] His main point, to which he returns a number of times (e.g., pp. 83, 132, 136), is that Rules impeded liberal legislation, not that it pushed conservative legislation. Even in the passage quoted by Schickler, Lapham refers to "unwanted or deficient" rules, not simply "unwanted" ones, and our detailed consideration of the dozen cases in question suggests that most of them were "deficient" (i.e., not aggressive enough in pushing bills the majority did want) rather than "unwanted" (i.e., too aggressive in pushing bills the majority did not want).[9] Another close observer of congressional politics at roughly the same time noted that it was only "seldom" that a rule would be given to a bill "opposed by the leadership" (Clapp 1964: 349). Thus, the qualitative evidence would seem consistent with our original position – that Rules seldom actively pushed bills that the majority-party leadership opposed.

Suppose we are wrong and the conservative coalition on the Rules Committee relatively often crafted special rules in order to *promote* conservative policies, per Schickler. In this case, liberal Democrats should have voted against adopting these rules and Republicans (and conservative Democrats) in favor. Indeed, if the special rules facilitated rightward policy changes, then one should sometimes find a majority of Democrats opposing them.[10]

In what follows we will examine votes on the adoption of special rules from a number of Congresses. If we find that the majority party suffered a significant number of rolls on the adoption of special rules during the 78th Congress, or other Congresses, we shall conclude that Schickler is correct – Rules was actively pushing conservative priorities. If, on the other hand, we find that the

---

[8] As Young (1956) notes, the 78th Congress was unusual in a number of respects. Because this Congress was in session during the height of World War II, it had to deal with a number of contentious issues, including wage rates, labor strikes, and soldier voting. The issue of soldier voting was particularly divisive because, as Young notes, "all Congressmen were interested in the issue, for the extent to which soldiers voted might determine the political fate of the members of Congress and of the presidential candidates" (Young 1956: 83).

[9] The majority party was rolled in connection with only two special rules. One rule pertained to the Soldiers' Ballot Bill of 1944. In this case, the majority leadership supported the Worley amendment to the bill and wanted a roll call vote on that amendment. However, the majority party was rolled on the previous question vote preceding consideration of the special rule and this led to adoption of a rule under which the Worley amendment was not considered. Another rule on which the majority was rolled (this time on the actual adoption vote) pertained to an anti–poll tax bill opposed by most Southern Democrats and favored by Northern Democrats and Republicans.

[10] We say "sometimes" because some rightward moves can be opposed just by a few of the furthest-left members of the House, when the status quo policy being targeted is itself "too far" left. As the status quo moves in from too far left, the number of leftist opponents to any bill changing that status quo increases, until eventually one reaches highly controversial changes that a majority of Democrats would oppose.

majority party suffered rolls on the adoption of special rules no more frequently than it suffered rolls on final passage, we shall conclude that Smith and his allies on Rules were constrained in how, and how hard, they pushed their legislative priorities. In particular, they usually made sure that the special rules they proposed did not roll the majority party.

Note that the point at issue here is a matter of degree. We have no doubt that Smith and his allies *favored* conservative policies in many respects. The question is whether they pushed for such policies completely unconstrained by their ties to the majority party, slightly constrained by such ties, or heavily constrained by such ties. If they were completely unconstrained, then we should see frequent scenarios of the following sort: A bill moving policy rightward is reported by a committee with a Southern Democratic chair; a favorable rule is granted by Rules; and the Democrats are rolled on final passage. If Smith and his Southern Democratic allies were heavily constrained (in particular, by the first commandment of party leadership), then any policy initiatives undertaken by the conservatives would be packaged in such a way so as not to roll the majority party on final passage. So, did Smith seek policies by constructing relatively narrow support coalitions and using Rules' powers to the hilt, producing majority-party rolls, or did he seek policies by constructing relatively broad support coalitions and using Rules' powers mostly to delay, thereby avoiding majority-party (and minority party) rolls? It is to these questions that we now turn.

## 7.4. DATA

As seen in the previous sections, different views of whether members of the Rules Committee behave as agents of their party lead to differing predictions regarding how key events in the history of the Rules Committee should have affected the majority party's roll rate on rule-adoption votes. In this and the next few sections, we examine *every* recorded vote on special rule adoption taken in the post-Reed period, the 54th–105th Congresses, focusing on how often each party was rolled.[11]

In analyzing the data, we look first at how the parties' roll rates changed at each of the four landmarks in committee history identified previously (1910, 1937, 1961, and the mid-1970s). We then provide a more comprehensive

---

[11] Recall that a party is rolled on a vote if the motion in question passes against the wishes of a majority of the party's voting members. The data for the 54th–82nd Congresses were compiled by searching the Voteview database (*voteview.ucsd.edu/default.htm*), as discussed in Poole and Rosenthal (1997), for all votes whose titles contained any reference to "H.Res" or "HRes" or "H.–Res" or "H-Res." Each of these votes was then examined to see which were rule adoption votes. The data for the 83rd–105th Congresses are from Rohde's House roll call dataset, maintained by the Political Institutions and Public Choice Program at Michigan State University. For access to this data set, contact David Rohde at *rohde@msu.edu* or visit *www.settingtheagenda.com*.

TABLE 7.1. *Majority-Party Roll Rates on Rule Adoption Votes, Congresses 54–74*

| Period | Number of Recorded Votes on Rule Adoption | Roll Rate on Rule Adoption Votes, Majority Party (%) | Roll Rate on Rule Adoption Votes, Minority Party (%) |
|---|---|---|---|
| Czar rule (54th–60th) | 25 | 0.0 | 92.0 |
| Postrevolt (61st–71st) | 76 | 1.3 | 57.9 |
| New Deal (72nd–74th) | 29 | 0.0 | 82.8 |

examination of whether or not changes in Rules' median affected each party's roll rate.

### 7.4.1. Party Roll Rates on Rule Adoption Votes and the Revolt Against Cannon

Did the revolt against Cannon affect the majority party's roll rate, the minority party's roll rate, both, or neither? We employ a standard research design with two nonequivalent groups to test for the effect of a single treatment, the revolt, on majority- and minority-party roll rates. A nonequivalent group design requires both pretest and post-test observations; that is, the design requires that we observe roll rates before and after the treatment (the revolt) for two groups (the majority and minority parties) for whom we have divergent predictions (cf. Trochim 2001: 216–21). Table 7.1 presents the relevant data.

As can be seen, there were no rolls of the majority party during the period of czar rule, exactly one roll of the majority between the end of czar rule and the New Deal, and again no rolls during the New Deal era. Given this lone counterexample, we are unable to reject the null hypothesis that the revolt against Cannon had *no* effect on the majority party's roll rate on rule-adoption votes.

In contrast, the minority party's roll rate decreases by 34 percentage points from the czar-rule level to the postrevolt period and then increases again by 29 percentage points during the New Deal era. Both changes are statistically significant. Together, these results provide a highly valid test of the causal impact of the revolt against Cannon on the behavior of the Rules Committee (cf. Trochim 2001: 216 on nonequivalent group designs).

This pattern – no significant change in the majority's roll rate but hefty changes in the minority's – is consistent with the assumption that members of Rules acted as limited agents of their parties. In contrast, our results allow us to argue that the Dion–Huber model (which assumes that they acted as independents because one would expect changes in *both* parties' roll rates, were that model true) lacks conclusion validity.

TABLE 7.2. *Majority-Party Roll Rates on Rule-Adoption Votes, Congresses 54–105*

| Period | Number of Recorded Votes on Rule Adoption | Number of Rule Adoption Votes Rolling the Majority Party | Majority Party's Roll Rate on Rule-Adoption Votes (%) | Number of Rule-Adoption Votes Rolling the Majority and Leading to a Majority Roll on the Associated Bill |
|---|---|---|---|---|
| Early (54th–74th) | 130 | 1 | 0.8 | 0 |
| Conservative coalition (75th–86th) | 134 | 9 | 6.7 | 1 |
| Postpacking (87th–93rd) | 195 | 4 | 2.1 | 3 |
| Postreform (94th–105th) | 1065 | 4 | 0.4 | 1 |
| TOTAL | 1524 | 18 | 1.2 | 5 |

### 7.4.2. Party Roll Rates on Rule-Adoption Votes: 1937, 1961, and the 1970s

How did the conservative "take-over" of Rules in 1937, the packing of the committee in 1961, and the reforms of the 1970s affect the parties' roll rates? The problem with constructing a test in this case is that there was not a single treatment, but rather a series of actions that lasted decades: the split between Northern and Southern Democrats over civil rights, the appointment of various Democrats to the committee, the election of 1946, and so on.

Tables 7.2 and 7.3 report roll rates for the majority and minority parties, respectively, on rule-adoption votes for the entire 1895–1997 period and for four different subperiods: the 54th–74th Congresses (the early period, detailed in Table 7.1); the 75th–86th Congresses (the heyday of the conservative coalition); the 87th–93rd Congresses (between the packing of the Rules Committee and the major reforms of the 94th Congress); and the 94th–105th Congresses (the postreform House).

As can be seen, the majority's overall roll rate for the entire century (1895–1997) is 1.2%, which is very similar to the majority roll rate reported in Chapter 5 for final-passage votes on bills. Looking at the figures for each period, we see a statistically significant increase in the majority party's roll rate, from 0.8 to 6.7 percent, following the take-over of the Rules Committee by the conservative coalition in 1937. Thereafter, the majority party's roll rate declines following the packing of the Rules Committee in 1961, and we see a slightly smaller decline following the adoption of more general reforms in 1974. However, neither of the latter two declines were significant in a binomial test of

TABLE 7.3. *Minority-Party Roll Rates on Rule Adoption Votes, Congresses 54–105*

| Period | Number of Recorded Votes on Rule Adoption | Number of Rule Adoption Votes Rolling the Minority Party | Minority Party's Roll Rate on Rule Adoption Votes (%) | Number of Rule Adoption Votes Rolling the Minority and Leading to a Minority Roll on the Associated Bill |
|---|---|---|---|---|
| Early (54th–74th) | 130 | 91 | 70.0 | — |
| Conservative coalition (75th–86th) | 134 | 39 | 29.1 | — |
| Postpacking (87th–93rd) | 195 | 33 | 16.9 | — |
| Postreform (94th–105th) | 1065 | 533 | 50.0 | — |
| TOTAL | 1524 | 696 | 45.7 | — |

proportions (although the overall roll rate for the 87th–105th Congresses is significantly lower than the roll rate in the era of conservative coalition).

The minority's overall roll rate for the entire century (1895–1997) is 45.7 percent, which is almost twice its roll rate for final-passage votes on bills (from Chapter 5). Looking at the figures for each period, we see a substantial (and statistically significant) decline in the minority party's roll rate following both the conservative coalition take-over in 1937 and, surprisingly, the packing of the Rules Committee in 1961. These declines were followed by a sharp increase in the minority party's roll rate on rule adoption in the postreform era.

Figure 7.2 shows kernel-density plots of each Congress's majority and minority roll rates on special rules, dividing the time series into the four periods described earlier. These kernel-density plots show the frequency with which a particular roll rate occurs within a particular congressional period. The majority and minority roll rates are clearly distinct with the majority commonly having its peak density near zero, while the minority's highest density is always greater than the majority's and is higher than zero.

The conservative take-over in 1937 does not fit our idealized Cartel Agenda Model of the Rules Committee as an agent of the majority party. Under our model, the majority-party roll rate should have remained essentially zero. Instead, it increases. Note, however, that, during the era of the conservative coalition, the majority's roll rate differs from the overall roll rate for the majority party by only 5.5 percentage points. To put it another way, there were only six excess majority-party rolls on rule adoptions beyond what the idealized Cartel Agenda Model would predict for the 24-year period of the conservative

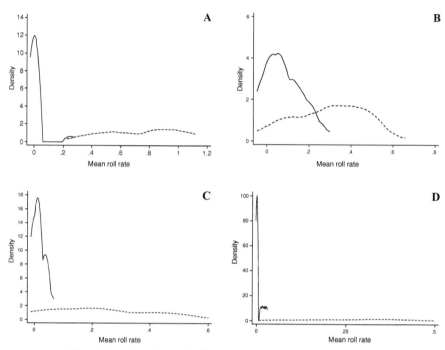

FIGURE 7.2. Kernel-density plots of roll rates on special rules votes: (a) majority and minority roll rate, 54th–74th Congress; (b) majority and minority roll rate, 75th–86th Congress; (c) majority and minority roll rate, 87th–93rd Congress; (d) majority and minority roll rate, 94th–105th Congress

coalition, with one third of these falling in the tumultuous 78th Congress. By contrast, the minority's roll rate varies greatly with each change, dropping by about 40 percentage points from 1937 to 1961. Thus, the main effect of the conservative take-over was to diminish the frequency of rules that rolled the minority, with only a secondary and small increase in the majority's roll rate.

If we take 1937 as the treatment and look at the entire 24-year period that follows as the post-test, then we would reject the null hypothesis that the creation of the conservative coalition had no effect on the behavior of the Rules Committee. The evidence for this period supports the Dion and Huber model of the Rules Committee as independent agents. If we take the period from the emergence of the conservative coalition in 1937 to the reforms in 1974 as the post-test (as Rohde 1991 suggests), then the difference in proportions for the majority party is insignificant, while there was a significant decline for the minority party's roll rate on rule adoption, again providing a highly valid test that the creation of the Conservative Coalition was consequential for the Rules Committee. Moreover, with this choice of post-test period, the evidence supports our idealized Cartel Agenda Model.

The reassertion of majority party control over Rules, beginning in 1961 and continuing after 1974, also shows a marked asymmetry between the parties. The majority party's roll rate does decline after both 1961 and 1974 – but by 4.6 and 1.7 percentage points, respectively (only the latter is significantly different from the series average of 1.2 percent in a binomial test). The minority party's roll rate shows much larger changes, declining by 12.2 and then increasing by 33.1 percentage points.

The main story we wish to emphasize concerns how aggressively Rules pushes the majority's legislative program,[12] as reflected in the large swings in the minority roll rate, rather than how often Rules betrays the majority and pushes special rules promoting cross-party bills, as reflected in the substantially smaller swings in the majority roll rate.

We do see considerable evidence for the textbook view of the Rules Committee (Galloway 1968; Fox and Clapp 1970; Matsunaga and Chen 1976; Oppenheimer 1977), as forcefully presented by Lapham (1954), that "the Rules Committee has always been regarded in a special sense as the agent of the party with the greater strength, in order to facilitate the conduct of business and the responsibilities of leadership" (p. 89). We do not find much evidence to support the claim that the Rules Committee was independent of the majority party, as argued by Schickler (2001), Dion (1997), and Dion and Huber (1996). The evidence shows that the Rules Committee only rarely took actions to roll the majority party, even during the period of the textbook Congress (six excess rolls on rule adoptions over a 24-year period), and that the Rules Committee acted to roll the minority party at a rate four times as frequently as it rolled the majority party. Again, we agree with Lapham-who argues that the House Committee on Rules has, at times, used its control over the agenda "to obstruct and weaken the program decided upon by the party leadership and the administration" (Lapham 1954: 83).

### 7.4.3. Party Rolls and the Location of Rules' Median

In the previous two sections, we examined how four important events in the history of the Rules Committee changed party roll rates on rule-adoption votes. Each of these events was assumed to have altered the ideological complexion of Rules, pushing it either toward the left (1910, 1961, 1970s) or toward the right (1937). In more technical lingo, each event can be viewed as shifting the median ideal point on Rules.

In the previous sections, however, we did not explicitly measure *how far* Rules' median ideal point moved. In this section, we do so, in order to test the

---

[12] In Chapter 10, we present an example of this phenomenon by discussing the Rules Committee in the 108th Congress. There, we emphasize that the Rules Committee often held post-midnight meetings in order to push the majority party's agenda and to keep minority members in the dark about legislation until the very last minute. Such a tactic has earned 108th Congress' Rules Committee the nickname "Dracula Congress" (Boston Globe 2004).

predictions of the Dion–Huber model against a variant of our idealized Cartel
Agenda Model.

To see the logic of our investigation, consider a version of our idealized model
from Chapter 3, with the following modifications. Rather than the majority-
party median or the floor median being the agenda setter, the agenda is set by a
two-stage process in which the Rules Committee median first decides whether
to grant a rule to bill $b$ (which proposes to amend the status quo on dimension $j$).
If the committee grants a rule, the floor then votes whether to adopt the rule.
If the floor adopts the rule, the bill is taken from a calendar, considered under
an open rule on the floor, and passes at the floor median's ideal point. If the
committee does not grant a rule, or if the floor rejects the rule, then the status
quo remains in place on dimension $j$.

The implications of this model depend crucially on whether or not the Rules
Committee acts as a faithful agent of the majority party. Suppose that the Rules
Committee is an *unfaithful* agent – that is, it pursues its own interests without
regard for the majority party's interests or goals as in the Dion–Huber model.
The implications of this assumption are illustrated by Figure 7.3, in which $R$
is the Rules Committee median's ideal point; as before, $M$, $F$, and $m$ are the
majority party, floor, and minority party medians; $g$ is the probability density
function of status quo points, and is assumed not to be skewed to the right of
$F$; and, for simplicity, $M < F < m$. First, note that the Rules Committee will
not grant a rule to a bill on any dimension on which the status quo is between
$2R_j - F$ and $F$, which is the Rules Committee's blockout zone.[13] This implies
that the majority party will never be rolled if $M$ is between $R$ and $F$, as is the case
with $R_1$ in Figure 7.3, since the entire set of status quos that the majority party
would like to block from being amended is a subset of the set that the Rules
Committee would like to block $(2R_1 - F)$. This also implies that the majority-
party roll rate will be unrelated to the distance between the party median's ideal
point and either $F$ or $R$. The minority party, on the other hand, is more likely
to be rolled as the distance between it and the Rules Committee blockout zone
(in this case, $|F - m|$) increases.

Now consider the case in which the Rules Committee median is between $M$
and $F$, as with $R_2$ in the figure. In this case, some of status quos the majority would like to protect – those between $2M - F$ and $2R_2 - F$ – are outside
the Rules Committee's blockout zone, and the majority party will be rolled on
adoption votes for rules that allow amendment of those status quos. It follows
directly that the majority's probability of being rolled increases as the distance
between $M$ and the majority party's blockout zone (here, $|M - R_2|$) increases.
More generally, when $M < R_j$, the majority is more likely to be rolled as
$|M - R_j|$ increases, all else constant. And again, the minority party is more
likely to be rolled as the distance between it and the Rules Committee blockout
zone (again, $|F - m|$) increases.

---

[13] For simplicity, and consistent with our emphasis on different locations of the Rules Committee
median, we dispense with subscripts for $M$, $F$, and $m$ for the rest of this discussion.

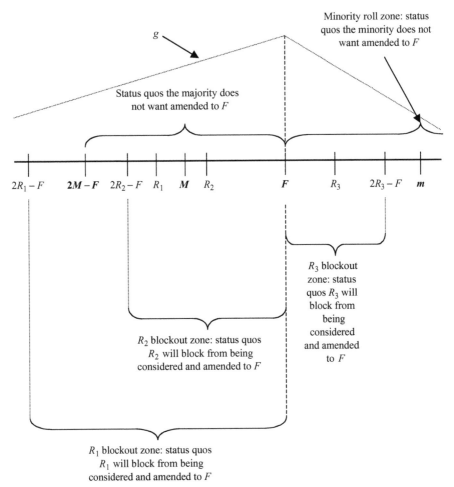

FIGURE 7.3. Location of the Rules Committee median and party rolls

Finally, consider the case in which the Rules Committee median is to the right of $F$, as illustrated by $R_3$ (and that is perhaps most consistent with the story typically told about the Rules Committee during the conservative coalition period). In this case, it is actually the *minority* party that benefits from Rules Committee agenda control, and *none* of the status quos that the majority party wants to protect are protected by the Rules Committee. Again, the majority party's likelihood of being rolled is a function of its distance from the Rules Committee blockout zone, which in this case is $|M - F|$. And the minority party's roll likelihood also remains a function of its distance from the Rules Committee blockout zone, which is $|R - m|$ in this case.[14]

---

[14] Because it does not arise empirically, we do not discuss the case in which $M < F < m < R$.

TABLE 7.4. *Effects of Distance from Rules Committee Blockout Zone on Majority- and Minority-Party Rolls on Rule-Adoption Votes, Congresses 62–100*

| Party | Distance from $(R, F)$ | Predicted Effect of Distance on Roll Rate If Agent | | Estimated Effect of Distance on Roll Rate | |
|---|---|---|---|---|---|
| | | Faithful | Unfaithful | Coefficient | Standard Error |
| | | If $R < M < F < m$ | | | |
| Majority | $\|R - M\|$[a] | 0 | 0 | $-2.47$ | $25.96$[b] |
| | | If $M < R < F < m$ | | | |
| Majority | $\|M - R\|$ | 0 | $+$ | $19.46$* | $7.64$[c] |
| | | If $M < F < R < m$ | | | |
| Majority | $\|M - F\|$ | 0 | $+$ | $3.579$ | $7.320$[d] |
| | For All Configurations of $M$, $F$, and $R$ | | | | |
| Minority | $\min(\|R - m\|,$ $F - m\|)$ | $+$ | $+$ | $5.586$* | $0.944$[e] |

* Indicates $p$ .05.
[a] For the majority party in cases characterized by $R < M < F$, we use the distance from $R$ to $M$ ($\|R - M\|$) as our measure of distance.
[b] $\alpha = (-4.60); N = 20; \text{Pseudo}\, R^2 = 0.0103; \text{Log likelihood} = -40.156$.
[c] $\alpha = -5.96\ (1.49); N = 11; \text{Pseudo}\, R^2 = 0.2144; \text{Log likelihood} = -13.934$.
[d] $\alpha = -3.67\ (1.778); N = 8; \text{Pseudo}\, R^2 = 0.0107; \text{Log likelihood} = -18.99$.
[e] $\alpha = (-2.449); N = 39; \text{Pseudo}\, R^2 = 0.1272; \text{Log likelihood} = -594.648$.

To this point, we have maintained the assumption put forth by Schickler (2001), Dion (1997), and Dion and Huber (1996) that the Rules Committee is an independent actor that pursues its own, rather than the majority party's, welfare. But what if the majority party, through some combination of selection and selective incentives, is able to induce its members on the Rules Committee to act as faithful (albeit limited) agents of the party? That is, what if the Rules Committee blocks consideration of bills that the majority party wants blocked, in addition to bills that the Rules Committee median wants to block?

Given this "faithful agent" assumption, some of the model's predictions change. As with the idealized Cartel Agenda Model, the majority party will never be rolled, regardless of its distance from the $(R, F)$ interval. Indeed, when $R$ is between $F$ and $M$, the model reduces to the idealized Cartel Agenda Model. When $R$ is to the left of $M$, though, some status quos that the majority would *like* to amend will be protected by the Rules Committee. This is also the case when $R$ is to the right of $F$. The minority party's probability of being rolled, on the other hand, continues to be positively related to the distance between the minority party median and the $(R, F)$ interval, regardless of the faithful agent assumption (so long as we assume that the minority median does not fall between the floor and Rules Committee medians).

Columns 3 and 4 of Table 7.4 show, for each configuration of ideal points, the effect of a party median's distance from the $(R, F)$ interval on that party's roll rates, under the faithful agent and unfaithful agent assumptions. As can be seen, the two models differ in their predictions when $R$ (the median of the Rules Committee) is to the right of $M$ (the majority party median), in which cases the faithful agent model predicts no relationship, and the unfaithful agent model predicts a positive relationship.

To test these predictions, we compiled a dataset, with an observation for each Congress from the 62nd to the 100th. We started the investigation in the 62nd, as this is the first Congress in which the speaker was not a member of the Rules Committee at the beginning of the session. When the speaker is on the committee, it is not possible to calculate Rules' median ideal point because the speaker so rarely votes that he is not given a DW-NOMINATE score. We end the investigation in the 100th Congress because our source of data on committee membership ends in that Congress.[15]

For each Congress, we used first-dimension DW-NOMINATE scores to identify the Rules Committee median, the floor median, and each party's median. From these, we created the variable,

$Dist(R, F)_{ct}$, which is the absolute value of the distance from the ideal point of party $c$'s median and the nearest point of the $(R, F)$ interval in Congress $t$, where $c$ is either the majority or the minority party. The exact measure of $Dist(R, F)_{ct}$ for each configuration of ideal points $M$, $R$, $F$, and $m$ is shown in column 2 of Table 7.4.

In addition, we created the variable,

*RulesRollRate$_{ct}$*, which is the proportion of rule-adoption votes on which a majority of party $c$'s members voted against adoption, but the rule was adopted nonetheless in Congress $t$.

Using extended beta binomial regression (King 1989; Palmquist 1999), we then estimate the equation

$$RulesRollRate_{ct} = \alpha_c + \beta_1 Dist(R, F)_{ct} + \varepsilon_{ct}$$

separately for the majority and minority parties. In addition, for the majority party, we estimate it separately for each of the three possible configurations of $R$, $M$, and $F$, since the hypothesized effect of $Dist(R, F)_c$ varies by configuration for the majority party.[16] Since the effect of $Dist(R, F)_c$ does not vary

---

[15] We used Nelson's committee data (as amended by Cox and McCubbins 1993) as our source for committee assignments.

[16] Our entire discussion to this point has assumed a Democratic majority (i.e., $M < F < m$). In sorting Republican-majority Congresses into the three categories of preference arrays, we accounted for this by reversing the inequality operators for each category. In other words, a Congress in which $m < F < R < M$ in the raw NOMINATE data would go into the $M < R < F$ category in the empirical results that we present.

by configuration for the minority party, we pool all Congresses into a single equation for the minority party. Appendix 7.A shows which Congresses in our time series are characterized by each of the three configurations of preferences, as well as the majority roll rate, minority roll rate, and number of rule-adoption votes, for each Congress.

The final two columns of Table 7.4 display the results of these regressions. We begin with the results of the two regressions in which the models predict the same outcomes. The first row of results shows that, as predicted by both models, the majority's median distance from the Rules Committee's median does not have a significant effect on the majority party's roll rate (the $p$-value is a meager .924) when the majority party's median is between the Rules Committee's median and the floor median (i.e., $R < M < F$).[17] Similarly, the final row of results shows that, as predicted by both models, the effect of $Dist(R, F)_c$ on minority-party roll rates is significant and positive (the $p$-value is less than .0001).

We now turn to the more interesting cases in which the faithful and unfaithful agency models make different predictions. The second row of results shows that, when $M < R < F$, the coefficient for $Dist(R, F)_c$ is positive and significant at almost the 99 percent level. These results are consistent with the unfaithful agent model, and inconsistent with the faithful agent model. For cases in which the Rules Committee median is to the right of the floor median ($M < F < R$), however, we see different results: The coefficient for $Dist(R, F)_c$ is positive but is significant only at the 37 percent level, which supports the faithful agent model and is inconsistent with the unfaithful model.

Given that the results are contrary to our expectations, we examine the cases in which $M < R < F$ in greater detail. First, in eight of the 11 Congresses characterized by these conditions, the majority party was never rolled on a rule adoption vote. In the other three Congresses (the 78th, the 83rd, and the 84th), its roll rates were .25, .14, and .14, respectively (see Appendix 7.A). Moreover, these rates are based on a small number of rule-adoption votes; in fact, the number of majority-party rolls in these Congresses was one, one, and two, respectively. In other words, the majority was not being rolled frequently.

Converting our EBB results for cases in which $M < R < F$ into probabilities that the majority party will be rolled on a rule-adoption vote, we find that the estimated probability is less than .015 in all Congresses except the 68th, 78th, and 84th, and in the 68th the probability is only .022. For the 78th and 84th, though, the roll probabilities are .16 and .13, respectively.

Thus, it seems that the 78th and 84th Congresses are distinct outliers. However, even in the tumultuous 78th – for which Lapham, Schickler, and Young portray the Rules Committee as an unruly agent of the majority party – the Rules Committee produced only one special rule that rolled the majority party. In the 84th (1955–7), in which the Democrats retook control of the House from the Republicans, there were only two rolls of the majority party on rule-adoption

---

[17] For Congresses in which $R < M < F$, we use $|R - M|$ as our measure of distance.

votes. These Congresses suggest a rough upper bound on the extent to which the Rules Committee ever acts as a bad agent of the majority party and suggests that this upper bound is still quite low. If we rerun the $M < R < F$ model without these two outlier Congresses, we find that the coefficient for $Dist(R, F)_c$ is no longer positive and significant; rather, it is negative and insignificant. Although we would not reject the unfaithful agent model of the Rules Committee on this evidence, neither would we reject the faithful agent model.

In addition, the 84th Congress is one of only three Congresses in our sample (the others are the 81st and 82nd) in which the minority party is more favorably positioned than the majority, relative to the Rules and floor medians. In both of these Congresses, the minority's median member was closer to the interval between the Rules and floor medians than was the majority's median member. By a purely spatial reckoning, then, the minority party's roll rate on rule-adoption votes should have been less than the majority party's. (A sufficient condition for this expectation is that the distribution of status quo points is symmetric on either side of the interval between the Rules and floor medians; or that any asymmetries put greater density on the majority-party side of that interval.) Empirically, however, one finds the opposite: In the 81st, the majority party was never rolled and the minority was rolled four times; in the 84th, both parties were rolled twice. Combining the results for these two Congresses, one can reject the null hypothesis that the majority party's roll rate was greater than or equal to the minority's in favor of the alternative hypothesis that its roll rate was lower, at the 0.07 level.

For the cases when $M < F < R$, there are only eight Congresses from which to conduct our test, so our test statistic showing that the mean effect of changes in the median of the Rules Committee is insignificant in predicting minority-party roll rates has very little power, and we are hesitant to reject the unfaithful agent hypothesis on the basis of this test alone. Looking at the majority roll rate, we see that it is zero in four Congresses (the 65th, 75th, 77th, and 81st). We just discussed the 81st Congress and how the outcomes at that time do not fit with the predictions of the unfaithful agent model.

Taken together, the results presented here do not allow us to reject either the faithful or unfaithful agency model of the Rules Committee. On balance, the data support the faithful model very well, as the Rules Committee has only very rarely acted unfaithfully, even under conditions when the Dion–Huber model could lead us to believe that the Rules Committee was in a running battle with the majority party.

### 7.4.4. Rules Committee Investigations

As Schickler notes, another part of the Rules Committee's jurisdiction concerns committee investigations. Most investigations, and the financing to conduct them, are authorized pursuant to resolutions reported by the Rules Committee. Schickler's discussion highlights several of the more contentious investigations (e.g., those conducted by the House Un-American Activities Committee), notes that none of them would have been loved by a liberal, and argues that they indeed damaged the electoral prospects of the Democratic Party.

We agree that there were investigations that displeased the majority party during the period Schickler examines. How frequently did this happen, however? In Chapter 4, we introduced a comprehensive dataset of organizational and rule changes effected pursuant to a roll call vote. Included in this dataset are 55 votes that both divided the two parties and concerned the funding of committees.[18] (For example, there were 16 controversial votes regarding investigations undertaken by the House Committee on Un-American Activities, one of the issues stressed by Schickler in his review of the conservative coalition's actions.) Of the 55 party votes on funding controversies, the majority party won 54 and lost 1.[19]

## 7.5. PATHWAYS AROUND THE MAJORITY PARTY?

Like those who suggest that the Rules Committee can be used to circumvent the majority party, others have argued that various rules of the House undercut the ability of the majority to control the agenda. First, it has been suggested that the discharge petition provides the means to bypass majority party agenda control, allowing bills onto the floor that could roll the majority (Krehbiel 1995). We discussed this measure at length in Chapter 4, emphasizing that discharge petitions are extremely difficult to use successfully and, as a result, are almost never undertaken (see Beth 2001).[20] Even where there have been attempts to strengthen the discharge petition, the actual procedure has been difficult, particularly if it is used against a similarly sized coalition that has the backing of the Rules Committee or majority leadership and seeks to keep the bill off the agenda. (See Appendix 4.B for further details.)

Second, others have argued that the motion to recommit (or the motion to recommit forthwith) gives the minority party a "last move" on any proposal, giving them take-it-or-leave-it powers similar to those of committee chairmen in Shepsle and Weingast's (1987) model of conference committees (Krehbiel and Meirowitz 2002). Again, if this were an accurate portrayal of the legislative process, then there would be good reason to doubt the potency of majority-party

---

[18] One of the investigations that Schickler discusses – the 1939 investigation of the National Labor Relations Board (NLRB) – which rolls the majority party, falls outside of the purview of our dataset, as it does not create or fund a committee, but instead simply authorizes an investigation. None of the other five House or Joint investigations discussed by Schickler made it into our dataset of rule changes, as none had "party votes" (See Schickler 2001: Appendix B.3).

[19] As an aside, we also note that Schickler's main claim – that the particular investigations on which he focuses damaged liberal electoral interests – is not quantified. It seems plausible that liberals would have disliked these investigations; it is less clear how large an electoral penalty they anticipated or actually paid.

[20] Since the late 1970s, discharge *motions* have been very common. Unlike the discharge procedure, however, which can be used by any member of the House, a discharge motion is entirely at the speaker's discretion and is used solely for discharging committees of bills that have been multiply referred (Oleszek 2001).

agenda control. For several reasons, however, we believe this model is inaccurate. First, the model's explicit predictions about the frequency of, and voting patterns on, recommittal motions are strongly at odds with empirical findings (Kiewiet and Roust 2003, Roberts 2003; Cox et al. 2004).[21] Second, in several different ways, the driving assumptions of the model do not match up to the procedural reality of the House. For example, motions to recommit with instructions are always subject to points of order on germaneness, which are always subject to interpretation and control by the majority party. Further, prior to 1994, motions to recommit were subject to the restrictions of special rules (Cox et al. 2004). After the 1994 Republican take-over of the House, when the motion to recommit was strengthened as a gesture to give the minority party some "power," the Republicans increasingly rejected the motions as nongermane (Wolfensberger 2003). Indeed, Kiewiet and Roust (2003) argue that the motion to recommit is little more than one of many opportunities for the minority party to offer an amendment, but that it is routinely voted down by the majority. Moreover, the motion to recommit is never the last move on any proposal because the majority party can use conference committees, to which the speaker controls appointments (Lazarus and Monroe 2003), to undo any unwanted amendments adopted through a motion to recommit (Kiewiet and McCubbins 1991). In the end, the motion to recommit is only as powerful as the majority party permits it to be (Wolfensberger 2003).

To address more specifically Krehbiel and Meirowitz's (2002) argument about the motion to recommit, we note that our theory can account for the use of motions to recommit and that the empirical evidence presented in this book demonstrates that motions to recommit are not used in the way that Krehbiel and Meirowitz hypothesize. First of all, our Cartel Agenda Model assumes the presence of an open rule; that is, all bills that the majority party puts on the agenda are ultimately amended to the floor median (see Chapter 3). Thus, under our one-dimensional spatial model, the motion to recommit merely functions as an amendment that moves the bill to the floor median. Furthermore, in multiple dimensions, our empirical findings demonstrate that Krehbiel and Meirowitz's argument cannot be correct. Specifically, Krehbiel and Meirowitz suggest that the minority party can use (or threaten to use) the motion to recommit to drive a wedge through the majority party and then ultimately prevail on final passage. For this to be true, however, there must be a pattern of results showing that the minority party wins votes and rolls the majority party at final passage. The results presented in Chapter 5 demonstrate that this pattern clearly does not exist in the U.S. House.

---

[21] As Cox et al. (2004) demonstrate, there is substantial evidence that cuts against Krehbiel and Meirowitz's conclusions. Indeed, they find that (1) only 27 percent of final-passage votes in Rohde's dataset are preceded by any motion to recommit, (2) only 13 percent of all recommittal motions are actually passed, and (3) of the 848 total recommittal motions, a majority of the minority party opposes nearly one out of five recommittal motions. Nothing in Krehbiel and Meirowitz's model can account for these results.

## 7.6. CONCLUSION

In the postreform Congress, there is ample evidence that the Rules Committee acts as an agent of the majority party. First, if one asks members, they will say that this is true. For example, one member quoted in 1998 put it this way: "Whoever is the top member on Rules executes whatever the party's game plan [is]. That's what the job is all about" (*Roll Call* 1998: 32). Second, if one looks systematically at the sorts of bills that get more favorable (i.e., more restrictive) rules, one finds that they are those in the majority party's interest (Marshall 2002). Third, if one examines the pattern of votes on special rule adoption and final passage, one finds further evidence of majority-party control (Sinclair 2002a; Cox and Poole 2002). Lastly, considering the 1,065 special rules recommended by the Rules Committee in the postreform period, one finds that the majority party was rolled 0.4 percent of the time (four times), while the minority party was rolled slightly more than half the time.

In this chapter, however, we focused on the Rules Committee in the prereform period, especially during the heyday of the conservative coalition (1937–60). At issue is whether Rules during this period simply blocked liberal legislation – a claim we do not dispute – or whether it also actively promoted conservative legislation. Schickler is the primary exponent of the latter view, and we take a three-pronged approach to rebutting his claim. First, we look at his primary source (Lapham 1954) and argue that few of the cases this source cites provide much support for the claim that Rules was actively promoting conservative policies that a majority of the Democratic Party would oppose. Second, we look at all votes on the adoption of special rules from the 54th–105th Congresses, showing that the majority's roll rate remained modest even during the heyday of the conservative coalition. Third, we look at all investigations authorized by Rules, finding that the majority party lost one out of the 55 recorded votes concerning such authorizations.

The debate here is certainly a matter of degree. We do not deny that Rules sometimes pushed rules that the majority party disliked and that it did so somewhat more frequently after 1937. Indeed, our data are the first to offer a systematic documentation of this point. What impresses us, however, is how *infrequently* the Rules Committee pushed conservative legislation during the 1937–60 period. Even during the nadir of majority-party control of Rules, the committee seldom reported special rules that rolled the majority party, and such actions became substantially rarer after the packing incident and again after reform. Even when the minority party's median was closer to the floor and Rules' medians than was the majority party's (in the 81st and 84th Congresses), the majority still had a lower roll rate. More generally, the majority's roll rate was lower for a given constellation of floor, Rules, and party medians than the minority's and showed a much smaller substantive response to variations in this constellation than did the minority's. All of this is consistent with the hypothesis that, although imperfect agents of their party, Rules' majority party members were still pulling their punches when it came to the promotion of an alternative legislative agenda. Thus, although Rules did become a less reliable agent of the majority in 1937, we conclude that almost all of the agency loss came in the form of blocking too much (blocking liberal legislation, hence lowering the Republicans' roll rate) rather than pushing too much (pushing conservative legislation, hence raising the Democrats' roll rate).

APPENDIX 7.A. MAJORITY AND MINORITY ROLLS ON RULE ADOPTION VOTES, BY ORDER OF RULES COMMITTEE, MAJORITY PARTY, AND FLOOR MEDIAN IDEAL POINTS, CONGRESSES 62–100[a]

| Congress | Majority Roll Rate | Minority Roll Rate | Rule-Adoption Votes |
|---|---|---|---|
| $R \leq M \leq F$ | | | |
| 62 | 0 | 0.63 | 8 |
| 69 | 0 | 1.00 | 3 |
| 70 | 0 | 1.00 | 1 |
| 71 | 0 | 1.00 | 2 |
| 72 | 0 | 0.60 | 5 |
| 73 | 0 | 0.89 | 9 |
| 74 | 0 | 0.87 | 15 |
| 87 | 0 | 0.4 | 10 |
| 88 | 0.05 | 0.37 | 19 |
| 90 | 0 | 0.05 | 19 |
| 91 | 0 | 0.11 | 18 |
| 92 | 0.03 | 0.06 | 35 |
| 93 | 0.03 | 0.07 | 72 |
| 94 | 0 | 0.15 | 109 |
| 95 | 0 | 0.15 | 124 |
| 96 | 0 | 0.27 | 96 |
| 97 | 0.02 | 0.34 | 50 |
| 98 | 0.03 | 0.51 | 72 |
| 99 | 0 | 0.52 | 99 |
| 100 | 0 | 0.66 | 85 |
| MEAN | 0.008 | 0.483 | 42.6 |
| $M \leq R \leq F$ | | | |
| 63 | 0 | 0.75 | 8 |
| 64 | 0 | 0.36 | 11 |
| 66 | 0 | 0.50 | 14 |
| 67 | 0 | 0.69 | 13 |
| 68 | 0 | 0.40 | 5 |
| 78 | 0.25 | 0 | 4 |
| 80 | 0 | 0.33 | 12 |
| 83 | 0.14 | 0.43 | 7 |
| 84 | 0.14 | 0.14 | 14 |
| 85 | 0 | 0.38 | 16 |
| 89 | 0 | 0.55 | 22 |
| MEAN | 0.048 | 0.412 | 11.5 |

(*continued*)

(*continued*)

| Congress | Majority Roll Rate | Minority Roll Rate | Rule Adoption Votes |
|---|---|---|---|
| | | $M \leq F \leq R$ | |
| 65 | 0 | 0.43 | 7 |
| 75 | 0 | 0 | 1 |
| 76 | 0.08 | 0.42 | 12 |
| 77 | 0 | 0.57 | 7 |
| 79 | 0.06 | 0.35 | 17 |
| 81 | 0 | 0.19 | 21 |
| 82 | 0.18 | 0.36 | 11 |
| 86 | 0.08 | 0.08 | 12 |
| MEAN | 0.05 | 0.30 | 11 |

[a] For ease of exposition, our discussion and tests are framed in terms that assume a Democratic majority (i.e., $M < F < m$). In sorting Republican-majority Congresses into the three categories of preference arrays, we accounted for this by reversing the inequality operators for each category. So, for example, a (Republican-majority) Congress in which $m < F < R < M$ in the raw NOMINATE data would go into the $M < R < F$ category in this table, as would the empirical results that we present.

# 8

# The Bills Reported from Committee[†]

[A] Republican Senate committee staff director put it this way: "Democratic bills are going nowhere when we have the gavel." A personal staff member for a powerful Democratic Senator corroborated that comment by saying, "We introduce our bills, but they get entirely ignored." Along similar lines, a House committee staffer said that: "Congressional committees can be a lonely place for minority members."

– Krutz 2001

One extremely important but subtle rule underpinning committee influence is its *power to veto proposals within its jurisdiction: any proposal that fails to make a committee majority better off is simply kept from coming to the floor for a vote.* [italics added]

– Shepsle and Weingast 1994c

*The single most important feature of the legislative process in the House and Senate is that, to succeed, a bill must survive a gauntlet of veto gates in each chamber*, each of which is supervised by members chosen by their peers to exercise gatekeeping authority. In each chamber of Congress, at least one subcommittee and one full committee have gatekeeping rights in that a bill normally will not be considered by the entire legislative body until it has been approved in committee. [italics added]

– McNollgast 1994

*Undoubtedly, the most important tool* possessed by committees is their *gatekeeping power*. Since bills are routinely referred to standing committees, committee members can defeat legislation by refusing to report. [italics added]

– Maltzman 1997

## 8.1. INTRODUCTION

In the 108th Congress, the different levels of success that majority- and minority-party members had in pushing their proposals out of committee and

[†] This chapter is based on Cox (2001).

through the rest of the legislative process are quite informative. Indeed, a brief comparison of two legislators' proposals reveals that regardless of the nature of the proposal (i.e., substantive, procedural, or commemorative), majority-party members enjoyed substantial agenda-setting advantages over their minority counterparts.

Consider, for example, the difficulties that Minority Leader Nancy Pelosi (D-CA) faced in getting her proposals out of committee. During the 108th Congress, Pelosi proposed 14 different pieces of legislation, 13 of which either were tabled or did not receive a hearing. As a glance at her legislative record reveals, Pelosi was not only unable to pass substantive legislation (e.g., her proposal to amend the Public Health Service Act did not receive a hearing), but she was also helpless to pass more routine procedural and commemorative pieces of legislation. Indeed, Pelosi could not even get hearings for her proposals to encourage the president to establish a "Read Across America Day," to honor the service of the U.S. Armed Forces in Iraq, or to designate the U.S. courthouse in San Francisco as the "James R. Browning United States Courthouse."

Pelosi's inability to push her proposals through the legislative process is even more glaring when we compare her record with that of her counterpart in the majority party. Specifically, a glance at Majority Leader Tom DeLay's (R-TX) proposals reveals that while Pelosi was virtually unable to get her proposals onto the legislative agenda, DeLay enjoyed substantial success, with 31 of his 32 proposals passing the House. Indeed, not only did many of DeLay's substantive proposals enjoy tremendous legislative success (e.g., his proposals to implement the U.S.–Chile Free Trade Agreement, the U.S.–Singapore Free Trade Agreement, the U.S.–Australia Free Trade Agreement, and the U.S.–Morocco Free Trade Agreement all eventually became law), but his commemorative and procedural proposals did, too. For example, DeLay's proposal to honor the courage and sacrifice of members of the U.S. armed forces who were held as prisoners of war during the Vietnam Conflict passed the House with flying colors, as did his proposal to offer condolences to the families of the crew of the space shuttle *Columbia*.[1]

The contrasting success of Pelosi and DeLay is consistent with our general emphasis on the procedural advantages enjoyed by the majority party. In Chapter 3, we modeled the majority's advantages by assuming that the majority party's senior partners occupy offices that give them the power to block bills and use that power to prevent rolls of their party. Chapter 5 then presented evidence focusing on final-passage votes *on the floor* consistent with Chapter 3's model.

In this chapter, we devise a formal model of the legislative process *in committee* that also embodies our key assumption. At the committee level, the key senior partners are the committee and subcommittee chairs. We assume that they prevent rolls of the majority-party contingent on their committee, just as the party's floor leaders (the Rules Committee and speaker) prevent rolls

---

[1] The data on proposals was retrieved from Thomas, the web site hosted by the Library of Congress.

of the overall party on the floor.[2] Thus, we predict that the bills scheduled for hearing and mark-up in each committee should have substantial backing within the majority-party contingent and that no bill should be reported from committee against the wishes of a majority of its majority-party contingent. In what follows, we provide evidence supporting these two claims, by considering who sponsors bills, who votes in committee in favor of (and against) reporting bills, and who signs the majority (and dissenting) opinions in committee reports on bills.

If we were to follow the technique of the rest of the book, we would spend the bulk of the chapter examining the majority and minority parties' roll rates

---

[2] For more than 125 years, congressional scholars (Cox and McCubbins 1993; McNollgast 1994; Shepsle and Weingast 1984c, 1994; Shepsle 1989; Kiewiet and McCubbins 1991; Maltzman 1997), Washington observers (Oleszek 2004; McConachie 1974 [1898]; Bryce 1888), and politicians (Wilson 1956 [1885]; Hastert 2004) have noted the extraordinary gatekeeping power of congressional committees. Despite this vast body of literature emphasizing that committees have such power, however, not all scholars agree. Specifically, Krehbiel (1998: 233) states: "strictly speaking, committees do not have gatekeeping rights.... The point, then, is that what sometimes may appear to be committee power via committee gatekeeping may instead be yet another manifestation of the implicit power of supermajority pivots in a much more open and egalitarian legislative setting."

In response to Krehbiel's claim, we present a pattern of results demonstrating that committees do in fact have gatekeeping power. Such a pattern is the hallmark of a nonequivalent dependent variables (NEDV) research design and is associated with very strong internal validity (Trochim 2001). NEDV designs derive their strength from making multiple predictions across many observable outcomes and testing to see if the pattern of outcomes matches the predictions of the theory.

Even though we do not fully explicate here a theory of committee gatekeeping and its predictions (see Cox and McCubbins, and NEDV Design to Test Congressional Committee Gatekeeping at *www.settingtheagenda.com*), the following results demonstrate the presence of gatekeeping power: Lobbyists expend significant resources on committee members to improve access to the legislative floor (Beckmann 2004; Hojnacki and Kimball 1998; Hall and Wayman 1990). Bureaucratic actors often report directly to committees and subcommittees in their dealings with Congress (Ripley and Franklin 1980; Aberbach and Rockman 1977; Davidson 1976), and change policy according to the directives of congressional committees and in anticipation of changes in their membership (Weingast and Moran 1983; Calvert, Moran, and Weingast 1987).

If we add the assumption that committees act as agents of the majority party (an assumption that is supported both in this book and elsewhere), we observe still more evidence of committee gatekeeping power. Specifically, we find that: The majority party manipulates the membership of committees to its advantage (Cox and McCubbins 1993: Chapter 8). The majority party chooses chairs and subcommittee chairs, sanctions and rewards on the basis of party loyalty (Cox and McCubbins 1993: Chapter 7). The floor median is rolled more often than the majority-party median on final-passage votes (Cox and McCubbins 2002). There are dramatic swings in majority- and minority-party bill sponsorship rates when party control of Congress shifts (Cox and McCubbins 1993: Chapter 10). The majority party is more likely to sponsor bills that are reported from committee and is extremely unlikely to be rolled at the committee stage (Chapter 8). The Rules Committee uses its power to secure passage of legislation that favors the majority party (Chapter 7). Restrictive rules are more likely to be granted to bills that were reported from committee following a party unity vote (Thorson and Nitzschke N.D.) Taken together, the pattern of these results (along with many others from the literature, posted on this book's web page, or discussed in the 2nd edition of *Legislative Leviathan*) test and affirm the hypothesis that congressional committees have gatekeeping powers.

on committee reports. For this analysis, however, we need not take an entire chapter. Indeed, there were only four bills (out of 5,628) that roll the majority-party contingent at the committee stage for the Congresses that we consider. This, in and of itself, is strong evidence for the Cartel Agenda Model.

However, we suspect that there is still more mileage to be had in analyzing the actions of committees in the agenda control process. Thus, we devote a good portion of this chapter to an examination of dissent by individual committee members. Specifically, we ask whether majority party status affects a member's probability of dissent, controlling for that member's ideological predisposition (as captured by his or her NOMINATE score). Consistent with the expectations of our Cartel Agenda Model, the main finding is that members of the majority party are significantly less likely to dissent on committee reports than ideologically similar members of the minority party.

## 8.2. BILL SPONSORSHIP AND REPORTS

Who sponsors the bills considered in committee? Although we do not have evidence on bills that are considered in, but not reported from, committee we can provide statistical evidence on the more numerous bills that are both considered and then reported.

We (1993: 261) have calculated the percentage of all bills reported from committee that were sponsored by members of the minority party in selected Congresses. For the Democratically controlled 82nd Congress, 26 percent were sponsored by minority-party members, while it was 13 percent in the Republican-controlled 83rd Congress. Thus, the Democrats' sponsorship rate fell from 74 percent to 13 percent when their seat share fell from 53.8 percent to 49.0 percent. Significantly, we also show that comparable seat swings (of 4 percent or more from one party to the other) that did *not* entail a change in majority status had very little effect on sponsorship rates.

Connelly and Pitney (1999: 175) find a similar pattern in two more recent Congresses that also saw a change in party control:

Of the 295 House bills and joint resolutions that President Clinton signed during the 103rd Congress, Republicans sponsored only 35 (or 14 percent), mostly dealing with minor matters. In the 104th Congress, the pattern flipped: Republicans sponsored 212 of 252 signed House measures, leaving Democrats with just 16 percent. While Republicans were making policy, Democrats were directing the Secretary of the Interior to convey the Carbon Hill National Fish Hatchery to the State of Alabama.[3]

All told, it is clear that the percentage of reported bills sponsored by members of the majority party substantially exceeds its percentage of seats. The members of the majority party get the lion's share of legislative opportunities.

---

[3] See also Richard Hall's work (Hall 1996), which shows the central role played by committee and subcommittee chairs – all majority-party members – in most deals within committee.

But what of the small percentage of bills sponsored by the minority? Were these bills (successfully) designed to split the majority party and create new ad hoc coalitions? Or were minority-sponsored bills either trivial (per Connelly and Pitney), or nearly unanimously supported (as in the case of Tom Lantos's (D-CA) measures, discussed in Chapter 5), or at least palatable to a majority of the majority-party contingent (per our claim that no bill will be scheduled in committee against the wishes of that contingent)?

A partial answer to these questions can be given by examining bill reports. As we reported earlier, out of a total of 5,628 bill reports issued in the 84th, 86th, 88th, 90th, 92nd, 94th, 96th, and 98th Congresses – all controlled by the Democrats – only *four* (or 0.07 percent) were reported from committee to the floor despite a majority of the committee Democrats dissenting from the committee's report.[4] Moreover, of the four bills reported out of committee against the wishes of the Democrats wishes, one was immediately reversed in the Rules Committee, one never made it to floor consideration, one was known to be headed for defeat at LBJ's hands in the Senate, and one died in the Senate, whether its fate was anticipated or not. Thus, none of the four became law. Consequently, none constitute prediction errors for our model.

From these figures, we conclude that the majority party's contingent on each committee does succeed in preventing the report of bills they dislike.[5] In the remaining sections of this chapter, we investigate which individual members dissent on bills reported by their committees. We go beyond the aggregate data presented previously, in that we control for each member's ideological location when assessing whether majority status affects the probability of dissent.

## 8.3. TWO MODELS OF HOW THE FLOOR AGENDA IS SET

In this section, we extend the idealized model of legislative decision making from Chapter 3 so as to include committee consideration of bills. The model we present here is based on the seminal work of Shepsle (1979). Shepsle's model begins with two main elements: a set of $w$ issues, or policy dimensions, that the legislature must decide (represented by a subset $W$ of Euclidean $w$-space); and a set of $n$ legislators, each with strictly quasi-concave preferences defined over the policy space, $W$. The members are divided into a number of committees (with membership on more than one committee possible), each with its own jurisdiction.[6]

---

[4] There were actually 5,789 bills reports in these Congresses, as reported in Cox and McCubbins (1993), but 161 have missing data for present purposes.

[5] We also examine in this chapter whether the minority-party contingent on each committee is similarly successful in blocking bills.

[6] Committees are given the exclusive right to propose bills in their jurisdictions, but a committee's jurisdiction may itself be the union of smaller subjurisdictions (possibly though not necessarily attached to subcommittees), with the committee debarred from proposing bills that cross sub-jurisdictional boundaries. A committee with a complex jurisdiction may propose a separate bill for each of its subjurisdictions, but it cannot propose one omnibus bill dealing with all at once.

As in our idealized model from Chapter 3, we consider only bills that seek to alter policy along a single dimension. If such a bill is reported to the floor, we again assume that it is considered under an open rule (with germaneness restrictions). With these assumptions, the outcome of a bill reported to the floor is easy to anticipate – via the median voter theorem – which then facilitates analyzing actions in committee.[7]

The sequence of events in Shepsle's model is (1) the committees propose bills (i.e., put them on the plenary agenda);[8] (2) the plenary amends each of the bills put on its agenda by the committees, as its members see fit; (3) each bill, as amended, is put to a final up-or-down vote. We alter Shepsle's model in three main ways.

First, we consider fully strategic actors, instead of "sincere" legislators. In this respect, we follow Denzau and Mackay (1983) and Krehbiel (1985).

Second, we divide Shepsle's committee stage into separate agenda-setting, amendment, and final-passage substages. Just as the floor legislative process can be divided into these stages, so too can the committee legislative process.

Third, we consider two polar distributions of agenda power at the committee stage – the local majoritarian model and the local partisan model. In the first model, each committee's agenda (i.e., the set of bills that it will consider) is determined as if by majority vote in the whole committee. This model ignores the ability of chairs to set their committees' agendas, in pursuit of either personal, bipartisan, or partisan objectives. It also ignores the agenda-setting role of subcommittees. If a majority on the committee wants a particular bill considered, it will force the chair and any recalcitrant subcommittees to schedule it. In the second model, the committee agenda is determined as if by majority vote in the majority-party contingent on the committee. One might interpret this as a model in which chairs have full control over the committee agenda but are responsive to the wishes of their party colleagues on the committee. To keep the analysis here simple, and to derive simple, testable propositions from these two polar opposite models of agenda formation, we ignore (for the present) the costs and benefits of various committee actions.

### 8.3.1. A Model of Committee Decision Making

- **Committee jurisdictions.** Each committee has a well-defined jurisdiction. Committee 1 has jurisdiction over policy dimensions 1 through $w_1$, committee 2 has jurisdiction over dimensions $w_1 + 1$ through $w_2$, and so forth.
- **Member preferences.** As in Shepsle (1979), each member of Congress has strictly quasi-concave preferences defined over the policy space, $W$. Thus,

---

[7] More complicated assumptions about what will happen on the floor could in principle be accommodated in some of our results that follow, as we note at the appropriate points.

[8] Shepsle's model is a simplification because it assumes that bills proposed by committees are guaranteed a hearing on the floor, as if all bills were privileged. The role of the Rules Committee, of the speaker, and of suspension of the rules is thus ignored. On the disputed ability of the majority party to rig the "special rules" issued by the Rules Committee, see Dion and Huber (1996, 1997); Krehbiel (1997); Sinclair (2002a); and Kiewiet (1998).

on any given issue or policy dimension, each member has strictly single-peaked preferences with a unique dimension-specific ideal point.

To explain the model further, consider a Congress in which the Democrats hold a majority of seats so that members of the majority party are generally to the left of members of the minority party on any given dimension. More formally, let $m_j$ denote the location of the median member of the minority party on the committee with jurisdiction over dimension $j$.[9] Let $M_j$ denote the location of the median member of the majority party on the committee with jurisdiction over dimension $j$. Finally, let $F_j$ denote the location of the median member of the House on dimension $j$. We again assume that $M_j < F_j < m_j$ for all $j$.[10] Note that the assumption allows some Democrats to be to the right of some Republicans. Indeed, it is possible for some Democrats to be to the right of a majority of Republicans on some, or even all, dimensions. Similarly, some Republicans may be to the left of some Democrats, or even a majority of the Democrats, on some or all dimensions. Note also that no assumption is made that the same member of Congress is the median on all dimensions, although this is possible. We shall continue with the example of a Democratic House but, of course, the model applies also to cases of Republican control, mutatis mutandis.

- **Status quo points.** The location of the status quo may vary from dimension to dimension.[11] The model is simplest if one assumes that the status quo on each dimension $j$, $q_j$, is common knowledge at the beginning of the game (as in Shepsle 1979).
- **Committee procedure.** In the majoritarian model, which is a mirror of the Floor Agenda Model in Chapter 3, we assume that any member of any committee can propose a bill on any dimension in the committee's jurisdiction. However, only unidimensional bills – those proposing changes on a single dimension – are allowed. We ignore the possibility that committee chairs might be able to "veto" consideration of a proposed bill. We also ignore the costs of committee consideration; thus, any bill that is proposed by a committee member is automatically voted upon. If a majority on the committee votes to report it, it is reported; otherwise, the bill dies.
- In the partisan model, which is a mirror of the Cartel Agenda Model from Chapter 3, *only bills that a majority of the majority-party members support can appear on the committee agenda.* Those bills are then voted upon, as in the majoritarian model, by the full committee membership. Committees can (again) only propose unidimensional bills. Thus, the only difference between the two models concerns the set of local veto groups – all majorities of the full membership in the majoritarian model, or all majorities of the majority party's committee caucus in the partisan model.

---

[9] For convenience, we shall assume that each median is a unique point rather than an interval.

[10] This assumption is used only in Section 8.3, not in Section 8.2.

[11] Throughout the paper, we assume that the status quo outcome on dimension $j$ is also the reversionary outcome on dimension $j$. That is, the status quo will obtain if no new legislation is enacted.

- **Floor procedure.** We make four assumptions about floor procedure. The first two are drawn from our model in Chapter 3. First, *there is an exogenous germaneness restriction* (à la Shepsle 1979). If a committee reports a bill that proposes alterations in the status quo on dimension *j*, then the only amendments that are in order are those pertaining to dimension *j*. Second, *all bills are considered under open rules.* The purpose of this assumption is to simplify the analysis in a way that stacks the deck in favor of majoritarian outcomes. If outcomes favoring the majority party can arise even with this assumption, they can also arise when restrictive rules are considered.

  To these two assumptions about floor consideration, we add two new assumptions. First, *the cost of discharging bills from committee is prohibitively high.* This last assumption incorporates the widespread belief that committees have real vetoes, rarely challengeable by actors off the committee. (Changing this assumption would be inconsequential for the majoritarian model, if the committee in question were representative of the House as a whole. We discuss its consequences for the partisan model.) Second, *bills are considered and voted on in sequence* (no bundling or simultaneous votes).

  The rest of the rules of procedure governing consideration of bills on the floor are assumed to be neutral as between the two parties. Thus, any member can move to consider any bill reported from committee, with such motions then voted up or down by majority rule. The majority party leadership has no ability to veto reported bills by denying them a place on the floor schedule. These assumptions hold for both the majoritarian and partisan models. Thus, the partisan model in this chapter is partisan only at the local, or committee, level, while the majoritarian model is majoritarian at both the committee and floor stages.

  If we were to retain the assumption of the Cartel Agenda Model in Chapter 3, in which majority-party leaders (representing the majority-party median) were able to decide which reported bills made it to the floor agenda, then the committee stage would be more complicated than it is here. Not all bills reported from committee would end up passing at the House median. Instead, those in the majority-party roll zone would be blocked by the majority-party leadership (i.e., left to die on a calendar). Assuming that committee chairs dislike having their bills languish on the calendars, they would avoid scheduling issues with status quo points in the majority-party roll zone. Thus, the bills reported from committee would clear not only a local (or committee) majority-party hurdle but also a global (or floor) majority-party hurdle. Here, we investigate only the local hurdle.

## 8.3.2. Summary

All told, the sequence of moves in the model is as follows. First, Nature chooses the status quo, $q_j$, for each dimension *j*, which then becomes common knowledge. Second, bills (dealing with a single dimension of policy) are proposed in each committee; only those not opposed by a majority of the majority-party contingent are actually considered. Third, each committee votes whether to report the various bills it considers. Fourth, the floor considers all bills reported, amending them one at a time as the members see fit, and then either passing or rejecting them.

## 8.4. PREDICTIONS

The majoritarian and partisan models lead to different predictions concerning the probability that a given member of a committee will dissent. To elucidate these predictions, we first deal with the last stage of the game – floor consideration of bills – then discuss how anticipation of this last-stage result affects decisions at earlier stages.

### 8.4.1. What Happens on the Floor?

When floor action begins, the members face a given set of bills reported from the various committees. Because discharge is prohibitively costly, and nongermane amendments are not allowed, the floor essentially deals with a subset of the full policy space, consisting of all those dimensions touched on by a reported bill. Call this policy subspace $H$ and relabel the dimensions (if necessary) so that $H$ comprises the first $h$ dimensions. Given that each dimension is considered separately and each member has single-peaked preferences on each dimension, there exists an equilibrium point in $H$ at $(F_1, \ldots, F_h)$, the dimension-by-dimension median. Moreover, any attempt to logroll away from this equilibrium, by trading votes across dimensions, would unravel under the model's assumptions.[12] *Thus, the outcome on each bill $j$ reported to the floor is easy to foresee: it is simply $F_j$, the floor median.* This is true under both versions of the model.

### 8.4.2. Voting in Committee

Each committee member recognizes that the consequence of reporting a bill – any bill – on dimension $j$ will be the eventual enactment of the floor median, $F_j$.[13] Members are in this sense "sophisticated," as defined in Denzau and Mackay

---

[12] Recall that the floor considers the bills put on its agenda sequentially. Once the order of consideration is fixed in this complete-information model, $(F_1, \ldots, F_h)$ becomes the unique equilibrium. Another condition sufficient to ensure that $(F_1, \ldots, F_h)$ is the unique equilibrium is that members' preferences are additively separable. What if one models the situation as something like a repeated game (consider a bill, then another with probability $p$, then another...)? In this case, multiple equilibria will presumably arise. At this point, one would need to deal with a model in which members have probabilistic beliefs about the outcome on the floor, conditional on a bill being reported, as in Denzau and Mackay (1983). Our belief is that the gist of the results presented here could be derived in such a model, too. The next part of the book develops stochastic versions of some of the models discussed in this part and serves to indicate how one might go about this sort of task.

[13] If the bill reported equals $F_j$, then the floor accepts it without amendment. If the bill reported differs from $F_j$, then the floor first amends the bill to $F_j$ and then passes it.

(1983) or Krehbiel (1985). Similarly, each committee member knows that the consequence of refusing to report a bill on dimension $j$ will be the continuance of the status quo policy $q_j$ (recall the assumption that the floor finds it too costly to discharge). *Thus, each committee member proposes a bill on dimension $j$ and votes to report such a bill, if and only if he or she prefers the outcome $F_j$ to the outcome $q_j$.*

In the following empirical work, it is natural to assume that there is some error in members' voting. That is, members' votes are not determined *completely* by their ideal points and the locations of the bill and status quo; instead, as in the standard spatial models in the literature (cf. Appendix 9.A), there is some residual uncertainty.

### 8.4.3. Predictions: The Majoritarian Model

In this section, we consider the majoritarian model's predictions concerning how members vote on final passage in committee and whether they dissent from the committee report. The technical mechanics of the model are relegated to an appendix. We just state the main results here.

Intuitively, the main message is just that *the more extreme a member is (relative to the floor median, F, and the committee median, C), the higher his or her dissent rate will be.* This implication can be empirically explored either with a quadratic or a linear specification. In the quadratic specification, one attempts to explain variation in a member's probability of dissent by a measure of that member's ideology, say $x$, plus a quadratic term, $x^2$, where $x$ is a hypothetical member's ideal policy position on dimension $j$. If $x$ is scaled so that $F = 0$ (i.e., negative values indicate leftists and positive values indicate rightists), then one expects the coefficient on $x^2$ to be positive, indicating greater dissent at either ideological extreme.[14]

In the linear specification, extremism is represented by a single variable, $E$, equal to the distance between a member's ideal point and the interval between $C$ and $F$. For leftist members, whose ideal point $x$ is located such that $x < \min(F, C)$, it follows that $E = \min(F, C) - x$ (the distance between the member's ideal point and the closer of the two medians). For centrist members, with $\min(F, C) \le x \le \max(F, C)$ (i.e., those with ideal points between F and C inclusive) $E = 0$. Finally, for rightist members, with ideal points $x > \max(F, C)$, then $E = x - \max(F, C)$ (again, the distance between the member's ideal point and the closer of the two medians). The $E$ score economically captures the basic intuition of the spatial model: Extremism relative to the relevant committee and floor medians should boost dissent. To test the idealized majoritarian model, we would estimate the equation

$$Dissent_{ij} = \alpha + \beta_1 E_{ij} + \varepsilon_{ij}$$

---

[14] This specification ignores the location of C, as would be justified if C tends to be near F (empirically often true). The linear specification considered next does not ignore C.

where

*Dissent*$_{ij}$ is member $i$'s dissent rate on dimension $j$

$E_{ij}$ is the distance between member $i$'s ideal point and the nearest point in the $(C, F)$ interval (inclusive)

The majoritarian model would expect $\beta_1$ to be positive and significant.

### 8.4.4. Predictions: The Partisan Model

The partisan model generates two expectations at variance with those arising under the majoritarian model. First, under the partisan model, one expects members of the majority party to dissent less often than ideologically comparable minority-party members simply because they have a vote in the setting of the agenda, and they are hence less likely to be faced with an unpleasant bill. If two members' ideal points are the same on all dimensions in the committee's jurisdiction, then this expectation disappears because the behavior of a Republican R and a Democratic D, both with ideological score $x$, would be identical. But if members' ideological scores indicate an average position on issues, and there is some variance, then D's vote in setting the agenda sometimes helps keep off the agenda bills that D dislikes but R likes, and sometimes helps put on the agenda bills that D likes but R dislikes.[15]

Another (nonspatial) reason to expect majority-party members to dissent less than ideologically comparable minority-party members has to do with side payments. Suppose that a majority of committee Democrats want a particular bill but that the conservative Democrats oppose it on ideological grounds. As between a Republican and a conservative Democrat of similar ideology, which does the Democratic caucus buy off? One expects that they will buy their fellow Democrat because he is equally cheap – both he and the Republican have the same ideological distaste to overcome – but the side payment will boost his probability of reelection, thus conferring an external benefit on the other Democrats (viz., an increased probability of majority status) (cf. Cox and McCubbins 1993). If in fact the Democratic caucus on each committee is often

---

[15] When members vote with some error (see Appendix 9.A), the probability that member $k$ is rolled on roll call $j$ equals the probability that $k$ prefers $q_j$ to $F_j$, while a majority of the majority party prefers $F_j$ to $q_j$. More formally, this can be written $\Pr[u_k(q_j) > u_k(F_j)\ \&\ \#\{h \in \text{MAJ}: u_h(q_j) < u_h(F_j)\} > \#\{h \in \text{MAJ}: u_h(q_j) > u_h(F_j)\}]$, where #A denotes the number of elements in the set A and MAJ denotes the set of all members of the majority party. Rewriting, this equals $\Pr[u_k(q_j) > u_k(F_j)]\Pr[\#\{h \in \text{MAJ}: u_h(q_j) < u_h(F_j)\} > \#\{h \in \text{MAJ}: u_h(q_j) > u_h(F_j)\}\ u_k(q_j) > u_k(F_j)]$. For two members with identical preferences, $k$ and $i$, $\Pr[u_k(q_j) > u_k(F_j)] = \Pr[u_i(q_j) > u_i(F_j)]$. If $k$ is a member of the majority party while $i$ is not, however, then $\Pr[\#\{h \in \text{MAJ}: u_h(q_j) < u_h(F_j)\} > \#\{h \in \text{MAJ}: u_h(q_j) > u_h(F_j)\}\ u_k(q_j) > u_k(F_j), k \in \text{MAJ}] < \Pr[\#\{h \in \text{MAJ}: u_h(q_j) < u_h(F_j)\} > \#\{h \in \text{MAJ}: u_h(q_j) > u_h(F_j)\}\ u_i(q_j) > u_i(F_j), i\text{MAJ}]$. Thus, the probability that the minority-party member $i$ will be rolled is higher than the probability that the majority-party member $k$ will be rolled.

in the position of buying extra votes from their right-wing members, one should find that such members dissent less than otherwise comparable Republicans.

A second difference between the majoritarian and partisan models can be expressed in terms of the representation of extremism, $E$. The majoritarian model predicts that a member's dissent rate should increase as $E$ increases. The partisan model also predicts that a member's dissent rate should increase as $E$ increases, *if* the member's ideal point does not fall between $M$ and $F$. If the member's ideal point does fall between $M$ and $F$, however, then the partisan model predicts that the member will never dissent, hence that his or her dissent probability will neither increase nor decrease with $E$. This implies a regression discontinuity design.[16] To test the idealized partisan model, we would estimate the equation

$$Dissent_{ij} = \alpha + \beta_1 Majstatus_{ij} + \beta_2 E_{ij} + \beta_3 E_{ij}{}^* Between_{ij} + \varepsilon_{ij}$$

where $Dissent_{ij}$ and $E_{ij}$ are as above,

> $Majstatus_{ij}$ is a dummy variable coded one if member $i$ is a member of the majority party
> $Between_{ij}$ is a dummy variable coded one if the member's ideological location lies between the majority party median, $\hat{M}$, and $\min(\hat{F}, \hat{C})$
> $E_{ij}{}^* Between_{ij}$ is an interaction term

## 8.5. RESULTS: FILING DISSENTS WITH COMMITTEE REPORTS

Note that the model just described subsumes the test of the idealized majoritarian model from Section 8.4.3, and that there are two factors – $E_{it}{}^* Between_{it}$ and $Majstatus_{it}$ – that distinguish the two models. We estimate the equation

$$Dissent_{ij} = \alpha + \beta_1 Dem_{ij} + \beta_2 E_{ij} + \beta_3 E_{ij}{}^* Between_{ij} + \varepsilon_{ij}$$

where the variables are as described in the previous section, except for

> $Dem_{it}$, a dummy variable equal to 1 for Democrats and 0 for Republicans, which we substitute for $Majstatus_{it}$ because the Democrats were the majority party in all the Congresses in our dataset.[17]

To operationalize the model, we used Nelson's dataset to identify each member's committee assignments in each of eight Congresses: the 84th, 86th, 88th, 90th, 92nd, 94th, 96th, and 98th (all controlled by the Democrats).[18] For each bill

---

[16] According to Trochim (2001: 221–2), a regression discontinuity design is a pretest–post-test program–comparison group strategy that is comparable in internal validity to a randomized experiment.

[17] The specification derived from the two models has two main effects and one interactive effect, without the corresponding main effect. We have reestimated the model with all the main effects included, which yields coefficients of the same sign and significance as the results presented here.

[18] See Nelson and Bensen (1993).

reported by each committee, we used a dataset we compiled (1993) to ascertain whether or not each committee member filed a dissent with each bill report.[19]

One could estimate a variant of the model as a straight logit, using a decision by an individual congressperson whether to dissent from a particular bill report (on a given committee during a particular Congress) as the unit of analysis and using a dummy variable for whether or not the member dissented from the bill report as the dependent variable.[20] Defined in this way, there are more than 180,000 observations in the dataset. But the independent variables vary only at the level of committee–Congress and so, in a sense, running the analysis as a straight logit exaggerates the true number of observations. Relatedly, the straight logit approach underestimates the standard errors.

Accordingly, we take the unit of analysis here to be a member's stint on a particular committee–Congress, as shown in the equation (and yielding 4,607 observations), and the dependent variable to be the percent of bills on which the member dissented. We estimate the model via the minimum logit chi-squared (or grouped logit) technique (cf. Maddala 1983: 28–31). This provides more realistic (larger) standard errors. (However, the actual parameter estimates from the grouped logit are qualitatively identical to those one gets from a straight logit estimated via maximum likelihood.)

### 8.5.1. Results: Linear Specification

Given each individual's ideological location, it was easy to calculate the floor median $\hat{F}$, in any given Congress, as well as the median of each committee, $\hat{C}$, in each Congress. From this information, in turn, it was possible to estimate each member's relative extremism from $\hat{F}$ and $\hat{C}$ – denoted $\hat{E}$.

With these operational variables, we then sought to explain each committee member's observed dissent rate in terms of $\hat{E}_{it}$, $\hat{E}^*_{it}$, $Between_{it}$, and $Dem_{it}$. The model includes fixed effects for each committee and each Congress. The results are given in Table 8.1.

We would stress three points about the results. First, the coefficient on $\hat{E}$ is positive and significant: Members' dissent probabilities do increase noticeably as they become more extreme relative to the relevant committee and floor medians.[21]

---

[19] The dataset includes only bills in the H.R. series (i.e., bills originating in the House). We thus exclude committee reports pertinent to House resolutions and bills originating in the Senate.

[20] It is not required that members sign the committee report, and often one will find no signatures. Thus, the dependent variable is defined in terms of the positive act of dissent, and failure to dissent is a mixed bag of passive and active assent.

[21] The model works less well in predicting the behavior of those with ideal points between C and F. In theory, these members should never dissent (under either model); in practice, they do, albeit at a low rate. To accommodate this finding, one might, for example, appeal to nonspatial idiosyncratic sources of dissent or (more problematically from an econometric viewpoint) argue that W-NOMINATE scores do not perfectly capture "true ideology."

TABLE 8.1. *Determinants of Dissent on Committee Reports,*
*Congresses 84–98 (even-numbered)*

| Independent Variables | Coefficient | Standard Error |
|---|---|---|
| E | 0.80 | 0.05 |
| E*Between | −0.58 | 0.20 |
| Dem | −1.23 | 0.03 |
| cong_86 | 0.47 | 0.07 |
| cong_88 | 0.89 | 0.08 |
| cong_90 | 0.73 | 0.07 |
| cong_92 | 0.62 | 0.07 |
| cong_94 | 1.12 | 0.07 |
| cong_96 | 1.09 | 0.07 |
| cong_98 | 1.19 | 0.08 |
| Appropriations | −1.01 | 0.09 |
| Armed Services | −1.04 | 0.12 |
| Banking | 0.53 | 0.09 |
| DC | −0.28 | 0.11 |
| Education | 0.40 | 0.11 |
| Foreign Affairs | 0.27 | 0.11 |
| Govt Operations | 0.71 | 0.10 |
| House Admin | 0.95 | 0.12 |
| Interior | −1.48 | 0.10 |
| HUAC | 2.51 | 0.21 |
| Commerce | −0.12 | 0.09 |
| Judiciary | −0.69 | 0.10 |
| Merchant Marine | −0.72 | 0.12 |
| Post Office | 0.09 | 0.11 |
| Public Works | −0.65 | 0.10 |
| Rules | 1.94 | 0.23 |
| Veterans' Affairs | 0.03 | 0.12 |
| Ways and Means | −1.03 | 0.10 |
| Constant | −2.98 | 0.09 |
| Number of observations | 4,607 | |
| $R^2$ | .60 | |

*Notes:* (1) The estimation was performed using the MLCS technique. The unit of observation can be thought of as a member of Congress's stint on a particular committee in a particular Congress. There were 4,607 stints in the dataset. The dependent variable is $\ln[p_{diss} + (2n)^{-1}/(1-p_{diss} + (2n)^{-1})]$, where $p_{diss}$ is the proportion of bill reports to which the member in question filed a dissent and $n$ is the number of bill reports made by the relevant committee during the stint. See Maddala (1983: 29–30), for more on this procedure. (2) The following committees were excluded from analysis because they did not exist during the entire period studied or had too few observations: Budget, Science, Small Business, and Official Conduct.

Second, the coefficient on $\hat{E}^{*}Between$ is negative, significant, and roughly equal in magnitude to the coefficient on $\hat{E}$. Indeed, an F-test shows that one cannot reject the null hypothesis that these two coefficients sum to zero. This is consistent with the partisan model's prediction that variations in $E$ should have no effect on dissent for members in the interval between $M$ and min $(C, F)$ and is contrary to the majoritarian model's expectation that such members should be little different from any others.

Third, the coefficient on *Dem* is negative and significant, as in the previous analysis. Three examples illustrate the size of the partisan difference. First, consider the committee with the fourth highest average dissent rate: Banking. A member of this committee with W-NOMINATE score equal to zero (near the median in most Congresses) was predicted to dissent 22.9 percent of the time if a Republican, 3.9 percent of the time if a Democrat. Second, consider the committee with the lowest average dissent rate: Appropriations. A member of this committee with W-NOMINATE score equal to zero was predicted to dissent 3.3 percent of the time if a Republican, 1.2 percent of the time if a Democrat. Finally, the corresponding figures for the committee with the median level of dissent (Agriculture) were 13.9 percent and 3.5 percent, respectively.

### 8.5.2. Results: Quadratic Specification

We used the first dimension of Poole and Rosenthal's W-NOMINATE score, denoted $\hat{x}$, to indicate the ideological location of each member of Congress (cf. Poole and Rosenthal 1997). To explain variation in each member's dissent on the various bills reported from committee, we first ran a MLCS regression in which the regressors were $\hat{x}_{it}$, $\hat{x}_{it}^2$, and $Dem_{it}$.[22]

The results of this regression (not reported in detail) can be summarized as follows. First, the coefficient on $\hat{x}^2$ is positive and significant: Dissent increases at both the left and right extremes, as expected under both models. Second, the coefficient on *Dem* is negative and significant: Holding constant each member's ideological location, Democrats were substantially less likely to dissent. For example, a member with W-NOMINATE score equal to zero was predicted to dissent 11.1 percent of the time if a Republican, 2.9 percent of the time if a Democrat. These results accord only with the partisan model. Figure 8.1 illustrates these results by plotting each member's predicted dissent rate against his or her W-NOMINATE score.[23]

It is worth stressing again that the *shape* of the curves in Figure 8.1 (specifically, that they bend upward at the ends) is predicted under both the majoritarian and the partisan models, as long as the status quo policies are widely

---

[22] Augmenting this specification with fixed effects for each Congress and for each committee has no effect on the qualitative results for the primary variables.

[23] The results are qualitatively similar if one allows Democrats and Republicans to have separate slope estimates for $\hat{x}$ and $\hat{x}^2$. Note that the W-NOMINATE scores are not normalized to lie in the $[-1, 1]$ range.

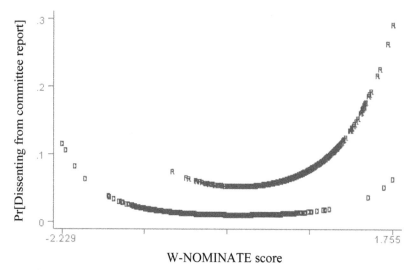

FIGURE 8.I. Estimated dissent rates for (majority) Democrats and (minority) Republicans, by W-NOMINATE score

dispersed with respect to members' ideal points. What distinguishes the two models is the distance between the Democrats' and Republicans' curves. The partisan model predicts that there should be a separation, as long as members' estimated ideals represent average positions across a number of related dimensions.[24]

### 8.6. RESULTS: VOTING IN COMMITTEE TO REPORT BILLS

Filing a written dissent with the committee report, explaining why one disagrees with the majority report, is costly. In this section, we examine what is perhaps a less costly form of dissent: voting against the motion in committee to report a bill to the House. Votes in committees were not recorded prior to the early 1970s. Here we use the dataset on committee votes compiled by Parker and Parker (1985) to investigate committee votes in the 94th and 96th Congresses.[25]

To study the incidence of such behavior, we examine the rates at which committee members vote against bills that are reported from the given committee. Is voting against a bill on final passage more common than filing a dissent? The average member in the 94th and 96th congresses (unsuccessfully) voted against 14.4 percent of the bills for which there is a recorded final-passage vote

---

[24] Neither the shape nor the separation of the curves depends on an assumption that there is some minimum percentage of status quo points to the left of *F*; such an assumption does play a role when it comes to interpreting aggregate roll rates, but it is not important here.

[25] Twelve committees are included in the analysis: Agriculture, Armed Services, Banking, Commerce, Education and Labor, Foreign Affairs, Government Operations, House Administration, Interior, Judiciary, Merchant Marine and Fisheries, and Post Office.

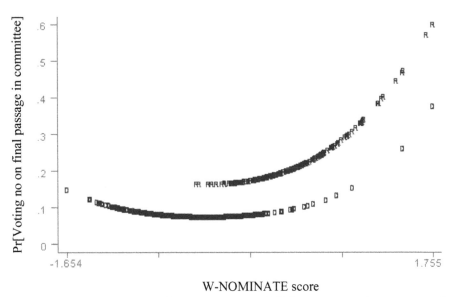

FIGURE 8.2. Estimated rate of voting against a bill for (majority) Democrats and (minority) Republicans, by W-NOMINATE score

in the relevant committee. By contrast, the average member filed a dissent with 6.8 percent of the bills reported by his or her committee. One cannot be too sure from these figures that members actually did vote against bills more often than they filed dissents with bill reports, however. After all, the average member saw 38 bills reported from his or her committee, but there were recorded votes held on only 10. Presumably, these 10 were the more controversial ones, on which dissent was more likely. From what individual-level data we have examined (the dataset is not structured to make this easy), it seems that members who voted "no" on final passage in committee also typically filed dissents to the committee report.

In any event, if one substitutes the rate of voting against a bill that is reported for the dissent rates we used in the previous section, and performs the same minimum logit chi-squared regressions with the same quadratic and linear specifications, the results are qualitatively similar: (1) Ideologically more extreme members dissent more often, but (2) increasing extremism in the interval between $M$ and $F$ has no discernible impact, and (3) Democrats are substantially less likely to dissent than Republicans. Figure 8.2 illustrates the first and third points by graphing the estimated probability of dissent as a (quadratic) function of each member's W-NOMINATE score and party affiliation.

## 8.7. RESULTS: THE 104TH AND 105TH CONGRESSES

All of the evidence presented thus far has concerned the even-numbered Congresses from the 84th through the 98th, all of which were controlled by the

Democrats. Are the results due to something about Democrats, rather than something about majority parties? Are they period-specific?

Anyone who has examined the committee reports and final-passage votes for the 104th and 105th Congresses will know that Republicans in the majority were at least as adept as had been Democrats at controlling the agenda. On the Committee on Educational and Economic Opportunities in the 104th, Congress for example, no Republican committee member voted against *any* bill on final passage, and none filed a dissent with *any* bill report. Experience on the other committees was similar. The average percentage of Republicans dissenting on final-passage votes in committee in this Congress was 1.4 percent.

The difference between the more recent period of Republican majorities and the earlier period of Democratic majorities appears primarily in the frequency with which the minority was rolled. In the eight even-numbered congresses between 1955 and 1984, the Republican minority was rolled 233 times, or an average of about 29 per Congress. In contrast, the Democrats were rolled 14 times just on the Committee on Educational and Economic Opportunities in the 104th Congress. The average percentage of Democrats dissenting on final-passage votes in committee in this Congress was 65.3 percent.

## 8.8. CONCLUSION

In this chapter, we have provided three sorts of evidence that the set of bills reported from committee changes substantially, indeed dramatically, depending on which party has a majority. The first bit of evidence is that relatively small changes in the membership of the House can produce large changes in bill sponsorship, if (and only if) they entail a change in majority status. The Republicans' seat share increased by only 4.8 percentage points between the 82nd and 83rd Houses, yet their sponsorship rate increased by 61 percentage points. Between the 103rd and 104th Houses, the Republicans' seat share increased by 12.4 percentage points, while their sponsorship rate increased by 70 percentage points. Seat swings that did not change which party controlled Congress, by contrast, had little effect on the sponsorship rate.

The second bit of evidence is that the majority party's committee contingents are virtually never rolled. That is, there is virtually never a bill reported from committee against the wishes of a majority of the majority-party members. The Cartel Agenda Model implies the absence of such majority rolls. Is it inconsistent with the majoritarian model? It is if one believes that there were some left-of-center federal policies that a coalition of Southern Democrats and Republicans might have wished to bring to the median of current congressional opinion. For, if there were such status quo policies, then a Southern chair unconstrained by the first commandment of party leadership could simply have scheduled it for consideration in his committee, whereupon it would have passed against the wishes of the Northern Democrats. Since Northern Democrats often constituted a majority of committee Democrats, a non-trivial number of majority rolls should have followed under the majoritarian model.

Note, moreover, that the situation is only slightly improved by adverting to a more sophisticated pivot model, such as that proposed by Krehbiel (1998). As long as there were any left-of-center status quo points outside the pivot zone but not so far left that even the Northern Democrats wanted to correct it, the same prediction – a nontrivial number of majority rolls in committee – is generated. All told, then, the virtually complete absence of such rolls is inconsistent with current partyless models of Congress.

A third sort of evidence concerns who dissents when committees report bills to the House calendars, either by voting against the motion to report in committee or filing a dissent to the bill report. The same picture arises for both forms of dissent. First, ideologically more extreme members dissent more. Second, as predicted by the Cartel Agenda Model, increasing extremism in the interval between the majority-party median, $M$, and the floor median, $F$, does *not* increase dissent. Third, also as predicted by the Cartel Agenda Model, majority-party members dissent less than ideologically comparable minority-party members. Moreover, it is not just a matter of rejecting the model in which the majority has *no advantage* for one in which it has *some advantage*. The formal model confers a *monopoly*, and the data, perhaps surprisingly, are consistent with it.

Before moving on to the next chapter, we also wish to note the majority party's advantage on one very special type of committee: the conference committee. As our analysis of the 83rd to the 105th Congresses reveals, the majority party was rolled on only 14 votes out of 1,011 total roll call votes on adoption of conference reports in the House. This means that the majority party was rolled only 1.4 percent of the time on such votes,[26] and this low roll rate clearly implies a significant majority party ex post veto by way of controlling the conference committee process.

APPENDIX 8.A

The conclusion in the text that committee members vote for a bill if and only if they prefer the floor median to the status quo can be restated with some further notation. Let $R_j(x) = 2x - F_j$ denote the point that is equally as far from $x$ as it is from $F_j$ but on the opposite side of $x$ from $F_j$. If $x < F_j$, then $R_j(x)$ is just as far to the left of $x$ as $F_j$ is to the right of $x$ (see Figure 8.A.1). If $x > F_j$, then

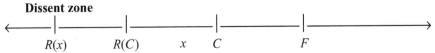

**Dissent zone**

**Committee report zone |Committee block zone |Committee report zone**

FIGURE 8.A.1. Illustrating the member dissent and committee block zones

---

[26] Our analysis is based on a House roll call dataset compiled by David Rohde and maintained by the Political Institutions and Public Choice Program at Michigan State University.

TABLE 8.A.1. *Determining the Dissent Zone as a Function of x, C, and F*

| Order of C, F, and $x$ | Member with Ideal Point $x$ Votes Against Reporting a Bill to Change $q$, if $q$ is in the Interval | Committee Will Not Report a Bill to Change $q$, if $q$ is in the Committee's "Block Zone," Given by | Member with Ideal Point $x$ Votes Against Reporting a Bill to Change $q$, but Loses, if $q$ is in the Dissent Zone, Given by |
|---|---|---|---|
| $x \le F \ \& \ C \le F$ | $[R(x), F]$ | $[R(C), F]$ | $[R(x), R(C)]$ |
| $x \le F \ \& \ C > F$ | $[R(x), F]$ | $[F, R(C)]$ | $[R(x), F]$ |
| $x > F \ \& \ C \le F$ | $[F, R(x)]$ | $[R(C), F]$ | $[F, R(x)]$ |
| $x > F \ \& \ C > F$ | $[F, R(x)]$ | $[F, R(C)]$ | $[R(C), R(x)]$ |

$R_j(x)$ is just as far to the right of $x$ as $F_j$ is to the left of $x$. In either case, $R_j(x)$ is utility-equivalent to $F_j$ for the member with ideal point $x$. Then:

**Lemma 1:** Consider a member with ideal point $x$ on dimension $j$.

(a) If $x < F_j$, the member votes in favor of reporting a bill on dimension $j$ if and only if $q_j \notin [R_j(x), F_j]$;

(b) If $x > F_j$, the member votes in favor of reporting a bill on dimension $j$ if and only if $q_j \notin [F_j, R_j(x)]$.

Lemma 1 holds under both models.

Because the committee with jurisdiction over dimension $j$ will not report a bill on that dimension if $C_j$ (the committee median) is closer to $q_j$ (the status quo) than to $F_j$ (the floor median), the set of dimensions for which bills are reported to the floor is a function of (dropping the subscripts) $C$, $q$, and $F$. If $C < F$, then the committee will not report a bill if the status quo lies in the "block zone" $[R(C), F]$, but it will report a bill if the status quo falls in the "report zone" $(-\infty, R(C)) \cup (F, \infty)$. If, on the other hand, $C \ge F$, then the committee will refuse to report all dimensions with status quo points in the range $[F, R(C)]$, but it will report all others. Figure 8.A.1. illustrates the $C < F$ case.

Recall that a committee member votes against reporting a bill on dimension $j$ if and only if his or her ideal point on dimension $j$ – call it $x$ – is closer to the status quo, $q$, than to the floor median, $F$. A member with ideal point $x$ will *dissent* (i.e., vote against reporting a bill, but lose) if and only if $x$ is closer to $q$ than $F$ but $C$ is closer to $F$ than to $q$. This condition yields four different "dissent zones," depending on the relative placement of $C$, $F$ and $x$, as indicated in column 4 of Table 8.A.1. The third column of the table also gives the committee's block zone.

As an example of how to read the table, suppose both $C$ and $x$ are less than $F$ (as in the first row of the table). In this case, the member will *dislike* reporting a bill if the status quo is in the region $[R(x), F]$, but a bill will in fact be reported only if the status quo lies outside the region $[R(C), F]$. Thus, the only status quo points that will provoke a dissent from the member are those lying in the interval $[R(x), R(C)]$. If $C \leq x$, so that $R(C) \leq R(x)$, then this interval will be empty: Members with ideal points lying between their committee's median and the floor median should never dissent. Otherwise, if $x < C$, then the dissent zone will be nonempty (and will grow in size as $x$ gets smaller and C gets larger). Figure 8.A.1. illustrates a nonempty dissent interval for this case.

If we knew the function G governing the distribution of status quo points and each member's ideal point, we could calculate the theoretical probability of dissent and then compare the result to each member's observed dissent rate.[27] Unfortunately, G is unknown.

Even without specifying much about G, however, the model generates clear predictions about how a member's rate of dissent on bills reported from his or her committee should change with changes in $x$. Consider the effect of increasing $x$ (the member's ideal point). If $x < F$ and $x < C$, then increasing $x$ decreases the dissent zone while leaving the report zone unchanged: Thus, as long as G has positive density over $[R(x), F]$, the member's dissent rate on reported bills should decline.[28] If $x$ is between F and C, then the dissent zone is empty; increasing $x$ in this range should have no effect on the dissent rate, which should be zero. Finally, if $x > F$ and $x > C$, then increasing $x$ increases the dissent zone while leaving the report zone unchanged: thus, the member's dissent rate should increase.

We should emphasize that more extreme members dissent more only if G has positive density over a fairly wide range. To see why, suppose all status quo points are in the interval $[M, m]$. In this case, there would be no votes that differentiated between M and members with ideals $x < M$. All "leftists" $(x \leq M)$ would vote against changing status quo points in the interval $[M, F]$ and for changing status quo points in the interval $[F, m]$. Thus, all "leftists" $(x \leq M)$ would dissent at the same frequency (given similar committees). The more dispersed is the distribution of status quo points, the more status quo points there are over which M and more extreme leftists differ, and all of these are such that the more extreme member dissents.

To see this, note that $M < F$, and assume that $M < C$ (the latter is empirically always true in the data). Now suppose that $x < M$. In this case, as E increases, the distance between $x$ and M increases. But any status quo point

---

[27] The probability $p$ that a member dissents, conditional on his or her committee reporting a bill on a given dimension, can be calculated using elementary probability theory: $p = \Pr[\text{Bill reported \& Member dissents}]/\Pr[\text{Bill reported}]$. Letting G denote the cumulative distribution function governing the location of $q$, $\Pr[\text{Bill reported}]$ is just the probability that $q$ lies outside the block zone: $1 - [G(F) - G(R(C))]$. Denoting the lower bound of a member's dissent zone by lower $(x, C, F)$, and the upper bound by upper$(x, C, F)$, one can write $\Pr[\text{Bill reported \& Member dissents}]$ as $G[\text{upper}(x, C, F)] - G[\text{lower}(x, C, F)]$. All told, $p = [G[\text{upper}(x, C, F)] - G[\text{lower} (x, C, F)]]/[1 - G(F) + G(R(C))]$.

[28] More formally, $\Pr[\text{Bill reported}]$ does not change, while $\Pr[\text{Bill reported \& Member dissents}]$ declines; thus, $p$ declines.

in the interval from $R(x)$ to $R(M)$ will spark a dissent; hence, the probability of dissent increases with $E$. Suppose instead that $x > \max(F, C)$. Increasing $E$ increases the distance between $x$ and $\max(F, C)$. But any status quo point in the interval from $R(\max(F, C))$ to $R(x)$ will spark a dissent; hence, the probability of dissent again increases with $E$.

# 9

# Which Way Does Policy Move?

> Since early in the nineteenth century, [the major political parties] have presented their programs formally in official party platforms. Asking for total power in the two elected branches, they have been eager to accept the total responsibility and accountability that would accompany it. That was the theory of party government; and not only the politicians, but the people accepted it.... The people listened to the arguments of the two parties and made their choices. And when they did, the party they elected had a full opportunity to carry out its mandate.
>
> – Sundquist, 1988

## 9.1. INTRODUCTION

Thus far in this book we have focused on party roll rates, which indicate how frequently each party has suffered unwanted policy changes. In this chapter, we consider policy directions, which indicate which way – left or right – bills reaching a final-passage vote propose to move policy. The reader may recall that we first considered policy directions in Chapter 4, finding that the adoption of Reed's rules sharply increased the proportion of bills moving policy toward the majority party (leftward for Democratic majorities, rightward for Republican majorities). In the post-Reed era, our data showed that Democratic speakers preside over mostly leftward moves, while Republican speakers preside over mostly rightward moves.

Does this marked pattern in policy moves arise simply because there are more leftist members when the Democrats have a majority, and more rightists when the Republicans do? A priori, there are reasons to expect that policy directions might react to more than just the distribution of preferences on the floor. Consider the life history of a typical bill. After it is introduced, the bill is referred to committee. As shown in Chapter 8, however, almost no bills are reported out of committee against the wishes of a majority of the majority-party contingent on the committee. After it is reported, a bill may need a special rule.

171

As shown in Chapter 7, however, almost no special rules are adopted against the wishes of a majority of majority-party members on the floor. Eventually the bill may be scheduled by the speaker for consideration on the floor and voted on. As shown in Chapter 5, however, the majority is rarely rolled on final-passage votes. The evidence on party roll rates at the various stages of the legislative process suggests that agenda control exerted by committee chairs, the Rules Committee, and the speaker is not neutral. Instead, the majority party's agents at these various stages seem to be loyal enough to filter out many, if not all, bills pushing policy in the "wrong" direction. Is there more systematic evidence of such an effect in the empirical record, once one controls for the locations of the median legislator and the veto and filibuster pivots?

In this chapter, we seek to answer this question, explicitly pitting our model against its main rival(s). At a very general level, the proportion of bills reaching a final-passage vote that propose to move policy leftward – which we denote $P_{Left}$ – should depend on (1) where the status quo policies are, (2) which bills reach the floor agenda, and (3) what happens to bills that do reach the floor agenda. Because our focus is on agenda setting, we can entertain several different hypotheses about what happens to bills after they reach the floor agenda. Perhaps bills are amended to conform to the House median's preferences, and the Senate and president then approve them. Perhaps bills put on the agenda must secure the approval of filibuster and veto pivots and are amended in order to do so. Perhaps bills are amended to reflect a weighted average of the views of the three main constitutional veto players – the Senate, the House, and the president. We shall show that, regardless of one's views on this matter, a partisan model of how the agenda is set outperforms the nonpartisan alternative. This provides perhaps the single most compelling test of the various theories that we present in this book.

## 9.2. POLICY MOVES

To set the stage for our analysis, Figure 9.1 shows the percentage of bills getting final-passage votes that moved policy leftward, which we denote $P_{Left}$. As can be seen, there is a clear difference between Congresses with a Democratic majority (marked with Ds) and those with Republican majorities (marked with Rs). After the adoption of Reed's rules, Democratic Congresses moved policy leftward 81 percent of the time while Republican Congresses did so only 17 percent of the time.[1] Thus, a naked-eye view of the raw data suggests that the majority party strongly pulls policy in its favored direction.

In the rest of the chapter, we undertake a more rigorous exploration of this basic finding. Do the shifts in policy direction displayed in Figure 9.1

---

[1] When we look at $P_{Left}$ for only votes on bills identified by Mayhew as "significant legislation," the patterns still hold. The post-Reed average $P_{Left}$ for Democrats was 87 percent, while it was 15 percent for Republicans.

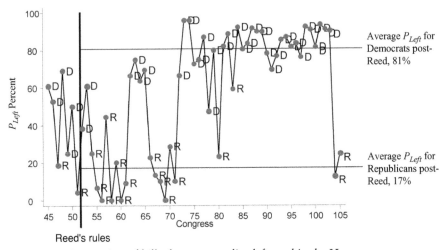

FIGURE 9.1. Proportion of bills that move policy leftward in the House

merely reflect shifts in the distribution of preferences within the House? Or is there a partisan effect (mediated by agenda control), even controlling for such shifts?

## 9.3. LEFTWARD MOVES

In this section, we consider various models of legislative decision making that generate different predictions about the proportion of leftward policy movements in a given House. Each of these models consists of two components: first, an agenda-setting model, which describes which bills are put on the agenda; second, a bill-mapping model, which describes what happens to any given bill, if it is put on the agenda (e.g., is it defeated, passed as introduced, passed with amendments?). Our main argument is that, regardless of which bill-mapping model one chooses (we try three different ones), a partisan model of agenda setting is preferable to a nonpartisan one.

Figure 9.2 illustrates the legislative process as represented in the models to come. Each legislature faces a given array of status quo policies, determined by laws enacted in previous legislative periods as well as by exogenous shocks (more on this later). In the agenda-setting stage, an agenda setter decides which status quo policies will be protected (by blocking all bills that seek to change them) and which status quo policies the legislature will be allowed to consider changing. If a status quo policy is not protected, there are various possible outcomes. For example, one might assume that all unprotected status quo policies are brought to the floor median's ideal point, or one might adopt the mapping from status quo policies to new policies proposed by Krehbiel (1998).

| DETERMINATION OF STATUS QUO POLICIES | AGENDA-SETTING STAGE | BILL-PASSAGE STAGE |
|---|---|---|
| The legislature faces a predetermined set of status quo policies. These status quo policies reflect bills enacted in the previous legislative period, as well as exogenous shocks. | On each dimension of policy, an agenda setter chooses whether proposals to change that dimension's status quo policy will be considered by the House. Examples of assumptions that may be made about the agenda-setting stage are that the agenda is set by the median voter of the House, by the median member of the majority party, or by the left and right pivots. | The House passes a bill (or fails to) concerning each issue dimension that the agenda setter(s) allowed to be considered on the floor. Essentially, each status quo policy is mapped into a new policy. Examples of assumptions that may be made about this mapping are that it produces outcomes at the median voter's ideal point (per the median voter theorem) or within a range of ideal points (e.g., the gridlock zone between the pivots). |

FIGURE 9.2. Agenda-setting and bill-passage stages of the legislative process

## 9.3.1. Modeling Elements

We now discuss the three distinct elements of the legislative process, illustrated in Figure 9.2: (1) the *status quo policies* the House faces; (2) the *agenda-setting process* it utilizes; and (3) the *bill-mapping process* it uses. We then consider some specific examples of models consistent with the general approach sketched here.

The status quo policies facing a given House can be conceived as the product of two factors. First, the previous House, Senate, and president will have set various policy instruments at various values. Second, Nature may have then perturbed the world, which can be modeled as perturbing prior policy decisions, yielding a new status quo. The notion is that a stream of events – such as the fall of the Berlin Wall, the terrorist attacks of September 11th, the invention of web-based methods of copyright evasion, or inflation – constantly alter politicians' evaluation of current government policies.[2] Formally, the process generating

---

[2] One way to view this is that it shifts all members' ideal points uniformly; an equivalent viewpoint is that it shifts the status quo policy.

the status quo on issue dimension $j$ can be represented by a random variable, $Q_j = q_{0j} + e_j$, where $q_{0j}$ represents the policy chosen previously by Congress and the president and $e_j \sim N(\mu, \sigma^2)$ represents a shock administered by Nature.[3] The realized value of $Q_j$, denoted $q_j$, is the status quo policy facing the agenda setter on issue $j$. (In our idealized models from previous chapters, this stage is omitted, which amounts to assuming that $\sigma^2 = 0$.)

After the status quo policy is realized, an *agenda setter* can choose either to block legislative action or to allow legislative action. If the setter blocks action, then the status quo policy is preserved. In contrast, if the setter allows legislation targeting the status quo to be considered, then the setter and $n$ other agents choose a new policy. Let $b(q; x)$ denote the policy that will result if the setter permits legislation targeting a change in the status quo, $q$, to be considered. The vector $x = (x_0, \ldots, x_n)$ consists of the ideal points of the agents involved in the legislative process (e.g., the filibuster pivot, the president, or the House median legislator) with $x_0$ being the ideal point of the agenda setter. We shall call the function $b$ the bill-mapping function.

### 9.3.2. Some General Results

There are many models in the literature (e.g., Shepsle 1979; Shepsle and Weingast 1981; Denzau and Mackey 1983; Krehbiel 1998; Cox and McCubbins 2002) that take the general form just described. We call these models, generally, Shepsle models of policy choice. The outcome of the legislative process in such models can be described as taking one of three values: (1) The agenda setter blocks action, and there is no policy change; (2) $b(q; x) < q$ and policy moves leftward; or (3) $b(q; x) > q$ and policy moves rightward. We are interested here in the probability of a leftward move, conditional on policy change occurring.

As it turns out, some general results within this class of bill-mapping models can be stated regarding the proportion of leftward moves.

- The proportion of leftward moves declines as the agenda setter becomes more conservative, all else equal.
- The proportion of leftward moves declines as the agent deciding new policy becomes more conservative, all else equal.
- The proportion of leftward moves increases as the distribution of status quo points shifts rightward.

The specific models elaborated in Appendix 9.B all comport with these more general propositions, as the more dedicated readers can verify. For less dedicated readers or those already willing to accept these relatively intuitive predictions, we proceed to describe the particular models we have empirically investigated.

---

[3] Note that $q_0$ is not stochastic.

### 9.3.3. Classifying Models of the Legislative Process

Substantively, the family of Shepsle models can be classified in terms of their assumptions about (1) who the agenda setter is and (2) what the $b(q; x)$ mapping is. We wish first to describe the range of assumptions utilized and then describe our empirical approach.

As regards the agenda setter, there are three main alternative assumptions in the literature: The median legislator sets the agenda (e.g., Black 1958; Downs 1957; Krehbiel 1998), the median member of the majority party sets the agenda (Cox and McCubbins 2002 and in Chapter 3), or the median member of the Rules Committee (Dion and Huber 1996) or of some other committee (Shepsle 1979; Shepsle and Weingast 1987; Weingast and Marshall 1988) sets the agenda. Here, we shall focus on the first two possibilities, in which either the median legislator or the majority median sets the agenda.

As regards the bill-mapping function, $b(q; x)$, there are again several to choose from. We shall give three examples. First, in the classic median-voter model (with an open rule),

$$b(q; x) = H \tag{9.1}$$

where $H$ is the median ideal point in the House. This formulation is used, for example, in some of the models in Shepsle (1979).

Second, in Krehbiel's (1998) pivot model, the mapping from status quo to new policy depends on the pivot structure of the House. Letting $LP$ denote the left pivot's ideal point and $RP$ denote the right pivot's ideal point,[4] one has

$$b(q; x) = \begin{cases} H & \text{if } q > 2RP - H \\ 2RP - q & \text{if } q \in (RP, 2RP - H] \\ \varnothing & \text{if } q \in [LP, RP] \\ 2LP - q & \text{if } q \in [2LP - H, LP) \\ H & \text{if } q < 2LP - H \end{cases} . \tag{9.2}$$

While more formidable in appearance, the intuition behind this formulation is simply that bills in the House will be constructed to pass muster both in the Senate (where they may be filibustered) and in the White House (where they may be vetoed).

Third, some scholars (e.g., Fiorina 1996; Alesina and Rosenthal 1995) have used weighted-average specifications that, in the present context, would look like:

$$b(q; x) = \beta_1 H + \beta_2 S + \beta_3 P \tag{9.3}$$

where $S$ denotes the median senator's ideal point, $P$ denotes the president's ideal point, and the weights (the $\beta$'s) are nonnegative and sum to unity. This

---

[4] One can assume either that $LP$ and $RP$ are among the ideal points listed in $x$ or that they are well-defined functions of $x$.

TABLE 9.1. *Six Models of the Legislative Process*

|  | Median Legislator Determines Outcome | Pivot Structure Determines Outcome | Weighted Average of Constitutional Actors' Ideal Points Determines Outcome |
|---|---|---|---|
|  | Status quo policies considered on the floor are changed to coincide with the median legislator's ideal point. | Status quo policies considered on the floor are mapped into new policies in accordance with Krehbiel's pivot model. | Status quo policies considered on the floor are mapped into new policies that coincide with a weighted average of the House, Senate, and president's ideal points. |
| Median Legislator Sets the Agenda | Model 1: Floor Agenda Model | Model 3: Floor agenda with pivot outcomes model | Model 5: Floor agenda with weighted average outcomes model |
| Median Majority-Party Legislator Sets the Agenda | Model 2: Cartel Agenda Model | Model 4: Cartel–pivot hybrid model | Model 6: Cartel–weighted-average-hybrid model |

formulation also reflects a concern for the preferences of other constitutional actors (the Senate and president) but prefers to view their interaction as a less-structured bargaining game.

In constructing a particular model of the House's legislative process, one can mix and match the assumptions about agenda setting (is it the median legislator or the median majority-party member who sets the agenda?) and bill making (is the mapping specified by the median voter model, the pivot model, or the weighted-average model?). As our primary aim is to clarify the nature of agenda power, we proceed as follows. We adopt each possible bill-mapping function, $b(q; x)$, in turn and unite it with the assumption that the median legislator sets the agenda, estimating the resulting model. We then take the same $b(q; x)$ function and unite it with the assumption that the median majority-party member sets the agenda, estimating the resulting model. This yields the six models categorized in Table 9.1 and provides us with answers to three different questions. First, if bill making in the House is largely a matter of setting policy to the median legislator's ideal point, which assumption about who sets the agenda better explains the data? Second, if bill making in the House is as stipulated in the pivot model, which assumption about who sets the agenda better explains the data? Third, if bill making in the House is an exercise in bargaining between the three main constitutional actors, which assumption about who sets the agenda better explains the data? We shall show that, regardless of the assumption one makes about how policies are changed, once they reach the floor, the most fruitful assumption about who sets the agenda is that the majority party median does (in a simplified contest in which the only competing assumption is that the floor median does).

## 9.4. LEFTWARD H0: EMPIRICAL RESULTS

In this section, we investigate how $P_{Left}$, the proportion of final-passage bills that propose to move policy leftward, varies from Congress to Congress. To identify the direction of policy movement that each bill proposes, we use the technique explained in Chapter 4, whereby a bill is classified as moving policy leftward if leftist members are significantly more likely to support it than rightist members. We then counted up the leftward moves so identified in each House and expressed it as a proportion. We explored three different codings of the dependent variable, with each yielding very similar results (and so we report only one here).[5]

We divide our results into three sections, each corresponding to one of the three assumptions about what happens to status quo policies that are considered on the floor of the House listed in Table 9.1. The data we use to estimate our models vary, depending on which assumption about bill mapping we use. When all bills are assumed to move policy to the House median, we use all final-passage votes in all 54 Houses operating under Reed's rules.[6] We restrict our attention to the Congresses in which the Reed's rules are in effect, as we have shown in Chapter 4 that the pre-Reed Congresses do not pool with the post-Reed Congresses. When all bills are assumed to move policy in accord with Krehbiel's pivot model, we likewise use all 54 post-Reed Houses.[7] However, when all bills are assumed to move policy to a weighted average of the House, Senate, and president's ideal points, we need to employ common-space NOMINATE scores and therefore must restrict the Congresses included

---

[5] Letting $N_L$, $N_R$, and $N_U$ denote the number of leftward, rightward, and undetermined policy moves in a given Congress, the dependent variable in our analyses is $P_L = N_L/(N_L + N_R)$. Note that $P_{Left} = (N_L + P_L * N_U)/(N_L + N_R + P_L * N_U + (1 - P_L) * N_U)$. Thus, our analysis as presented in Table 9.1 assumes that the proportion of unclear votes that move policy leftward equals the proportion of undetermined votes that move policy leftward. An alternative assumption about the unclear votes is that they break down in a way that is maximally inconsistent with the cartel model's expectations: All unclear moves are rightward under Democratic speakers but leftward under Republican speakers. With this recoding of the dependent variable, none of our qualitative results change. Yet another alternative coding of the dependent variable is to look not at the significance of the coefficients in Equation (4.1) but just at the sign of the relationship between ideal point and vote. If the sign of the relationship is negative, the vote is considered a leftward move; otherwise, it is a rightward move. With this dependent variable, too, our results remain unchanged from those presented in Table 9.1.

[6] Recall, as in Chapter 4, we use here our Post-Reconstruction data so that only bills in the H.R. series, which accounts for the bulk of all bills, are included.

[7] There is an issue regarding how to identify the left and right pivots operationally. To address this, we also rerun the analyses for just the 83rd–105th Congresses, for which we can identify the filibuster and veto pivots using common-space NOMINATE scores. Our results are similar. See the book's web page for exact results (*www.settingtheagenda.com*).

in the analysis to those for which such scores are available – greatly reducing our sample size.

### 9.4.1. Status Quo Policies are Mapped to the Floor Median

Suppose that the House's agenda-setting agents anticipate that any policy considered on the floor will be changed to jibe with the median legislator's preference. In this case, how will they behave? Which status quo policies will they refer to the floor to be changed and which will they not refer, thereby preserving the status quo?

If the median legislator sets the agenda, then the general results articulated previously yield two expectations: (1) the further right is the current floor median, the lower will be the proportion of leftward policy moves (because it is *harder* to find status quo policies to the right of the current median that she will wish to move left); (2) the further right is the lagged floor median, the further right will be the status quo policies (as these were established by the previous House), hence the higher will be the proportion of leftward policy moves (because it is *easier* to find status quo policies to the right of the current median that she will wish to move left).

If the majority-party median sets the agenda, expectations (1) and (2) just noted are maintained. The first remains because the median legislator still determines what the new policy will be, for any status quo referred to the floor. The second remains because the lagged median legislator determined what policies would be in the previous House, hence affecting the distribution of status quo policies facing the current House.[8] The new feature in this model is that the majority-party median sets the agenda. Thus, one expects (per the general results articulated previously) that the further right is the majority party median, the lower will be the proportion of leftward moves.

Table 9.2 displays results of an EBB estimation of the proportion of leftward moves across 54 post-Reed Houses, with one specification corresponding to each of our two hypotheses about who sets the agenda (the floor or majority-party median).[9] In both specifications, the status quo policy is represented by the House median from the previous Congress (given the assumption about bill mapping in the specification).

We note four points. First, the farther right the current floor median is, the smaller the proportion of bills proposing leftward moves, as expected under

---

[8] One caveat must be registered. In the previous House, some status quo policies will have been protected from change by the agenda setter (the previous median majority-party member). These status quo policies will thus not be brought to the lagged floor median. Thus, the lagged floor median indicates the location of all status quo policies changed in the previous House but not the location of others.

[9] In addition, to capture any autocorrelation in the data, we include the first lag of the dependent variable, $P_{Left}$. Excluding the lagged dependent variable does not change the main results we report. The second lag of $P_{Left}$ proved insignificant, and including it did not change any of the main results, either.

TABLE 9.2. *Explaining Variations in the Proportion of Final-Passage Bills That Propose to Move Policy Leftward, If Bills Move Policy to the Floor Median*

| Independent Variables | Specification 1 (floor median sets agenda) | Specification 2 (majority-party median sets agenda) |
|---|---|---|
| Lagged floor median | 3.44** | 3.02*** |
| (status quo defining) | (1.12) | (0.92) |
| Majority-party median | — | −3.65*** |
| (agenda setter) | | (0.59) |
| Floor median (agenda | −7.2*** | −1.35 |
| setter in Specification 1 | (1.0) | (1.26) |
| and bill mapping in | | |
| Specification 2) | | |
| $P_{Left}$ Lagged | 3.01*** | 2.31*** |
| | (0.57) | (0.48) |
| Constant | −.88*** | −.88** |
| | (0.343) | (0.29) |
| $\gamma$ | 0.073*** | 0.024** |
| | (0.023) | (0.011) |
| Log likelihood | −1248.05 | −1232.45 |
| Pseudo $R^2$ | 0.235 | 0.245 |
| N | 54 | 54 |

Standard errors are given in parentheses; $*p < .10$; $**p < .05$; $***p < .01$.
The estimation technique is Extended Beta Binomial.
Dependent variable: $P_{Left}$, the proportion of final-passage bills that move policy left.

both models. However, this effect is statistically significant only in the first specification. Second, the farther right the lagged floor median is, the higher the proportion of bills proposing leftward moves, as expected under both models. This effect is statistically significant in both specifications. Third, the farther right the majority-party median is, the lower the proportion of bills proposing leftward moves, as expected under the Cartel Agenda Model (but contrary to the Floor Agenda Model). Finally, the higher the value of $P_{Left}$ in the previous Congress, the higher its value in the current Congress is (holding constant the other regressors).

All told, then, one can state that the Floor Agenda Model lacks conclusion validity because the coefficient on the majority-party median should be zero in specification 2 if the Floor Agenda Model is correct. The Cartel Agenda Model performs well, however.[10] Interestingly, the data do not strongly support the median voter bill-mapping hypothesis in that the floor median's influence on $P_{Left}$ is not statistically significant. We cannot reject this hypothesis about bill mapping, however, because we lack the statistical power in this case to do so

[10] Note that Covington and Bargen (2004) use a different measure of policy change and find similar results.

(power is only about 38 percent). The tenuous statistical relationship between $P_{Left}$ and the floor median's location may arise because it is too much of a simplification to say that bills reaching the final-passage stage all propose to move policy to the House median. Perhaps such bills sometimes reflect the Senate and president's preferences as well, as the next two bill-mapping models would suggest.

### 9.4.2. Status Quo Policies Are Mapped per Krehbiel's Pivot Model

In this section, we assume that agenda-setting agents anticipate that any policy considered on the floor will be changed in accord with Krehbiel's pivot mapping, given in Equation (2). The intuition behind this mapping is similar to that in the median voter theorem, except that a simple House majority is not viewed as sufficient for enacting a bill; instead, enactment requires enough support to overcome two further legislative roadblocks: Senate filibusters and presidential vetoes.

If the median legislator sets the agenda, anticipating a pivot mapping of any issue dimensions he allows to be considered on the floor, what proportion of bills will propose to move policy leftward? The median legislator will propose to move any status quo policy that is to the right (respectively, left) of the gridlock zone leftward (respectively, rightward). Assuming that it is costly to propose bills that will fail, the median legislator will not propose any changes to status quo points lying within the gridlock zone because he knows these will fail later in the process anyway.[11] Thus, the proportion of leftward moves is equal to the proportion of status quo policies that lie to the right of the current gridlock zone, among those that do not lie in the gridlock zone. Statistically, $P_{Left}$ should be a function of four variables: the lagged pivots (which indicate where the lagged gridlock zone is and hence where the status quo policies are) and the current pivots.

If the majority-party median sets the agenda, anticipating a pivot mapping of any issue dimensions she allows to be considered on the floor, then $P_{Left}$ should be a function of the same four variables – the lagged and current pivots – *plus* the location of the majority-party median.

The key finding from Table 9.3, which estimates the two models just described, is again that the location of the majority-party median is a statistically significant predictor of the proportion of final-passage bills that propose to move policy leftward. This again allows us to argue that the Floor Agenda Model for agenda setting lacks conclusion validity. Thus, if one believes that Krehbiel's pivot model accurately describes how status quo policies are transformed on the floor, the evidence suggests that the agenda is set by the majority party rather than the floor median. In other words, the median-pivot

---

[11] If one assumes that the median legislator will propose changes, even when he knows they will fail, then the model is no different than the Floor Agenda Model, in terms of the agenda of bills that will result.

TABLE 9.3. *Explaining Variations in the Proportion of Final-Passage Bills That Propose to Move Policy Leftward, If Bills Move Policy as per the Pivot Model*

| Independent Variables | Specification 1 (floor median sets agenda) | Specification 2 (majority-party median sets agenda) |
| --- | --- | --- |
| Lagged left pivot | −0.16 | 0.51 |
| (status quo defining) | (1.09) | (0.89) |
| Lagged right pivot | 2.06*** | 0.95 |
| (status quo defining) | (0.80) | (0.59) |
| Majority-party median | — | −3.87*** |
| (agenda setter) | | (0.39) |
| Left pivot | 1.03 | 1.73* |
| (bill mapping) | (1.13) | (0.91) |
| Right pivot | −2.63*** | −0.87 |
| (bill mapping) | (0.79) | (0.60) |
| $P_{Left}$ Lagged | 3.19*** | 1.70*** |
| | (0.56) | (0.43) |
| Constant | −.98** | −0.09 |
| | (0.44) | (0.33) |
| $\gamma$ | 0.186*** | 0.031** |
| | (0.044) | (0.012) |
| Log likelihood | −1262.6 | −1234.1 |
| Pseudo $R^2$ | 0.226 | 0.243 |
| N | 54 | 54 |

Standard errors are given in parentheses; *$p < .10$; **$p < .05$; ***$p < .01$.
The estimation technique is Extended Beta Binomial.
Dependent variable: $P_{Left}$, the proportion of final-passage bills that move policy left.

hybrid mode l (the model put forth by Krehbiel 1998) lacks conclusion validity, whereas the cartel-pivot hybrid does not.

### 9.4.3. Status Quo Policies are Mapped to a "Constitutional Weighted Average"

In this section, we assume that agenda-setting agents anticipate that any policy considered on the floor will be moved to a "constitutional weighted average" of the House, Senate, and president's ideal points, given in Equation (3). For this analysis, we obviously need a way to locate the House, Senate, and president's ideal points on a comparable scale. We chose to use common-space NOMINATE scores, currently the best solution to the cross-chamber and cross-branch comparability problem (see Poole and Rosenthal 1997). There is a cost involved in using common-space scores, however: Scores for both the president and Senate are available only for the 83rd–105th Congresses. We thus must restrict our analysis to this period.

TABLE 9.4. *Explaining Variations in the Proportion of Final-Passage Bills That Propose to Move Policy Leftward, if Bills Move Policy to a Constitutional Weighted Average*

| Independent Variables | Specification 1 (floor median sets agenda) | Specification 2 (majority-party median sets agenda) |
|---|---|---|
| Floor median (agenda setter in Specification 1; bill mapping in Specification 2) | −8.79*** (1.93) | −3.03* (1.64) |
| Senate median (bill mapping) | −5.87** (2.61) | −1.17 (1.86) |
| Presidential ideal point (bill mapping) | −0.058 (0.30) | −0.46** (0.21) |
| Majority-party median (agenda setter) | — | −3.94*** (0.72) |
| Lagged floor median (status quo defining) | 1.22 (1.59) | 1.05 (1.10) |
| Lagged Senate median (status quo defining) | 7.15** (3.21) | 4.32* (2.21) |
| Lagged presidential ideal point (status quo defining) | (0.40) (0.40) | (0.27) (0.27) |
| Constant | 1.57*** (0.22) | 0.96*** (0.18) |
| $\gamma$ | 0.024** (0.011) | 0.003 (0.004) |
| Log likelihood | −937.33 | −926.22 |
| Pseudo $R^2$ | 0.179 | 0.189 |
| N | 22 | 22 |

Standard errors are given in parentheses; *$p < .10$; **$p < .05$; ***$p < .01$.
The estimation technique is Extended Beta Binomial.
Dependent variable: $P_{Left}$, the proportion of bills that move policy left.

The results of two "constitutional weighted average" models, one in which the floor median sets the agenda and one in which the majority-party median sets the agenda, are displayed in Table 9.4. All of the variables intended to capture the bill-mapping part of the model have the correct signs. However, of the three current "pulls" on policy – the House median, Senate median, and president's ideal point – only the first is statistically significant in both specifications; while of the three lagged "pulls" on policy – the lagged House median, lagged Senate median, and lagged presidential ideal point – only the second is statistically significant in both specifications. For our purposes, the most important finding is that, controlling for the "constitutional weighted average" specification of where new policies are located, the majority-party median in the House is a significant predictor – indeed, the single most important predictor – of leftward policy moves.[12]

## 9.5. DIGRESSION: REED'S RULES REDUX

As an aside, we note that the analysis of Reed's rules conducted in Chapter 4 can be reframed with the proportion of leftward moves ($P_{Left}$) instead of the proportion of moves toward the majority ($P_{Maj}$) as the dependent variable and with the regressors introduced in this chapter as controls. We have done this, adapting the specification as needed, and found the same qualitative results as reported in Chapter 4. The extended beta-binomial regression includes the majority median as one factor, with the lagged floor median and the lagged value of $P_{Left}$ as covariates. The second factors of primary interest are two indicator variables, *Reed* and *Revolt*, defined in Chapter 4, along with the interactions of the factors, *Reed × Majority_Median* and *Revolt × Majority_Median*. We expect the majority-party median to have an effect on the proportion of leftward policy moves only after the Reed rules, which gave the majority the ability to control the agenda. We do not expect the relationship between the majority-party median and the proportion of leftward moves to be significantly affected by the revolt against Speaker Cannon, for the reasons detailed in Chapter 4. The rule changes should not themselves have an effect on the proportion of leftward policy moves, as the direction of policy change is mediated by agenda control. So, we expect the main effects of $Reed_t$ and $Revolt_t$ to be indistinguishable from zero. The results are as given in Table 9.5 (for the 45th–105th Congresses). Note that the majority-party median did have some impact before Reed's rules (the coefficient on the majority median is correctly signed, but it is not significant at the .05 level), but that this impact grew dramatically after Reed's rules were adopted (the coefficient on the interaction between Reed's rules and the majority median is correctly signed and significant at the .005 level). The main effects (*Reed* and *Revolt*) showed no independent impact on $P_{Left}$.

## 9.6. DISCUSSION: HOW BIG ARE THE POLICY MOVEMENTS?

Just because most final-passage bills propose to move policy toward the majority party does not say how large or important such moves are. What can one say about the size of policy movements?

Throughout this chapter, we have presented statistical evidence that agenda control enables majority parties to move policy in their preferred direction: left for Democrats and right for Republicans. A closer look at three legislative epochs (New Deal, Great Society, and Contract with America) in U.S. history provides further evidence that the majority party is able to move policy in its preferred direction.

---

[12] Of course, by estimating two equations, we used up a considerable number of degrees of freedom and reduced our confidence in the coefficients estimated.

TABLE 9.5. *The Effect of Reed's Rules on the Proportion of Leftward Moves*

| Independent Variables | Majority Median | Lagged floor median | Lag of $P_{Left}$ | Reed | Revolt | Reed × Majority-Median | Revolt × Majority-Median | Constant |
|---|---|---|---|---|---|---|---|---|
| Coefficient estimates (z scores) | −1.45 (−1.82) | 2.69 (3.74) | 2.21 (4.57) | 0.264 (0.71 = 0) | −0.011 (−0.06) | −2.74 (−3.05) | −0.002 (−0.00) | −1.15 (−3.49) |

$N = 61$; Pseudo $R^2 = 0.245$.

Historical accounts of the New Deal often discuss the significant leftward moves of policy that were frequent during this period. Importantly, our measures of policy movement capture this direction as well. Our measures also capture the highly partisan nature of most of the significant legislation from this time period.

The following pieces of legislation, all considered significant during the New Deal, rolled the Republican party: creation of the Tennessee Valley Authority, Agricultural Adjustment Act, Securities Exchange Act of 1934, Social Security Act, National Recovery Act, Fair Labor Standards Act, Works Progress Administration, Indian Reorganization Act, and Banking Act of 1934. Furthermore, all these votes were highly partisan in nature with the vast majority of Democrats supporting them and Republicans opposing them. Some of the important legislation from the New Deal was relatively bipartisan and did not roll either party. For instance, the Federal Emergency Relief Agency, National Recovery Act, Civil Works Administration, and Social Security Act did not roll either the majority or minority party. Of the preceding bills that originated in the House, and that are in our dataset, the following legislation moved policy to the left: the Agriculture Adjustment Act, National Recovery Act, Securities Act of 1933, Banking Act of 1934, Social Security Act, and the 1934 act to regulate securities. The combination of rolls and policy moves to the left suggests that the majority party was able to move policy in its preferred direction throughout the New Deal.

During the Great Society, there were three general types of legislative outcomes on significant legislation: unanimous votes, rolls of the Southern Democrats, and partisan legislation. Unanimous legislation included the Higher Education Act, Water Quality Act, Clean Air Act, Truth in Packaging Act, and Highway Safety Act.

The second type of legislation, which rolled the Southern Democrats but did not roll the entire Democratic majority, included the Civil Rights Act of 1964, Voting Rights Act of 1965, and Immigration Act of 1965. All three of these pieces of legislation moved policy to the left.

The third category of legislation during the Great Society was partisan. Republicans were rolled on all of the following legislation: the Economic Opportunity Act of 1964, Medicare, Medicaid, Omnibus Housing Act of 1965, Housing and Urban Development Act, and Education Act. These pieces of legislation all moved policy significantly to the left, as well.

In contrast with the two previous legislative epochs we considered, the 1994 Contract with America featured a Republican majority. Consistent with our story regarding the ability of the majority to control the legislative agenda and move policy in its preferred direction, the vast majority of the legislation central to the Contract with America did indeed move policy rightward.

Of the 17 major votes of the Contract with America, 16 of them moved policy toward the right. These votes include passage of the Balanced Budget Amendment, Budget Impoundment Control (line-item veto), Exclusionary Rule Reform, Death Penalty Appeal Reform, Prison Construction, Anticrime

Block Grants, relationship between UN and U.S. troops, Regulatory Moratorium, Regulatory Overhaul, Takings Revision, Civil Litigation Reform, Securities Litigation Reform, and Term Limits. One of the 17 major bills, Unfunded Mandates, originated in the Senate, and although it appears to move policy to the left based on the breakdown of votes, we do not know if the relationship would scale using our $P_{Left}$ technique.

The review of major legislation during the New Deal, Great Society, and Contract with America strongly suggests that the majority party is able to move policy in its preferred direction, and that our measures of policy direction capture that effect.

Further, we can report that bills that appear on Howell et al.'s (2000) list of the most significant legislation obey the same basic patterns as do bills in general. Thus, the bills that move policy leftward under Democratic majorities and rightward under Republican majorities do not consist disproportionately of the least important bills; they include landmark enactments as well.[13]

Another perspective on the importance of majority-direction policy moves can be gained by considering a series of policy areas in which substantial and long-lasting partisan differences have been documented. Studenski and Krooss (1963), for example, in their account of the financial history of the United States, show consistent patterns of partisan differences in tax and monetary policy since the Civil War.[14] Republicans have pursued high tariffs and low (but more progressive) income taxes and have opted for sales, payroll, or excise taxes rather than income taxes (especially corporate income taxes).[15] Democrats, on the other hand, have sought to reduce or eliminate tariffs, to substitute higher income taxes across all income brackets, and to impose higher payroll taxes, with high tax incidence down through the middle-income tax brackets for other forms of taxation. Republicans have favored tight monetary policy, with hard currency and expensive money, while Democrats have sought lower and easier credit, expansion in the money supply, and loose money with soft currency. Additionally, bankruptcy bills have, for the most part, only been enacted into law when parties on the right (Whigs, Federalists, Republicans) have unified control of government (Berglof and Rosenthal 2004).

Similarly, partisan divisions over both agricultural policy (*Congressional Quarterly* 1984) and labor policy have remained relatively consistent over this period. Democrats have favored easy credit for farmers, creating several farm credit agencies prior to World War I and during the New Deal and high levels of income support and production controls, while Republicans have generally supported a low level of income support for farmers that protects them against

---

[13] Results of this analysis can be found on the book's web page: *www.settingtheagenda.com*.

[14] Indeed, it is interesting to note that the general tax and monetary policy positions of the two parties have remained essentially unchanged for well over a century (Studenski and Krooss 1963).

[15] See also Cox and McCubbins (1991) for an account of Republican and Democratic differences over fiscal policy.

precipitous drops in income but does not guarantee a high income (*Congressional Quarterly* 1984). Further, the Department of Labor and the National Labor Relations Board were both created under Democratic governments. In addition, Democrats tend to support higher minimum-wage policies, unemployment insurance, and government-employee pensions. Republicans, on the other hand, have opposed federal intervention in the labor market and now disagree with Democrats on issues of economic concern, such as changes in the minimum wage (Douglas and Hackman 1938, 1939; Poole and Rosenthal 1991).

Spending decisions also vary significantly by party. Kiewiet and McCubbins (1991) show, for example, that when Democrats are in the majority in both the House and Senate, appropriations awarded to domestic programs and agencies increase by about 8 percent a year more than during Republican Congresses.[16] Similarly, Browning (1986) shows that Democratic presidents and Democratic Congresses have initiated almost all federal programs related to nutrition, social services, education, and health. More generally, new social-program initiatives occurred nearly twice as frequently under unified Democratic governments as when a Democratic Congress faced a Republican president, and there have been virtually no attempts to create new social-welfare programs when Republicans have controlled Congress.

Recent work by Den Hartog and Monroe (2004) and Monroe (2004) has shown that changes in party control lead to significant changes in the prospects for energy policy. Specifically, when Republicans captured unified control of government after the 2000 election, the values of oil and gas stocks increased dramatically, while renewable-energy stocks fell sharply (Monroe 2004). When Senator James Jeffords defected from the Republican Party several months later, however, giving majority control of the Senate to the Democrats, renewable-energy stocks rallied, while oil and gas stocks plummeted (Den Hartog and Monroe 2004).

The politics of health policy has seen Republicans focused on employer mandates and extension of private insurance (aspects of insurance market reform), whereas Democratic policy has focused on attempts to advance National Health Insurance and extend government provision or regulation of health care (Peterson 1994). Similarly, Democrats have tended to favor a larger federal role in education and increased spending, while the Republican Party has traditionally placed greater emphasis on standards and testing, choice and competition, and reducing the federal government's role in education (Bresnick 1979; Sullivan and O'Connor 1972).

As a final illustration, control of the federal government also entails the ability to appoint judges to the federal court system. As a result, the ability of presidents to appoint judges with harmonious policy preferences depends on the willingness of the Senate to approve the president's nominations. As the policy

---

[16] See also Kiewiet and McCubbins (1985, 1988) and McCubbins (1991) on the effect of divided government on deficits and Stewart (1991) on the effect of divided government on taxing and spending.

differences between the president and the controlling majority of the Senate increase, the likelihood grows that the president will be forced to compromise with the Senate on the appointee's policy preferences. In turn, presidents will be most likely to fill vacancies with appointees having like preferences when the same party controls both the executive branch and the Senate (Cameron, Cover, and Segal 1990; Labaton 1993; Zuk, Gryski, and Barrow 1993; Gryski, Zuk, and Barrow 1996). Further, there is evidence that both Democrats and Republicans tend to increase the number of federal judges during periods of unified control so that they can "pack" the judiciary with fellow partisans (McNollgast 1995).

### 9.7. CONCLUSION

The literature offers various perspectives on "where" new policies are located when bills are enacted. Each is in the nature of a first-order approximation: Perhaps new policies are located at the House median (ignoring bicameral and presidential influence); perhaps new polices are located as Krehbiel's pivot model suggests (one way to incorporate the other constitutional actors); or perhaps new policies are located at a weighted average of House, Senate, and presidential preferences (another way to incorporate other constitutional actors). Regardless of which perspective one takes on what the central tendency is if an issue gets on the agenda, a separate question is which issues get on the agenda to begin with.

For each of the three bill-mapping assumptions noted here, we pit two different assumptions about agenda setting against one another. One assumption is that the House agenda is set as if by majority vote on the House floor (empowering the median legislator). Another is that the House agenda is set as if by majority vote in the majority party's caucus (empowering the majority party median).

Empirically, we find that the most successful bill-mapping model appears to be defined by a constitutional weighted average. Regardless of which bill-mapping assumption one chooses, the choice between Floor and Cartel Agenda Models is clearly in favor of the latter. As predicted by the Cartel Agenda Model, when the Democrats have a majority, the vast bulk of bills that reach final passage propose to move policy leftward. In contrast, when the Republicans have a majority, the vast bulk of final-passage bills propose to move policy rightward. Given these results, we are able to claim that those models that assume that the House agenda is set on the floor lack conclusion validity and that those models that assume that the House agenda is set by the majority party should be accepted.

### APPENDIX 9.A. A STOCHASTIC SPATIAL MODEL

Up to this point in the book, we have assumed that legislators know each other's preferences. In this section, we incorporate some conventional assumptions from the scaling literature (e.g., Ladha 1991; Poole and Rosenthal 1997; Londregan 2000; Poole 2001; Cox and Poole 2002) to relax the assumption that members of Congress have complete information about each other's preferences. After sketching the model's elements, we note how our previous results (C1 and C2 from Chapter 3) change with the introduction of uncertainty.

The model takes as given (and fixed throughout the analysis) the following elements: the legislators, indexed $k = 1, \ldots, T$; the policy dimensions, indexed $j = 1, \ldots, n$; the legislators' ideal points on each dimension, $\{x_j^k : 1 \leq k \leq T, 1 \leq j \leq n\}$; the legislators' standard errors, $\{s_k : 1 \leq k \leq T\}$; and the status quo policies on each dimension, $\{q_j : 1 \leq j \leq n\}$. We provide a fuller discussion of some of these elements in the next section.

### 9.A.1. Elements

The utility to legislator $k$ of policy alternative $a$ on dimension $j$ is $u_i(a; x_j^k) = -(a - x_j^k)^2 + e_{ak}$, where $e_{ak} \sim N(0, 2\sqrt{2}s_k)$ for all $a$. The error $e_{ak}$ is independent of $e_{bk}$ for all alternatives $a \neq b$. We refer to the parameter $s_k$ as member $k$'s standard error.

An important assumption is that members' errors are statistically independent. Formally, if $i \neq k$, then $e_{ai}$ and $e_{ak}$ are independent for all $a$. Thus, knowing whether legislator $i$ evaluated proposal $a$ more favorably than would have been expected, based on the distance between the policy and his ideal point, tells one nothing about whether legislator $k$ will evaluate that proposal more or less favorably. This is a standard, if sometimes implicit, assumption in most of the scaling literature.

There are $p \leq n$ votes held. No vote is held if the agenda-setting agent on dimension $j$ decides not to report a bill to the floor. Otherwise, vote $j$ pits an alternative on the left, $l_j$, against an alternative on the right, $r_j$. The vote is more conveniently characterized by a cutpoint, $c_j = (l_j + r_j)/2$, and a distance (or gap), $d_j > 0$, where $l_j = c_j - d_j < r_j = c_j + d_j$.

Legislator $k$'s voting behavior on roll call $j$ can be characterized by his probability of voting for alternative $l_j$ : $p_{kj} = \Pr[k$ votes for $l_j]$. That is, $p_{kj}$ is the probability of voting for the left-of-cutpoint alternative. As it turns out (see, e.g., Londregan 2000), $p_{kj} = \Phi(d_j(c_j - x_j^k)/s_k)$, where $\Phi$ is the standard normal cumulative distribution function.

### 9.A.2. Sequence of Events

The following sequence of events occurs under each of the models we consider for each dimension $j$ sequentially ($j = 1, \ldots, n$). First, an agenda-setting agent decides either not to report a bill on dimension $j$ at all, which we denote by $bj = \emptyset$, or to report some bill, $b_j \in \Re$. We assume that, if the agent reports a bill, it is consistent with the bill-mapping process she anticipates; that is, $b_j = b(q_j; x)$. When the agenda-setting agent does report $b_j$ to the floor, she anticipates that each member $k$ will vote for the leftmost alternative (whether the bill or the status quo) with probability $p_{kj}$ defined earlier.

Second, Nature draws the "errors" $\{e_{ak}: 1 \leq k \leq T, a = q_j\}$ and $\{e_{bk}: 1 \leq k \leq T, b = F_j\}$. That is, each member learns the additional considerations that affect her decision. It is not necessary that these become common knowledge.

Third, members vote either for $q_j$ or for $b_j$ at final passage. If $q_j$ wins, then policy remains unchanged on dimension $j$. If $b_j$ wins, then policy on dimension $j$ moves from $q_j$ to $b_j$. This move is either leftward or rightward.

### 9.A.3. The Majority Party's Roll Rate under the Cartel Agenda Model

How does the introduction of uncertainty about members' utilities affect our previous results? In order to clarify this matter, we make the following assumptions. First, the floor agenda is set as if by the median member(s) of the majority party. That is, a bill addressing dimension $j$ is allowed on the floor if and only if the member with ideal point $M_j$ (whom we henceforth refer to as $M_j$) prefers to do so, rather than block action.[17] Second, $M_j$ must decide whether to allow a bill on the floor *before* he knows even his own "additional considerations," much less those of other members (i.e., before he knows $\{e_{a1}, \ldots, e_{aT}\}$). The notion is that the additional considerations come in the form of opinions and pressures from constituents and interest groups, and some of these sources do not weigh in until the bill reaches final passage.[18] Third, we continue to assume that all bills are considered under open rules.

Given these assumptions, $M_j$ will schedule a bill if and only if the floor median is closer to $M_j$ than is the status quo policy, which is the same as our result C1 from Chapter 3.[19] Thus, the characterization of the majority block zone remains unaffected by the introduction of (this particular kind of) uncertainty.

In contrast, result C2, which concludes that the majority party will *never* be rolled, does change. Because of the additional considerations $\{e_{a1}, \ldots, e_{aT}\}$, there is a positive probability that the majority will be rolled on *any* final-passage vote. Consider, for example, a policy dimension on which $M_j < F_j < q_j$ – consistent with our maintained assumption of a Democratic majority – and a bill proposing to move policy leftward from $q_j$ to $F_j$. Albeit approximating a zero-probability event as voting errors shrink, all Republicans might vote

---

[17] Note that $M_j$ is the median of $\{x_k^k: k$ is a member of the majority party$\}$.

[18] A more realistic depiction of the legislative process would have new information regarding constituents' and interest groups' preferences being revealed at each stage. Here, we simplify by having only two stages and one point at which new information is revealed.

[19] The expected utility to $M_j$ of proposing a bill to move policy on dimension $j$ from the status quo, $q_j$, to the floor median, $F_j$, can be written as $\Pr[\text{Bill proposing } F_j \text{ passes}]E[u(F_j; M_j)] + \Pr[\text{Bill proposing } F_j \text{ fails}]E[u(q_j; M_j)]$. The expected utility of blocking action is $E[u(q_j; M_j)]$. The $E[u(\bullet; \bullet)]$ terms are straightforward to calculate; for example, $E[u(q_j; M_j)] = -(q_j - M_j)^2$, since $E[e_{qk}] = 0$ for all $k$ by assumption. Letting $\pi_j = \Pr[\text{Bill proposing } F_j \text{ passes}]$, $M_j$ will schedule a bill if and only if $\pi_j[(q_j - M_j)^2 - (F_j - M_j)^2] > 0$. Since $\pi_j > 0$, this leads to the conclusion in the text.

for this bill (due to unusually large additional considerations) while a bare majority of Democrats vote against it (again, due to unusually large additional considerations) – resulting in a majority-party roll. The incomplete-information Cartel Agenda Model does predict a "low" majority party roll rate, but it does not predict, as the complete-information model did, a zero roll rate.

To get some notion of what "low" means in practice, note that a rough upper bound on the majority-party roll rate, in the case of a Democratic majority, would be $(1 - P_{Left})/2$. A proportion, $P_{Left}$, of the final-passage bills propose to move policy leftward, and the majority's roll probability on these bills is essentially zero (given spatial errors and gaps equal to those empirically estimated in conventional models).[20] A proportion, $1 - P_{Left}$, of the final-passage bills propose to move policy rightward, and the largest possible roll probability for such bills (consistent with their being scheduled to begin with) is .5.[21] Empirically, the average value for $P_{Left}$ in Democratic Congresses is about .82 after the adoption of Reed's rules, yielding an upper bound on the majority party's roll rate of .09. This compares to the actual roll rate of about .013 reported in Chapter 5.

## APPENDIX 9.B. MODELING THE PROPORTION OF LEFTWARD PROPOSALS: THREE MODELS

What determines the proportion of bills proposing to move policy leftward, $P_{Left}$? In this appendix, we consider the answer to this question given by the first three models listed in Table 9.1.

### 9.B.1. The Floor Model

In the floor model, the only factors determining $P_{Left}$ are the status quo policies $\{q_{1t}, q_{2t}, \ldots, q_{nt}\}$ and floor medians $\{F_{1t}, F_{2t}, \ldots, F_{nt}\}$ in Congress $t$. Ignoring the possibility that a particular status quo point, $q_{jt}$, coincides exactly with the current floor median, $F_{jt}$, there are only two possibilities: $q_{jt} < F_{jt}$ and $q_{jt} > F_{jt}$. In the first case, the median legislator will propose a bill moving policy rightward; in the second, the median legislator will propose a bill moving policy leftward.[22] All bills will reach final passage in this model. Thus, $P_{Left}$ does not depend at all on which party has a majority, on the location of pivot points,

---

[20] Poole and Rosenthal (1997), among others, estimate member parameters $(x_k, s_k)$ and roll call parameters $(c_j, d_j)$. Given their estimates, the probability of a majority roll can be calculated.

[21] Consider a status quo $q_j < 2M_j - F_j$. As $q_j$ approaches $2M_j - F_j$, the probability of a majority of the majority voting against it approaches .5. As the bill passes with near certainty (again, assuming standard errors and gaps near empirically estimated levels), the majority-party roll rate also approaches .5, for a bill proposing to alter such a status quo point.

[22] Recall that proposals are made knowing how Nature has perturbed the status quo policies (i.e., knowing the $q_{jt}$) but without knowing each member's nonspatial error utilities (the $e$'s). The median legislator will propose a bill moving policy leftward for any $q_{jt} > F_{jt}$. This increases his *expected* utility (cf. footnote 19 in this chapter), although the nonspatial errors may result in the bill passing and the median legislator disliking it, all things considered.

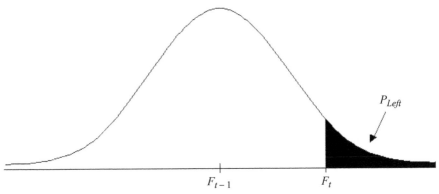

FIGURE 9.B.I. Proportion of leftward moves under the Floor Agenda Model

or any other consideration. All that matters is how many current status quo points are to the left (right) of the current floor median.

In general, the floor median might differ from dimension to dimension, as in Chapter 6, but here we assume that the median is constant across dimensions. This is largely for practical reasons: We can estimate the overall median via NOMINATE scores but have no way of identifying separate dimensions, much less the medians on each.

What determines the status quo policies $\{q_{1t}, q_{2t}, \ldots, q_{nt}\}$? We assume that the previous Congress has set all policies to its median, denoted $F_{t-1}$, but that these have then been perturbed by Nature. Thus, $q_{jt} = F_{t-1} + \varepsilon_{jt}$, where $\varepsilon_{1t}, \varepsilon_{2t}, \ldots, \varepsilon_{nt}$ are independently and identically distributed variates with zero mean.

All told, then, the only two systematic factors that affect $P_{Left}$ are $F_t$ and $F_{t-1}$. Figure 9.B.1 illustrates one case, in which $F_{t-1} < F_t$ (the floor median has shifted rightward). The normal distribution pictured in the figure, centered on $F_{t-1}$, shows the distribution of status quo points. The shaded area under the curve to the right of the current floor median, $F_t$, equals the proportion of final-passage bills that will propose leftward moves.

We can easily test this model by regressing $P_{Left}$ on $F_t$ and $F_{t-1}$ (in practice, we use an extended beta binomial model). The model predicts a negative coefficient on $F_t$: The further right the House median, the harder it is to find status quo points to the right of the median that can be moved left (and the easier it is to find status quo points to the left of the median that can be moved right). It predicts a positive coefficient on $F_{t-1}$: The further right the lagged House median, the easier it is to find status quo points to the right of the current median that can be moved left (and the harder it is to find status quo points that can be moved right).

### 9.B.2. The Pivot Model

Krehbiel's (1998) pivot model is designed to explain enactments (the production of laws) within the U.S. constitutional structure. In particular, it highlights two nonmajoritarian features of U.S. policy making: the filibuster in the Senate and the presidential veto. Consciously simplifying the complexities of bicameralism and presidentialism, Krehbiel assumes that a bill can be enacted only if it either (1) is preferred to the status quo by the president, a majority in the House, and at least 60 percent of the Senate (and hence is filibuster-proof and not vetoed) or (2) is preferred to the status quo by at least two thirds in both chambers of Congress (and hence is filibuster-proof and veto-proof).

When one focuses on the *passage of bills* in the House of Representatives, rather than the *enactment of laws* in the United States, what should one make of filibusters and vetoes? One obvious point is that members of the House may anticipate Senate filibusters and presidential vetoes and fashion their bills accordingly. Yet, how should we model this anticipation? How will House members "fashion their bills accordingly" when they anticipate a filibuster or veto?

The simplest reaction that members of the House might have is to propose only bills that will be filibuster-proof in the Senate and either acceptable to the president or veto-proof. In this chapter, we focus on this simplest possibility, which essentially extends the pivot model to the internal legislative process of the House.[23]

There are of course reasons that the House might pass bills that are not filibuster-proof (or not veto-proof). Perhaps members seek to stake out a position, rather than enact policy, as in the models of Magar (2001) and Groseclose and McCarty (2001). Or, perhaps they view passing a filibuster- or veto-vulnerable bill as the opening gambit in an extended negotiation, as in Cameron's (2000) model of veto bargaining. Nonetheless, the simpler model of anticipation just proposed highlights what are plausibly important influences on House legislation – the anticipation of filibusters and vetoes – in a straight-forward way. Moreover, the model's implications can be empirically tested – something we did in this chapter.

In the pivot model, the only factors determining $P_{Left}$ are the status quo points $\{q_{1t}, q_{2t}, \ldots, q_{mt}\}$ that face Congress $t$; and the location of the left and right pivots, $LP_t$ and $RP_t$, in Congress $t$. In general, the pivots might differ from dimension to dimension, but here we assume that they are constant across dimensions. This again is largely for practical reasons: We can estimate the overall pivots via NOMINATE scores but have no way of identifying separate dimensions, much less the pivots on each.

Ignoring the possibility that a particular status quo point, $q_{jt}$, coincides exactly with one of the current pivot points, there are only three possibilities: $q_{jt} < LP_t$ and the median legislator will propose a bill moving policy rightward;

---

[23] Extending the pivot model to the House produces a model that is essentially the analog of Cameron's first model of veto politics (Cameron 2000). Players have complete information, and actual vetoes and filibusters never occur in equilibrium (unless the veto can be overridden), yet the possibility of vetoes and filibusters prompts the House to anticipate and partially accommodate presidential and Senate-pivot preferences.

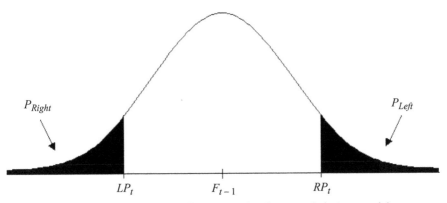

$P_{Right}$

$P_{Left}$

$LP_t$        $F_{t-1}$        $RP_t$

FIGURE 9.B.2. Proportion of leftward moves under the extended pivot model

$q_{jt} > RP_t$ and the median legislator will propose a bill moving policy leftward; or neither and no bill will be proposed.[24] Thus, $P_{Left}$ does not depend at all on which party has a majority, on the location of the floor median, or on any other consideration. All that matters is how many current status quo points are to the left (right) of the current gridlock zone.

What determines the status quo policies $\{q_{1t}, q_{2t}, \ldots, q_{nt}\}$? We assume that the previous Congress has adjusted all policies so that they lie within the previous gridlock zone, $[LP_{t-1}, RP_{t-1}]$. Within this zone, it is especially likely to find policies at the lagged floor median, $F_{t-1}$. After the previous Congress sets policy on each dimension, Nature then perturbs it before the next Congress convenes.

All told, then, we can test the pivot model by regressing $P_{Left}$ on $LP_t$ and $RP_t$, to capture the current gridlock zone, and either $F_{t-1}$ alone or perhaps $F_{t-1}$, $LP_{t-1}$, and $RP_{t-1}$, to reflect the distribution of status quo points faced by Congress $t$. Figure 9.B.2 illustrates one case, in which $F_{t-1}$ lies between $LP_t$ and $RP_t$. The normal distribution pictured in the figure, centered on $F_{t-1}$, shows the distribution of status quo points. The shaded area under the curve to the right of the current right pivot, $RP_t$, equals the proportion of final-passage bills that will propose leftward moves.[25]

The extended pivot model predicts a positive coefficient on the lagged variables: As the distribution of status quo points shifts rightward, more of them can be moved left in Congress $t$. It predicts a negative coefficient on both $LP_t$ and $RP_t$: As the gridlock zone shifts right, more status quo points are available to move right, and fewer are available to move left.

---

[24] We assume that no bill is proposed if the status quo lies in the gridlock zone.

[25] This is true only if one bill is proposed for each dimension, even if the relevant status quo point lies in the gridlock zone. If gridlocked status quo policies are left alone (no bill targeting them is allowed to the final-passage stage), then $P_{Left}$ would equal the shaded area in Figure 9.B.2, divided by the sum of this area plus the analogous area to the left of the left pivot.

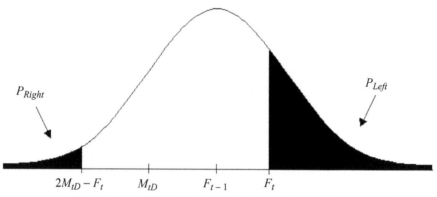

$$2M_{tD} - F_t \qquad M_{tD} \qquad F_{t-1} \qquad F_t$$

FIGURE 9.B.3. Proportion of leftward moves under the Cartel Agenda Model

## 9.B.3. The Cartel Agenda Model

In the Cartel Agenda Model, the only factors determining $P_{Left}$ are the status quo points $\{q_{1t}, q_{2t}, \ldots, q_{nt}\}$ that face Congress $t$ and the location of the majority party and floor medians, $M_t$ and $F_t$, in Congress $t$.[26] Ignoring the possibility that a particular status quo point, $q_{jt}$, coincides exactly with either $M_t$ or $F_t$, there are only three possibilities: $q_{jt} < \min(M_t, F_t)$, and the majority-party median will propose a bill moving policy rightward; $q_{jt} > \max(M_t, F_t)$, and the majority-party median will propose a bill moving policy leftward; or neither and no bill will be proposed. Thus, $P_{Left}$ depends only on how many current status quo points are to the left (right) of the current majority block zone.

What determines the status quo policies $\{q_{1t}, q_{2t}, \ldots, q_{nt}\}$? We assume that the previous Congress has adjusted all policies so that they lie within the previous majority block zone, $[\min(M_{t-1}, F_{t-1}), \max(M_{t-1}, F_{t-1})]$. Moreover, all policies adopted under an open rule will cluster at $F_{t-1}$.[27] Thus, the lagged floor median is a natural indicator of the distribution of status quo points in the Cartel Agenda Model – as in the Floor Agenda and pivot models.

All told, then, we can test the Cartel Agenda Model by regressing $P_{Left}$ on $F_{t-1}$, as an indicator of the distribution of status quo points, and on $M_t$ and $F_t$, as indicators of the current majority block zone. Figure 9.B.3 illustrates the case in which $M_{tD} < F_{t-1} < F_t$: The majority-party (Democratic) median is to the left of the lagged floor median, which in turn is to the left of the current floor median. The normal distribution centered on $F_{t-1}$ again shows the distribution of status quo points. In this case, the proportion of status quo points that will be targeted by bills proposing leftward moves is given by the area under the distribution to the right of the current floor median, $F_t$. The proportion of status quo points that will be targeted by no bills, as they lie in

---

[26] We again assume that these medians are constant across dimensions, as in the previous two models.

[27] Closed rules are needed to support outcomes between $F_{t-1}$ and $M_{t-1}$ (or at $M_{t-1}$).

the majority block zone, is given by the area under the curve between $F_t$ and $2M_{tD} - F_t$.[28] Finally, the proportion of status quo points that will be targeted by bills proposing rightward moves is given by the area under the curve to the left of $2M_{tD} - F_t$. Putting these three results together, the proportion of final-passage bills proposing leftward moves can be calculated as the first area (right of $F_t$) divided by the sum of the first and third (left of $2M_{tD} - F_t$) areas.

---

[28] We continue to assume open rules for all bills. Relaxing this assumption means that status quo points between $2M_{tD} - F_t$ and $M_{tD}$ can be altered (with suitable closed rules). See Chapter 10.

# PART III

# THE CONSEQUENCES OF POSITIVE AGENDA POWER AND CONDITIONAL PARTY GOVERNMENT

# 10

## Positive Agenda Power

The central feature of representative government is a mediating assembly of legislators that stands between the citizenry and decisions on public policy.... Such an assembly presents a serious challenge to democratic accountability. Since no single legislator can make policy decisions unilaterally, voters cannot reasonably hold any one legislator responsible for overall policy outcomes.... One way to meet this challenge is with responsible party government. Here political parties serve as collective agents of the electorate by designing alternative policy agendas and implementing them, once in power. If successful, the parties can offer voters clear options and accomplishments as guides at election time.

– Patterson, Magleby, and Thurber 2002

With $400 billion set aside for Medicare, with the 2004 campaign looming in the future, and with President Bush dubbing prescription drug coverage his number-one domestic priority, Republicans in the 108th Congress faced enormous pressure to pass legislation that would add prescription drug coverage to Medicare (*Congressional Quarterly Weekly* 2003). Republicans had tried to pass similar legislation since 1999, but with President Clinton occupying the White House, their attempts were unsuccessful. When President Bush took office in 2000, the Republicans saw an opportunity to pass the legislation, but this time a slim Democratic majority in the Senate (owing to Senator Jeffords' decision to help them organize the chamber) stymied their efforts. In 2003, however, the Republicans had their chance, as they finally controlled the House, Senate, and White House.

Recognizing that "it was now or never" for Medicare reform, Speaker of the House Dennis Hastert (R-IL) used a broad range of legislative maneuvers to push Medicare legislation through to enactment against determined resistance from the Democratic minority (Hastert 2004: 254; Carey 2003a, 2003b; Koszczuk and Allen 2003; Adams and Carey 2003; *Congressional Quarterly Weekly* 2003). The Republicans' efforts to roll over the Democrats began with a post-midnight meeting of the Rules Committee, prompting minority members to complain about the 108th being a "Dracula Congress" (*Boston Globe* 2004). During this meeting, the Rules Committee adopted a rule regulating House floor debate and ignored Democratic objections about being left, quite literally, in the dark about the legislation. After the Rules Committee's graveyard shift, Speaker Hastert and Majority Leader Tom DeLay (R-TX) still needed to corner wayward Republicans during the floor vote, in order to persuade them to support the Medicare bill. In the end, Hastert garnered just enough votes to pass the bill, which cleared the House by a one-vote margin of 216–215 (Carey and Adams 2003).

Following the House–Senate conference (where Republicans excluded all but two Democrats from the negotiations), House Republicans continued to steamroll the Democrats. Facing substantial opposition from Democrats and key GOP conservatives, Republican leaders again lived up to their "Dracula" nickname by putting off a roll call vote on the conference report until 3 A.M. on a Saturday. They then left the vote open for 2 hours and 53 minutes (which is thought to be the longest recorded vote in the history of electronic voting) in order to pressure those Republicans who had voted against the report to change their minds (*Congressional Quarterly Weekly* 2003; Koszczuk and Allen 2003). And pressure they did. As Republican leaders and President Bush worked the phones and confronted Republican holdouts, Hastert scoured the aisles for votes. In describing the dramatic events of that night, Hastert stated:

When the roll call vote started it was about 3 o'clock Saturday morning. I was watching the red and green lights on the voting board in the House chamber. I counted more red than green, so I decided to prowl the aisles myself to look for additional votes.... One prairie state Member, a fourth-term Representative from a solidly Republican district, voted no, then ran and hid. I sent people to find him; they couldn't.

(Hastert 2004: 265)

By dawn, Hastert had tracked down the votes that his party needed to win, enabling the Republicans to enact Medicare legislation just in time for it to become a major plank in the Republicans' 2004 reelection campaign.

In keeping with the theme of this anecdote, we now shift our focus from negative agenda power (the ability to prevent bills from reaching a final-passage vote on the floor) to positive agenda power (the ability to ensure that bills reach a final-passage vote on the floor, even though these bills ultimately may not pass). Empirical examples of positive agenda power include the Rules Committee's ability to craft special rules, the Brazilian president's right under the urgency procedure to send bills to the top of the assembly's agenda (cf. Amorim Neto et al. 2003), and the U.S. speaker's ability to allow motions to "suspend the rules and pass" a particular bill.

This chapter pursues two main questions related to positive agenda power. First, what are the differences between our theory and the theory of conditional party government (CPG)? As we will explain, CPG differs from our theory in that it has positive agenda power at its core. CPG is thus closely related to the theory of responsible party government, which emphasizes the enactment of the party's platform as a key element in the story line of party government. In contrast to CPG, procedural cartel theory has negative agenda power at its core, although it, too, makes predictions about the use of positive agenda power. In this chapter, we discuss how these two types of agenda power are related and how their use should (and should not) change under our theory, as the key condition in the theory of conditional party government varies. We then compare our theory's predictions to the corresponding predictions of CPG.

Second, to ensure the passage of the bills that it puts on the agenda, the majority party may need to corral a few votes on the margin; that is, it may need to use not only agenda power but also some mix of party discipline and side payments to minority-party members. Is there any evidence that it can do this? Specifically, is there any evidence that the majority party controls resources that are important to its members and that can be used to ensure the passage of legislation? We review recent investigations of party influence in roll call voting, by way of an answer.

## 10.1. WHAT CHANGES WHEN THE MAJORITY PARTY BECOMES MORE HOMOGENEOUS?

In this and the next two sections, we explore some differences between our theory and CPG. The main difference is that, in our model, there is a constant level of party government that is always present and not conditional on the condition stipulated in CPG. We seek to explain this point by first considering what does and does not change when the majority party becomes more homogeneous, according to our theory (Sections 10.1 and 10.2). We then contrast our predictions with those of CPG (Section 10.3).

### 10.1.1. The Mix of Positive and Negative Agenda Powers

In Chapter 2, we argued that special agenda powers are attached to various offices within the House, that the majority party's senior partners take the lion's share of these offices, and that these senior officeholders are not completely free to use their official powers but, instead, have some fiduciary responsibilities to their parties. In the idealized model in Chapter 3, we elaborated on these fiduciary responsibilities, specifying that (1) agents with veto power are expected to block bills that would roll the majority party, even if they themselves favor the bill, and (2) agents with proposal power are expected to refrain from using such power to advance bills that would roll the majority party, even if they themselves favor the bill.

Notice that these normative restrictions on behavior focus on crimes of commission: They bar officeholders from using their official powers actively to harm the majority party's interests. Crimes of omission – failures to help – are still allowed. In particular, agents with veto power can block bills that they dislike, even if a majority of their party would prefer to see the bill advanced to the floor. Similarly, agents with proposal power can refrain from using this power to push bills that they dislike, even if most in their party favor the bill. Thus, in our original model, the majority party may face a considerable problem of *excess* blocking (veto agents using their delegated powers to block issues the party as a whole would like to consider).

If the majority party could be sure its officeholders would never use their official powers in such a way as to roll the majority party, then it could get around the problem of excess blocking, simply by distributing extraordinary proposal powers to others in the party. In practice, however, the majority allocates proposal powers very sparingly and only to carefully designed bodies, never to individuals. This contrasts with veto powers, which are distributed widely, including to individuals.

We believe the reason for this difference is that abuse of veto power is less costly than abuse of proposal power. If a single veto agent refuses to block a bill that will roll the majority party, the bill merely advances one stage in the legislative process. If the next veto agent has a personal incentive to block it or is more loyal, then the majority will not suffer substantial damage from the first agent's bad behavior. In contrast, if a single agent has the right to place bills directly on the floor for a vote, then once that single agent has chosen to violate the minimal fiduciary standard, the damage is already done (in the sense that a floor vote that rolls the party has occurred; it may still be possible to block the bill in the Senate, at conference, or on the president's desk).

As we have noted previously, there is an inherent trade-off between positive and negative agenda power. The more a procedural cartel distributes veto rights (at the expense of proposal rights), the harder it is to negotiate and pass a program of legislation. The more it distributes proposal rights (at the expense of veto rights), the greater the risk that some proposals will impose external costs on other members of the cartel – even to the point of rolling the majority. Thus, a procedural cartel always faces the question of the optimal mix of veto and proposal powers.

We do not aim to provide a theory that provides point predictions about the optimal mix. We do, however, wish to provide some intuition about what should happen to the mix of positive and negative agenda powers when the majority party becomes generally more homogeneous in preference.

Aldrich and Rohde conjecture that the majority party will tend to delegate greater positive agenda power to their central agents, at the expense of blocking powers, when the party becomes more homogeneous. To see why, note that, as the members of a cartel become more homogeneous in preference, they can better trust one another with proposal powers – simply because they agree on a wider range of issues. They can also better trust one another with veto powers – for the same reason. However, the increasing similarity of preference should have a much bigger impact on the use of proposal powers. The probability of a painful misuse of veto powers was already relatively low because there are multiple veto points. Thus, increasing homogeneity only slightly reduces this probability. In contrast, increasing homogeneity more substantially lowers the probability of painful misuse of proposal powers. If the mix of positive and negative agenda powers is chosen by the majority party to minimize agency loss, then increasing homogeneity prompts the majority to readjust the mix in favor of more proposal powers.

Note two additional features of our argument. First, we are not claiming that the mix of agenda powers responds continuously to variations in majority party homogeneity. The formal and informal rules governing agenda powers may be costly to change, so small variations in homogeneity produce little or no effect. However, when homogeneity increases and there is a subsequent change in the rules, we expect such changes to increase proposal powers.

Second, proposal powers can be increased either through rule changes (such as the 21-day rule) or through changes in the fiduciary standard to which office-holders are held. Such a change in fiduciary standard occurred during the 1970s reform period (cf. Rohde 1991). The opening shot, announcing a raising of the bar on what was expected by the Democratic caucus of its chairs, was the removal of four Southern Democrats from their positions as chairmen. These chairs had not pushed bills out of their committee that rolled the majority on the floor. Rather, they were foot-draggers in jurisdictions in which a newly coherent party majority wished to move bills. Crook and Hibbing (1985) show that Democratic chairs in general got the message and changed their behavior to conform to the new standard.[1]

Having clarified some of the logical aspects of our argument, we can ask whether there is any evidence in favor of it. Does increasing homogeneity lead to better (or at least no worse) proposal powers?

Clearly, David Rohde's (1991) masterful account of the House reforms of the 1970s provides evidence in favor of such a view. On the other hand, Schickler and Rich (1997), in a statistical study covering a much larger time frame, do not find any consistent relationship between promajority rule changes and a measure of majority-party homogeneity. Possibly the difference in these two studies can be explained by Rohde's focus on a very large increase in the homogeneity of the Democratic Party, pursuant to Southern realignment, in contrast to Schickler and Rich's focus on sometimes small and sometimes large variations in homogeneity. Moreover, one might wonder whether all rule changes are equally important (as Schickler and Rich's coding scheme assumes) and whether the results would change if one recoded the rule changes systematically with an eye to the distinction between positive and negative agenda power.[2]

---

[1] To see how the change in incentives and party control played out, consider the case of Jaime Whitten of Mississippi. Whitten had a low party support score (even for Southern Democrats) prior to the House reforms of the 1970s. When Whitten was nominated to be chair of Appropriations in 1979, his support score had slightly increased, but liberal Democrats challenged his nomination. After his appointment, his party loyalty score further increased until he was more loyal than most other Southerners (Rohde 1991).

[2] Consider, for example, the Calendar Wednesday rule (as described in more detail in Chapter 4). It is well documented that Calendar Wednesday never proved to be a workable pathway for passing legislation (see Oleszek 2004). Yet, Schickler and Rich (1997) and Schickler (2000) count Calendar Wednesday the same as every other rule change, no matter how big or small, in their statistical analyses. Moreover, Calendar Wednesday is coded as a change that went against the majority party (Binder 1997; Schickler and Rich 1997; Schickler 2000). Yet, while

In short, the discussion about rule changes is intended to make a very simple point. We need a better theory of the effect of rule changes before we can be confident in the conclusions that are drawn from analyses of the timing of such changes. If we can begin to understand both the relative weight and the nature of the distribution of these changes, then we can begin to test our predictions about what should happen when they occur. Indeed, this is a line of investigation that we intend to pursue in future work.

## 10.1.2. The Size of the Majority Party's Agenda

In this section, we consider how the size of the majority party's legislative agenda changes as the party becomes more homogeneous. The majority party's agenda consists of all bills pushed onto the floor as priorities of the majority-party leadership. It is easy in some systems, such as the United Kingdom, to identify the government's agenda, as it is simply a matter of seeing if the whips were put on or not. In the United States, it is not so easy, but we have suggested previously (Cox and McCubbins 1993) that bills on which the majority leader and majority whip vote together can be considered part of the party's agenda. Ideally, we would like to know exactly how many bills the majority is getting on the agenda of those it wants on the agenda. With no means to ascertain this exact quantity, dividing the number of bills on the agenda by the number of bills reaching a final-passage vote provides a convenient measure of the size of the majority party's agenda. This should be a reasonably good measure of positive agenda power.

We have previously argued that the party's agenda should increase in size as the party becomes more homogeneous. Moreover, we have shown that this is the case empirically. Recall that in our previous work (Cox and McCubbins 2002) we regressed the size of the majority party's agenda on the distance between the majority-party median and the floor median, which we employed as a measure of majority-party heterogeneity. Specifically, we estimated the following regression (results are in parentheses):

$$AggendaSize_{ct} = X_c(0.389) + \beta_c(-0.656; se = 0.242)D_{ct} + \varepsilon_{ct}$$

and we found an inverse relationship.[3] That is, as the majority party gets more heterogeneous, the size of its agenda shrinks.

supporters of Calendar Wednesday may have hoped to circumvent the central veto authority of the majority party, the principal recipients of new agenda-setting powers were the committee chairs, all of whom were part of the majority party leadership. Thus, rather than viewing Calendar Wednesday as taking away from the power of the majority party in an absolute sense, it might better be understood (and coded) as a redistribution of power within the majority party. Indeed, this is a particularly relevant distinction given that these codings have been used to test the predictions of CPG, where the core of the theory lies in assumptions about the redistribution of authority *within* the majority party.

[3] The results are from an OLS regression. The dependent variable is size of the majority party's positive agenda, which is measured as the number of roll calls (in a given Congress) on which (1) the majority leader and majority whip vote the same way, *and* (2) the minority leader and/or the minority whip vote in opposition to the position of the majority leaders (Cox and McCubbins 1993: 145–6).

### 10.1.3. The Minority Party's Roll Rate

We cannot always measure the size of the majority party's agenda. But, we should be able to trace its effects on other measures. Consider that, as the majority becomes more homogeneous and increases the amount of delegated proposal power, relative to delegated veto power, there should be more minority party rolls. To see why, imagine that prior to the increase in proposal rights, a Democratic majority has $N$ veto players, with ideal points ranging from $x_1$ to $x_N$. Assume for convenience that $x_1 < x_2 < \cdots < x_N$ and also that $F < x_N$ (i.e., the Nth veto player is to the right of the floor median). In this case, the Nth veto player will block consideration of some bills that would roll the minority party. After the increase in proposal rights, $N$'s veto may be weakened or removed (think of Jaime Whitten as chair of the House Appropriations Committee, for example). This means that more bills rolling the minority can now pass the gauntlet of veto (or delay) points. Assuming a relatively constant number of bills, the minority party's roll rate should increase with greater proposal rights.

To investigate this hypothesis, we construct three variables for the 45th–105th Congresses. As in previous chapters, our dependent variable – the minority party's roll rate – is constructed as the number of times the minority party is rolled as a percentage of the total final-passage votes in a given Congress. To capture majority-party homogeneity, we use *MajStDev*, which measures the standard deviation of first-dimension DW-NOMINATE scores for the majority party. As majority-party members become more tightly bunched – and thus *MajStDev* decreases – majority-party homogeneity increases. Thus, we expect a negative relationship (and thus a negative coefficient) between *MajStDev* and the minority party's roll rate. We also calculated *InterPartyDist*, which measures the distance between the majority-party median and the minority-party median first-dimension DW-NOMINATE scores. Aldrich and Rohde (1998) suggest that as this distance increases, and thus the parties become more polarized, the party "condition" should be increasingly met. Since the logic of conditional party government is fundamentally about positive agenda power, we should see an increase in the minority party's roll rate. Thus, we expect a positive coefficient on *InterPartyDist*.

Table 10.1 shows the results of our extended beta binomial analysis of this relationship.[4] In Model 1, we see that, as predicted, there is a negative and highly significant relationship between *MajStDev* and the minority-party roll rate. As *MajStDev* decreases, and thus majority-party homogeneity increases, there is a significant increase in minority-party roll rate. In model 2, we include both *MajStDev* and *InterPartyDist*. Though *MajStDev* remains negative, it is no longer significant (which is unsurprising, given that *MajStDev* and *InterPartyDist* are correlated at $-0.76$). As expected, however, *InterPartyDist* is positive and highly significant. As the distance between the two parties increases, the minority party is significantly more likely to be rolled.

---

[4] For a discussion of the logic of employing extended beta binomial, see Chapter 4.

TABLE 10.1. *Extended Beta Binomial Estimation of the Minority-Party Roll Rate, Congresses 45–105*

| Independent Variables | Model 1 | Model 2 |
|---|---|---|
| MajStDev | −7.36*** | −2.75 |
| | (1.41) | (2.14) |
| InterPartyDis | | 2.18*** |
| | | (0.76) |
| MajFloorDist | | |
| Constant | 0.50** | −1.72** |
| | (0.26) | (0.82) |
| Γ | 0.06*** | 0.05*** |
| | (0.02) | (0.01) |
| N | 61 | 61 |
| Log likelihood | −2,058.24 | −2,054.07 |
| Pseudo $R^2$ | 0.05 | 0.05 |

Standard errors in parentheses; $^*p < .10$; $^{**}p < .05$; $^{***}p < .01$, two-tailed tests.
Our estimation technique is Extended Beta Binomial regression.
The dependent variable is the proportion of bills that roll the minority party in a given Congress.

### 10.1.4. Summary

All told, then, we expect the following as consequences of an increase in majority-party homogeneity: (1) a shift in the balance of delegated agenda powers toward greater positive (hence less negative) powers, accomplished either through changes in the rules, or through changes in the fiduciary standard expected of officeholders, or both; (2) an increase in the size of the majority party's agenda; and (3) an increase in the minority-party roll rate. We cannot claim to have presented definitive evidence in favor of any of these propositions here, only correlational studies. However, each passes at least the preliminary investigations we have undertaken here.

### 10.2. WHAT DOES NOT CHANGE WHEN THE MAJORITY PARTY BECOMES MORE HOMOGENEOUS?

Having just said what should change, we can now consider what should not change when the majority party becomes more homogeneous. These aspects of party government should not be conditional on majority-party homogeneity.

### 10.2.1. The Rules "Base"

The basic structural advantages of the majority party embedded in the rules – what we have called the rules "base" (Cox and McCubbins 1997) – should not change, as the party becomes more or less homogeneous. To put it another way, although the mix of positive and negative agenda powers may shift, the vast bulk of all agenda powers, positive or negative, will be delegated to members of the majority party, regardless of how internally divided it may become.

The reasoning behind this claim is as follows. In our view, agenda powers are a resource, hence subject to the general theory of resource allocation we advanced in Chapter 2. Because agenda powers are an extremely important resource, the majority is inclined to take a very disproportionate share. The only thing in our model that prevents the majority from taking *all* such powers is the risk that the opposition might be able to convince the public that the majority is greedy or unfair. In some polities, such as the United Kingdom, the majority party takes virtually all agenda powers. In others with more proportional norms, such as Sweden, the opposition retains significant agenda powers. In the U.S. House, Thomas Brackett Reed seized substantial agenda power for the majority party by establishing what came to be known as Reed's rules, but his party then suffered a loss of public support during the next two elections. Indeed, following the establishment of Reed's rules in the 51st Congress, the Republican Party lost control of the House for the next two Congresses. In his writings, Reed maintained that one of the central issues of the election campaigns for the 52nd and 53rd Congresses was the creation of Reed's rules and the significant advantage that they gave the majority party (Den Hartog 2004). Although the Republicans eventually regained majority-party status in the 54th Congress, this episode nonetheless illustrates the potential tension between seizing agenda power and losing public support.

Empirically, we have already argued that the rules "base" has two key features: first, that the minority party's powers of delay are weak; second, that the majority party's leaders (broadly construed) have flexible means at their disposal to bring bills to the floor out of "regular order." We have also already argued that neither of these features has changed significantly since the adoption of Reed's rules in 1890.

### 10.2.2. The Minimal Fiduciary Standard

The minimal fiduciary standard – debarring officeholders from using their powers to roll the majority party – should remain unaltered, regardless of the majority's degree of homogeneity. To put it another way, although the standard regarding how much officeholders should use their powers to aid the majority party's agenda may wax and wane, the standard debarring them from using their powers to roll the majority should not.

The reasoning behind this claim is as follows. The fiduciary standards in question here are up to the majority party's members to determine, formally or informally. There are many possible standards regarding crimes of commission. An officeholder might get in trouble for pushing bills that a fraction, $W$, of the majority party disliked, with $W$ being anything from $(N-1)/N$ (you only get in trouble if everyone else in the party dislikes your bill) to 0.5 (our suggested standard) to $1/N$ (you get in trouble if any single member of the majority dislikes your bill). We have argued for $W = 0.5$ earlier. The reason is that a majority of the majority party can vote in caucus to deny renomination to the offending officeholder, for any $W \geq 0.5$. This remains true, regardless of how homogeneous or heterogeneous the majority's members are.

### 10.2.3. The Majority Party's Roll Rate

The majority-party roll rate should not change. This, of course, is the argument made at length in Chapters 3 and 5. The evidence is straightforward. There are very few majority party rolls, and they do not vary significantly with majority-party homogeneity. Indeed, in our previous work (Cox and McCubbins 2002), we regressed the majority party's roll rate on the distance between the majority-party median and the floor median (results are in parentheses):

$$Rollrate_{ct} = \mathcal{X}_c(0.022) + \beta_c(0.91; se = .091)D_{ct} + \varepsilon_{ct}$$

Based on these results, we could not reject the null hypothesis of no relationship, and as we demonstrated in Chapter 6, there are no unexplained consequential majority-party rolls; thus, they do not vary with homogeneity either.

### 10.3. HOW DOES PROCEDURAL CARTEL THEORY DIFFER FROM CONDITIONAL PARTY GOVERNMENT?

How does the theory sketched in the preceding chapters differ from the theory of conditional party government, as first stated by Cooper and Brady (1981) and advanced most prominently by Rohde (1991), Aldrich (1995), and Aldrich and Rohde (1998, 2001)? Under CPG, responsible party government is conditional on a sufficient degree of preference agreement within the majority party and preference disagreement between the two parties. When "the condition" is not met (i.e., when intraparty agreement and interparty disagreement fall below a minimum threshold), responsible party government fades away.

Exactly what replaces party government, when a party system falls below the threshold, is not entirely clear to us from reading the various works generally collected under the rubric of CPG. One reading is that, when party government fades away, it is replaced by the shifting coalitions, committee government, and ineffective majority parties of the textbook Congress. Sundquist (1981) argued it was replaced with coalition (bipartisan) government. We believe this is a common reading, and it is certainly suggested by Rohde (1991: 7, 31), who argues that "by the 1960's the House was characterized by a system of committee government, dominated by a working coalition of Southern Democrats and Republicans" and that "there would be party responsibility only if there were widespread policy agreement among House Democrats."

What does "committee government" mean? A common interpretation in the literature is that committees had both negative and positive agenda power during the textbook era. Although it was often noted that the Rules Committee blocked liberal legislation during this period, most committees were viewed as able to get their measures to the floor most of the time. Formal models of committees, such as Shepsle (1979), Shepsle and Weingast (1987), Weingast and Marshall (1988), or Denzau and Mackay (1983), had no Rules Committee stage built into them. Thus, the committees in these models had the right to report bills directly to the floor. It was also common to assume, both in informal and formal accounts, that committee members pursued their own interests, rather than being agents of their parties (see, most prominently, Mayhew 1974 and Arnold 1979). However, proposal power plus the pursuit of personal interest plus diversity in committee preferences leads directly to the prediction that the majority party will be rolled.

To see how, suppose that the Democrats have a majority with median $M$ and that there exists a committee with median $C > M$. The easiest case to consider arises when $C > F$; that is, the committee in question has a median to the right of the floor median. Empirical examples of such committees during the textbook era include Armed Services and Agriculture. Given the assumption of self-interestedness, a rightist committee would prefer to report a bill seeking to change a moderate leftist status quo policy $q$ (such that $M < q < F$) to a new policy $b$ (say, $b = F$), rather than leave the status quo in place. Given the assumption of proposal power, the committee would be able to push such a bill to a final-passage vote. The consequence of this, however, would be that the bill passed and rolled the majority party. If one is willing to assume that the distribution of status quo points is symmetric about $F$, or that there is greater density on the side of the majority party median, then the majority party's roll rate, on the bills reported by a rightist committee, will exceed 50 percent. Thus, a committee government model leads to the prediction that the majority party's roll rate on bills reported from rightist committees should be quite large.

Empirically, however, we know that the majority-party roll rate is nowhere near 50 percent for any committee, including rightist ones. Table 10.2 shows majority- and minority-party roll rates on final-passage votes by committee for the 84th–98th even-numbered Congresses. Note that the highest majority-party roll rate on any committee is 10 percent, from the Joint Committee on Economic Energy. Even the committees that we have shown to be majority-party outliers (e.g., Armed Services, Agriculture) never have a roll rate higher than 5 percent.[5] And, as predicted, control committees (e.g., Appropriations, Ways and Means) never roll the majority but do produce very high minority roll rates. We can thus state that the committee government model (self-interested committee members plus committees with proposal power) lacks conclusion validity. Hence, we can say the same about the version of CPG – call it CPG/committee government – in which failure to meet "the condition" leads to committee government.

What if failure to meet "the condition" leads, not to a pure committee government model, but to committee government modified by a self-interested

---

[5] See Cox and McCubbins (1993: 208–11) for a full list of outlier and representative committees.

TABLE 10.2. *Majority- and Minority-Party Roll Rates by Committee, Congresses 84–98 (even-numbered)*

| Committee | Majority Rolls | Minority Rolls | Bills That Got Final-Passage Votes | Majority Roll Rate (%) | Minority Roll Rate (%) |
|---|---|---|---|---|---|
| Agriculture | 3 | 13 | 59 | 5 | 22 |
| Appropriations | 0 | 30 | 157 | 0 | 19 |
| Armed Services | 0 | 1 | 47 | 0 | 2 |
| Banking and Currency | 1 | 22 | 57 | 2 | 39 |
| Budget | 0 | 0 | 1 | 0 | 0 |
| D.C. | 0 | 6 | 34 | 0 | 18 |
| Education and Labor | 0 | 19 | 63 | 0 | 30 |
| Foreign Affairs | 2 | 13 | 47 | 4 | 28 |
| Government Operations | 0 | 6 | 18 | 0 | 33 |
| Interior | 0 | 8 | 48 | 0 | 17 |
| Interstate and Foreign Commerce | 2 | 16 | 97 | 2 | 16 |
| Joint Committee on Atomic Energy | 1 | 0 | 10 | 10 | 0 |
| Judiciary | 3 | 4 | 52 | 6 | 8 |
| Merchant Marine and Fisheries | 0 | 3 | 28 | 0 | 11 |
| Post Office | 1 | 6 | 23 | 4 | 26 |
| Public Work | 0 | 7 | 32 | 0 | 22 |
| Science | 0 | 6 | 35 | 0 | 17 |
| Ways and Means | 2 | 33 | 89 | 2 | 37 |

*Note:* Committees with fewer than 10 bills that made it to final passage were dropped from the table. Rolls reported are on final-passage votes in the House, with the bills sorted by committee of origin.

Rules Committee, as in the Dion–Huber model discussed in Chapter 7? Theoretically, adding such a Rules Committee does not change the basic story, as long as Rules' median, $R$, is also right-of-center ($R > F$). As long as $R = C > F$ (both Rules and the policy committee in question have similar right-of-center median preferences), then one again expects that the majority-party roll rate on bills reported from conservative committees should exceed 50 percent. One can thus claim that the CPG/committee government plus a self-interested Rules Committee lacks conclusion validity.

What if failure to meet "the condition" leads to a purely atomistic legislature, dominated by the median legislator? In such a case, one again expects a majority-party roll rate in excess of 50 percent (given the assumption that the distribution of status quo points is either symmetric or skewed toward the majority party). Thus, one can state that the CPG/floor government model lacks conclusion validity.

More generally, let CPG/X stand for the theory in which X is what happens when "the condition" is not met. One can argue that any CPG/X for which X entails that the majority party's consequential roll rate is more than trivial lacks conclusion validity.

What if X = procedural cartel theory (PCT)? Is CPG/PCT a viable theory? Well, yes. This is what we think of as our theory. At times, this seems also to be what Aldrich has in mind. Consider the following passage from Aldrich (1995), describing what happens when the majority party is internally divided:

> In this case, the majority party might still be "strong," but it will be strong to the extent that it can ensure that the status quo remains in effect. A strong majority party would be primarily a blocking coalition. Having already "won" what they want to win and can win, they will seek to control the agenda and hold on to their already established gains. If the party is to be strong, then it will be strongly inactive. That means we should expect to see a strong party employing mechanisms that keep the gates closed. In other words, a strong party would be one that used the committee system heavily, probably by empowering committee chairs to be recalcitrant, or that empowered party leaders to exert substantial control over the floor agenda, or that did both.... This case is most likely sometime after a realignment. For example, after the two waves of New Deal legislation in the 1930's, the Democratic majority may have extracted nearly as much as it could in legislation. (Aldrich 1995: 223–4)

The view Aldrich expresses in this passage is consistent with our findings and previous descriptions. However, it seems at odds with Rohde's view expressed earlier. Moreover, it is not clear why, if parties can still be "strong" even when divided, there is a need for conditional party government. Two points follow.

First, if all one means by conditional party government is that when "the condition" is not met, party government assumes a different and more conservative character, then we agree. Second, even if there is this degree of agreement between CPG and our theory, the causal mechanism that Aldrich and Rohde (2001) stipulate differs in important ways from that which we envision here. Specifically, they focus on floor discipline:

> If members are independent entrepreneurs concerned about being reelected, they will be reluctant to delegate significant power to party leaders for fear that that power could be used to force them to support policies (or identify with policies) that would make them vulnerable. When a party is quite diverse, the risk that a significant number of members would be put in such a position is considerable. This is the insight and conclusion Mayhew offered, and CPG offers the same conclusion.
> (Aldrich and Rohde 2001: 275)

In this passage, the focus is on delegated powers being used to "force [members] to support policies ... that would make them vulnerable." That is, members fear party discipline being imposed on the floor, forcing them to cast votes that their opponents might exploit in the next election. Our focus is quite different. We believe that the powers delegated to party leaders are used primarily to select which issues are voted on and only secondarily to twist arms (and then just enough to win, as is discussed later). Thus, the primary causal mechanism is not issue-by-issue arm-twisting but rather deciding what issues will see the light of day to begin with.

## 10.4. FLOOR VOTING DISCIPLINE

The majority party will want the rules to delegate *some* positive agenda power to offices held by its senior partners. For example, if there is widespread agreement within the majority-party caucus that a particular bill is desirable, the party will want enough positive agenda power to be delegated to its officeholders so that they can push such a bill to the floor. Prior to adoption of Reed's rules, this condition was *not* met: nonprivileged bills on the calendars came to the floor under the "regular order" (basically, a first in, first out system); and breaking out of the regular-order straitjacket was difficult against determined opposition from the minority (see Chapter 4; Den Hartog 2004). After Reed's rules, however, the majority could push bills to the floor via privileged committees, via special rules, and via suspension of the rules – an array of positive agenda powers sufficient to enable the majority to advance a legislative agenda when there was widespread agreement within the party on that agenda.

It is at this point that the parties as floor-voting coalitions make an entrance into our theory. If all the party is doing is blocking changes to status quo policies that its members either agree to preserve or cannot agree on how to change, then it does not need much in the way of arm-twisting, cajoling, or rational argumentation in the run-up to floor votes. The majority party keeps unwanted issues off the agenda mostly by the *inaction* of its officeholders. Only occasionally will the minority challenge that inaction (e.g., through a discharge petition); even then, the minority's challenge will not often lead to a roll call vote. Thus, negative agenda control does not require a great deal of floor-voting discipline.

Positive agenda control is another matter. If the party wants to put a particular bill onto the floor, it may need a special rule – and there will often be votes on adopting the rule (and on the previous-question motion before rule adoption). Once on the floor, the party may need to fend off motions to amend or kill its bills (e.g., to table or to recommit them), and it will again need to marshal its troops on the floor in such efforts. Thus, floor discipline is a natural complement to positive agenda power.

We consider two specific predictions about floor discipline consistent with our general approach (i.e., consistent with the six assumptions articulated in Chapter 2). First, parties should exert some influence over their members' votes on the floor. Second, parties should exert only enough influence to win floor victories (expending effort and incurring costs to add unneeded votes is inefficient); they should not be interested in maximizing floor cohesion per se.

Both of these predictions find anecdotal support. Returning to our earlier discussion of the Republicans' efforts to pass Medicare legislation, we see that Speaker Dennis Hastert exerted tremendous influence over his members' floor votes and that he also corralled just enough votes to pass the legislation. In describing the events surrounding the passage of the legislation, Hastert noted that "the hallmark of effective [majority-party] leadership is one that can deliver the votes" (Hastert 2004: 250). He then described exactly how he obtained the few votes that his party needed to win:

> At one point my side had 185 votes. We had to get to 218. Going over the names, all I had left were no's. When you face a problem like that, you don't accept its apparent hopelessness. You don't let it overwhelm you. You go after it incrementally, talking to Members about their votes individually, persuading them to change.
>
> (Hastert 2004: 264)

Such anecdotal evidence suggests that there is significant party influence in roll call voting. In what follows, we present more systematic evidence of this phenomenon.

### 10.4.1. How Much do Parties Influence Their Members' Votes?

Our theory does not predict that floor voting discipline in the House will be nil, just that it will be secondary to agenda manipulation. In this section, we consider whether there is detectable party discipline in the U.S. House.

Arnold (1990: 226) probably spoke for many scholars when he noted that, "whenever legislators see a conflict between making themselves look good and making their party look good they naturally choose the former, for . . . they can always do more to affect their own images than they can to affect their party's performance in office." Such a statement implicitly downplays the ability of the parties to punish their members for pursuing individual benefits at the expense of collective benefits – something that Arnold made explicit by elsewhere citing Mayhew's (1974) discussion of party debility and member independence.[6] We (Cox and McCubbins 1993) took a different view. We agreed that members are always tempted to make themselves look good, even at the expense of their parties. However, we argued that the parties exist precisely to overcome the electoral externalities that copartisans would impose upon one another, were each unconstrained. Such a position naturally entailed a concern for the resources that parties deployed, such as committee assignments, to affect members' incentives on the margin.

So which view better fits the facts? We have long known that party correlates highly with roll call voting behavior – indeed, it is prominently cited as the single best predictor of members' votes (Poole and Rosenthal 1997; Snyder and Groseclose 2001). However, if parties consist of like-minded legislators

---

[6] The view that congressional parties do not influence their members' behavior, of course, predates Mayhew. A prominent earlier example would be Schattschneider (1942: 196).

facing similar constituencies, a strong correlation would arise, even if parties had no independent influence on their members' votes. So how can one detect the independent influence of party, if any, on roll call voting?

This methodological problem has been clear for some time (see, e.g., Kingdon 1973; Cox 1987: 29; Krehbiel 2000) but only recently has serious progress been made in solving it. We discuss five different approaches next.

First, if parties do not influence their members, then congresspersons' voting behavior should not change when they switch parties. Yet analyses of party switchers over the postwar era have found very substantial changes in their voting behavior, toward greater agreement with their new party (McCarty, Poole, and Rosenthal 2001; Hager and Talbert 2000; Nokken 2000). The weakness of this evidence is that there have been fewer than 20 postwar party switchers. Nonetheless, the changes in behavior documented have been large and consistent enough so that they are statistically significant at conventional levels.

Second, suppose no member casts "tough" (i.e., electorally costly) votes for his party. Given this premise, if one member is more loyal to his party than another on key votes, this can only be because his constituency is more in tune with the party's position. Such loyalist members will be no more likely to lose votes at the next election, or suffer actual defeat, than less loyal members. Yet Jacobson (1996) finds systematic correlations between party loyalty on key issues and electoral performance: loyalists pay a price. Moreover, Brady, Canes-Wrone, and Cogan (2000) find that "losing Democratic incumbents generally vote too liberally for their district [while] losing Republican incumbents vote too conservative[ly]" (p. 179).

Why would members vote too liberally or too conservatively for their constituents, thus incurring electoral risk? Perhaps the answer is that party leaders compensate electoral risk takers with internal side payments, such as better committee assignments. We (Cox and McCubbins 1993) provide evidence that more loyal Democrats do receive better assignments (and review the literature to the early 1990s). More recently, Brady and Burchett (2001) find that members who vote more loyally *than their district characteristics suggest they should* are rewarded with better committee assignments.[7]

Third, if parties do not influence their members' votes, then members should be no more likely to support their parties than would be expected on the basis of the positions they advocate in their election campaigns. However, Ansolabehere et al. (2001) find that members of the U.S. House in the 103rd–105th Congresses were more likely to support their party than would be expected from their responses to electoral questionnaires on about 45 percent of all roll calls. The weakness of this evidence is that it is confined to three recent Congresses – those

---

[7] Another recent study corroborates the notion that members exchange loyalty for better assignment probabilities. Stratmann (2000) finds that more junior legislators – those more likely to still be in the queue for power committee appointments – are also more likely to be loyal. As Stratmann includes legislator-specific fixed effects, his results are unlikely to reflect mere preference phenomena.

for which a suitable electoral questionnaire could be found. The strength is that the authors examine all roll calls and not only find significant party effects on a substantial subset of them but, more important, they find party effects in precisely those areas where partisan theories would expect such effects to arise. In particular, the impact of party is the strongest on close votes, on votes affecting the value of the party reputation, and on procedural votes.

Fourth, if parties do not influence their members' votes, then the aggregate difference in voting behavior between the parties, as measured by the standard Rice index of party dissimilarity, should be just what one expects on the basis of members' ideologies (technically, their ideal points) and the nature of the issue at hand (technically, the issue cutpoint). Yet Cox and Poole (2002) find that, in almost every Congress from 1877 to 1999, larger-than-expected Rice indices crop up far more frequently than can be explained by a null model of no party influence. The advantage of the Cox–Poole estimator is that it is based solely on roll call voting data and thus covers by far the largest time span of the studies canvassed thus far.

Fifth, Cox and Poole (2002) also find that the parties tend to vote differently than expected on precisely the sorts of roll calls that procedural cartel theory would predict: procedural votes (e.g., motions of the previous question, motions to table, or adoptions of special rules), organizational votes (e.g., the election of the speaker; regulation of committee staff, funding, and procedure; and adoption of House rules), and label-defining votes (e.g., votes on taxes).

In sum, the conventional wisdom among congressional scholars has long been that legislative parties in the U.S. Congress are substantially weaker than their European counterparts. Indeed, a prominent and perhaps the dominant view has long been that U.S. parties are so weak as to be analytically negligible. Among many others one might cite, consider Mayhew (1974: 100): "Party 'pressure' to vote one way or another is minimal. Party 'whipping' hardly deserves the name. Leaders in both houses have a habit of counseling members to 'vote their constituencies'." More recently, Mayhew (2000: 252) has reiterated his skepticism about the efficacy of party pressure, even in the more partisan 90s: "I have not seen any evidence that today's congressional party leaders 'whip' or 'pressure' their members more often or effectively than did their predecessors 30 years ago. Instead, today's pattern of high roll-call loyalty seems to owe to a post-1960s increase in each party's 'natural' ideological homogeneity across its universe of home constituencies."

The works cited here are among the first systematic studies that have seriously addressed the methodological problem of separating party effects from mere coincidence of opinion. Taken together, these studies show that parties do significantly affect the voting behavior of their members. Moreover, party effects are more likely to arise on precisely those roll calls that party theories would expect. Finally, party loyalty is, as party theorists have claimed, part of an exchange relationship: it is costly to members to supply loyalty (i.e., they run electoral risks by voting with their parties); thus, members expect and receive something in return (e.g., better committee assignments).

## 10.4.2. Buying Just Enough Votes to Win

When a party *successfully* influences one of its members' votes this typically means that the member will cast a vote at odds with her constituents' opinions.[8] Casting such votes, however, entails electoral risk for the member. We have assumed (Assumption 1 in Chapter 2) that legislators value majority status. Thus, party leaders should be reluctant to "force" members to vote with the party, as such votes lower the probability that that member will be reelected, hence the probability that the party will secure a majority. There has to be a payoff to changing the member's vote, large enough to offset the damage. In our theory, the payoff has to be a legislative accomplishment that enhances the party's legislative record, hence its reputation, hence its collective electoral performance (Assumptions 2 and 3). Since legislative accomplishments imply actually *winning* legislative votes, the majority party's leadership should often be interested only in corralling just enough votes to win, not in maximizing the party's cohesion. (The exceptions to this rule of thumb would arise when the party decided that presenting a united front was a valuable signal in itself.) In other words, we believe U.S. party leaders wish to allow their followers maximal freedom in voting, subject only to the party being able to push its bills through the legislative process successfully.

Is there evidence that such a practice is common in the U.S. House? Yes. King and Zeckhauser (2003) have an extensive discussion of this practice, and we refer the reader there for the details.

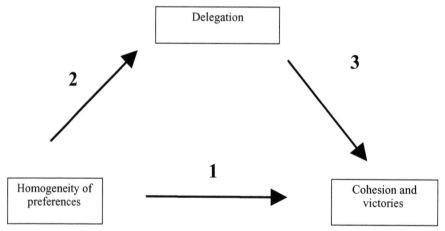

FIGURE 10.1. The consequences of increasing homogeneity

---

[8] If the party and constituency agreed, there would typically be no need to exert any influence, except perhaps in the case of strong personal beliefs at odds with both party and constituency.

## 10.5. CONCLUSION

We conclude by noting a key difference between conditional party government theory and procedural cartel theory. The main logical sequence in conditional party government theory is as follows: more homogeneous majority parties delegate more (positive) power to their central leaders, and this delegated power is used to push a legislative program through to passage (see Figure 10.1). Procedural cartel theory differs in arguing that even the least homogeneous majorities delegate a substantial amount of *blocking* power to their central and committee leaders, sufficient to ensure that the bulk of bills propose to move policy toward the majority and that the majority is rarely rolled.

To put the point another way, consider a time period during which both the majority and minority parties are internally divided, so that the "condition" in conditional party government is not met – for example, the heyday of the conservative coalition (1937–60). As we understand it, conditional party government theory in this case predicts that members will act in a primarily bipartisan or nonpartisan mode, each pursuing his own conception of good legislation, cutting deals with any available partners. Now imagine that some majority of members prefers that a particular bill be passed, and that this majority *excludes* a majority of the majority party. Presumably, conditional party government theory would agree with partyless models in this instance and predict that the bill in question would pass, thereby rolling the majority party. In contrast, procedural cartel theory would predict that the bill would never see the light of day on the floor, at least not in a form that would be opposed unsuccessfully by a majority of the majority party. As we have seen, this central prediction is borne out.

# 11

# Conclusion

In this book, we have argued for a fundamental rethinking of how political parties operate in Congress. Traditional conceptions of parties, stretching back to the theory of "responsible party government" (e.g., Ranney 1951; American Political Science Association 1950), focus on the ability of party leaders to command loyalty from their rank and file. In this view, parties matter only if they can vote as cohesive blocs, as they do in most Western European countries. Scholarship in this tradition focuses on the sociological and institutional devices by which loyalty might be maintained, on the tension that members feel between party loyalty and service to their constituents, and on documenting the extent to which parties are indeed able to hold their lines.

The key result in this long line of research is negative. As forcibly argued over 60 years ago by E. E. Schattschneider (1942: 131–2): "when all is said, it remains true that . . . *the parties are unable to hold their lines in a controversial public issue when the pressure is on.* [This is] *the most important single fact concerning the American parties.* He who knows this fact, and knows nothing else, knows more about American parties than he who knows everything except this fact" (italics in original).

The prevalence of this Schattschneiderian view led generations of researchers, from mid century to the 1990s, to turn their analytic focus away from the parties to individual legislators, standing committees, interest groups, and other possible actors on the legislative stage. Many studied the bipartisan alliances that emerged on the floor, especially the so-called *conservative coalition* (a combination of conservative Southern Democrats and Republicans). Indeed, some (e.g., Shelley 1983) viewed the conservative coalition, rather than the Democratic majority, as ruling the congressional roost from 1937 until the mid 1970s. The logical culmination of this scholarly emphasis on party debility emerged in the 1970s, 1980s, and 1990s, when scholars built formal models of Congress that explicitly omitted political parties as inappropriate or unnecessary "analytic units" (e.g., Mayhew 1974; Weingast and Marshall 1988; Krehbiel 1998).

Coexisting uneasily with this vein of research deemphasizing parties was an equally long tradition of scholarship that focused on the parties' internal organization and legislative behavior. In this tradition were both institutional studies – for example, how the parties chose their leaders (Sinclair 1983), how the whip organizations operated (Ripley 1964), various aspects of leadership strategy (Sinclair 1995; Jones 1968) – and behavioral studies – especially those documenting the ups and downs of "party voting" across congressional history (Cooper, et al. 1977; Brady, Cooper, and Hurley 1979). Many scholars writing about parties took it for granted that the parties were important players on the congressional stage. Nonetheless, some – perhaps most – of those working on parties tacitly acknowledged or explicitly agreed with the Schattschneiderian judgment that "it is impossible to speak realistically of party responsibility for legislation in the United States" (Odegard and Helms 1938: 153).

In this book, we have sided with the partisan tradition in congressional scholarship but sought to add a new edge to it. We argue that the key events of the legislative process do not occur on the floor of Congress, when members vote for or against the bills that are put on the floor agenda. Rather, the key events occur beforehand, when senior members of the majority party determine which bills will be considered on the floor and which will not. Parties matter, in our view, not so much because they influence how their members vote on bills (although they do), but rather because the majority party controls which bills their (and other) members have an opportunity to vote on to begin with.

Although our claim that the prefloor stages of the legislative process are both crucial and dominated by the majority party's senior partners resonates with much of the previous literature taking a partisan perspective, the dominance of traditional floor-centric theories has been such that some of the most fundamental consequences of majority-party agenda control have not been investigated. By examining all bills reaching the floor of the House of Representatives from the 45th to 105th Congress (1877–1999), we show something surprising. The majority party almost never suffers the *passage* of a bill that most of its members dislike, with *enactment* of such bills being even rarer. In many Congresses (9 out of 23), the majority party literally suffers *no* enactment that most of its members oppose. Further, in the remaining 14 Congresses in which the majority party does suffer a consequential roll, it is rolled on average only 1.7 times. These simple facts, we would argue, are more important to know than Schattschneider's single fact; they speak more clearly to who controls the legislative process.

Of course, we do not wish to leave matters at symbolic facts any more than did Schattschneider. In *Legislative Leviathan* and *Setting the Agenda*, we have sought to explore the mechanics of party government, in addition to documenting its strengths and weaknesses. In the remainder of this conclusion, we survey some of the issues that we have raised and results we have established.

## 11.2. HOW MUCH AGENDA POWER WILL A MAJORITY TAKE?

In our view, a political party always has an incentive to take more key legislative resources, such as high offices and staff. However, in democratic systems, parties are restrained in their pursuit of office and emolument, by the anticipated reactions of the electorate. Even in artificially contrived (experimental) situations in which humans allocate resources among themselves, norms of "fairness," proportionality, and the like seem to play an important role (Frohlich et al. 1971; Smith 2003). Such norms, we believe, translate into the political realm. They do not, however, always determine outcomes. As we argue in the second edition of *Legislative Leviathan*, political parties take super-proportional shares of resources, when those resources are worth the risk of public criticism that taking them entails. Exactly what share is judged the maximum consistent with prevailing norms varies from system to system, but the tendency for majority coalitions to take super-proportional shares of internal legislative offices is quite general, extending even into consensus democracies (Carroll et al. 2004).

In the case of the U.S. House, we have argued that, since the adoption of Reed's rules, offices wielding special agenda powers have been crucial resources of which the majority party has consistently taken a controlling share. Although we have not attempted to explain why Reed's rules were adopted – on that, see Den Hartog (2004) – we have sought to document their status as the central watershed in House procedural history. To put it simply, we believe that House procedure prior to Reed's rules set up a legislative game in which both parties had potent abilities to delay, and hence could bargain to have their views reflected in any bills reaching the floor. Reed's rules gravely and permanently weakened the minority's ability to delay (most famously, by outlawing the "disappearing quorum"), and substantially and permanently improved the majority's ability to put bills on the floor (chiefly through enabling the Rules Committee to report special rules).[1] These changes, as we documented in Chapters 4 and 6, abruptly decreased the majority's roll rate, increased the minority's roll rate, and increased the proportion of final-passage bills proposing to move policy toward the majority (leftward if the Democrats held the gavel, rightward if the Republicans did).

## 11.3. THE TWO TYPES OF AGENDA POWER

In exploring agenda power in the U.S. House, we have found it useful to classify special agenda powers into two main categories, positive and negative. Positive agenda powers allow their wielders to push bills through the gauntlet of legislative stages to a final-passage vote on the floor. Negative agenda powers allow their wielders to block bills from reaching a final-passage vote on the floor.

---

[1] We have argued that innovations in the Senate have accomplished the latter of Reed's effects but not the former.

Since the adoption of Reed's rules, the rules of the U.S. House have assured a substantial advantage in setting the agenda for the majority party, chiefly by setting up an "electoral system" in which the majority party can always win a super-proportional share of the most important offices (e.g., committee chairs, seats on conference committees). However, the mix of positive and negative agenda powers has varied, as has the degree to which agenda powers have been centralized or decentralized.

We have argued that changes in the homogeneity of preference within the majority party have driven the mix of positive and negative powers. The more heterogeneous are preferences within the majority party, the more dangerous it is for the party to distribute positive agenda power, since the possessors of that power may push bills to the floor that will then displease substantial portions of their copartisans. The more homogeneous are preferences within the majority party, the more dangerous it is for the party to distribute negative agenda power, since the possessors of that power may block bills that would please substantial portions of their copartisans. Thus, *as the majority party becomes more homogenous, it is more likely to adjust the balance of positive and negative agenda powers in favor of the former.*

### 11.3.1. The Bedrock of Party Government: Negative Agenda Power

Given the precept just articulated, there is a sense in which negative agenda power forms the bedrock of party government. Even when the majority is internally divided, our theory predicts that the rules of the House will ensure that the majority is able to block bills it dislikes, and that it will exact a minimal fiduciary standard from its officeholders that is essentially negative (viz., not pushing bills that would roll the party). Even coalition partners who disagree on fundamental policy issues can agree to take a super-proportional share of agenda-setting offices. However, such partners will want to ensure that no office (not under their control) has proposal power, lest one or more of their partners use that power to promote bills that will roll them.

### 11.3.2. The Superstructure of Party Government: Positive Agenda Power

As the various elements of the majority party become more alike in preference, they can agree on two improvements to the basic model of party government: first, adjusting the rules to endow more officers with positive agenda powers; second, raising the fiduciary standard expected of those officers, by adding a requirement that they proactively aid party measures.

### 11.4. AGENDA POWER AND PARTY GOVERNMENT

Thus, there are two stories in the edifice of party government. The first, or bedrock, story consists in securing a super-proportional share of offices, securing a veto for the party, and successfully imposing a negative fiduciary standard on the party's officeholders. The second, or superstructural, story consists in enhancing the positive agenda powers of the party's officeholders and successfully imposing a positive fiduciary standard upon them.

The previous literature on responsible party government and on conditional party government has stressed the second story at the expense of the first. In these theories, the only party government worth the name is one in which the majority party or coalition enacts a substantial program of new legislation, successfully overcoming any internal disagreements along the way. If a party lacks sufficient internal preference similarity, and also lacks the big guns of discipline (e.g., denial of renomination or expulsion from the party), then – in both the responsible party and conditional party government theories – party government falls away, to be replaced by something else: committee government, floor government, or whatever.

In our view, party government continues, even when the majority party is internally divided. It continues in three main senses: The majority party still takes a super-proportional share of key offices, the majority party still has a substantial advantage over the minority in blocking legislation, and the majority party's officeholders still obey a minimal fiduciary standard (that of not using their powers to roll their own party).

By envisioning two stories of party government, our conception of responsible party government demands less of the governing party than does the traditional conception. To switch metaphors, traditional theories require the majority party to be squarely in the driver's seat and fully in control of the brake, the steering wheel, and the accelerator. In our theory, the majority party always controls the brake and the steering: It can stop bills from reaching the floor and, hence, control the direction of possible policy movements. However, it may not always be able to step on the accelerator. Internal divisions within the majority, combined with unfavorable rules (in the Senate), may prevent the legislative machine from moving forward in the direction in which the majority has pointed it.

## 11.5. NEGATIVE AGENDA POWER: CONSEQUENCES

### 11.5.1. Background

The recent literature on legislatures has highlighted the importance of veto players – for example, see Heller (1997), Krehbiel (1998), Cox and McCubbins (2001), Tsebelis (2002), and the literature cited therein. Most models of veto power focus on relatively distal consequences, such as the rate at which laws are produced, arguing that the more veto players there are, and the more diverse their preferences, the fewer will be the laws that can pass through the legislative process (Tsebelis 2002; Krehbiel 1998; Döring 1995).

In this book, we have instead focused on several simpler and more immediate consequences of veto power. First, if an agent has veto power, then he should never suffer unwanted policy changes (although he may want some changes that he cannot get). Second, if an agent has veto power, then all bills must propose to move policy closer to that agent's ideal policy.

Before we review the evidence bearing on these predictions, we make two interpretive points. First, in the simplest version of our model, negative agenda power means the ability to block bills from ever appearing on the plenary agenda (presidential strong-arming or public opinion notwithstanding). In the more nuanced version of our model, negative agenda power entails at least the following moves: blocking outright; allowing bills onto the floor but assuring their demise there (quasi-rolls); packaging sour pills with sweeteners and allowing the (acceptable) omnibus to pass; allowing the bill onto the floor, voting against it unsuccessfully, and relying on the Senate or president to kill it (inconsequential rolls).

Second, we stress that these moves – all effective in preventing actual policy change contrary to the wishes of the bulk of the majority party – are not necessarily made by the top party leadership. Many readers of our first book, through faults in our exposition, came away with the impression that we were arguing that the House has consistently featured an iron-fisted central leadership, à la Uncle Joe Cannon. In this book, we have tried to express more clearly our agnosticism regarding the distribution of agenda power *within* the majority party, insisting only that the vast bulk of the rule-based ability to manipulate the agenda inheres in offices held by members of the majority party. When combined with two crucial assertions – (1) the rule-based advantages of majority-party officeholders are collectively substantial, and (2) majority-party officeholders are significantly more responsive to their own party (above and beyond mere congruence of preference) – our argument is set in train.

### 11.5.2. Evidence

Now consider the evidence marshaled in Part II of the book. We would stress five major findings consistent with our view of House organization.

First, as noted previously, upon the adoption of Reed's rules, there was an abrupt, large, and permanent increase in the proportion of final-passage bills proposing to move policy toward the majority party, an abrupt and permanent decline in the majority party's roll rate on final passage, and an abrupt and permanent increase in the minority party's roll rate. In our view, Reed's rules established the modern structure of agenda power in the House and installed within that structure significant advantages for the majority party. These advantages – at least those affecting the majority party's negative agenda power – have changed only marginally since the 1890s.

Second, since the adoption of Reed's rules, the majority party has been rolled very rarely. Looking at each of the key agenda-setting steps in the House's legislative process, Table 11.1 displays both the overall roll rate of the majority party (number of rolls divided by number of votes) and its consequential roll rate (number of rolls on bills ultimately enacted, divided by number of votes). As can be seen, these rates are low at every stage: standing committee reports to the House (0.07 and 0 percent), Rules Committee reports to the House (N/A), floor votes on the previous question for special rules (2.5 percent and N/A), floor votes on special rule adoption (1.2 and 0.3 percent), floor votes to pass bills (1.7 and 0.8 percent), conference committee votes to report bills to the House (0 and 0 percent), and floor votes to adopt conference reports (1.4 and 1.4 percent).

It is worth noting that there may be bills that should have qualified as consequential rolls that we were not able to capture as such. For example, the majority party may have expected a bill to become law should it get beyond the House, and thus made genuine (but unsuccessful) efforts to stop it, only to have it unexpectedly die at some other stage of the process. These instances, if they exist, should count against our theory because they do not conform to the "costly blocking" amendment that we offer in Chapter 6; however, we are not able to determine systematically if and when this occurs (although we did try). Still, from our review, it seems unlikely that there would be enough of these cases to cast doubt on the majority party's negative agenda control, particularly given that the upper bound on these types of classification errors is defined by the consistently low roll rate presented in the left-hand column of Table 11.1.

Third, most majority-party rolls in the postwar era occur under divided government. We assume that presidents can raise the salience of certain bills by "going public" (cf. Kernell 1997), thus raising the cost to the House majority party of denying the bill consideration on the floor. In other words, even though the president does not have any formal power to set the House's agenda, he can make it electorally costly to block certain bills. In some cases, the House majority can assure such a bill's demise on the floor through delay and other tactics. In other cases, it may strike a deal with the president, allowing the bill to be scheduled and passed, with mostly minority votes supporting it, in return for other considerations (e.g., the president's not vetoing another piece of legislation). In yet other cases, albeit rare, the president may rout the majority, getting much of what he wanted without needing to logroll.

Fourth, considering bills that reached a final-passage vote in the post-Reed Congresses studied here (51st, 53rd–105th), on average 81 percent of them proposed to move policy leftward, when the Democrats held the gavel, while 84 percent of them proposed rightward moves, when the Republicans held a majority.

Fifth, the main determinants of Congress-to-Congress variations in the proportion of bills moving policy leftward (after Reed's rules) are the location of the majority party's median and the lagged floor median. The lagged floor median serves as a crude indicator of where the status quo policies are located. The current majority party's median indicates the direction in which the majority would like to move policy.

Some of these findings are consistent with the floor or pivot models, the two alternative models we consider. But only the Cartel Agenda Model is consistent with the full range of evidence.

TABLE 11.1. *Majority-Party Roll Rates Throughout the Legislative Process*

| Stage in Legislative Process | Majority Party's Roll Rate<br>Time period<br>Data covered<br>Relevant chapter | Majority Party's Consequential Roll Rate<br>Time period<br>Data covered<br>Relevant chapter |
|---|---|---|
| Vote on floor to adopt conference report | 1.4%<br>83rd–105th Congresses<br>All conference reports | 1.4%<br>83rd–105th Congresses<br>All conference reports |
| Vote in conference committee to report bill to House | 0%<br>96th–104th Congresses<br>All conferences<br>See Hennig (1997) | 0%<br>96th–104th Congresses<br>All conferences<br>See Hennig (1997) |
| Vote on floor to pass bill | 1.7%<br>83rd–105th Congresses<br>All joint resolutions<br>See Chapter 6 | 0.8%<br>83rd–105th Congresses<br>All joint resolutions<br>See Chapter 6 |
| Vote on floor to adopt rule | 1.2%<br>54th–105th Congresses<br>See Chapter 7, Table 7.2 | 0.3%<br>54th–105th Congresses<br>See Chapter 7, Table 7.2 |
| Vote on floor to adopt previous question on motion to adopt special rule | 2.5%[a]<br>83rd –106th Congresses<br>All votes on previous question on motion to adopt special rules<br>See Chapter 4, Section 4.2.6.3.6 | N/A |
| Vote in Rules Committee to report special rule to House | N/A[b] | N/A |
| Vote in standing committee to report bill to House[c] | 0.07%<br>84th, 86th, 88th, 90th, 92nd, 94th, 96th, and 98th Congresses<br>All bills reported from standing committee<br>See Chapter 8 | 0%<br>84th, 86th, 88th, 90th, 92nd, 94th, 96th, and 98th Congresses<br>All bills reported from standing committee<br>See Chapter 8 |

[a] See Finocchiaro and Rohde (2002). This may overcount consequentiality as we cannot delineate between consequential and inconsequential rolls from this data.

[b] Votes in the Rules Committee present another good test of the various models of legislative organization and would be worth examining; however, we could not find systematic data for such analysis.

[c] Votes in this case are signatures on dissenting or majority opinions in bill report, as explained in Chapter 8.

## 11.6. COMPARATIVE THEMES

Many of the themes we have struck in this study of the U.S. House of Representatives apply, in varying degree, to other democratic assemblies. Majority coalitions worldwide take a larger-than-proportional share of the most important offices wielding agenda power. Majority coalitions worldwide combine efforts to wield agenda-setting powers with efforts to discipline their members' votes, in order to steer their legislative agenda through to passage (and ultimately enactment). Majority coalitions worldwide face an architectural decision, regarding how much positive and how much negative agenda power to delegate to their respective officeholders. Majority coalitions worldwide ensure that at least the bedrock of party government – the ability to block – is secured. They do this either by preventing bills from reaching a floor vote to begin with, thus economizing on discipline but exercising (at some cost) their agenda powers, or by defeating bills that do reach a floor vote, thus economizing on agenda power but exercising (at some cost) discipline.

Our preliminary research suggests that majority coalitions always employ agenda power to some degree; none relies solely on discipline, as traditional views of responsible party government seem to suggest. Moreover, if a majority coalition forms, then it will take a controlling share of whatever high offices and special agenda-setting powers are to be had. If the coalition's discipline is good, it may need only to take a proportional share of some agenda-setting offices. However, the worse its disciplinary abilities are, the more it will seek to supplement them with super-proportional shares of all key agenda-setting offices. Regardless of the coalition's disciplinary abilities, we believe they will seek first to ensure good negative control over the legislative agenda. Having secured such control, majority coalitions can avoid issues that would split them, provide cover to their members on tough votes, and otherwise aid their cause.[2]

In future work, we hope to further explore the interplay between coalitional government and agenda power. Among the key topics for investigation, we would note the following: the role of minority governments, the balance struck between agenda power and discipline, the mix of positive and negative agenda power, the connection between agenda power (and the structure thereof) and legislative productivity, and committee influence.

## 11.7. THE FINAL WORD

The stakes involved in party government are high. When political parties are weak and "irresponsible," the most important integrating and coordinating mechanism in democratic politics does not work. Absent effective political parties, the more parochial forces in political life have freer rein, with consequences that have been decried in the *Federalist No. 10* (Hamilton, Madison,

---

[2] On agenda power in assemblies other than the U.S. House, see, e.g., Huber 1996; Döring 1995; Amorim Neto et al. 2003; Cox et al. 2000; Campbell et al. 2002.

and Jay 1961 [1787]), in the extensive literature on subgovernments and iron triangles (see Cox and McCubbins 1993: Chapter 1) and in work on interest-group liberalism (Lowi 1969; McConnell 1966) – to cite just a few selected gelid chips from an enormous scholarly iceberg. As Bryce (1888) noted long ago, "No one has shown how representative government could be worked without [political parties]."

The clear and present dangers of "factions," interest groups, special favors, cronyism, and many other kindred ills – all rooted in self-interest construed too narrowly and pursued too vigorously – have simultaneously fueled scholars' admiration for parties' role in theory and sharpened their disappointment at parties' performance in practice. Indeed, in the American literature, parties have often been judged completely unsuccessful in their integrative function – helpless to prevent and often conniving in various special-interest feasts at public expense.

We argue that the conditions required to sustain a form of responsible party government are different and less severe than those traditionally demanded. The traditional standard requires that a majority party be able to marshal brute voting strength on the floor of the assembly and use that strength to pursue its electoral platform. Our standard requires that a majority party delegate agenda powers to its senior partners and that those senior partners employ their off-the-floor powers to set the agenda in a way that protects the party's broader interests. We believe that agenda power is the bedrock of party government – not just in the United States, as we have argued here, but also in many other assemblies worldwide. But that is the topic for another book.

# Appendix

## Construct Validity and External Validity

In this appendix, we address the construct validity and external validity of our theory and measures.[1] We also respond to an alternative theory recently developed by Krehbiel.

### A.1. CONSTRUCT VALIDITY

Our ability to draw legitimate (believable) inferences from our results depends on our ability to demonstrate construct validity – that is, that our empirical measures reflect accurately the theoretical notions they are intended to capture (Trochim 2001: 64). This aspect of construct validity is often misunderstood, for it is widely believed that measures should reflect the world around us. However, valid measures must reflect one's theory, and one's theory, in turn, must be an analogy to the real world. Thus, construct validity raises questions about how to measure *theoretical*, not real-world, constructs.

### A.1.1. Face Validity

The most basic type of construct validity is face validity. As an example of how our measures satisfy face validity, consider a party roll. For this measure to be facially valid, it must appear "on its face" to be a good translation of the theoretical construct that it purports to measure (Trochim 2001: 67).

What is the theoretical construct that a party roll measures? The answer, in short, is that a roll measures legislators' ability (or inability) to block bills from progressing through the legislative process. Our model of legislative politics

---

[1] Our measures are derived from public sources, such as the House Journal or House Calendars, or the digital collection of House roll call votes archived by the Interuniversity Consortium on Political Research (ICPSR). Regarding the reliability and reproducibility of our results, see our web page at *www.settingtheagenda.com* for datasets, programs, lab notes, and replication materials.

(along with many others) assumes that a given legislator or group of legislators (e.g., a committee or party or faction) has the ability to block bills that they dislike. In each instance of a roll, a legislator or group of legislators opposed a bill that passed nonetheless – a finding that indicates a lack of blocking ability. Rolls and roll rates, therefore, are, on their face, measures of (lack of) blocking ability.

Although we maintain that our measures of rolls and roll rates are valid on their face, we recognize that our measures are imperfect. In our idealized model (Chapter 3), we define rolls in terms of members' *preferences*. For example, let us say that a particular legislator is *theoretically rolled* on a particular final-passage vote if (a) the bill in question passes and yet (b) the legislator prefers the status quo to the bill. Similarly, let us say that the majority party is *theoretically rolled* if a bill passes, even though a majority of the majority party's total membership prefers the status quo to the bill.

We cannot directly observe each legislator's true preference between the status quo and the bill on each vote. Thus, we use *how each member voted* as an indicator of her preference. For our present purposes, let us say that the majority party is rolled – or, in this appendix, *observationally rolled* – if a majority of its voting members vote against the bill in question, yet the bill passes.

Despite the impossibility of using theoretical rolls to measure blocking ability, we maintain that observed rolls are a valid measure of this construct.[2] This use of votes as a revelation of legislators' preferences is largely justified by the fact that members have few, if any, opportunities for strategic behavior on a final-passage vote. Thus, most final-passage votes, most of the time, will reveal legislators' true preferences for a bill or the status quo.

### A.1.2. Convergent and Divergent Validity

Going beyond the face validity of our measures, we need to establish that the pattern of observations on our key dependent and independent variables matches the pattern expected by our theory. To do this, we show that our measures are related to measures that our theory suggests they should be related to (convergent validity) and unrelated to measures that our theory suggests they should not be related to (divergent validity). In what follows, we discuss the convergent and divergent validity of our two key dependent variables – roll rates and policy moves.

As for the convergent validity of roll rates, we have shown in our previous work that roll rates are correlated with measures to which they should be related. Specifically, we have shown that they are correlated with: being in and out of government (Cox et al. 2000; Cox and McCubbins 2002; Amorim Neto et al. 2003), holding a veto (Cox et al. 2000: Chapter 7), having a copartisan hold a veto (Cox et al. 2000: Chapter 7), and switching from the minority to

---

[2] We refer the reader to Poole and Rosenthal (1997) and Poole (2005) for a discussion of the construct validity of their measures of the spatial locations of political actors. For an analysis of measuring legislators' preferences, see Cox and Poole (2002).

majority party and vice versa (Den Hartog and Monroe 2004). Roll rates are also highly correlated with win rates $(-0.9293)$,[3] as defined by Lawrence et al. (1999, in press).[4]

Now consider the divergent validity of roll rates. Roll rates should not be related to (1) preference homogeneity within the majority party, (2) the number of votes in a given session, or (3) the number of bills passed. Indeed, roll rates are not related with any of these other measures (bivariate correlations of $-0.28$, $-0.22$, and $-0.22$, respectively). Additionally, roll rates should not be related to the position of the House pivot, and indeed they are not (correlation of 0.18). Roll rates also should not be related to the specific party in the majority,[5] and they are not (correlation of $-0.03$). Thus, we have demonstrated that roll rates are characterized by both convergent and divergent validity.

As for leftward and rightward policy moves, we are able to show that they, too, have strong convergent and divergent validity.[6] For example, leftward and rightward policy moves should be (and are) correlated with the identity of the majority and minority party and with changes in the identity of the majority party. Indeed, the correlation between $P_{Left}$ and Democratic control of the House is 0.87. Policy moves should also be related to the majority and minority

---

[3] When comparing Lawrence et al.'s (1999, in press) dataset with our own, we found that for 96th–105th Congresses there were 21 observations in their dataset that were not included in ours and 87 observations in our dataset that were not included in theirs. All told, however, there were 4,336 observations in common, and a regression of roll rates on win rates produced an $R$-squared of 0.8635 and a $p$-value of 0. 

[4] The relationship between win rates, roll rates, and disappointments is quite precise. Consider the following table:

|  |  | Vote of Member | |
|---|---|---|---|
|  |  | Yes | No |
| Fate of bill | Win | Positive win | Roll |
|  | Loss | Disappointment | Negative win |

If defined on the same sample of bills, then (Positive win + Negative win + Disappointment + Roll)/Number of bills in the sample $= 1$. Lawrence et al. (1999, in press) do not use the same sample of bills as we do (they sample all votes rather than just final-passage votes). Nonetheless, we would expect a high correlation between the two measures, and we do in fact observe this.

[5] This is true in the U.S. House of Representatives, although it may not hold in a comparative context where parties have different means for controlling the agenda and different relationships to the executive and other chambers. These factors may influence roll rates; thus the theory must relate to the specific form of legislative organization.

[6] We also assessed the convergent validity of the proportion of bills moving policy toward the majority party in the Senate (a measure that we dub $SP_{maj}$). Specifically, $SP_{maj}$ should be positively related to minority roll rates in the Senate and negatively related to majority roll rates in the Senate. When we regressed $SP_{maj}$ on these two variables, we found that this is indeed the case (the coefficient of Senate minority roll rates is 0.376 and is significant at the 0.05 level, whereas the coefficient of Senate majority party roll rates is $-1.124$ and is significant at the 0.01 level). Thus, we have substantial evidence for the convergent validity of $SP_{maj}$.

party in the Senate (correlation between $P_{Left}$ and Democratic Senate $= 0.75$). Furthermore, policy moves should be related to party roll rates, win rates, and disappointment rates; in fact, there is a strong relationship among these measures. For example, when Democrats are the majority party, $P_{Left}$ and the majority's roll rate correlate at $-0.63$; when the Republicans are the majority, $P_{Left}$ and the majority's roll rate correlate at $0.83$. Given this pattern of correlations that theoretically should exist and that empirically do exist, we have considerable evidence for the convergent validity of our measure of policy moves.

We can also demonstrate the divergent validity of our measure of policy moves. The proportion of bills moving policy leftward should not be highly correlated with time (after the invention of Reed's rules). Our results demonstrate that it is not, with a correlation of only $0.34$ between $P_{Left}$ and a trend variable representing the 45th–105th Congresses.

## A.2. EXTERNAL VALIDITY

We have received several dozen reviews of our manuscript, and some raised important challenges and questions regarding the external validity of our theory. In this section, we provide a brief description of external validity and a response to some of these challenges.

Unlike construct validity, external validity is not an issue of measurement but one of theory. Like construct validity, external validity is about generalization. Specifically, external validity is the extent to which our conclusions are generalizable both to other periods and to other legislative bodies. Concerns about external validity imply that one questions our theory, either because our constructs are misspecified (i.e., we have oversimplified our model and are missing key relationships that ultimately affect our measures) or because our results stem from a biased sample. The presence of either problem suggests that we cannot draw the inferences that we do about the existence of agenda control in the U.S. House.

### A.2.1. Sample Bias

Although generalizing our model and measures of the post-Reconstruction House of Representatives to other legislatures (see Cox et al. 2000 for generalizations to Japan, the United Kingdom, and Sweden) or to the House at other times (see Den Hartog 2004) will be problematic, we do not see this as potential sample bias. Rather, each legislature offers a variation to our idealized model. Each legislature has different politics, operates under different constitutional and legal structures, and has adopted its own rules and practices. Thus, our idealized model and our measures need to be adapted to each new setting. We have, for example, noticed that in many legislatures (e.g., the Bundesrat in Germany, the House of Representatives in Texas) the key up-or-down, pass-or-fail vote on a bill is on the second reading and not the third reading as in the U.S. House. With such adaptations, our theory of agenda power and policy choice should be broadly applicable.

We have applied our idealized model in Chapter 3 to the post-Reconstruction Senate (Campbell et al. 2002; Chapters 4, 5, 6, and 9). Even though we have found much support for the idealized Cartel Agenda Model in these results, we have also found that, for various eras, we cannot reject the Floor Agenda Model, and that, for other eras, we cannot reject a dual-veto model. Changes in Senate rules and practices, changes in the behavior of Senators, and the relationship among the parties in the Senate, the majority party in the House, and the occupant of the White House seem to have broad, systematic effects on the organization of the Senate and the behavior of its members.

Others have challenged our sampling of observations in different ways. The direct translation of the final voting stage in the idealized models in Chapter 3, at least in the U.S. House, is third-reading or final-passage votes. Rather than sample all final-passage roll call votes in the House, we were asked to use a sample of significant legislation (as defined by Mayhew 1991), on the assumption that not all final-passage votes are created equal. This new sampling did not materially affect our results. We also examined final-passage votes on platform issues for the New Deal, Great Society, and Contract with America. Again, our results remained similar despite the new sampling. We also sampled only House-originated bills, only Senate-originated bills, bills that became law, and ones that did not. We examined substantive and nonbudget bills, as opposed to appropriations and budget bills, and we also sampled rules and procedure votes versus substantive policy votes. Again, the results we describe in the preceding chapters were unaffected, substantively, by any new sampling.

### A.2.2. Misspecification

The most frequent misspecification critique that we have received pertains to the dimensionality of our theory; that is, we rely on a one-dimensional spatial model, but some argue that congressional voting is not one-dimensional.[7] This critique often takes the following form: Suppose that there are two votes on two separate bills, both of which would roll the majority party; however, because there is a logroll between these bills (i.e., because two or more dimensions are implicitly or explicitly tied together in a legislative deal), the majority party is not observed to be rolled even though it would have been rolled, in theory, if these bills had been considered separately. If this situation were to occur, then we would underestimate majority-party rolls. On the flip side, if the logroll involves the minority party, then the minority party may appear to be rolled, even though they ultimately get the legislative package they desire. This would cause us to overestimate minority-party rolls. This extension to our idealized

---

[7] Poole (2005) and Poole and Rosenthal (1991, 1997) argue that voting in the U.S. Congress, for a significant part of its history, has indeed been unidimensional, although between 1937 and the mid 1980s there is a second dimension to congressional voting.

model could complicate our results and affect the generalizations that we draw from our analysis.

In this section, we respond to a variety of these multidimensional challenges that have been (or could be) leveled against roll rates. Several of these challenges in some form or another ask, "If a vote on a given bill does not produce a roll for one party or the other, can one safely conclude that the vote is consistent with that party having veto power?" Still others ask, "Is our theory of legislative organization a good analogy to the world?" In what follows, we marshal considerable theoretical and empirical evidence demonstrating that one can in fact answer these questions in the affirmative.

Specifically, we offer theoretical reasons for why logrolls, sophisticated voting, and side payments do not affect our general inferences; empirical evidence that abstentions and voice votes are infrequent events; and a mix of both theoretical and empirical responses to concerns about "constituency-forced voting" and "bad combinations." Note that our theoretical evidence demonstrates that even if the legislative process is multidimensional, our measures will almost always accurately characterize the existence of veto power if we consider the net effect of legislative changes. Further, our empirical evidence demonstrates that despite the logical possibility of such multidimensionality, we do not find evidence of its existence in the U.S. House of Representatives.


### A.2.2.1. *Theoretical Responses*

A.2.2.1.1. LOGROLLS. Let's consider logrolls first. It is easy to envision circumstances under which a legislator who truly possesses blocking power would nonetheless allow herself to be theoretically, but not observationally, rolled. In particular, suppose that one legislator with blocking power has cut a deal with another, whereby the first legislator allows bill $b_1$ to pass, even though she prefers the status quo $q_1$ on that issue, while the second legislator allows bill $b_2$ to pass, even though she prefers the status quo $q_2$. Their hypothesized vote in favor of the package reveals that each legislator prefers the package $(b_1, b_2)$ to the status quo pair $(q_1, q_2)$. Thus, each is pleased with the overall logroll, even though each finds part of it undesirable (which is the essence of a logroll). Their votes on $b_1$ and $b_2$ are not rolls, either theoretically or empirically, and therefore should not be considered rolls, as together they improve the overall approximation between each legislator's ideal point and the enacted policies. The legislators are theoretically rolled only in the narrow, and perhaps, mistaken view of taking one bill at a time.

Is the converse possible? That is, is it possible that a legislator will be observationally rolled, even though theoretically she is not rolled? If this is possible, then the legislator would not be voting her true preferences over the logroll and would, therefore, bear a cost for the strategic behavior to the extent that her vote was determinative. Thus, a pivotal player would not behave in a manner so as to be observationally rolled when she is theoretically not rolled, given the assumptions just described. Thus, for logrolls, theoretical and observed rolls coincide, and our observed measure, therefore, captures these theoretical extensions.

A.2.2.1.2. SOPHISTICATED VOTING. As we discussed in Chapter 8, legislators may also be sophisticated; that is, they may look ahead to the ultimate consequences of passing legislation. For example, suppose a legislator with veto power believes that if the bill $b$ fails, then the status quo $q$ will be preserved, whereas if $b$ passes, then the ultimate policy outcome (e.g., after further bargaining with the Senate and president) will be $b'$. Furthermore, even though the legislator prefers $q$ to $b$, he also prefers $b'$ to $q$. In this case, a legislator with veto power would again allow himself to be theoretically, but not observationally, rolled on the final-passage vote (i.e., his unsophisticated preferences would lead us to believe that he preferred $q$ to $b$ and was thus rolled, in theory, while his sophisticated preference was to prefer $b$, and thus ultimately $b'$, to $q$, and thus he would not oppose the bill and would not be rolled). Again, the end result is not a roll because the legislator is ultimately made better off by voting in favor of the original bill, $b$. Also, the converse, where the legislator prefers $b'$ to $q$, he would not vote against the bill if his vote affected the outcome. Thus, for sophisticated voting, theoretical and observed rolls again coincide, and our measure should capture sophisticated behavior.

A.2.2.1.3. SIDE PAYMENTS. Now consider a bill $b$ that is not part of a logroll and that, when passed, leads to the enactment of $b'$. Further suppose that a legislator possessing veto power prefers $q$ to $b'$. Is it possible for this legislator to be theoretically rolled on such a bill? *No.* Our model does not admit the possibility that a legislator possessing veto power is bribed (although side payments that are embodied in the bill itself are of course allowed). Absent a source of utility extraneous to the bill and status quo in question and absent uncertainty about the true nature of how the original bill, $b$, will be transformed into the final outcome, $b'$, a legislator with veto power has no reason to allow the passage of a bill when the ultimate consequence will be a policy that is worse for that veto player than is the status quo policy.

Our model does not capture the absence of rolls due to side payments (nor does it capture rolls that are observed as a consequence of side payments inducing a vote against a bill that nonetheless passes). Only if the side payments are in the form of a vote trade, across another dimension, does our measure still account for this type of behavior. If nonpolicy side payments are a common form of voting currency, then we may need to examine the type of bias introduced into our measures as a consequence (e.g., if legislators buy votes on amendments, but not final passage; if votes are bought on amendments, but not on rules; if majority party leaders are able to buy votes, but the opposition-party leaders are not, and so on). However, we foresee no systematic effects on majority- or minority-party roll rates, given the literature on side payments, except perhaps to lower minority-party roll rates (as it would seem that the majority is better able to provide side payments than is the minority and so it should be the case that minority votes are bought to support majority proposals).

### A.2.2.2. *Theoretical and Empirical Responses*

A.2.2.2.1. CONSTITUENCY-FORCED VOTING. If passing bill $b$ leads to a final outcome $b'$ and most of the majority party's members prefer $q$ to $b'$, then passage would be inconsistent with the notion that the majority party has a veto and is able to foresee legislative outcomes correctly (an ability we generally assume in our models). The majority knows that passing the good bill, $b$, leads to the enactment of the bad bill, $b'$ (a bill they would reject if they could), and so they should vote to prevent $b$'s passage. Why would the majority allow $b$ to pass, knowing that $b'$ is the ultimate outcome? Again, we are asking, "When will a theoretical roll not coincide with an observed roll, and thus, under what conditions does our measure not capture blocking power or incorrectly capture blocking power?" Perhaps some individual members of the majority party vote for $b$ because (1) their constituents favor $b$ over $q$; (2) their constituents will punish the member for voting against $b$, even after the member tries to explain what the ultimate consequence of passing $b$ would be; and (3) the expected electoral risk is too large, relative to the utility loss in getting $b'$ rather than $q$ as the final outcome. If enough members of the majority party are "forced" to vote with their constituents – for the bill, $b$ – rather than strategically – against the ultimate outcome, $b'$ – then a vote that is not an observed roll can still represent a "defeat" for the majority party.

How common is this scenario of constituency-forced voting? Denzau, Riker, and Shepsle (1985) have considered this possibility, and their conclusion is that, theoretically, it is rare. We have not found, in admittedly unsystematic examinations of nonrolls for the majority party, any clear evidence of constituency-forced voting. We also examined legislation appearing on Mayhew's (1991) list of significant legislation, as well as the key legislation passed during the New Deal, Great Society, and Contract with America. In none of these cases did we find evidence that the majority party was defeated at the early stages of the legislative process and then forced to pass legislation at the final stage. In fact, the typical pattern during these three time periods is that the majority party passes legislation with huge majorities and the minority party gets rolled.[8] Consider the following example: On 10 of 17 key New Deal votes, the majority party rolled the minority. On those 17 votes, the average vote totals were 320 votes for the bill and 67 against it. This is clearly inconsistent with the theory that majority-party members were forced by their constituents to vote a certain way. Other scholars are, of course, free to marshal more systematic evidence on this score – but we do not think that it will add significantly to

---

[8] Indeed, minority-party members frequently decried the majority party's ability to push their agenda through the legislative process during these three great moments. For example, during the passage of Great Society legislation, Representative Melvin B. Laird (R-WI) sadly noted that "we in the minority, 140 strong, have no illusions about preventing the majority from working its will" (Hunter 1965, quoting Laird). Similarly, as the majority party rolled its Contract with America agenda through the legislative process, minority member Representative Melvin Watt (D-NC) claimed, "I've been banging my head against the wall all day" (Seelye 1995, quoting Watt).

the total number of recorded votes on which the majority party appears to be rolled.

A.2.2.2.2. BAD COMBINATIONS. Next, consider a scenario of the following form: A small majority of the majority party prefers $b_1$ to $q_1$ and prefers $b_2$ to $q_2$. Meanwhile, large minorities of the majority party intensely prefer $q_1$ to $b_1$ and $q_2$ to $b_2$. The intense minorities in the two cases do not intersect. Thus, overall, a (large) majority of the majority party prefers $(q_1, q_2)$ to $(b_1, b_2)$. By hypothesis, the majority party is not theoretically rolled on either $b_1$ or $b_2$. Yet, considering the two-dimensional move from $(q_1, q_2)$ to $(b_1, b_2)$, one can say that the majority is theoretically rolled.

If "bad combinations" of the preceding form are frequently forced upon the majority party, then conclusions based on vote-by-vote rolls would indeed overstate the majority's success. To put it another way, a possible conclusion from our empirical evidence showing extremely low majority-party roll rates is that (1) the majority has no agenda-setting advantage[9]; (2) the majority is relatively often forced to accept logrolls of the above form; but for some reason (3) the majority is never forced to accept straight defeats on single votes. This is possible, but no alternative model – median voter, pivot, conditional party government – would predict such a pattern, nor does it seem plausible on its face. If this type of logroll were a common occurrence, we would expect to find either direct evidence (e.g., intense, large, and non-overlapping minorities within the majority party opposed to various bills) or observable implications (e.g., leaders of the majority party commenting on how they were hoodwinked or a rationalization, after the fact, of the legislation through the reconciliation process). If we found such evidence, we would then question roll rates as an appropriate measure of agenda control. However, we do not find such evidence and so do not reject the usefulness of roll rates as indicators of agenda power.

### A.2.2.3. *Empirical Responses*

A.2.2.3.1. ABSTENTIONS. The challenge that abstentions might affect roll rates has no theoretical analog in our model, but we nonetheless investigate abstentions empirically in order to demonstrate that our model is indeed a good analogy to the real world. To see how abstentions might affect our measures, suppose there are 220 majority-party members in all, and 210 majority-party members vote, with 106 voting against the bill and 104 voting in favor. The bill passes nonetheless. Thus, the majority party is observationally rolled. However, all of the 10 nonvoting members of the majority prefer the bill to the status quo. In this case, we observe a roll of the majority party (more members vote against the bill than for it), but in fact more members prefer the bill to the status quo

---

[9] Another possibility is that there are multiple agenda setters within one legislative body. For example, the Danish parliament had one majority coalition partner handle domestic affairs, while another handled foreign affairs, and this could theoretically generate rolls of the majority party (Damgaard and Svensson 1989). Even in this instance, however, those controlling the agenda did not typically roll the other members of the majority coalition.

than the reverse. It is only because turnout is low that the majority's preference for the bill is obscured. In this case, our measure overestimates the true roll rate of the majority party. This problem is actually more likely for the minority party because its members are more likely to abstain than are majority-party members. In this case, members of the minority party who would vote in favor of a bill choose to abstain, as their vote would go against their party. Thus, the minority party is observed to be rolled when, in truth, it would not be rolled had those who abstained actually voted.

To find evidence of this phenomenon we, again, examined significant legislation and legislation occurring during the New Deal, Great Society, and Contract with America. We looked at all votes with greater than 10 percent abstention rates and tried to examine how a nonroll could be converted into a roll (or a roll converted into a nonroll) if the abstainers had voted. From this analysis, we reached the following conclusions. First, unless a vote is relatively close, even the addition of abstainers into the vote totals will not change the final outcome. Second, we find that it would take between 72 and 100 percent of abstainers voting differently from how members of their own party voted to affect our measures. This suggests that the abstainers must have dramatically different positions on these issues from the rest of their party, and there is no evidence for such a systematic pattern of abstention.[10] Further, there are no results in the literature that show a strategic pattern for abstentions in the House (Cohen and Noll 1991).

A.2.2.3.2. VOICE VOTES IN LIEU OF RECORDED VOTES. We now consider cases in which a bill passes by a voice vote on final passage. We do not count such cases as majority-party rolls or minority-party rolls because there is no evidence that either party opposed the bill's passage.[11] Nonetheless, it is possible that the majority party, faced with certain defeat, chose not to demand a recorded vote on final passage; that is, it was well and truly defeated, but the legislative record does not reveal that fact. Were such a "hidden roll" to occur, it would be inconsistent with the notion that the majority party has veto power over placement of bills on the floor agenda; thus, we have no theoretical analog to this conjecture. However, it is worth noting that any member of the House can call for a recorded vote, and if supported by one fifth (which amounts to 25 members) of a quorum, such a vote is taken (Rule XX of House procedures). Thus, in the event that the majority party will be rolled on a voice vote, the minority party can easily request a recorded vote. This low hurdle to obtain such votes makes it unlikely that there are many hidden rolls. As a matter of fact, there is good reason to believe that when the minority party is able to control

---

[10] In other governments, we know that when an entire faction of the in-party government abstains, it typically means they do not want to support a bill, but also do not want it to be a no-confidence vote against the government. This is not the case in the U.S. House of Representatives, however. This is another example of where we must understand the specifics of the legislature that we are studying when we construct a theory and interpret data.

[11] Indeed, voice votes tend to be unanimous.

the legislative agenda successfully and pass its policies against the wishes of the majority, it would call for a recorded vote to trumpet its success.

Further, we again looked at the record to see if we could find examples of this behavior. We have looked systematically for cases in which (1) a bill passes by voice vote, (2) there is a recorded vote earlier in the bill's legislative history, and (3) the majority party is rolled on the last such vote. These would seem to be the only plausible candidates for "hidden rolls." In an analysis of legislation in the postwar House, studying votes and reports for every even-numbered Congress, we found none. We know of no cases where the majority was rolled early in the legislative process (i.e., in committee), which is in itself an extremely rare occurrence, and then not rolled later on. Rather, the members of the majority party (like the members of the minority party) seem to go down swinging, losing every vote as it comes up.

A variant of the notion of a hidden roll is the claim that the majority party does not insist on a recorded final-passage vote because it knows that the bill in question will fail later in the legislative process. Such cases, to the extent that they arise, would, by assumption, not be consequential rolls. Thus, they are consistent with the costly-blocking model developed in Chapter 6.

### A.2.3. Further Investigation of Roll Rates

This theoretical and empirical investigation of roll rates notwithstanding, could it be that the majority party has suffered actual changes in policy that it dislikes, through routes that are subtler than overt rolls? In the preceding section, we considered several such routes, two of which appear to warrant further empirical consideration. First, it is *possible* that the majority party suffers from constituency-forced voting, but we await proof or argument that it does. Even if it does, however, note that the notion of constituency-forced voting relies on the pressure of public opinion, presumably marshaled by the minority party. Appealing outside the legislature to the public is the classic minority strategy in legislatures worldwide and is consistent with the minority's inability to act through the legislative process itself. Indeed, the minority, lacking the cards to play at the legislative table, seeks to change the venue of the game to the electoral table, whenever it can. Thus, constituency-forced votes may occur, but they arise as a natural consequence of the majority party's stranglehold on the internal agenda-setting process. Second, it is possible that the majority party may occasionally accept defeat without forcing a vote on final passage. Again, we await proof or argument that it does.

### A.2.4. Direction of Policy Movement

Another measure that we introduce in this book is our method of identifying whether a particular bill moves policy leftward or rightward on the left–right scale of politics. The method is simple: We simply regress each member's vote on a given final-passage vote (coded 1 if the member votes for the bill, 0 if the member votes against the bill) on the member's first-dimension DW-NOMINATE score. If there is a significant negative relationship, the policy movement is classified as leftward. If there is a significant positive relationship, the policy movement is classified as rightward. If there is no significant relationship, the policy movement is classified as unrelated to the left–right scale.

### A.2.5. Objections to Our Measure of Policy Movements

When will the method described in the preceding section fail to identify a policy movement correctly? Is it possible, for example, that rightists are significantly more likely to support a bill on final passage and yet the bill moves policy leftward?

Suppose first that the bill, $b$, is part of a logroll. The rightists in the House have been asked to support the bill, even though it moves policy leftward. In return, the Senate will approve a bill that moves policy rightward on another issue dimension (that they would not otherwise approve). Moreover, the far left in the House dislikes the logroll (finding the rightward move on the other bill too high a price to pay) and votes strategically – that is, against $b$ – in an attempt to scuttle the deal. With this conjunction of assumptions, one might find that rightists are significantly more likely to support $b$, even though $b$ itself moves policy leftward. Again, this is an issue of whether one considers logrolls to be individual pieces of legislation or packages. On a bill-by-bill basis, our measure will misclassify bills falling into the preceding category; however, taken as a package, a view more consistent with our assumption of sophisticated voting, our measure correctly classifies the overall direction of policy movement.

The preceding example is limited to times when different political parties control the Senate and House, a situation that occurred in 10 of the 61 Congresses we examined. More comprehensive evidence for the existence of inter-congressional logrolls is the greater existence of omnibus legislation during periods of divided government (Kiewiet and McCubbins 1991). However, as in the previous consideration of logrolls, it makes sense to consider this omnibus legislation as a package, in which case we expect packages that move policy significantly to the left or right will be captured by our measure of policy direction.

Suppose next that $b$ is not part of a logroll. Members foresee that $b$ will lead to the ultimate enactment of $b'$, and leftists dislike $b'$, while rightists like it. In this case, sophisticated voting would mean that rightists are significantly more likely to support $b$, even though $b$ itself moves policy leftward. Note, however, that our method correctly indicates that the ultimate consequence of passing $b$ will be a rightward policy move, $b'$. If one defines the policy direction as the ultimate direction (moving from $q$ to $b'$), rather than the proximal direction (moving from $q$ to $b$), then our method gets the direction right again.

Can strategic voting cause us to interpret mistakenly the direction of policy movement? Yes, if moving from $q$ to $b$ is rightward and members vote sincerely, then our measure will classify $b$ as a rightward policy move. However, if the ultimately enacted bill $b'$ is actually to the left of $q$, then our measure will classify $b$ when members vote sincerely.

### A.2.6. Summary of External Validity

In this section, we have considered various objections to the external validity of our theory and measures. We have considered the general objection that we oversimplify reality by focusing on a unidimensional model of politics, and we have shown that even in the case of a multidimensional U.S. House, our measures still capture the constructs to which they are analogies. First, it makes sense to consider logrolls and other evidence of multidimensionality as a net change in utility, in which case sophisticated actors can be expected to anticipate the ultimate consequences of their actions correctly and vote accordingly. We have shown that in such cases our measures work well. Second, many logically possible multidimensional situations seem not to exist empirically. Third, our measure of policy movement captures the essential distinction between policies supported by leftist and rightist members of Congress. There may be occasional votes that we mistakenly classify because of multidimensionality, but our measure accurately captures the net change as perceived by sophisticated actors. In sum, our measures stand up to the various critiques against them, and our theory's external validity is not damaged.

### A.3. RESPONSE TO KREHBIEL

Another challenge to our measures is based on Krehbiel's "partyless" theory of legislative organization. Krehbiel suggests an alternative explanation for our findings, rather than directly calling into question the validity of our measures and results. However, he then uses his model to argue that roll rates are not useful measures of party influence. In this section, we respond to his arguments.

Before going further, we wish to emphasize that Krehbiel's critique is an alternative theory and should be judged as such. We are not alone in this view. Indeed, Groseclose and Snyder (2003), in their response to Krehbiel, correctly note that "if a researcher claims that a test is consistent with his or her theory, it is always possible for another researcher to claim that the same test is consistent with an alternative theory." Even though we agree with Groseclose and Snyder's claim (it *is* always possible for other researchers to claim that a given test or empirical finding is consistent with an alternative theory), we also emphasize that the plausibility of the alternative theory must be considered and that the theory must be evaluated against the full range of empirical evidence. We take up both of these tasks in the remainder of this appendix.

Krehbiel, offering an alternative theory of legislative organization, has argued that roll rates similar to the ones we observe can be generated without the majority party controlling the legislative agenda (Krehbiel 2003). His key claims are as follows:

- A partyless model can explain the low majority-party roll rates and high minority-party roll rates that we observe.
- This partyless model establishes the baseline theory of legislative organization.

In response to his claims, we will argue the following:

- His model relies on the heroic assumption that legislators within a given party have a common ideal point – an assumption that we know to be empirically false (see Poole and Rosenthal 1997).[12]
- His model merely explains the stylized fact of low majority-party roll rates and high minority-party roll rates; it does not (and cannot) account for the many other empirical findings that our Cartel Agenda Model explains.

Specifically, the Cartel Agenda Model accounts for the following empirical findings that Krehbiel's model cannot explain:

- The dramatic change in roll rates (for both minority and majority party) after the implementation of Reed's rules.
- The increase in the proportion of bills moving policy toward the majority party after the implementation of Reed's rules.
- Changes in roll rates during periods of divided and unified government.
- The ability of the majority party to move policy towards itself, as measured by $P_{Left}$.
- The effect of changes in party control on roll rates.

Although Krehbiel's work presents an important challenge to our theory, we take a Lakatosian view here and, for the reasons summarized earlier and elaborated later, reject it.

### A.3.1. Krehbiel's Critique

Krehbiel's (2003) argument is a response to our 2002 article that used roll rates as indicators of party influence (primarily through agenda control) in the U.S. House. He does not challenge the data in our earlier article, and presumably the data in this book as well, on the majority party's roll rate. He also has not

---

[12] For further refutation of this assumption, see our web site (*www.settingtheagenda.com*). There, we demonstrate that the probability of being rolled is related to distance from the majority median – a finding that is inconsistent with Krehbiel's assumption of common ideological preferences.

attacked the logical validity of our model, nor has he sought to test any of the four main propositions that we advanced in the work to which he responded. The purpose of his critique has been to argue that roll rates are poor measures of "party strength" and to provide an alternative explanation of a portion of our findings.[13]

The alternative model put forward by Krehbiel can be stated succinctly: (1) The majority party consists of $J$ members, the minority party consists of $N$ members, and there are no third-party members, so the total number of legislators is $J + N$; (2) there are $K$ final-passage votes held and on the $k$th roll call, all majority party members vote "yes" with probability $p_k$ and all minority party members vote "yes" with probability $q_k$.

For given values of $p_k$, $q_k$, $J$, and $N$, it is easy to calculate the probability that the majority party is *rolled* – that is, the probability that a majority of the majority party's members vote against a bill that nonetheless passes (call this $R_{Maj,k}$). Similarly, it is easy to calculate the probability that the minority party is rolled (call this $R_{Min,k}$). Krehbiel examines a range of $(p_k, q_k, J, N)$ values, computes for each the associated roll probabilities $(R_{Min,k}, R_{Maj,k})$, and, on this basis, launches two main criticisms of our analysis.

The first challenge centers on how the roll probabilities $(R_{Min,k}, R_{Maj,k})$ change in response to the parameters $(p_k, q_k, J, N)$. For example, Krehbiel shows that $R_{Maj,k}$ does not respond monotonically to changes in $p_k$ and concludes that $R_{Maj,k}$ is therefore a poor measure of majority-party agenda power. Krehbiel's second challenge is that small differences between $p_k$ and $q_k$ can generate majority and minority roll rates that approximate those we have found empirically for the House, thus showing that a partyless (or "baseline") model might account for our results. Our responses are elaborated next.

### A.3.1.1. The Microfoundations of Krehbiel's Model

In interpreting Krehbiel's model, one can either take the probabilities $p_k$ and $q_k$ as primitives not to be further analyzed or view them as derived from some more basic considerations (albeit implicitly). If one takes them as primitives, then the model essentially analogizes legislators to coin flips with coins weighted

---

[13] We have put dozens of predictions to the test within the pages of this manuscript. Krehbiel's probabilistic model would either fail to have corresponding predictions to ours or it would flatly fail many of the corresponding tests. For example, how would the introduction of Reed's rules affect outcomes in his model? How would committee outcomes or conference committee outcomes or the outcomes on votes over recommendations from the Rules Committee come about in Krehbiel's model? Results on our web page, *www.settingtheagenda.com*, which contains tests deleted from the manuscript to save space, signal further troubles for Krehbiel's probabilistic theory of congressional voting, specifically, why would the pattern of individual roll rates follow the Nike "Swoosh" shapes depicted in the chapter on "Individual Roll Rates" on our web page? How would Krehbiel's model explain the findings of Lawrence et al. (1999, in press) regarding individual win rates?

to $p_k$ and $q_k$, which does not seem an attractive option.[14] If one takes them as derivative, then from what do they derive?

By far the most commonly used model in legislative studies is the spatial model. Beginning with the work of Black (1958) and the famous median voter theorem and continuing through to the present generation, spatial models have been employed to analyze informational issues (e.g., Krehbiel 1991), to estimate members' ideological predispositions (e.g., Poole and Rosenthal 1997; Londregan 2000), to identify partisan influence over roll call votes (e.g., Cox and Poole 2002; Snyder and Groseclose 2000), to explore gridlock (e.g., Krehbiel 1998), and so on.

The basic elements of the spatial model are simple: each legislator $j$ has an ideal point $x_j$ (and a standard error $s_j$), and each roll call $k$ is characterized by the policy $y_k$ that would obtain were the motion in question to pass and the policy $n_k$ that would obtain were the motion to fail. In the stochastic literature, motions pitting $y_k$ against $n_k$ are usually described in terms of their cutpoint $c_k$ (the midpoint between the "yes" and "no" positions, or $(y_k + n_k)/2$) and their gap $d_k$ (the distance between the "yes" and "no" positions, or $y_k - n_k$). In this model, it is well known that the probability of member $j$ voting "yes" on roll call $k$, $p_{jk}$, is $\Phi(d_k(x_j - c_k)/s_j)$, where $\Phi$ is the standard cumulative normal distribution.[15]

What assumptions about individual members' preferences must one add to the standard spatial model described earlier in order to yield Krehbiel's model – in particular, the assumption that all members of a given party have the same probability of voting "yes" on any given roll call? To answer this question, suppose that at least two distinct roll calls are held per Congress ($K > 1$), and let $N$ denote the set of minority party members.[16] If, for each roll call, all members of the minority party have the same probability of voting "yes" ($p_{jk} = p_{Nk}$ for all $j$ in $N$ and all $k = 1, \ldots, K$), then the only possible conclusion is that $x_j = x_N$ and $s_j = s_N$ for all $j$ in $N$ (where $x_N$ is a common ideal point shared by all members of $N$ and $s_N$ is a common standard error).[17] Thus,

---

[14] Indeed, few scholars have suggested a purely probabilistic voting model for explaining congressional behavior (or voting behavior in general), including Krehbiel who, in his past work, has relied extensively on simple, unidimensional, spatial models of voting. This is not to say that the spatial model is the "end of political science," rather, it is a well-defended and well-accepted analogy in the social sciences. Further, spatial analogies and metaphors are the most commonly used in all languages and cultures and thus capture a common, well-used way of discussing things (Lakoff and Johnson 1980). Probabilistic voting models, indeed, purely probabilistic models of human choice, which deny free will, individuality, and strategic behavior, are not at all common in the literature or language.

[15] Cf. Londregan (2000) for an explicit derivation of this formulation.

[16] Two roll calls are distinct if they differ in their cutpoints.

[17] To prove this assertion, let $(d_1, c_1)$ and $(d_2, c_2)$ be two distinct roll calls (i.e., such that $c_1 \neq c_2$). Let $j$ and $h$ be two legislators. It is given that $\Phi(d_k(x_j - c_k)/s_j) = \Phi(d_k(x_h - c_k)/s_h)$, for $k = 1, 2$. This implies $d_k(x_j - c_k)/s_j = d_k(x_h - c_k)/s_h$, for $k = 1, 2$. Hence, letting $s = s_j/s_h$, we have $x_j = c_k(1 - s) + sx_h$, for $k = 1, 2$. Without loss of generality, assume that $c_1 < c_2$, and renormalize so that $c_1 = 0$. Then we have (1) $x_j = sx_h$ and (2) $x_j = c_2(1 - s) + sx_h$. Both equations can

*Krehbiel's model is a special case of the standard spatial model in which there is perfect preference homogeneity within each party.* Two points follow.

First, one can neither interpret $p_k$ as measuring the majority party's preference homogeneity nor interpret $q_k$ as measuring the minority party's preference homogeneity, even if Krehbiel is tempted to do so. Viewed from a spatial perspective, both parties are already perfectly homogeneous and that fact is held constant throughout the analysis. (For the reader curious as to what *does* drive the value of $p_k$ across $k$ within a given Congress, the answer is the roll call parameters $c_k$ and $d_k$. These are quite distinct from the members' preference parameters, hence from any notion of preference homogeneity.)

Second, one can easily reject the restriction that Krehbiel imposes in his model on empirical grounds. For example, members' estimated ideal points do differ significantly from one another, even within a given party (cf. Poole and Rosenthal 1997). Further, individuals' probabilities of voting "yes," even within one party, are not identical, as must straightforwardly be true as a result in Krehbiel's model.

### A.3.1.2. Roll Rates as a Measure of Party Agenda Power

Having made these initial observations, we proceed in this section to consider Krehbiel's first main challenge of our model. Krehbiel views us as using the majority-party roll rate as a general measure of the majority party's agenda power, as one might use a ruler to measure height. Motivated by this view, he explores at length the relationship between $p_k$ and $q_k$, on the one hand, and $R_{Maj,k}$ and $R_{Min,k}$, on the other – finding that the relationships are nonmonotonic. On this basis, he rejects our analysis.

Our response is twofold. First, we use roll rates primarily to test explicit hypotheses: that the majority roll rate will be zero; that the majority roll rate will be unaffected by how far the majority-party median is from the overall House median; that the minority roll rate will be significantly affected by how far the minority-party median is from the House median.[18] We do not use the roll rate as a continuous measure of agenda power in any of our tests (although we are open to the possibility of using them as such in comparative research).

Second, the argument for viewing roll rates as measures of agenda power would presumably be roughly as follows. The better control the majority party has over which bills do and do not make it onto the floor agenda, the more it should be able to prevent the appearance of bills that will roll it on final passage; hence – all else equal – the lower its roll rate should be. Put differently,

---

hold simultaneously only if $c_2(1 - s) = 0$. Since $c_1 \neq c_2$, it must be that $s = 1$, which implies $s_j = s_h$, from the definition of $s$ and $x_j = x_h$.

[18] We test other hypotheses derived from the Cartel Agenda Model and from extensions of the original model. For example, we test the cartel and pivot models' predictions about individuals' roll rates in different regions of the policy space. In addition, we test hypotheses derived from extensions to the model in which there is incomplete information, and in which the majority party can bring bills to the floor under a closed rule.

a veto player should never lose, and the more closely a particular legislator approximates a veto player, the less often she should lose. In this limited sense, roll rates would appear to be "measures" of agenda power.

Krehbiel, however, articulates an alternate standard that measures should meet: "A weaker criterion for a measure is that it should respond to competing influences consistently, predictably, and in a correctable fashion" (p. 12). He then shows that roll rates do not respond monotonically to the parameters, $p_k$ and $q_k$, in his model. However, we believe the question of validity that he raises is not with our measure (indeed, it is hard to see how or why his model undermines our use of roll rates as measures of agenda power) but rather with the validity of his own constructs in his probabilistic model, $p_k$ and $q_k$.

### A.3.1.3. *The Partyless Baseline?*
Krehbiel's second challenge is that our results can be generated within his probabilistic, partyless model – a model that he claims is the "baseline" explanation of legislative organization.[19] However, given the broad range of results that our theory explains (and that Krehbiel's theory does not), we cannot agree that Krehbiel's probabilistic model is the baseline. Indeed, we will demonstrate shortly that Krehbiel's model is inadequate in explaining our empirical results.

From a theoretical standpoint, we also see no reason why Krehbiel's model should be considered the baseline. As an illustration of our reasoning, consider the following analogy: There exist two different types of thermometers, each of which measures temperature. One type of thermometer is based on a theory that relates the expansion or contraction of liquid to the measurement of temperature. Thus, when we use this type of thermometer, our measurement of temperature is based on a theory of how heat affects a liquid's volume. Note, however, that this type of thermometer will not work in all environments because some liquids will become solids if the temperature drops below a certain point and because air pressure can affect the liquid within this type of thermometer. Accordingly, we must match our liquid and thermometer to the environment in which they are used.

A second variety of thermometer is based on a theory that relates the movement of electrons across metal to temperature. This type of thermometer may be more useful than liquid thermometers because ambient temperature and air

---

[19] Note that in his other work, Krehbiel claims *more* baseline models for himself. Specifically, he states, "for the policy shift to be unambiguously partisan, the *magnitude* of the shift must be greater than that predicted by a baseline nonpartisan model. Elsewhere, I have used the median voter model as the baseline (Krehbiel 1993, 1996). Here it makes more sense to think of the pivotal politics theory as the baseline. Then the issue becomes whether a suitably defined, outcome-consequential party theory makes predictions that differ meaningfully from the pivotal politics theory" (Krehbiel 1998: 197; emphasis in original). So this would be yet a third "theoretical baseline" that Krehbiel would insist "partisan" theories beat. Again, each of these actually presents an alternative theory, subject to test, validation, refutation, and comparison.

pressure do not affect its measurements. As long as the metal does not melt and the temperature is above absolute zero, there will be electrons moving across its metal surface. Therefore, from our theory about electron movement, we can also calculate temperature.

These two different thermometers, based on two different theories of temperature, are analogous to Krehbiel's (2000, 2003, 2004) critiques of Aldrich and Rohde (2000), Snyder and Groseclose (2001), and Cox and McCubbins (1993, 2002). In his critiques, Krehbiel suggests a different theory (i.e., he designs a new thermometer), which in certain situations returns the same results (i.e., temperature) as these other theories do. However, rather than acknowledge that his approach is an alternative theory, Krehbiel claims that his theory, or "thermometer," should be considered the baseline.

As this analogy demonstrates, this assertion is unwarranted. Demonstrating that one's thermometer can measure temperature is evidence for the theory that underpins that thermometer, but it is not evidence against another thermometer. Stated differently, that both liquid and digital thermometers accurately measure San Diego's temperature does not tell us that one thermometer is wrong. Indeed, in order to make comparative claims, the two thermometers must be tested *against one another*, especially in situations where the theories differ in their predictions. We have conducted such tests throughout this book (pitting the Cartel Agenda Model against both the Floor Agenda Model and the pivot model), and our tests have led us to reject those other theories in favor of our own. Krehbiel, on the other hand, has not pitted his theory against others in empirical tests.[20]

Returning to the specific theories at hand, Krehbiel posits that $p_k = 0.52$ and $q_k = 0.48$ in row 5 of his Table 1 and computes the relevant roll rates within the model. Recall, however, that all majority-party members have a common ideal point, say $x_J$, and all minority-party members have a common ideal point, say $x_N \neq x_J$, in Krehbiel's model (interpreted from a spatial perspective). For *any* given $(x_N, x_J)$, with $x_N \neq x_J$, it is possible to generate the sequence of $(p_k, q_k)$ values that Krehbiel displays in his Table 1, by varying the issue voted on.[21] Thus, the particular values $p_k = 0.52$ and $q_k = 0.48$ do not necessarily say anything about how mild or great are the differences in parties' preferences.

---

[20] Although reminders to be skeptical about research are important, by themselves they do not contribute to the scientific enterprise. Proposing alternative theories and claiming preeminence for them, without comparing them to alternative theories, does not advance our understanding of the issues under study. Only when a theory is judged to perform better than alternatives does it constitute a scientific advance.

[21] For example, let $x = (x_N + x_J)/2$, and assume that the bill being voted on is $b_k = x - e_k$, while the status quo policy is $q_k = x + e_k$. With these assumptions, the cutpoint $c_k = x = (x_N + x_J)/2$, for all stipulated values of $e_k$. Now start with a value of $e_k = 0$, implying a gap parameter $d_k = 0$. This would generate the first row of Table 1, in which $p_k = q_k = 0.5$. By slowly increasing $e_k$, and hence $d_k$, holding all else constant, one could generate each successive row in Table 1. Note that this is possible for any values of $x_N$ and $x_J$, hence for any degree of preference disagreement between the parties (except perfect consensus, $x_N = x_J$).

$x_N$ and $x_J$ could be arbitrarily far apart, and yet it could be true that $p_k = 0.52$ and $q_k = 0.48$.[22]

In our view, the correct statement of Krehbiel's result is as follows: If both parties are completely homogeneous internally, then it is possible to generate low majority-party and high minority-party roll rates. We agree that this conditional statement is valid. However, his premise – that both parties are completely homogeneous internally – is observably false. Moreover, the only parameter values that Krehbiel finds to be consistent with our results on roll rates imply observably false things about the percentage of members in each party voting "yes." Thus, Krehbiel does not offer a plausible alternative account for the low observed majority-party roll rates that survives even a cursory examination of the data. Nor does he in any way refute our account. He merely offers a logically possible, though false, alternative account.

It is certainly fair to ask whether a 1.3 percent majority-party roll rate can arise in a partyless world. We have in our own work explained at length what one would have to assume in a general spatial model in which the majority party enjoys no special agenda-setting advantages in order to generate our empirical results. We point out that a partyless spatial model is consistent with *any* observed majority-party roll rate (from 0 to 100), in the sense that one can find parameter values that generate any given value. However, we characterize the particular conditions needed to generate very low majority-party roll rates as restrictive and far-fetched. We believe that until better models are developed and shown to beat the partisan approach, the debate about legislative organization, and the resulting measures of legislative activity, should center on the more plausible and general spatial model.

### A.3.1.4. Empirical Results

As noted previously, Krehbiel's model incorporates four parameters – ($p_k$, $q_k$, $J$, $N$). The last two of these refer to the number of members in the majority and minority parties, respectively. As $J + N = 435$, one can combine these two parameters into a single variable, $m = J/(J + N)$, reflecting the size of the majority party.

Krehbiel runs two bivariate regressions in order to analyze how the size of the majority party ($m$) affects the two parties' roll rates. The observations for the analysis are the 62 Congresses from the 45th to the 106th. For each Congress, the dependent variables are (1) the majority party's roll rate and (2) the minority party's roll rate on a sample of final-passage votes.

Krehbiel reports that both parties' roll rates are significantly influenced by the size of the majority, less strongly in the case of the majority and more

---

[22] Presumably, Krehbiel wishes to consider a sequence of votes in which the same issue is at stake and all that varies are the two parties' ideal points. Even in this case, however, the difference between the two parties' ideal points that implies a given ($p_k$, $q_k$) value depends on the posited roll call parameters, so Krehbiel has yet to state clearly what can be inferred about the mildness of the parties' differences.

strongly in the case of the minority. He concludes (p. 24) that "[t]he size of the majority party accounts for a statistically significant portion of variation in roll rates [the $R^2$s in his regressions range from 0.072 to 0.098]. Existing research interprets roll rates as indicative of party strength but ignores size effects and thereby overstates the former."

We would make two points in response. First, we do not "ignore size effects," although we have not previously published our findings. Indeed, we included the size of the majority as a regressor in our early analyses of roll rates. We found, however, that once one includes other theoretically motivated variables – in particular, the distance between the House median and the median of the party whose roll rate is being analyzed – *the majority's size no longer has any significant effect*. We have also found that if one restricts the analysis to Congresses after the adoption of Reed's rules – a key event in our view – *then variations in the size of the majority do not affect the majority-party roll rate, even in a bivariate regression*. Thus, we have omitted the size of the majority from our published analyses with good reason. Furthermore, including this variable changes none of our qualitative findings.

Second, note that Krehbiel's regressions predict, when the majority party has 218 of the 435 seats ($m = 0.501$), that the majority party's roll rate will be 0.10, while the minority party's roll rate will be 0.28.[23] Is this sort of gap to be expected under a model in which neither party has any particular advantage in setting the agenda?

### A.3.1.5. Summary
We have found that the majority party in the U.S. House of Representatives very rarely unsuccessfully opposes the passage of a bill or joint resolution. Conditional on the bill or joint resolution passing, the majority favors it roughly 99 percent of the time. This finding is consistent with our theoretical model, which posits that the majority party has significant advantages in setting the floor agenda. Krehbiel (2003) offers an alternative "partyless" explanation of our finding.

As we have shown, however, Krehbiel's critique is based on a special case of the spatial model in which all Democrats have identical preferences and all Republicans have identical preferences. It is thus not surprising that the larger party would suffer fewer rolls. Indeed, such a result follows directly from his assumptions.

Krehbiel also argues that the rate at which the majority party is rolled is a poor general measure of the majority's agenda power. The basis for his critique is that variations in a parameter in his model, which he construes as representing the homogeneity of preference within the majority party, do not lead reliably to decreases in the majority-party roll rate. However, as we have shown, the parameter in question cannot be interpreted as a measure of homogeneity of preference. So, the premise in this argument does not hold.

---

[23] These are the results computed from his models (2) and (4) in Table 2.

# Addendum

## Majority and Minority Rolls, 45th–105th Congresses

| Sequential Roll Call Number | Bill | Significant Law | Enacted |
|---|---|---|---|
| **Majority Rolls** | | | |

---

### 45th Congress 1877–1879 Democratic majority

| Sequential Roll Call Number | Bill | Significant Law | Enacted |
|---|---|---|---|
| 85 | Allow women lawyers before Supreme Court | N | Y |
| 184 | Publicize acts of the government | N | N |
| 209 | Deficiency appropriations | N | Y |
| 281 | Issues CDs to aid refunding of debt | N | Y |
| 287 | Distribute money from Great Britain | N | N |

### 46th Congress 1879–1881 Democratic majority

| Sequential Roll Call Number | Bill | Significant Law | Enacted |
|---|---|---|---|
| 51 | Money exchange | N | N |
| 156 | Declare all public roads are post routes | N | N |
| 160 | Private relief | N | Y |
| 274 | Indian treaty | N | Y |
| 434 | Reapportionment bill | N | N |

| Sequential Roll Call Number | Bill | Significant Law | Enacted |
|---|---|---|---|
| **47th Congress 1881–1883 Republican majority** | | | |
| 27 | Army appointments | N | Y |
| 250 | Refund defense money to Georgia | N | Y |
| 290 | U.S. court jurisdiction | N | N |
| 292 | Private relief | N | N |
| 331 | Rivers and harbors | N | N |
| **48th Congress 1883–1885 Democratic majority** | | | |
| 33 | Regulate shipment of diseased animals | Y | Y |
| **49th Congress 1885–1887 Democratic majority** | | | |
| 19 | Enable national banking association to increase stock | N | Y |
| 31 | Pension to Margaret B. Harwood | N | Y |
| 70 | Pension to Loren Burritt | N | N |
| 82 | Regulate importing/landing of mackerel | N | Y |
| 97 | Regulate oleomargarine | N | Y |
| 138 | Pension to Catherine Waters | N | Y |
| **50th Congress 1887–1889 Democratic majority** | | | |
| 26 | Private relief | N | N |
| 34 | Private relief | N | N |
| 167 | Individual military retirement | N | Y |
| **51st Congress 1889–1891 Republican majority** | | | |
| 522 | Public building in Dallas | N | N |
| **52nd Congress 1891–1893 Democratic majority** | | | |
| 223 | Money for Columbian Exposition | N | N |
| **53rd Congress 1893–1895 Democratic majority** | | | |
| 355 | Private pension | N | N |
| **55th Congress 1897–1899 Republican majority** | | | |
| 50 | Relief for book agents of Methodist Episcopal | N | Y |

| Sequential Roll Call Number | Bill | Significant Law | Enacted |
|---|---|---|---|
| **57th Congress 1901–1903 Republican majority** | | | |
| 37 | Correct military record of Michael Mullet | N | N |
| 89 | Authorize to pay claim of heirs of Peter Johnson | N | N |
| 90 | Claim of representatives of John L. Young | N | Y |
| **59th Congress 1905–1907 Republican majority** | | | |
| 41 | Extend irrigation to Texas | N | Y |
| **61st Congress 1909–1911 Republican majority** | | | |
| 166 | Reciprocal trade with Canada | N | N |
| **63rd Congress 1913–1915 Democratic majority** | | | |
| 179 | Provide for moving Botanical Garden | N | N |
| **64th Congress 1915–1917 Democratic majority** | | | |
| 11 | Establish Army and Navy Medal of Honor roll | N | Y |
| 14 | Provide pension for survivors of Indian Wars | N | Y |
| **66th Congress 1919–1921 Republican majority** | | | |
| 134 | Army appropriations | N | Y |
| **68th Congress 1923–1925 Republican majority** | | | |
| 34 | Authorize contract with Henry Ford for steam plant | N | N |
| **72nd Congress 1931–1933 Democratic majority** | | | |
| 65 | Develop American air transport service | N | N |
| **74th Congress 1935–1937 Democratic majority** | | | |
| 70 | Develop strong American Merchant Marine | N | Y |
| 116 | Provide reimbursement of certain military people for earthquake | N | N |
| **76th Congress 1939–1941 Democratic majority** | | | |
| 96 | Make lynching a federal crime | N | N |
| 175 | Amend National Labor Relations Act | N | N |

| Sequential Roll Call Number | Bill | Significant Law | Enacted |
|---|---|---|---|
| **78th Congress 1943–1945 Democratic majority** | | | |
| 13 | Increase debt limit | N | Y |
| 42 | Poll tax unlawful | N | N |
| 85 | Forbid general consumer subsidies from government funds | N | N |
| 154 | Jackson Hole part of national forest | N | N |
| **79th Congress 1945–1947 Democratic majority** | | | |
| 107 | Return public employee offices to states | N | N |
| 111 | Board to investigate labor disputes | N | N |
| **81st Congress 1949–1951 Democratic majority** | | | |
| 86 | Amend Natural Gas Act | N/A | N |
| 148 | Prohibit discrimination | N/A | N |
| **84th Congress 1955–1957 Democratic majority** | | | |
| 71 | Exempt natural gas from utility regulations | N | N |
| 125 | Postal rates | N | N |
| **85th Congress 1957–1959 Democratic majority** | | | |
| 78 | Postal rate increase | N/A | Y |
| 164 | Federal law does not nullify state law | N/A | N |
| **86th Congress 1959–1961 Democratic majority** | | | |
| 47 | Federal preemption doctrine and subversion | N | N |
| 170 | Authorize Federal Aviation Administration to pay people for moving off land | N | N |
| **88th Congress 1963–1965 Democratic majority** | | | |
| 84 | Extend Mexican farm labor recruitment program | N | N |
| 220 | Bar federal court jurisdiction over state legislative reapportionment | N | N |
| **90th Congress 1967–1969 Democratic majority** | | | |
| 278 | Prohibit unfair trade practices in agriculture | N | N |

| Sequential Roll Call Number | Bill | Significant Law | Enacted |
|---|---|---|---|
| **91st Congress 1969–1971 Democratic majority** | | | |
| 44 | Continue income tax surcharge and excise tax | N/A | N |
| 59 | Amend D.C. minimum wage law for hospital workers | N/A | N |
| 151 | Extend Voting Rights Act (tests and devices) | N/A | Y |
| 189 | Labor and Health, Education, and Welfare department appropriations | N/A | Y |
| **92nd Congress 1971–1973 Democratic majority** | | | |
| 152 | Authorize emergency loan guarantees to business | Y | Y |
| 436 | Amend Subversive Control Act | N | N |
| 513 | Provide pay for losses from cyclamate ban | N | N |
| 619 | Temporarily increase debt ceiling | N | Y |
| **93rd Congress 1973–1975 Democratic majority** | | | |
| 475 | Trade Reform Act | N/A | Y |
| **94th Congress 1975–1977 Democratic majority** | | | |
| 108 | Authorize funds for assistance and evacuation in Vietnam | N | N |
| 430 | Enable cattle producers to promote meat | N | Y |
| 1067 | Certain energy appropriations | N | N |
| **95th Congress 1977–1979 Democratic majority** | | | |
| 770 | Amend overseas private investment corporation act | N/A | Y |
| 1044 | Tuition Tax Credit Act | N/A | N |
| **97th Congress 1981–1983 Democratic majority** | | | |
| 104 | Provide for budget reconciliation bill | N/A | Y |
| 800 | Promote economic revitalization/expansion Caribbean | N/A | N |

| Sequential Roll Call Number | Bill | Significant Law | Enacted |
|---|---|---|---|
| **98th Congress 1983–1985 Democratic majority** | | | |
| 615 | Authorize foreign aid (international development and security assistance) | N | N |
| 714 | Revise/reform Immigration and Nationality Act | N | N |
| 758 | Increase public debt limit | N | Y |
| **99th Congress 1985–1987 Democratic majority** | | | |
| 621 | Defense appropriations | N/A | N |
| **100th Congress 1987–1989 Democratic majority** | | | |
| 210 | D.C. appropriations (prohibit use of funds for abortion) | N/A | N |
| 216 | Legislative appropriations (reduce capitol architect fund) | N/A | N |
| **101st Congress 1989–1991 Democratic majority** | | | |
| 260 | Amend budget reconciliation regarding health plans | N/A | Y |
| **103rd Congress 1993–1995 Democratic majority** | | | |
| 558 | NAFTA implementation | N/A | Y |
| **104th Congress 1995–1997 Republican majority** | | | |
| 1061 | Amend Portal-to-Portal Act of 1947 | N/A | N |
| **105th Congress 1997–1999 Republican majority** | | | |
| 397 | Treasury and Post Office Appropriations | N/A | Y |
| 667 | Puerto Rico political status | N/A | N |
| 1025 | Campaign finance reform | N/A | N |

### Minority Rolls

| | | | |
|---|---|---|---|
| **45th Congress 1877–1879 Democratic majority** | | | |
| 30 | Resume specie payments | N | N/A |
| 75 | Provide for special term of federal court in Mississippi | N | N/A |
| 83 | Pay private claim | N | N/A |

| Sequential Roll Call Number | Bill | Significant Law | Enacted |
|---|---|---|---|
| 140 | Supply convenient currency | N | N/A |
| 238 | Taxes | N | N/A |
| 293 | Limit Chinese immigration | N | N/A |
| 349 | Government appropriations | N | N/A |

### 46th Congress 1879–1881 Democratic majority

| | | | |
|---|---|---|---|
| 6 | Army appropriations | N | N/A |
| 18 | Government appropriations | N | N/A |
| 23 | No military interference in elections | N | N/A |
| 80 | Coinage/bullion/treasury | N | N/A |
| 84 | Government appropriations | N | N/A |
| 98 | Pay of judges | N | N/A |
| 123 | Judicial appointments | N | N/A |
| 124 | Pay fees of U.S. Marshals | N | N/A |
| 157 | Remove political disabilities of an individual | N | N/A |
| 159 | Remove political disabilities of an individual | N | N/A |
| 164 | Establish titles in Hot Springs | N | N/A |
| 180 | U.S. court jurisdiction | N | N/A |
| 193 | Deficiency appropriations | N | N/A |
| 229 | Army appropriations | N | N/A |
| 252 | Taxes | N | N/A |
| 259 | Regulate distillery salaries | N | N/A |
| 288 | Civil appropriations | N | N/A |
| 293 | Deficiency appropriations | N | N/A |
| 347 | Refunding national debt | N | N/A |

### 47th Congress 1881–1883 Republican majority

| | | | |
|---|---|---|---|
| 14 | Discharge individual of liability for acts in office | N | N/A |
| 22 | Authorize Capitol architectural changes | N | N/A |

| Sequential Roll Call Number | Bill | Significant Law | Enacted |
|---|---|---|---|
| 52 | Private relief | N | N/A |
| 89 | Increase D.C. police force | N | N/A |
| 103 | Tariffs | Y | N/A |
| 108 | Court of commissioners Alabama claims | N | N/A |
| 129 | Extend incorporation of national banking association | N | N/A |
| 191 | Deficiency appropriations | N | N/A |
| 194 | Government appropriations | N | N/A |
| 202 | Reduce taxes | N | N/A |
| 207 | Navy appropriations | N | N/A |
| 209 | Civil appropriations | N | N/A |
| 287 | Amend pension laws | N | N/A |
| 296 | Navy appropriations | N | N/A |
| 310 | Government appropriations | N | N/A |

48th Congress 1883–1885 Democratic majority

| | | | |
|---|---|---|---|
| 13 | Negate court-martial | N | N/A |
| 51 | Post office appropriations | N | N/A |
| 67 | Appoint Texas border commission | N | N/A |
| 91 | Diplomatic appropriations | N | N/A |
| 107 | Government appropriations | N | N/A |
| 142 | Repeal preemption laws relating to public lands | N | N/A |
| 156 | Defense appropriations | N | N/A |
| 225 | Regulate interstate commerce and establish commission | N | N/A |

49th Congress 1885–1887 Democratic majority

| | | | |
|---|---|---|---|
| 22 | Relief of Fitz-John Porter | N | N/A |
| 214 | Settle with McMinnville and Manchester Railroad Company | N | N/A |

| Sequential Roll Call Number | Bill | Significant Law | Enacted |
|---|---|---|---|
| 249 | Appropriations for improvements to rivers and harbors | N | N/A |
| 256 | Additional term for D.C. circuit court | N | N/A |

**50th Congress 1887–1889 Democratic majority**

| | | | |
|---|---|---|---|
| 29 | Post office appropriations | N | N/A |
| 43 | Money for Virginia school/hospital | N | N/A |
| 169 | Reduce taxes | N | N/A |

**51st Congress 1889–1891 Republican majority**

| | | | |
|---|---|---|---|
| 17 | Simplify revenue laws | Y | N/A |
| 18 | Build federal prisons | N | N/A |
| 92 | Erect public building in Maine | N | N/A |
| 111 | Admit Wyoming to Union | Y | N/A |
| 120 | Admit Idaho to Union | N | N/A |
| 132 | U.S. court jurisdiction | N | N/A |
| 143 | Remove charges against individual | N | N/A |
| 184 | Tariffs | N | N/A |
| 197 | Issue treasury notes on deposit of silver bullion | N | N/A |
| 235 | U.S. election laws | N | N/A |
| 280 | Bankruptcy law (uniform) | N | N/A |
| 311 | Deficiency appropriations | N | N/A |
| 347 | Define lard | N | N/A |
| 425 | Revise copyright law | N | N/A |
| 429 | Punish embezzling pension money | N | N/A |
| 445 | Reapportionment | N | N/A |
| 503 | D.C. appropriations | N | N/A |

| Sequential Roll Call Number | Bill | Significant Law | Enacted |
|---|---|---|---|
| **52nd Congress 1891–1893 Democratic majority** | | | |
| 42 | Private relief | N | N/A |
| 45 | Money for college | N | N/A |
| 70 | Reduce duty woolen goods | N | N/A |
| 72 | No duty for cotton-producing resources | N | N/A |
| **53rd Congress 1893–1895 Democratic majority** | | | |
| 55 | Marshal and supervise elections | N | N/A |
| 76 | Admit Arizona to union | N | N/A |
| 99 | Reduce taxes | N | N/A |
| 162 | Coin silver/issue notes | N | N/A |
| 285 | Uniform bankruptcy law | N | N/A |
| 286 | Uniform bankruptcy law | N | N/A |
| 296 | Reinstate railroad clerks | N | N/A |
| 298 | Reinstate railroad clerks | N | N/A |
| 323 | Place iron ore on free list | N | N/A |
| 324 | Place barbed wire and wire rods on free list | N | N/A |
| 339 | Authorize appointment of cadets at military academy | N | N/A |
| **54th Congress 1895–1897 Republican majority** | | | |
| 5 | Increase taxes | N | N/A |
| 7 | Coin redemption fund and debt credits | N | N/A |
| 35 | Define and regulate cheese | N | N/A |
| 42 | Invalid pensions | N | N/A |
| 43 | Private relief | N | N/A |
| 45 | Uniform bankruptcy law | N | N/A |
| 137 | Incorporate railroad company | N | N/A |
| 155 | Increase circulation of national banks | N | N/A |

| Sequential Roll Call Number | Bill | Significant Law | Enacted |
|---|---|---|---|
| 55th Congress 1897–1899 Republican majority ||||
| 5 | Sundry civil appropriations | N | N/A |
| 10 | Tariffs | N | N/A |
| 77 | Authorize extending lines of Capitol Traction Company D.C. | N | N/A |
| 79 | Post Office appropriations | N | N/A |
| 91 | Additional powers to railroad companies | N | N/A |
| 105 | Income tax for war | N | N/A |
| 117 | Government taxes on liquor | N | N/A |
| 130 | Let Spanish-American War veterans vote in congressional elections | N | N/A |
| 137 | Extend 11th St. NW | N | N/A |
| 148 | Regulate interstate commerce | N | N/A |
| 161 | Reorganize the army | N | N/A |
| 170 | Provide for erection of public building in Blair, Nebraska | N | N/A |
| 56th Congress 1899–1901 Republican majority ||||
| 5 | Parity of all forms of U.S. money | N | N/A |
| 21 | Regulate tariffs and customs for Puerto Rico | N | N/A |
| 26 | Puerto Rico appropriations | N | N/A |
| 51 | Provide depositories public funds Cuba, Philippines, Puerto Rico | N | N/A |
| 91 | Subject oleomargarine to state laws | N | N/A |
| 113 | Claim of Wilson Cramp and Sons | N | N/A |
| 57th Congress 1901–1903 Republican majority ||||
| 5 | Provide revenue for Philippines | N | N/A |
| 38 | Provide for removal of overhead wires in D.C. | N | N/A |
| 76 | Promote army efficiency | Y | N/A |

| Sequential Roll Call Number | Bill | Significant Law | Enacted |
|---|---|---|---|
| 86 | Diplomatic appropriations | N | N/A |
| 38 | Provide for revenue, civil government of Philippines | N | N/A |

**58th Congress 1903–1905 Republican majority**

| | | | |
|---|---|---|---|
| 42 | Admit Oklahoma, New Mexico, and Arizona into union | N | N/A |
| 47 | Commission to consider developing Merchant Marine | N | N/A |

**59th Congress 1905–1907 Republican majority**

| | | | |
|---|---|---|---|
| 8 | Admit Oklahoma into union | Y | N/A |
| 25 | Incorporate Lake Erie and Ohio River Ship Canal | N | N/A |
| 53 | Relief of Henry E. Rhoades | N | N/A |
| 58 | Claim of estate of Samuel Lee | N | N/A |
| 106 | Provide for free evening lectures in D.C. | N | N/A |

**60th Congress 1907–1909 Republican majority**

| | | | |
|---|---|---|---|
| 164 | Protect bank depositors | N | N/A |
| 273 | Punish conspiracies against aliens | N | N/A |
| 288 | Provide for construction of Panama Canal and zone government | N | N/A |

**61st Congress 1909–1911 Republican majority**

| | | | |
|---|---|---|---|
| 19 | Tariffs | N | N/A |
| 24 | Census appropriations | N | N/A |
| 39 | Construct Panama Canal | N | N/A |
| 42 | Army appropriations | N | N/A |
| 105 | Regulate interstate commerce | Y | N/A |
| 107 | Sell Indian land for town site | N | N/A |
| 109 | Commerce court | N | N/A |
| 132 | Protect Appalachian streams/forests | N | N/A |

| Sequential Roll Call Number | Bill | Significant Law | Enacted |
|---|---|---|---|
| 153 | Establish tariff board | N | N/A |
| 192 | Increase efficiency of militia | N | N/A |

### 62nd Congress 1911–1913 Democratic majority

| | | | |
|---|---|---|---|
| 11 | Reciprocal trade with Canada | Y | N/A |
| 14 | Agriculture tools on free list | N | N/A |
| 24 | Reduce duty on wool | N | N/A |
| 28 | Reduce duty on cotton | N | N/A |
| 61 | Revise judiciary laws | N | N/A |
| 67 | Equalize duties | N | N/A |
| 87 | Equalize duties | N | N/A |
| 104 | Equalize duties | N | N/A |
| 109 | Reduce duties on wool | N | N/A |
| 169 | Duty on cotton manufacture | N | N/A |

### 63rd Congress 1913–1915 Democratic majority

| | | | |
|---|---|---|---|
| 3 | Consider sundry civil and Indian Department appropriations | N | N/A |
| 6 | Tariffs | N | N/A |
| 33 | Establish federal reserve banks | N | N/A |
| 78 | Require recital of real consideration in deeds to property in D.C. | N | N/A |
| 104 | Provide for maintenance and operation of Panama Canal | N | N/A |
| 124 | Laws against restraints and monopolies | N | N/A |
| 192 | Increase internal revenue | N | N/A |
| 202 | Declare U.S. purpose in Philippines and government there | N | N/A |
| 221 | Establish additional court in Steubenville, Ohio | N | N/A |
| 236 | Prohibit miscegenation in D.C. | N | N/A |

| Sequential Roll Call Number | Bill | Significant Law | Enacted |
|---|---|---|---|
| **64th Congress 1915–1917 Democratic majority** | | | |
| 38 | Appropriations for public works on rivers and harbors | N | N/A |
| 64 | Develop Merchant Marines for U.S. commerce | N | N/A |
| 66 | D.C. appropriations | N | N/A |
| 80 | Transfer two counties in Oklahoma to different judicial districts | N | N/A |
| 84 | Increase taxes | Y | N/A |
| 98 | Establish fish hatcheries in various states | N | N/A |
| 120 | Defense appropriations and taxes | N | N/A |
| **65th Congress 1917–1919 Democratic majority** | | | |
| 19 | Ban publishing defense information | N | N/A |
| 42 | Rivers and harbors | N | N/A |
| 97 | D.C. taxes | N | N/A |
| 130 | D.C. garbage disposal | N | N/A |
| 144 | Regulate convict labor | N | N/A |
| 224 | Military hospital | N | N/A |
| **66th Congress 1919–1921 Republican majority** | | | |
| 71 | Promote tungsten production | N | N/A |
| 76 | Tariff on shell and pearl buttons | N | N/A |
| 88 | Controls on dyes | N | N/A |
| 95 | Duty on magnetite | N | N/A |
| 104 | Vocational rehabilitation for disabled | N | N/A |
| 130 | Return railroads to private ownership | N | N/A |
| 131 | Weights and measures standards | N | N/A |
| 178 | Lincoln's birthday a D.C. holiday | N | N/A |
| 182 | Reorganize army | N | N/A |
| 249 | Temporary immigration suspension | N | N/A |
| 258 | Agricultural duties | N | N/A |

| Sequential Roll Call Number | Bill | Significant Law | Enacted |
|---|---|---|---|
| **67th Congress 1921–1923 Republican majority** | | | |
| 4 | Temporary duties on certain agricultural products | N | N/A |
| 69 | Tariffs | N | N/A |
| 86 | Control import of dyes and chemicals | N | N/A |
| 88 | Deficiencies in appropriations | N | N/A |
| 94 | Equalize taxes | N | N/A |
| 97 | Amend Transportation Act of 1920 | N | N/A |
| 112 | Extend Tariff Act of 1921 | N | N/A |
| 116 | Create committee to refund/convert foreign obligations | N | N/A |
| 123 | Authorize president to locate and construct railroads in Alaska | N | N/A |
| 136 | Appoint additional judges to certain U.S. courts | N | N/A |
| 141 | Provide for relief of starving Russians | N | N/A |
| 169 | Punish crime of lynching | N | N/A |
| 181 | Authorize president to provide housing for war needs | N | N/A |
| 277 | Establish U.S. Coal Commission | N | N/A |
| 284 | Declare national emergency coal production | N | N/A |
| 302 | Amend Merchant Marine Act of 1920 | N | N/A |
| **68th Congress 1923–1925 Republican majority** | | | |
| 16 | Create two judicial districts in Indiana | N | N/A |
| 88 | Provide for purchase of Cape Cod Canal property | N | N/A |
| 113 | Authorize alterations to and provide for building of naval vessels | N | N/A |
| 141 | Authorize Agriculture Department to disburse agents outside D.C. | N | N/A |
| 146 | Provide for erecting certain public buildings | N | N/A |

| Sequential Roll Call Number | Bill | Significant Law | Enacted |
|---|---|---|---|
| 159 | Amend China Trade Act of 1922 | N | N/A |
| 167 | Establish migratory bird refuges | N | N/A |

### 69th Congress 1925–1927 Republican majority

| | | | |
|---|---|---|---|
| 7 | Settle Italy's debts to U.S. | N | N/A |
| 26 | Regulate radio communications | Y | N/A |
| 49 | Authorize erection of military monument in France | N | N/A |
| 60 | Settle French debts to U.S. | N | N/A |
| 68 | Appoint additional judges | N | N/A |
| 104 | Government control of medicinal spirits | N | N/A |

### 70th Congress 1927–1929 Republican majority

| | | | |
|---|---|---|---|
| 35 | Amend act incorporating Howard University in D.C. | N | N/A |
| 55 | Settle debts with Greece | N | N/A |

### 71st Congress 1929–1931 Republican majority

| | | | |
|---|---|---|---|
| 7 | Tariffs | N | N/A |
| 15 | Settle French debts to U.S. | N | N/A |
| 17 | Report on conservation of public domain | N | N/A |
| 24 | Regulate carriers on public highways | N | N/A |
| 54 | Summary prosecution of slight Prohibition violations | N | N/A |

### 72nd Congress 1931–1933 Democratic majority

| | | | |
|---|---|---|---|
| 7 | Tariffs | N | N/A |
| 8 | Tariffs | N | N/A |
| 17 | Highway/jobs program | N | N/A |
| 60 | Powers of Reconstruction Finance Corporation | N | N/A |
| 64 | Immediate payment to veterans | N | N/A |
| 90 | Tax nonintoxicating liquors | N | N/A |

| Sequential Roll Call Number | Bill | Significant Law | Enacted |
|---|---|---|---|
| 97 | Independence of Philippines | Y | N/A |
| 118 | Regulate prescription of medicinal liquor | N | N/A |

### 73rd Congress 1933–1935 Democratic majority

| | | | |
|---|---|---|---|
| 7 | Provide for farm relief | Y | N/A |
| 34 | Sundry executive branch appropriations | N | N/A |
| 53 | Deficiencies in appropriations | N | N/A |
| 76 | Authorize postmaster to use War Department equipment | N | N/A |
| 86 | Aid cotton growers and prevent unfair competition | N | N/A |
| 91 | Tariffs (reciprocal trade agreements) | N | N/A |
| 94 | Regulate grazing on public lands | Y | N/A |
| 102 | Regulate securities exchanges | Y | N/A |
| 109 | Establish Everglades National Park in Florida | N | N/A |
| 111 | Establish foreign trade zones in U.S. ports | N | N/A |
| 115 | Authorize Secretary of Treasury to issue silver certificates | Y | N/A |
| 120 | Diversification of prison industries | N | N/A |
| 134 | Take employment census | N | N/A |

### 74th Congress 1935–1937 Democratic majority

| | | | |
|---|---|---|---|
| 47 | Sound and Effective Banking System | Y | N/A |
| 62 | Establish central statistical committee and board | N | N/A |
| 77 | Amend Tennessee Valley Authority Act | N | N/A |
| 92 | Regulate alcohol | N | N/A |
| 93 | Control Mississippi River floods | N | N/A |
| 98 | Equalize taxation | N | N/A |
| 108 | Stabilize bituminous coal mining industry | N | N/A |

| Sequential Roll Call Number | Bill | Significant Law | Enacted |
|---|---|---|---|
| 156 | Filing of copies of income tax returns | N | N/A |
| 167 | Agreements among tobacco-producing states | N | N/A |
| 176 | 1936 revenue bill | N | N/A |
| 205 | Private bill | N | N/A |
| 212 | Provide for administration and maintenance of Blue Ridge Parkway | N | N/A |

**75th Congress 1937–1939 Democratic majority**

| | | | |
|---|---|---|---|
| 11 | Provide for retirement of Supreme Court justices | N | N/A |
| 16 | Authorize purchase of 640 acres for Santa Rosa Indians | N | N/A |
| 17 | Study for hydroelectric project at Cabinet Gorge | N | N/A |
| 33 | Development of farm forestry | N | N/A |
| 50 | Provide for acquisition of lands for Yosemite National Park | N | N/A |
| 56 | Look into impeachment charges of certain judge | N | N/A |
| 79 | Authorize president to appoint up to six administrative assistants | N | N/A |
| 84 | Establish Department of Welfare | N | N/A |
| 94 | Farmers to grow soil-conserving crops | N | N/A |
| 115 | U.S. Navy appropriations | N | N/A |

**76th Congress 1939–1941 Democratic majority**

| | | | |
|---|---|---|---|
| 9 | Federal employees subject to income tax | N | N/A |
| 12 | Extend export–import bank and commodity credit | N | N/A |
| 20 | Provide for government reorganization | Y | N/A |
| 25 | Interior Department appropriations | N | N/A |
| 106 | Extend classified executive civil service | N | N/A |

| Sequential Roll Call Number | Bill | Significant Law | Enacted |
|---|---|---|---|
| 113 | $30,000 for tourist facilities Mt. McKinley National Park | N | N/A |
| 118 | Appoint additional judges | N | N/A |
| 134 | Include cotton growers in federal crop insurance program | N | N/A |
| 204 | Increase lending authority of export–import bank | N | N/A |
| 213 | Military draft | N | N/A |

77th Congress 1941–1943 Democratic majority

| | | | |
|---|---|---|---|
| 6 | Limit lend-lease to Great Britain to $2 billion, promote defense | N | N/A |
| 11 | Limit house to 435 members | N | N/A |
| 17 | Office of Government Reports appropriations | N | N/A |
| 23 | Certain D.C. officials need not live in D.C. | N | N/A |
| 26 | Authorize acquisition of merchant vessels | N | N/A |
| 32 | Stabilizing fund for dollar | N | N/A |
| 69 | Procedures for badly behaving federal judges | N | N/A |
| 72 | Establish price controls | N | N/A |
| 105 | Increase salaries of D.C. police | N | N/A |

78th Congress 1943–1945 Democratic majority

| | | | |
|---|---|---|---|
| 103 | Provide additional Secretary of the Interior | N | N/A |

79th Congress 1945–1947 Democratic majority

| | | | |
|---|---|---|---|
| 5 | Selective service | N | N/A |
| 43 | Extend trade agreements | N | N/A |
| 66 | Postage on catalogs | N | N/A |
| 74 | Add federal judge in Missouri | N | N/A |
| 75 | Health programs for federal employees | N | N/A |

| Sequential Roll Call Number | Bill | Significant Law | Enacted |
|---|---|---|---|

### 80th Congress 1947–1949 Republican majority

| Sequential Roll Call Number | Bill | Significant Law | Enacted |
|---|---|---|---|
| 24 | Reduce income tax | N/A | N/A |
| 36 | Repeal housing rent control | N/A | N/A |
| 56 | Admit Hawaii into Union | N/A | N/A |
| 60 | Reduce income tax | N/A | N/A |
| 87 | Amend Reclamation Act | N/A | N/A |
| 89 | Reduce income tax | N/A | N/A |
| 133 | Trade agreement authority to president | N/A | N/A |

### 81st Congress 1949–1951 Democratic majority

| | | | |
|---|---|---|---|
| 12 | Regulate exports | N/A | N/A |
| 21 | Extend Housing Act | N/A | N/A |
| 62 | Establish national housing objectives | N/A | N/A |
| 66 | Provide rural telephones | N/A | N/A |
| 98 | For military assistance | N/A | N/A |
| 153 | Promote science | N/A | N/A |
| 154 | Admit Alaska into Union | N/A | N/A |
| 193 | Extend Housing Act | N/A | N/A |
| 208 | Export–Import Bank | N/A | N/A |
| 217 | Appoint additional judges for Illinois | N/A | N/A |
| 222 | Appoint judge for Missouri | N/A | N/A |
| 258 | Authorize president to appoint Secretary of Defense | N/A | N/A |
| 268 | Extend Housing Act | N/A | N/A |
| 269 | Emergency aid to Yugoslavia | N/A | N/A |

### 82nd Congress 1951–1953 Democratic majority

| | | | |
|---|---|---|---|
| 42 | Revenue | N/A | N/A |
| 43 | D.C. Emergency Rent Act | N/A | N/A |
| 85 | Foreign aid | N/A | N/A |

| Sequential Roll Call Number | Bill | Significant Law | Enacted |
|---|---|---|---|
| 145 | Authorize government to lease buildings | N/A | N/A |
| 150 | Foreign military aid | N/A | N/A |
| 164 | Define production and rent control | N/A | N/A |
| 171 | Parity on prices of agricultural commodities | N/A | N/A |

**83rd Congress 1953–1955 Republican majority**

| Sequential Roll Call Number | Bill | Significant Law | Enacted |
|---|---|---|---|
| 10 | Admit Hawaii | N/A | N/A |
| 47 | Niagara power plant | N/A | N/A |
| 64 | Immigration | N/A | N/A |
| 69 | Increase debt limit | N/A | N/A |
| 97 | Establish commission on education | N/A | N/A |
| 126 | Amend Atomic Energy Act | N/A | N/A |
| 134 | Tariffs on hardboard | N/A | N/A |
| 136 | River project | N/A | N/A |

**84th Congress 1955–1957 Democratic majority**

| Sequential Roll Call Number | Bill | Significant Law | Enacted |
|---|---|---|---|
| 12 | Tax reduction | N | N/A |
| 28 | Agricultural price supports | N | N |
| 49 | California central valley project | N | Y |

**85th Congress 1957–1959 Democratic majority**

| Sequential Roll Call Number | Bill | Significant Law | Enacted |
|---|---|---|---|
| 5 | Pay ranchers not to graze on drought land | N/A | N/A |
| 27 | Provide funds for new bridge across Potomac | N/A | N/A |
| 33 | Legislative branch appropriations | N/A | N/A |
| 36 | Increase diversion of water from Lake Michigan | N/A | N/A |
| 59 | Authorize irrigation and municipal water project in Texas | N/A | N/A |

**86th Congress 1959–1961 Democratic majority**

| Sequential Roll Call Number | Bill | Significant Law | Enacted |
|---|---|---|---|
| 3 | Veterans housing bill | N | Y |
| 7 | Authorize a study of effects of diverting Lake Michigan water | N | N |

| Sequential Roll Call Number | Bill | Significant Law | Enacted |
|---|---|---|---|
| 11 | Extend Federal Airport Construction Act | N | N |
| 12 | Pan Am Games in Chicago appropriations | N | Y |
| 14 | Authority to rural electrification administrative head | N | N |
| 18 | TVA can issue revenue bonds for construction | N | Y |
| 19 | NASA appropriations | N | Y |
| 30 | Require states to match federal grants for sewage treatment plants | N | N |
| 38 | Wheat price controls | N | N/A |
| 67 | Authorize subsidies for construction of fishing vessels | N | Y |
| 70 | Give property to Sacto City for sewage agreement | N | Y |
| 82 | Revised public works appropriations | N | N/A |
| 110 | Emergency housing | N | N |
| 131 | Foreign investment incentive tax | N | N |
| 140 | Give states cigarette tax for school construction | N | N |
| 157 | Authorize subsidies for lead and zinc | N | N |

**87th Congress 1961–1963 Democratic majority**

| | | | |
|---|---|---|---|
| 8 | Provide price supports for feed grains | N/A | N/A |
| 25 | Increase grants for sewage plant construction | N/A | N/A |
| 28 | Salary for Council of Economic Advisors | N/A | N/A |
| 31 | Establish Office of International Travel and Tourism | N/A | N/A |
| 47 | Housing Act | N/A | N/A |
| 48 | Increase national debt ceiling | N/A | N/A |
| 61 | No funds for transfer of U.S. Army Food Institute | N/A | N/A |

| Sequential Roll Call Number | Bill | Significant Law | Enacted |
|---|---|---|---|
| 67 | Reorganize Federal Communication Commission | N/A | N/A |
| 68 | Authorize military to sell aircraft supplies in emergency | N/A | N/A |
| 71 | Reorganize Interstate Commerce Commission | N/A | N/A |
| 78 | Authorize subsidy for small lead and zinc mines | N/A | N/A |
| 80 | Authorize construction of National Fisheries Center and Aquarium in D.C. | N/A | N/A |
| 91 | Welfare and Pension Plans Disclosure Act | N/A | N/A |
| 122 | Increase debt ceiling to $300 billion | N/A | N/A |
| 137 | Tax revisions | N/A | N/A |
| 143 | Appropriations to NYC for police at UN assembly | N/A | N/A |
| 157 | Increase debt ceiling to $308 billion | N/A | N/A |
| 166 | Trade Expansion Act | N/A | N/A |
| 212 | Foreign aid | N/A | N/A |

**88th Congress 1963–1965 Democratic majority**

| | | | |
|---|---|---|---|
| 13 | Authorize issue of Federal Reserve notes | N | Y |
| 15 | Health Professionals Education Assistance Act education loans | Y | Y |
| 17 | Authorize feed grains acreage diversion program | N | Y |
| 28 | Increase debt ceiling | N | Y |
| 35 | Legislative appropriations | N | Y |
| 37 | Extend temporary excise and corporate income taxes | N | Y |
| 47 | Clean Air Act | N | Y |
| 58 | Extend temporary debt limit | N | Y |
| 62 | Authorize appropriations for foreign aid | Y | Y |

| Sequential Roll Call Number | Bill | Significant Law | Enacted |
|---|---|---|---|
| 69 | Revenue Act | Y | Y |
| 77 | Authorize appropriations to compile and publish U.S. documents | N | Y |
| 89 | Increase debt ceiling to $315 billion | N | Y |
| 90 | Authorize president to limit coffee imports | N | N |
| 99 | Authorize government to pay cotton subsidies and price supports | Y | Y |
| 112 | Foreign aid appropriations | N | Y |
| 127 | Civil Rights Act | N | Y |
| 135 | Temporary tax on purchase of certified foreign securities | Y | Y |
| 141 | Change certification and administrative procedure for National Bureau of Standards | N | N |
| 149 | Food stamp bill | Y | Y |
| 171 | Foreign Assistance Act | N | Y |
| 172 | Raise salaries of federal employees, Congress' and judges | Y | Y |
| 175 | Increase debt limit to $324 billion | N | Y |
| 178 | Federal mass transit aid | Y | N |
| 181 | Foreign economic aid reduction | N | Y |
| 193 | Authorize Secretary of Interior to administer national scientific reserve | N | |
| 199 | Provide state veto power over poverty programs | N | N |
| 213 | Extend federal regulations to small coal mines | N | N |
| 221 | Establish National Council of the Arts in executive office | N | Y |
| 228 | Authorize Secretary of Interior to administer national scientific reserve | N | Y |

| Sequential Roll Call Number | Bill | Significant Law | Enacted |
|---|---|---|---|
| **89th Congress 1965–1967 Democratic majority** | | | |
| 8 | Federal reserve banks not required to have gold certified reserves | N/A | N/A |
| 11 | Amend Inter-American Development Bank Act | N/A | N/A |
| 23 | Provide for acreage-poundage tobacco quotas | N/A | N/A |
| 26 | Strengthen and improve education | N/A | N/A |
| 35 | Provide hospital insurance for aged under Social Security | N/A | N/A |
| 44 | Amend authorization of arts and culture appropriations | N/A | N/A |
| 56 | Amend Foreign Assistance Act | N/A | N/A |
| 62 | Appointment General Wm F. McKee administrator for FAA | N/A | N/A |
| 67 | Increase public debt limit | N/A | N/A |
| 71 | Create Housing and Urban Development cabinet-level department | N/A | N/A |
| 81 | Create Housing and Urban Development cabinet-level department | N/A | N/A |
| 92 | Coinage act fixing level of silver in coins | N/A | N/A |
| 95 | Economic opportunity amendments | N/A | N/A |
| 101 | Repeal right-to-work section of Taft–Hartley Act | N/A | N/A |
| 102 | Amend Atomic Eenergy Act | N/A | N/A |
| 112 | Extend interest equalization tax | N/A | N/A |
| 122 | Food and Agriculture Act | N/A | N/A |
| 136 | Foreign aid authorization | N/A | N/A |
| 163 | Permit U.S. participation in Inter-American culture center | N/A | N/A |
| 193 | Sugar Act amendments | N/A | N/A |

| Sequential Roll Call Number | Bill | Significant Law | Enacted |
|---|---|---|---|
| 195 | Supplemental appropriations | N/A | N/A |
| 212 | Tax Adjustment Act | N/A | N/A |
| 218 | Provide for U.S. participation in Alaska Exposition | N/A | N/A |
| 220 | Cotton research and promotion | N/A | N/A |
| 228 | Second supplemental appropriations bill | N/A | N/A |
| 257 | Participation Sales Act | N/A | N/A |
| 270 | Temporary increase in public debt limit | N/A | N/A |
| 285 | Foreign Assistance Act | N/A | N/A |
| 302 | Urban Mass Transportation Act | N/A | N/A |
| 343 | Foreign assistance appropriations | N/A | N/A |
| 351 | Economic opportunity amendments | N/A | N/A |
| 353 | Suspension of investment credit and accelerate depreciation | N/A | N/A |
| 363 | Elementary and secondary education amendments | N/A | N/A |
| 369 | Create Indiana Dunes National Lakeshore | N/A | N/A |

**90th Congress 1967–1969 Democratic majority**

| Sequential Roll Call Number | Bill | Significant Law | Enacted |
|---|---|---|---|
| 8 | Increase public debt limit to $336 billion | N | Y |
| 21 | Extend interest equalization tax and presidential authority | N | Y |
| 73 | Authorize adjustment in amount of outstanding silver certificates | N | N |
| 82 | Increase federal debt limit to $358 billion | Y | Y |
| 102 | Authorize increase to Inter-American Development Bank | N | Y |
| 121 | Foreign assistance and military aid authorization | N | N |
| 122 | Increase federal money to Potomac protecting sewer | N | N |
| 210 | Foreign aid appropriations | Y | Y |

| Sequential Roll Call Number | Bill | Significant Law | Enacted |
|---|---|---|---|
| 258 | Eliminate reserve requirement for Federal Reserve Notes | N | Y |
| 282 | Market orders for cherries | N | N |
| 299 | Extend authorization for Corporation for Public Broadcasting | N | N |
| 391 | Foreign Assistance Act | N | Y |
| 394 | Transportation of schoolchildren | N | Y |
| 404 | Permit employer contributions to promote industry | N | N |
| 412 | Amend Food and Agriculture Act | Y | Y |
| 445 | Foreign aid appropriations | N | Y |

**91st Congress 1969–1971 Democratic majority**

| | | | |
|---|---|---|---|
| 12 | Increase U.S. participation in International Development Association | N/A | N/A |
| 46 | Authorize additional funds for JFK Center | N/A | N/A |
| 84 | Legislative branch appropriations | N/A | N/A |
| 121 | Administrative conference of U.S. to remove the ceiling on appropriations | N/A | N/A |
| 137 | Foreign aid authorization | N/A | N/A |
| 148 | Foreign aid appropriations | N/A | N/A |
| 163 | Lower interest rates for housing and business assistance | N/A | N/A |
| 179 | Amend Taft–Hartley Act (employer contribution) | N/A | N/A |
| 261 | Foreign aid appropriations | N/A | N/A |
| 321 | Agricultural Act | N/A | N/A |
| 339 | Pay rates of government employees | N/A | N/A |
| 382 | Trade Act of 1970 | N/A | N/A |

| Sequential Roll Call Number | Bill | Significant Law | Enacted |
|---|---|---|---|
| **92nd Congress 1971–1973 Democratic majority** | | | |
| 18 | Provide additional financing for rural telephone program | N | N |
| 159 | Amend Foreign Assistance Act | N | N |
| 305 | Storage of grain in hungry people's houses | N | N |
| 343 | Establish Office of Technology Assessment for Congress | N | Y |
| 348 | Extend Economic Opportunity Act programs | Y | Y |
| 400 | Increase federal government contribution to health benefits | N | N |
| 606 | Provide for construction of D.C. civic center | N | N |
| **93rd Congress 1973–1975 Democratic majority** | | | |
| 10 | Require a rural environmental assistance program | N/A | N/A |
| 14 | Amend emergency loan program for farmers | N/A | N/A |
| 30 | Extend authorization of Public Works and Economic Development Act | N/A | N/A |
| 71 | Appointment to Office of Management and Budget must be confirmed | N/A | N/A |
| 92 | Supplemental appropriations | N/A | N/A |
| 115 | Authorize assistance for development of emergency health care | N/A | N/A |
| 129 | Increase minimum wage for agricultural employees | N/A | N/A |
| 141 | Regulate maximum D.C. rents | N/A | N/A |
| 147 | Regulate unions and legal services | N/A | N/A |
| 241 | Provision for retirement of Immigration and Naturalization Service employees in hazardous jobs | N/A | N/A |
| 259 | Amend Agriculture Act | N/A | N/A |
| 277 | President and impoundment of funds | N/A | N/A |

| Sequential Roll Call Number | Bill | Significant Law | Enacted |
|---|---|---|---|
| 284 | Amend foreign aid (reduce population planning fund) | N/A | N/A |
| 326 | Prohibit state discriminatory burden on wine | N/A | N/A |
| 349 | Increase federal government contribution to health benefits | N/A | N/A |
| 367 | Urban Mass Transportation Act | N/A | N/A |
| 481 | Foreign aid appropriations | N/A | N/A |
| 604 | Regarding Tennessee Valley Authority expenditures for pollution control | N/A | N/A |
| 609 | Regarding D.C. referendum on advisory neighborhood councils | N/A | N/A |
| 610 | Create law revision commission for D.C. | N/A | N/A |
| 683 | Percentage of U.S. oil import must be in U.S. vessels | N/A | N/A |
| 691 | Establish legal services corporation | N/A | N/A |
| 704 | Temporary increase in public debt limit | N/A | N/A |
| 743 | Authorize appropriations for International Economic Policy Act | N/A | N/A |
| 810 | Provide emergency guaranteed livestock loans | N/A | N/A |
| 937 | Authorize change the penny and grants to a college | N/A | N/A |
| 982 | Amend National Visitor Facility Act | N/A | N/A |
| 1028 | Provide for U.S. participation in Asian Development Bank | N/A | N/A |
| 1038 | Amend Foreign Assistance Act | N/A | N/A |
| 1059 | Establish Harry S. Truman Memorial Scholarship program | N/A | N/A |

94th Congress 1975–1977 Democratic majority

| | | | |
|---|---|---|---|
| 5 | Suspend authority of president to adjust petroleum tariffs | N | N |
| 6 | Increase temporary debt limit | N | Y |

| Sequential Roll Call Number | Bill | Significant Law | Enacted |
|---|---|---|---|
| 29 | Emergency employment appropriations | N | |
| 30 | Foreign aid appropriations | N | Y |
| 48 | Target prices and price support for certain agricultural products | N | N |
| 56 | Expand Emergency Home Purchase Assistance Act | N | N |
| 87 | Provide for development of youth camp safety | N | N |
| 140 | Prohibit federal savings and loans from offering variable interest rate | N | N |
| 145 | Authorize Secretary of Commerce to promote tourism | N | N |
| 163 | Authorize local public works development program | N | N |
| 175 | Establish independent and regional U.S. parole commission | N | Y |
| 195 | Provide for congressional review of oil-related acts | N | N |
| 235 | National energy conservation and conversion program | N | N |
| 253 | Increase temporary debt limit | N | Y |
| 326 | Craft and industry worker rights (Common–Situs) | N | N |
| 353 | Extend council on wage and price stability | N | N |
| 378 | Assist low-income people to insulate homes | N | N |
| 379 | Establish American Folklife Center in Library of Congress | N | N/A |
| 384 | International Development and Food Assistance Act | Y | Y |
| 401 | Relating to construction of mint buildings | N | N |
| 405 | Energy Conservation and Oil Policy Act | N | N |
| 444 | Stabilize labor–management relations in construction | N | N |

| Sequential Roll Call Number | Bill | Significant Law | Enacted |
|---|---|---|---|
| 463 | Regarding federal employees running for office | N | N |
| 475 | Emergency Rail Transport Improvement and Employee Act | N | N |
| 476 | Right to representation for federal employees under investigation | N | N |
| 484 | Limit postal rate increase and other USPS matters | N | Y |
| 488 | Regulation of interest rates and marketing disclosure | N | N |
| 497 | Consumer Protection Act | N | N |
| 518 | Increase temporary debt limit | N | Y |
| 534 | Increase federal assistance to community action agencies | N | N |
| 537 | Extend National Foundation Art and Humanities Act | N | N |
| 541 | Intergovernmental Emergency Assistance Act | Y | Y |
| 552 | Reform tax laws | Y | Y |
| 562 | Increase U.S. participation in Inter-American Development Bank | N | Y |
| 568 | Direct commission to organize national women's conference | N | Y |
| 615 | Authorize and modify various reclamation projects | N | N |
| 640 | Ensure adequate supply of natural gas | N | N |
| 649 | Amendment providing further unemployment benefits | N | N |
| 659 | Increase temporary debt limit | N | Y |
| 664 | Increase black lung compensation for coal miners | N | N |
| 669 | Amendments to foreign military aid | N | N |
| 676 | Foreign aid appropriations | Y | Y |

| Sequential Roll Call Number | Bill | Significant Law | Enacted |
|---|---|---|---|
| 704 | Regarding Legal Services Corporation spending | N | N |
| 724 | Federal Election Campaign Act amendments | N | N |
| 849 | International Security Assistance and Arms Export Control Act | N | Y |
| 879 | Authorize appropriations for Lake Placid Winter Olympics | N | N |
| 884 | Treasury, postal, and general government appropriations | N | Y |
| 886 | Increase temporary debt limit | N | Y |
| 970 | Foreign aid appropriations | N | Y |
| 1008 | Unemployment compensation | Y | Y |
| 1014 | Amend Outer Continental Shelf Land Act (oil) | N | N/A |
| 1022 | Amend Pennsylvania Avenue Development Corporation Act | N | N |
| 1031 | Prohibit abusive practices by debt collectors | N | N |
| 1034 | Regarding mine health and safety | N | N |
| 1044 | Regarding California supplemental Social Security payments | N | Y |
| 1085 | Establish voter registration commission in FEC | N | N |
| 1096 | Extend D.C. authority to borrow from U.S. Treasury | N | N/A |

**95th Congress 1977–1979 Democratic majority**

| | | | |
|---|---|---|---|
| 24 | Increase authority for emergency public works job program | N/A | N/A |
| 38 | Appropriations for repairing JFK center | N/A | N/A |
| 46 | Reduce and simplify taxes | N/A | N/A |
| 58 | Amend UN participation act to stop import of Rhodesian chrome | N/A | N/A |
| 63 | Appropriations for economic stimulus | N/A | N/A |

| Sequential Roll Call Number | Bill | Significant Law | Enacted |
|---|---|---|---|
| 68 | Supplemental appropriations | N/A | N/A |
| 106 | Prohibit abusive practices by debt collectors | N/A | N/A |
| 116 | Authorize U.S. contributions to international financial institutions | N/A | N/A |
| 176 | Foreign aid authorization | N/A | N/A |
| 208 | International Development and Food Assistance Act | N/A | N/A |
| 212 | Antirecession Assistance Act | N/A | N/A |
| 259 | Amend foreign military aid | N/A | N/A |
| 295 | Amend Hatch Act (political participation of federal employees) | N/A | N/A |
| 348 | Foreign aid appropriations | N/A | N/A |
| 358 | Authorize appropriations to Legal Service Corporation | N/A | N/A |
| 367 | Legislative branch appropriations | N/A | N/A |
| 387 | National Consumer Coop Bank Act | N/A | N/A |
| 394 | Federal Mine Safety and Health Act | N/A | N/A |
| 447 | Agricultural appropriations | N/A | N/A |
| 482 | Establish comprehensive national energy program | N/A | N/A |
| 496 | Earthquake Hazards Reduction Act | N/A | N/A |
| 516 | Minimum wage | N/A | N/A |
| 523 | Improve black lung benefits | N/A | N/A |
| 545 | Regarding D.C. borrowing authority | N/A | N/A |
| 559 | Increase temporary debt limit | N/A | N/A |
| 570 | Victims of Crime act | N/A | N/A |
| 573 | Extend council on wage and price stability | N/A | N/A |
| 591 | Labor Reform Act | N/A | N/A |
| 601 | Congress can veto Federal Trade Commission rulings | N/A | N/A |

| Sequential Roll Call Number | Bill | Significant Law | Enacted |
|---|---|---|---|
| 649 | Increase in Social Security taxes and benefits | N/A | N/A |
| 758 | Providing for development of agriculture in U.S. | N/A | N/A |
| 767 | Authorize U.S. participation in support of financing of IMF | N/A | N/A |
| 841 | Promote full employment and balanced growth | N/A | N/A |
| 847 | Increase public debt limit | N/A | N/A |
| 884 | Reduce workweek of federal firefighters | N/A | N/A |
| 889 | President, White House staff appropriations | N/A | N/A |
| 972 | Amend International Development and Food Assistance Act | N/A | N/A |
| 973 | Establish H.H. Humphrey Fellowship | N/A | N/A |
| 1039 | State Department appropriations | N/A | N/A |
| 1077 | New York Financial Assistance Act | N/A | N/A |
| 1203 | Temporary increase in public debt limit | N/A | N/A |
| 1323 | Foreign aid appropriations | N/A | N/A |
| 1354 | Foreign intelligence surveillance | N/A | N/A |
| 1491 | Sugar Stabilization Act | N/A | N/A |

**96th Congress 1979–1981 Democratic majority**

| Sequential Roll Call Number | Bill | Significant Law | Enacted |
|---|---|---|---|
| 81 | Authorize foreign economic assistance appropriations | N | Y |
| 89 | Authorize State Department appropriations | N | Y |
| 183 | Authorize Treasury Department international affairs appropriations | N | N |
| 251 | Provide for operation and maintenance of Panama Canal | Y | Y |
| 289 | Establish Department of Education | N | N |
| 313 | D.C. appropriations | N | Y |
| 406 | Foreign aid appropriations | N | N |

| Sequential Roll Call Number | Bill | Significant Law | Enacted |
|---|---|---|---|
| 465 | Temporary increase in public debt limit | N | Y |
| 533 | Department of Energy civilian authorities | N | N |
| 548 | Benefits of certain Department of Indian Affairs employees | N | Y |
| 567 | Reform social welfare and support Social Security programs | N | N |
| 590 | Amend and extend Public Works and Economic Development Act | N | N |
| 603 | Extend borrowing authority of D.C. | N | Y |
| 643 | Provide for activities to prevent domestic violence | N | N |
| 661 | Chrysler Corporation loan guarantees | Y | Y |
| 692 | Anti-recession fiscal assistance | N | N |
| 700 | Retirement benefits reduce unemployment compensation | N | N |
| 718 | Improve and expand federal crop insurance program | N | N |
| 749 | Central American aid | N | Y |
| 783 | Provide for increased U.S. participation in various international banks | N | N |
| 817 | Amend IRS code (mortgage subsidy bonds interest) | N | N |
| 937 | Extend public debt limit | N | Y |
| 944 | Foreign aid (international security and development) | N | Y |
| 960 | Prejudgment interest in antitrust litigation | N | N |
| 985 | Supplemental appropriations and recissions | N | Y |
| 1019 | Regarding supplemental appropriations | N | |
| 1053 | State, Justice, and Commerce Department appropriations | N | N |
| 1125 | D.C. appropriations | N | Y |

| Sequential Roll Call Number | Bill | Significant Law | Enacted |
|---|---|---|---|
| 1168 | Authorize increase in U.S. quota in International Monetary Fund | N | N |
| 1188 | Increase authority for council on wage and price stability | N | N |
| 1192 | Amend National Capital Transportation Act (extend rail) | N | N |

**97th Congress 1981–1983 Democratic majority**

| | | | |
|---|---|---|---|
| 83 | Reauthorize Legal Services Corporation Act | N/A | N/A |
| 153 | Increase authorized federal payment to D.C. | N/A | N/A |
| 154 | Authorize D.C. mayor to accept certified U.S. loans | N/A | N/A |
| 183 | Commerce, Justice, State, Judiciary, etc., appropriations | N/A | N/A |
| 210 | Authorize $1.08 billion for National Science Foundation | N/A | N/A |
| 253 | Authorize money to Kennedy Center for non-arts functions | N/A | N/A |
| 270 | Expand daylight saving time to save energy | N/A | N/A |
| 338 | Appropriations for fiscal year 1982 | N/A | N/A |
| 344 | Authorize president to control oil supplies and prices | N/A | N/A |
| 433 | Authorize National Science Foundation appropriations | N/A | N/A |
| 436 | Authorize National Bureau of Standards appropriations | N/A | N/A |
| 480 | Provide for conservation and improvement of Indian lands | N/A | N/A |
| 491 | Amendment to clarify secret service functions | N/A | N/A |
| 519 | Urgent supplemental appropriations | N/A | N/A |
| 578 | Reduce funding for certified civil service programs | N/A | N/A |

| Sequential Roll Call Number | Bill | Significant Law | Enacted |
|---|---|---|---|
| 599 | Changes in legislation for reconciliation requirements | N/A | N/A |
| 652 | Override presidential veto of supplemental appropriations | N/A | N/A |
| 655 | Additional authority for Library of Congress building | N/A | N/A |
| 676 | Department of Transportation appropriations | N/A | N/A |
| 708 | Lift economic sanctions on USSR | N/A | N/A |
| 709 | Establish Ocean and Coastal Resources Management Fund | N/A | N/A |
| 759 | Commerce, Justice, State, Judiciary, etc., appropriations | N/A | N/A |
| 788 | Establish domestic content requirement for motor vehicles | N/A | N/A |
| 794 | Amend IRS code (tax deduction for conventions) | N/A | N/A |

**98th Congress 1983–1985 Democratic majority**

| | | | |
|---|---|---|---|
| 18 | Emergency supplemental appropriations for jobs and homeless | Y | Y |
| 35 | Designate certain Oregon land national wilderness | N | Y |
| 47 | Designate national forestland in California | N | Y |
| 98 | Emergency mortgage and shelter assistance | N | N |
| 103 | Authorize National Science Foundation appropriations | N | N |
| 108 | Department of Energy research appropriations | N | N |
| 143 | HUD and sundry agencies appropriations | N | Y |
| 153 | Legislative branch appropriations | N | Y |
| 167 | Agriculture and related appropriations | N | N |
| 199 | Department of Transportation appropriations | N | Y |

| Sequential Roll Call Number | Bill | Significant Law | Enacted |
|---|---|---|---|
| 207 | Amend IRS code to limit tax cuts | N | N |
| 213 | Department of Interior appropriations | N | Y |
| 219 | D.C. appropriations | N | Y |
| 228 | Amend Public Works and Appalachian Development acts | N | N |
| 235 | Extend laws to establish housing and community programs | N | N |
| 270 | Prohibit U.S. support for military/paramilitary operations in Nicaragua | N | N |
| 300 | Equalize House/Senate honaria income and salary | N | N |
| 304 | U.S. participation in international development banks | N | N |
| 317 | Establish Ocean and Coastal Resources Management Fund | N | N |
| 333 | Provide for employment opportunities for certain people | N | N |
| 345 | Extend Federal Supplemental Compensation Act | N | Y |
| 379 | Authorize government intelligence and related appropriations | Y | Y |
| 382 | Authorize grants for certain law-related education programs | N | N |
| 417 | Establish domestic content requirement for motor vehicles | N | N |
| 494 | Authorize appropriations for weatherization program for housing | N | N |
| 497 | Improve productivity of American farmers | N | N |
| 507 | Amend Federal Power Act regarding public utility rate increase | N | N |
| 515 | Provide grants for foreign language education | N | N |

| Sequential Roll Call Number | Bill | Significant Law | Enacted |
|---|---|---|---|
| 545 | Set forth and revise congressional budgets | N | N/A |
| 563 | Budget reconciliation | N | N |
| 570 | Authorize National Science Foundation appropriations | N | N |
| 647 | Temporary increase in public debt limit | N | Y |
| 656 | Housing and Urban Development and sundry agencies appropriations | N | Y |
| 664 | Commerce, Justice, State, Judiciary, etc., appropriations | N | Y |
| 681 | Legislative branch appropriations | N | Y |
| 751 | D.C. appropriations | N | N |
| 759 | Increase federal funds to political party conventions | N | Y |
| 767 | Extend authorization for certain communications appropriations | N | N |
| 780 | Extend authorization for certain educational programs | N | N |
| 782 | Reform remedies for unfair import competition | N | N |
| 787 | Labor, Health and Human Services, Education departments appropriations | N | Y |
| 789 | Supplemental appropriations | N | Y |
| 794 | Authorize government intelligence and related appropriations | N | Y |
| 874 | Authorize president to restrict import of carbon and steel | N | N |

99th Congress 1985–1987 Democratic majority

| | | | |
|---|---|---|---|
| 17 | Emergency credit and debt adjustment to farmers | N/A | N/A |
| 20 | Additional emergency credit to farm producers | N/A | N/A |
| 33 | Authorize increased funding for House committees | N/A | N/A |

| Sequential Roll Call Number | Bill | Significant Law | Enacted |
|---|---|---|---|
| 53 | Authorize National Bureau of Standards appropriations | N/A | N/A |
| 130 | Express opposition to South African apartheid | N/A | N/A |
| 205 | Provide for conservation and improvement of Indian lands | N/A | N/A |
| 218 | Commerce, Justice, State, Judiciary, etc., appropriations | N/A | N/A |
| 223 | Legislative branch appropriations | N/A | N/A |
| 245 | Treasury, postal, and general government appropriations | N/A | N/A |
| 248 | D.C. appropriations | N/A | N/A |
| 258 | Department of Interior appropriations | N/A | N/A |
| 277 | Department of Transportation appropriations | N/A | N/A |
| 299 | Labor, Health and Human Services, and Education Departments appropriations | N/A | N/A |
| 318 | Commission to study race/sex discrimination in federal jobs | N/A | N/A |
| 320 | Establish new quotas on textile imports | N/A | N/A |
| 330 | Extend daylight saving time | N/A | N/A |
| 347 | Deficit reduction | N/A | N/A |
| 362 | Treasury, postal, and general government appropriations | N/A | N/A |
| 369 | Temporary increase in public debt limit | N/A | N/A |
| 446 | Uniform poll closing time | N/A | N/A |
| 481 | Prohibit polygraph testing | N/A | N/A |
| 519 | Amend National Labor Relations Act | N/A | N/A |
| 527 | Redesign Garrison Diversion Unit | N/A | N/A |
| 547 | Supplemental appropriations | N/A | N/A |
| 567 | Omnibus trade bill | N/A | N/A |

| Sequential Roll Call Number | Bill | Significant Law | Enacted |
|---|---|---|---|
| 576 | Transfer D.C. property for homeless shelters | N/A | N/A |
| 627 | Establish National Nutrition Monitoring and Research Program | N/A | N/A |
| 667 | D.C. appropriations | N/A | N/A |
| 675 | Legislative branch appropriations | N/A | N/A |
| 720 | Authorize economic and military assistance to the Philippines | N/A | N/A |
| 760 | Increase the statutory limit on public debt | N/A | N/A |
| 767 | Armed forces appropriations | N/A | N/A |
| 841 | Settle land claims of Wampanoag Indians | N/A | N/A |
| 860 | Amend Immigration and Nationality Act | N/A | N/A |
| 884 | Protect and enhance Columbia River | N/A | N/A |

100th Congress 1987–1989 Democratic majority

| Sequential Roll Call Number | Bill | Significant Law | Enacted |
|---|---|---|---|
| 23 | Authorize funds for urgent relief for homeless | N/A | N/A |
| 63 | Supplemental appropriations | N/A | N/A |
| 74 | Improve competitiveness of U.S. industry | N/A | N/A |
| 112 | Temporary increase in federal debt limit | N/A | N/A |
| 135 | Defense Department appropriations | N/A | N/A |
| 152 | Regarding mineral lands leasing | N/A | N/A |
| 158 | Require fairness in broadcasting (air both sides) | N/A | N/A |
| 171 | Authorize funds for housing and community development | N/A | N/A |
| 184 | Amend National Labor Relations Act (construction) | N/A | N/A |
| 208 | Department of Interior appropriations | N/A | N/A |
| 212 | D.C. appropriations | N/A | N/A |
| 218 | Legislative branch appropriations | N/A | N/A |

| Sequential Roll Call Number | Bill | Significant Law | Enacted |
|---|---|---|---|
| 233 | Commerce, Justice, State, Judiciary, etc., appropriations | N/A | N/A |
| 238 | Authorize Coast Guard appropriations | N/A | N/A |
| 251 | Transportation Department appropriations | N/A | N/A |
| 261 | Treasury and postal service appropriations | N/A | N/A |
| 266 | Protect Medicare people from catastrophic costs | N/A | N/A |
| 271 | Suspend deportation of El Salvadoran and Nicaraguan aliens | N/A | N/A |
| 273 | Temporary increase in federal debt limit | N/A | N/A |
| 302 | Limit textile, apparel, and shoe imports | N/A | N/A |
| 304 | Japanese-American civil liberties (re: WW II camps) | N/A | N/A |
| 340 | Establish system to prevent disease in high-risk occupations | N/A | N/A |
| 354 | Extend independent counsel law to investigate wrongdoing | N/A | N/A |
| 356 | Authorize federal water resource development | N/A | N/A |
| 372 | Budget reconciliation | N/A | N/A |
| 394 | Prohibit use of polygraph in interstate commerce | N/A | N/A |
| 408 | Establish uniform poll closing times for presidential election | N/A | N/A |
| 453 | Foreign aid authorization | N/A | N/A |
| 465 | Family welfare reform | N/A | N/A |
| 506 | Civil Rights Restoration Act (clarify laws) | N/A | N/A |
| 534 | Former air traffic controllers rehiring | N/A | N/A |
| 547 | Extend alien legalization application program | N/A | N/A |
| 611 | Set military personnel and appropriations authority | N/A | N/A |

| Sequential Roll Call Number | Bill | Significant Law | Enacted |
|---|---|---|---|
| 663 | Treasury, postal, and executive office appropriations | N/A | N/A |
| 686 | D.C. appropriations | N/A | N/A |
| 710 | Require 60-day notice for large plant closings | N/A | N/A |
| 726 | Give more independence to National Park Service | N/A | N/A |
| 766 | South Africa sanctions (prevent almost all trade) | N/A | N/A |
| 846 | Equitable pay (study federal job system) | N/A | N/A |
| 902 | Foreign investments disclosure (require registration) | N/A | N/A |

**101st Congress 1989–1991 Democratic majority**

| | | | |
|---|---|---|---|
| 6 | Establish emergency board to mediate Eastern Airlines strike | N/A | N/A |
| 7 | Establish emergency board to mediate Eastern Airlines strike | N/A | N/A |
| 14 | Increase minimum wage | N/A | N/A |
| 16 | Establish uniform poll closing times for presidential election | N/A | N/A |
| 58 | Supplemental appropriations | N/A | N/A |
| 63 | Restrict sales of public oil-shale lands | N/A | N/A |
| 78 | Increase minimum wage over presidential veto | N/A | N/A |
| 175 | Authorize Department of Defense funds | N/A | N/A |
| 183 | Legislative branch appropriations | N/A | N/A |
| 187 | Commerce, state, justice appropriations | N/A | N/A |
| 190 | Increase national debt limit | N/A | N/A |
| 201 | D.C. appropriations | N/A | N/A |
| 204 | Reform federal deposit insurance system | N/A | N/A |
| 214 | Extend favored-nation status for Hungary | N/A | N/A |

| Sequential Roll Call Number | Bill | Significant Law | Enacted |
|---|---|---|---|
| 283 | International development and finance (Tied Aid Credit Fund) | N/A | N/A |
| 297 | Investigation into condition of displaced Salvadorans and Nicaraguans | N/A | N/A |
| 318 | Review some airlines stock acquisition | N/A | N/A |
| 345 | D.C. appropriations | N/A | N/A |
| 347 | Implement government ethics reform | N/A | N/A |
| 373 | Establish national voter registration procedures | N/A | N/A |
| 378 | Establish national voter registration procedures | N/A | N/A |
| 415 | Amend transportation act regarding Washington Metrorail | N/A | N/A |
| 423 | Authorize appropriations to expand Head Start programs | N/A | N/A |
| 436 | Establish evidence standards for price-fixing claims | N/A | N/A |
| 466 | Family and Medical Leave Act | N/A | N/A |
| 576 | Enhance position of American industry | N/A | N/A |
| 601 | Balanced Budget Act | N/A | N/A |
| 627 | D.C. appropriations | N/A | N/A |
| 639 | Increase public debt limit | N/A | N/A |
| 661 | Strengthen civil rights laws (employer discrimination) | N/A | N/A |
| 664 | Temporary increase in public debt limit | N/A | N/A |
| 669 | Campaign Cost Reduction and Reform Act | N/A | N/A |
| 702 | Authorize Department of Defense appropriations | N/A | N/A |
| 704 | Regarding Department of Energy metal casting research | N/A | N/A |
| 705 | Amend Defense Production Act | N/A | N/A |

| Sequential Roll Call Number | Bill | Significant Law | Enacted |
|---|---|---|---|
| 754 | Revise immigration based on family reunification | N/A | N/A |
| 811 | Increase authorization for reclamation projects appropriations | N/A | N/A |
| 818 | Budget reconciliation | N/A | N/A |
| 844 | Legislative branch appropriations | N/A | N/A |

**102nd Congress 1991–1993 Democratic majority**

| | | | |
|---|---|---|---|
| 80 | Require waiting period to purchase handgun | N/A | N/A |
| 106 | Authorize Department of Defense appropriations | N/A | N/A |
| 127 | Strengthen civil rights laws (employer discrimination) | N/A | N/A |
| 132 | Legislative branch appropriations | N/A | N/A |
| 191 | D.C. appropriations | N/A | N/A |
| 206 | Prevent discrimination based on participation in labor disputes | N/A | N/A |
| 220 | Revise and extend National Institute of Health programs | N/A | N/A |
| 241 | Establish limitations on duty time of flight attendants | N/A | N/A |
| 255 | Provide program of federal supplemental compensation | N/A | N/A |
| 267 | Provide emergency unemployment compensation | N/A | N/A |
| 269 | Provide for recognition of Lumbee Indian tribe | N/A | N/A |
| 293 | Establish Flint Hills Prairie national monument | N/A | N/A |
| 339 | Emergency supplemental and Desert Storm appropriations | N/A | N/A |
| 379 | Family and medical leave | N/A | N/A |

| Sequential Roll Call Number | Bill | Significant Law | Enacted |
|---|---|---|---|
| 411 | Regarding spending on election campaigns | N/A | N/A |
| 419 | Designate certain California national parks and wilderness | N/A | N/A |
| 456 | Amend IRS code tax relief for families | N/A | N/A |
| 459 | Assure protection of Haitians in U.S. | N/A | N/A |
| 519 | Revise and extend family planning services assistance | N/A | N/A |
| 542 | Authorize Legal Services Corporation appropriations | N/A | N/A |
| 549 | Emergency supplemental appropriations for disaster assistance | N/A | N/A |
| 594 | Authorize Department of Defense appropriations | N/A | N/A |
| 601 | Extend and revise emergency unemployment compensation | N/A | N/A |
| 648 | Legislative branch appropriations | N/A | N/A |
| 657 | Establish National Undersea Research Program | N/A | N/A |
| 667 | Agriculture, rural development, FDA, and related appropriations | N/A | N/A |
| 679 | Treasury, USPS, executive office appropriations | N/A | N/A |
| 690 | Strengthen U.S. international trade position | N/A | N/A |
| 735 | Amend Voting Rights Act regarding bilingual election requirements | N/A | N/A |
| 742 | Supplemental appropriations and recissions | N/A | N/A |
| 770 | Commerce, Justice, State, Judiciary, etc., appropriations | N/A | N/A |
| 773 | Miscellaneous amendments to Harmonized Tariff Schedule | N/A | N/A |
| 788 | Promote family preservation and child welfare | N/A | N/A |

| Sequential Roll Call Number | Bill | Significant Law | Enacted |
|---|---|---|---|
| 800 | Restructure education system | N/A | N/A |
| 801 | Enhance competition among air carriers | N/A | N/A |
| 826 | Authorize Technology Administration appropriations | N/A | N/A |
| 851 | D.C. appropriations | N/A | N/A |
| 860 | Authorize Interior to establish Abraham Lincoln Research Center | N/A | N/A |
| 900 | Amend Wild and Scenic Rivers Act | N/A | N/A |

**103rd Congress 1993–1995 Democratic majority**

| | | | |
|---|---|---|---|
| 20 | Family and medical leave | N/A | N/A |
| 24 | Voter registration | N/A | N/A |
| 39 | Unemployment | N/A | N/A |
| 67 | Public health (National Institute of Health) | N/A | N/A |
| 85 | Emergency supplemental appropriations | N/A | N/A |
| 103 | Treatment of pregnant women | N/A | N/A |
| 129 | Increase debt limit | N/A | N/A |
| 145 | Amend Budget and Impoundment Act | N/A | N/A |
| 166 | Manufacturing and technology development | N/A | N/A |
| 168 | Gallatin Range consolidation and protection | N/A | N/A |
| 186 | Supplemental appropriations | N/A | N/A |
| 191 | Budget reconciliation | N/A | N/A |
| 208 | Legislative appropriations | N/A | N/A |
| 215 | Amend National Labor Relations Act | N/A | N/A |
| 242 | Authorize State Department spending | N/A | N/A |
| 250 | Government appropriations | N/A | N/A |
| 279 | Government appropriations | N/A | N/A |
| 291 | Government appropriations | N/A | N/A |

| Sequential Roll Call Number | Bill | Significant Law | Enacted |
|---|---|---|---|
| 299 | Government appropriations | N/A | N/A |
| 305 | D.C. appropriations | N/A | N/A |
| 327 | Government appropriations | N/A | N/A |
| 334 | Government appropriations | N/A | N/A |
| 367 | Establish National Service Corporation | N/A | N/A |
| 377 | Low-income housing | N/A | N/A |
| 419 | Money for failed savings associations | N/A | N/A |
| 459 | Authorize military appropriations | N/A | N/A |
| 481 | Education programs | N/A | N/A |
| 487 | Authorize money for arts and humanities | N/A | N/A |
| 514 | Establish Department of Interior program | N/A | N/A |
| 522 | Recognize North Carolina Indian tribe | N/A | N/A |
| 538 | Amend Employee Retirement Income Security Act | N/A | N/A |
| 548 | Handgun waiting period | N/A | N/A |
| 560 | Minerals on public lands | N/A | N/A |
| 587 | Amend Federal Election Campaign Act of 1971 | N/A | N/A |
| 689 | Authorize extension of education spending | N/A | N/A |
| 694 | Establish Great Falls Historic District | N/A | N/A |
| 738 | Crime bill | N/A | N/A |
| 750 | Gun control | N/A | N/A |
| 768 | National forest management | N/A | N/A |
| 780 | Black lung program | N/A | N/A |
| 810 | Legislative appropriations | N/A | N/A |
| 820 | Authorize military appropriations | N/A | N/A |
| 841 | Government appropriations | N/A | N/A |
| 850 | Government appropriations | N/A | N/A |

| Sequential Roll Call Number | Bill | Significant Law | Enacted |
|---|---|---|---|
| 885 | Government appropriations | N/A | N/A |
| 915 | D.C. appropriations | N/A | N/A |
| 939 | Establish spending targets | N/A | N/A |
| 948 | Designate California wilderness areas | N/A | N/A |
| 951 | Radon testing | N/A | N/A |
| 961 | Authorize Department of Transportation appropriations | N/A | N/A |
| 987 | Authorize high-speed rail appropriations | N/A | N/A |
| 1000 | Manage Presidio | N/A | N/A |
| 1022 | Manage forests and rivers | N/A | N/A |
| 1029 | Amend National Park Act | N/A | N/A |
| 1074 | Establish American Heritage areas program | N/A | N/A |
| 1076 | Amend Postal Service code | N/A | N/A |

**104th Congress 1995–1997 Republican majority**

| | | | |
|---|---|---|---|
| 90 | President line-item authority | N/A | N/A |
| 98 | Exclusionary rule reform | N/A | N/A |
| 104 | Death penalty | N/A | N/A |
| 112 | Incarceration of violent criminals | N/A | N/A |
| 123 | Law enforcement block grants | N/A | N/A |
| 138 | Revitalize national security | N/A | N/A |
| 147 | Department of Defense appropriations | N/A | N/A |
| 167 | Moratorium on regulatory actions | N/A | N/A |
| 176 | Human health, safety, environment risks | N/A | N/A |
| 190 | Compensate private property owners | N/A | N/A |
| 192 | Decentralize government | N/A | N/A |
| 200 | Reform federal civil justice system | N/A | N/A |
| 222 | Product liability litigation standards | N/A | N/A |
| 243 | Disaster assistance | N/A | N/A |

| Sequential Roll Call Number | Bill | Significant Law | Enacted |
|---|---|---|---|
| 261 | Welfare | N/A | N/A |
| 286 | Amend IRS code | N/A | N/A |
| 328 | Amend Federal Water Pollution Control Act | N/A | N/A |
| 356 | Foreign affairs agencies | N/A | N/A |
| 375 | Department of Defense appropriations | N/A | N/A |
| 451 | Oklahoma City disaster assistance | N/A | N/A |
| 510 | Department of Interior appropriations | N/A | N/A |
| 521 | President, Postal Service, Treasury Department appropriations | N/A | N/A |
| 551 | Amend Federal Water Pollution Control Act | N/A | N/A |
| 571 | Department of Commerce, Justice, State appropriations | N/A | N/A |
| 593 | HUD and Veterans' Affairs appropriations | N/A | N/A |
| 612 | Labor, education, health appropriations | N/A | N/A |
| 621 | Legislative branch appropriations | N/A | N/A |
| 632 | Department of Defense appropriations | N/A | N/A |
| 638 | Restrictions on employee benefits promotion | N/A | N/A |
| 669 | Sanctions against Cuba | N/A | N/A |
| 677 | Amend National Labor Relations Act | N/A | N/A |
| 679 | Challenges to state referendums | N/A | N/A |
| 697 | Federal civilian science appropriations | N/A | N/A |
| 714 | Social Security amendments (Medicare) | N/A | N/A |
| 726 | Budget reconciliation | N/A | N/A |
| 733 | Waive points of order | N/A | N/A |
| 739 | Ban partial-birth abortion | N/A | N/A |
| 747 | D.C. appropriations | N/A | N/A |
| 764 | Increase debt limit | N/A | N/A |

| Sequential Roll Call Number | Bill | Significant Law | Enacted |
|---|---|---|---|
| 796 | Prohibit ground forces in Bosnia | N/A | N/A |
| 844 | Protect Social Security trust funds | N/A | N/A |
| 908 | Modify agriculture practices | N/A | N/A |
| 921 | Balanced budget appropriations | N/A | N/A |
| 932 | Terrorism | N/A | N/A |
| 958 | Department of Education layoffs | N/A | N/A |
| 972 | Amend IRS code (medical) | N/A | N/A |
| 997 | Amend National Wildlife Refuge Administration Act | N/A | N/A |
| 1010 | International ocean transportation system | N/A | N/A |
| 1027 | Deregulate public housing program | N/A | N/A |
| 1040 | Department of Defense appropriations | N/A | N/A |
| 1048 | Amend IRS code (fuel tax) | N/A | N/A |
| 1087 | Wisconsin Works | N/A | N/A |
| 1113 | Department of Defense appropriations | N/A | N/A |
| 1134 | Department of Interior appropriations | N/A | N/A |
| 1148 | HUD and Veterans' Affairs appropriations | N/A | N/A |
| 1179 | Labor, Health, Education appropriations | N/A | N/A |
| 1189 | Treasury, Postal Service, presidential appropriations | N/A | N/A |
| 1197 | Budget reconciliation | N/A | N/A |
| 1218 | Commerce, Justice, State appropriations | N/A | N/A |
| 1236 | Amend Fair Labor Standards Act | N/A | N/A |
| 1257 | English official government language | N/A | N/A |
| 1271 | Limit UN control of U.S. military | N/A | N/A |
| 1299 | Amend Immigration Act | N/A | N/A |

| Sequential Roll Call Number | Bill | Significant Law | Enacted |
|---|---|---|---|
| 105th Congress 1997–1999 Republican majority | | | |
| 22 | Family planning appropriations | N/A | N/A |
| 58 | Working Families Flexibility Act | N/A | N/A |
| 64 | Partial-birth abortion | N/A | N/A |
| 116 | Juvenile crime | N/A | N/A |
| 125 | Housing | N/A | N/A |
| 134 | Supplemental appropriations | N/A | N/A |
| 149 | Dolphin protection | N/A | N/A |
| 234 | Defense appropriations | N/A | N/A |
| 239 | Balanced Budget Act | N/A | N/A |
| 243 | Budget reconciliation | N/A | N/A |
| 273 | Interior appropriations | N/A | N/A |
| 333 | Legislative appropriations | N/A | N/A |
| 470 | Government appropriations | N/A | N/A |
| 489 | Limit president's ability to create national monuments | N/A | N/A |
| 498 | Land management | N/A | N/A |
| 507 | DC appropriations | N/A | N/A |
| 513 | Legal rights of property owners | N/A | N/A |
| 518 | Education | N/A | N/A |
| 543 | Livestock on federal lands | N/A | N/A |
| 594 | U.S.–Taiwan missile cooperation | N/A | N/A |
| 611 | Agriculture research, education | N/A | N/A |
| 638 | Rename National Airport | N/A | N/A |
| 641 | Prohibit federal spending for national education testing | N/A | N/A |
| 655 | Make federal agencies subject to federal courts | N/A | N/A |
| 677 | Foreign policy | N/A | N/A |

| Sequential Roll Call Number | Bill | Significant Law | Enacted |
|---|---|---|---|
| 680 | Government performance | N/A | N/A |
| 682 | End Tucker Act shuffle | N/A | N/A |
| 704 | Small business paperwork reduction | N/A | N/A |
| 708 | Assist small business | N/A | N/A |
| 718 | Emergency supplemental appropriations | N/A | N/A |
| 742 | Prohibit federal distribution of drug needles | N/A | N/A |
| 779 | Financial services regulation | N/A | N/A |
| 788 | Facilitate disclosure of federal mandates on business | N/A | N/A |
| 853 | Bankruptcy reform | N/A | N/A |
| 856 | Limit minimum wage | N/A | N/A |
| 866 | Taxes | N/A | N/A |
| 898 | Legislative appropriations | N/A | N/A |
| 906 | Child custody | N/A | N/A |
| 908 | Salton Sea project | N/A | N/A |
| 919 | Government appropriations | N/A | N/A |
| 955 | Government appropriations | N/A | N/A |
| 962 | Patient protection | N/A | N/A |
| 973 | Government appropriations | N/A | N/A |
| 1022 | Government appropriations | N/A | N/A |
| 1036 | D.C. appropriations | N/A | N/A |
| 1041 | Land claims | N/A | N/A |
| 1044 | English language programs | N/A | N/A |
| 1069 | Foreign operations appropriations | N/A | N/A |
| 1072 | Authorize education spending | N/A | N/A |
| 1084 | Protect Social Security | N/A | N/A |
| 1089 | Taxpayer relief | N/A | N/A |

# Bibliography

Aberbach, Joel D., and Bert A. Rockman. 1977. "The Overlapping Worlds of American Federal Executives and Congressmen." *British Journal of Political Science*, 7(1): 23–47.

Adams, Rebecca, and Mary Agnes Carey. 2003. "Compromise Will Come Hard in Medicare-Overhaul Conference." *CQ Weekly*, June 28.

Alchian, Armen, and Harold Demsetz. 1972. "Production, Information Costs, and Economic Organization." *The American Economic Review* 62: 777–95.

Aldrich, John H. 1995. *Why Parties? The Origin and Transformation of Party Politics in America*. Chicago: University of Chicago Press.

Aldrich, John H., and David W. Rohde. 1997. "Balance of Power: Republican Party Leadership and the Committee System in the 104th House." Paper presented at the annual meeting of the Midwest Political Science Association, April 10–13, Chicago.

　1998. "Measuring Conditional Party Government." Paper presented at the annual meeting of the Midwest Political Science Association, April 23–25, Chicago.

　2000. "The Consequences of Party Organization in the House: The Role of the Majority and Minority Parties in Conditional Party Government." In *Polarized Politics: Congress and the President in a Partisan Era*, eds. Jon Bond and Richard Fleisher. Washington, DC: CQ Press, pp. 31–72.

　2001. "The Logic of Conditional Party Government." In *Congress Reconsidered*, 7th ed., eds. Lawrence C. Dodd and Bruce I. Oppenheimer. Washington, DC: Congressional Quarterly, pp. 269–92.

Aldrich, John H., Mark M. Berger, and David W. Rohde. 2002. "The Historical Variability in Conditional Party Government, 1877–1994." In *Party, Process, and Political Change in Congress: New Perspectives on the History of Congress*, eds. David Brady and Mathew D. McCubbins. Stanford, CA: Stanford University Press, pp. 17–35.

Aldrich, John H., Calvin C. Jillson, and Rick Wilson. 2002. "Why Congress? What the Failure of the Confederation Congress and the Survival of the Federal Congress Tell Us about the New Institutionalism." In *Party, Process, and Political Change in Congress: New Perspectives on the History of Congress*, eds. David Brady and Mathew D. McCubbins. Stanford, CA: Stanford University Press, pp. 315–42.

Aldrich, John H., David W. Rohde, and Michael W. Tofias. 2003. "One D Is Not Enough: Conditional Party Government 1887–2002." Paper presented at the History of Congress conference December 5–6, San Diego.

Alesina, Alberto, and Howard Rosenthal. 1995. *Partisan Politics, Divided Government, and the Economy*. Cambridge: Cambridge University Press.

Alexander, DeAlva Stanwood. 1970 [1916]. *History and Procedure of the House of Representatives*. New York: Houghton Mifflin Company.

Alvarez, R. Michael, and Jason L. Saving. 1997. "Deficits, Democrats, and Distributive Benefits: Congressional Elections and the Pork Barrel in the 1980s." *Political Research Quarterly* 50: 809–31.

American Political Science Association. 1950. *Toward a More Responsible Party System, A Report*. New York: Rinehart.

Amorim Neto, Octavio, Gary W. Cox, and Mathew D. McCubbins. 2003. "Agenda Power in Brazil's Câmara dos Deputados, 1989 to 1999." *World Politics* 55: 550–78.

Anderson, William, Janet M. Box-Steffensmeier, and Valeria N. Sinclair. 2003. "The Keys to Legislative Success in the U.S. House of Representatives." *Legislative Studies Quarterly* 28(3, August): 357–86.

Ansolabehere, Stephen, and James Snyder. 2000. "Money and Office: The Sources of the Incumbency Advantage in Congressional Campaign Finance." In *Continuity and Change in House Elections*, eds. David Brady, John Cogan, and Morris Fiorina. Palo Alto, CA: Stanford University Press: 65–86.

Ansolabehere, Stephen, Alan Gerber, and James Snyder. 2002. "Equal Votes, Equal Money: Court-Ordered Redistricting and Public Expenditures in the American States." *American Political Science Review* 96: 767–78.

Ansolabehere, Stephen, Shigeo Hirano, and James Snyder. 2003. "What Did the Direct Primary Do to Congress?" Paper presented at the History of Congress conference, December 5–6, San Diego.

Ansolabehere, Stephen, James Snyder, and Charles Stewart. 2001. "The Effects of Party and Preferences on Congressional Roll-Call Voting." *Legislative Studies Quarterly* 26: 533–72.

Arnold, R. Douglas. 1979. *Congress and the Bureaucracy: A Theory of Influence*, New Haven, CT: Yale University Press.

1990. *The Logic of Congressional Action*. New Haven, CT: Yale University Press.

Babington, Charles. 2004. "Hastert Launches a Partisan Policy." Downloaded 11/27/04 from: *www.washingtonpost.com*.

Bach, Stanley. 1990. "From Special Orders to Special Rules: Pictures of House Procedures in Transition." Paper presented at the annual meeting of the American Political Science Association, August 30–September 2, San Francisco.

1991. "Resolving Legislative Differences in Congress: Conference Committees and Amendments Between the Houses." Congressional Research Service. Report no. 91–538.

Bader, Anne. 2002. "Conference Committees and Party Politics in the U.S. House of Representatives." Paper completed in fulfillment of the requirements for the UCSD Department of Political Science Faculty Mentor Program.

Baker, John D. 1973. "The Character of the Congressional Revolution of 1910." *Journal of American History* 60: 679–91.

Balla, Steven J., Eric Lawrence, Forrest Maltzman, and Lee Sigelman. 2002. "Partisanship, Blame Avoidance, and the Distribution of Legislative Pork." *American Journal of Political Science* 46(July): 515–25.

Baron, David P., and John A. Ferejohn. 1989. "Bargaining in Legislatures," *American Political Science Review* 83(4): 1181–1206.

Bartels, Larry M. 2000. "Partisanship and Voting Behavior, 1952–1996." *American Journal of Political Science* 44: 35–50.

Becker, Gary S. 1983. "A Theory of Competition Among Pressure Groups for Political Influence." *Quarterly Journal of Economics* 98: 371–400.

Beckmann, Matthew N. 2004. "Presidential Lobbying: How White House Officials Prosecute the President's Legislative Agenda." Paper presented November 16 at the University of California, San Diego.

Berglof, Eric, and Howard Rosenthal. 2004. "Congress and the History of Bankruptcy Law in the United States: From the Federalists to the Whigs." Paper presented at the History of Congress conference, April 9–10, Stanford, CA.

Berkson, J. 1953. "A Statistically Precise and Relatively Simple Method of Estimating the Bioassay with Quantal Response, Based on the Logistic Function." *Journal of the American Statistical Association* 48: 565–99.

Bernhard, William, and Brian Sala. 2003. "The Dynamics of Senate Voting." Paper presented at the History of Congress Conference, December 5–6, San Diego.

Beth, Richard. 1998. "The Discharge Rule in the House: Recent Use in Historical Context." Congressional Research Service. Report no. 97-856.

1999. "*Discharge Rule in the House: Recent Use in Historical Context*." CRS Report for Congress. November. Congressional Research Service. The Library of Congress.

2001. "The Discharge Rule in the House: Recent Use in Historical Context." Congressional Research Service. Report no. 97-856.

2003. "The Discharge Rule in the House: Recent Use in Historical Context." Congressional Research Service. Report no. 97-856.

Binder, Sarah A. 1996. "The Partisan Basis of Procedural Choice: Allocating Parliamentary Rights in the House, 1789–1990." *American Political Science Review* 90(March): 8–20.

1997. *Minority Rights, Majority Rule: Partisanship and the Development of Congress.* New York: Cambridge University Press.

1999. "The Dynamics of Legislative Gridlock, 1947–1996." *American Political Science Review*, 93(September): 519–33.

2003. *Stalemate: Causes and Consequences of Legislative Gridlock.* Washington, DC: Brookings Institution Press.

Binder, Sarah A., and Steven S. Smith. 1997. *Politics or Principle? Filibustering in the United States Senate.* Washington, DC: Brookings Institution Press.

Binder, Sarah A., Eric D. Lawrence, and Forrest Maltzman. 1999. "Uncovering the Hidden Effect of Party." *Journal of Politics* 61(August): 815–31.

Black, Duncan. 1958. *The Theory of Committee and Elections.* Cambridge: Cambridge University Press.

Bolling, Richard. 1965. *House Out of Order.* New York: E. P. Dutton & Co.

Bond, Jon R., and Richard Fleisher. 1990. *The President in the Legislative Arena.* Chicago: University of Chicago Press.

*Boston Globe.* 2004. "The Globe's Major Findings." October 3.

Brady, David W., and Justin Burchett. 2001. "The Benefits of Party Voting: Representation, Roll Calls, and Valued Committee Seats in the U.S. House." Unpublished typescript, Stanford University.

Brady, David W., and Mathew D. McCubbins. 2002a. "Party, Process, and Political Change: New Perspectives on the History of Congress." In *Party, Process, and Political Change in Congress: New Perspectives on the History of Congress*, eds. David Brady and Mathew D. McCubbins, Stanford, CA: Stanford University Press, pp. 1–14.

    2002b. "Afterword: History as a Laboratory." In *Party, Process, and Political Change in Congress: New Perspectives on the History of Congress*, eds. David Brady and Mathew D. McCubbins. Stanford, CA: Stanford University Press, pp. 471–2.

Brady, David, Kara Buckley, and Douglas Rivers. 2004. "Elections and Insurance Incentives: Parties at the Turn of the Century." Paper presented at the History of Congress conference April 9–10, Stanford, CA.

Brady, David W., Brandice Canes-Wrone, and John F. Cogan. 2000. "Differences in Legislative Voting Behavior Between Winning and Losing House Incumbents." In *Continuity and Change in House Elections*, eds. David Brady, John Cogan, and Morris Fiorina. Palo Alto, CA: Stanford University Press.

Brady, David W., Joseph Cooper, and Patricia A. Hurley. 1979. "The Decline of Party in the U.S. House of Representatives, 1887–1968." *Legislative Studies Quarterly* 4: 381–408.

Bresnick, David. 1979. "The Federal Educational Policy System: Enacting and Revising Title I." *Western Political Quarterly* 32: 189–202.

Broder, David S. 1972. *The Party's Over: The Failure of Politics in America*. New York: Harper and Row.

Brown, William Holmes. 1996. *House Practice: A Guide to the Rules, Precedents and Procedures of the House*. Washington, DC: U.S. Government Printing Office.

Browning, Clyde I. 1973. *The Geography of Federal Outlays*. Studies in Geography No. 4. Chapel Hill: University of North Carolina.

Browning, Robert. 1986. *Politics and Social Welfare Policy in the United States*. Knoxville: University of Tennessee Press.

Bryce, James. 1888. *The American Commonwealth*. New York: Macmillan and Company.

    1921. *Modern Democracies*, vol. 1. New York: The Macmillan Company.

Buchanan, James. 1968. *The Demand and Supply of Public Goods*. Chicago: Rand McNally.

Buchanan, James M., and Gordon Tullock. 1962. *The Calculus of Consent*. Ann Arbor: University of Michigan Press.

Burger, Timothy. 1995. "After a Defeat, House Leaders Must Regroup." *Roll Call*, July 17.

Calvert, Randall. 1995. "The Rational Choice Theory of Social Institutions: Cooperation, Coordination, and Communication." In *Modern Political Economy: Old Topics, New Directions*, eds. J. Banks and E. Hanushek. Cambridge: Cambridge University Press, pp. 216–68.

Calvert, Randall, and Justin Fox. 2000. "Effective Parties in a Model of Repeated Legislative Bargaining." Presented at the annual meeting of the American Political Science Association, August 31–September 3, Washington, DC.

Calvert, Randall L., Mark J. Moran, and Barry R. Weingast. 1987. "Congressional Influence over Policy Making: The Case of the FTC." In *Congress: Structure and*

*Policy*, eds. Mathew D. McCubbins and Terry Sullivan. Cambridge: Cambridge University Press, pp. 493–522.

Cameron, Charles. 2000. *Veto Bargaining: Presidents and the Politics of Negative Power*. Cambridge: Cambridge University Press.

Cameron, Charles M., Albert D. Cover, and Jeffrey A. Segal. 1990. "Senate Voting on Supreme Court Nominees: A Neoinstitutional Model." *American Political Science Review* 84: 525–34.

Campbell, Andrea, Gary Cox, and Mathew McCubbins. 2002. "Agenda Power in the US Senate. 1877–1986." In *Party, Process and Political Change in Congress*, eds. David Brady and Mathew McCubbins. Stanford, CA: Stanford University Press, pp. 146–65.

Cannon, Clarence. 1936. *Cannon's Precedents of the House of Representatives of the United States*. Washington, DC: U.S. Government Printing Office.

Carey, Mary Agnes. 2003a. "GOP Wins Battle, Not War." *CQ Weekly*, November 29. 2003b. "Medicare Deal Goes to Wire in Late-Night House Vote." *CQ Weekly*, November 22.

Carroll, Royce, Gary W. Cox, and Mónica Pachón. 2004. "How Parties Create Electoral Democracy." Paper presented at the 2004 meetings of the American Political Science Association, September 1–4, Chicago.

Carson, Jamie, and Jason Roberts. 2003. "Using History as a Laboratory to Study Congressional Elections and Institutional Development." Paper presented at the History of Congress conference, December 5–6, San Diego.

Carson, Jamie, and Ryan J. Vander Wielen. 2002. "Legislative Politics in a Bicameral System: Strategic Conferee Appointments in the U.S. Congress." Paper presented at the annual meeting of the Northeastern Political Science Association, November 7–9, Providence, RI.

Castle, David, and Patrick Fett. 2000. "Member Goals and Party Switching in the U.S. Congress." In *Congress on Display, Congress at Work*, ed. William T. Bianco. Ann Arbor: University of Michigan Press, pp. 231–42.

Cheney, Richard B., and Lynne V. Cheney. 1983. *Kings of the Hill: Power and Personality in the House of Representatives*. New York: Continuum.

Clapp, Charles. 1964. *The Congressman: His Work as He Sees It*. Garden City, NY: Doubleday.

Clark, Joseph S. 1964. *Congress: The Sapless Branch*. New York: Harper & Row.

Cleveland, W. S. 1979. "Robust Locally Weighted Regression and Smoothing Scatterplots." *Journal of the American Statistical Association* 74: 829–36.

Cohen, Linda R., and Roger G. Noll. 1991. "How to Vote, Whether to Vote: Strategies for Voting and Abstaining on Congressional Roll Calls." *Political Behavior* 13: 97–127.

Collie, Melissa P. 1988. "Universalism and the Parties in the U.S. House of Representatives, 1921–80." *American Journal of Political Science* 32: 865–83.

*Congressional Quarterly*. 1984. *Farm Policy: The Politics of Soil, Surpluses, and Subsidies*. Washington, DC: Congressional Quarterly.

*Congressional Quarterly Almanac*. 1964. Volume 20.

*Congressional Quarterly Almanac*. 1973. Volume 29.

*Congressional Quarterly Almanac*. 1998. Volume 54.

*Congressional Quarterly Weekly*. 1993. "Decisive Vote Brings Down Trade Walls with Mexico." November 20, pp. 3174–9.

*Congressional Quarterly Weekly.* 2003. "2003 Legislative Summary: Medicare Prescription Drug Coverage." December 13.

*Congressional Record,* 46th Congress, 2d sess., April 22, 1880.

*Congressional Record,* 51st Congress, 1st sess., June 5, 1890.

Connelly, William, and John Pitney. 1999. "The House Republicans: Lessons for Political Science." In *New Majority or Old Minority? The Impact of Republicans on Congress,* eds. Nicol C. Rae and Colton C. Campbell. Lanham, MD: Rowman and Littlefield, pp. 173–94.

Cooper, Joseph. 1970. *The Origins of the Standing Committees and the Development of the Modern House.* Houston: Rice University.

Cooper, Joseph, and David W. Brady. 1981. "Institutional Context and Leadership Style: The House from Cannon to Rayburn." *American Political Science Review* 75: 411–25.

Cooper, Joseph, and Garry Young. 2002. "Party and Preference in Congressional Decision Making: Roll Call Voting in the House of Representatives, 1889–1999." In *Party, Process, and Political Change in Congress: New Perspectives on the History of Congress,* eds. David Brady and Mathew D. McCubbins, Stanford, CA: Stanford University Press, pp. 64–106.

Cooper, Joseph, David W. Brady, and Patricia A. Hurley. 1977. "The Electoral Basis of Party Voting." In *The Impact of the Electoral Process,* eds. Louis Maisel and Joseph Cooper. Beverly Hills: Sage Press, pp. 135–67.

Covington, Cary R., and Andrew A. Bargen. 2004. "Comparing Floor-Dominated and Party-Dominated Explanations of Policy Change in the House of Representatives." *Journal of Politics* 66(4): 1069–88.

Cox, Gary W. 1987. *The Efficient Secret: The Cabinet and the Development of Political Parties in Victorian England.* Cambridge: Cambridge University Press.

    1999. "Agenda Setting in the U.S. House: A Majority-Party Monopoly?" Paper presented at the annual meeting of the American Political Science Association, September 2–5, Atlanta.

    2001. "Agenda Setting in the U.S. House: A Majority-Party Monopoly?" *Legislative Studies Quarterly* 25: 185–211.

Cox, Gary W., and Samuel Kernell. 1991. *The Politics of Divided Government.* Boulder: Westview Press.

Cox, Gary W., and Eric Magar. 1999. "How Much Is Majority Status in the U.S. Congress Worth?" *American Political Science Review* 93: 299–310.

Cox, Gary W., and Mathew D. McCubbins. 1991. "Fiscal Policy and Divided Government." In *The Politics of Divided Government,* eds. Gary W. Cox and Samuel Kernell. Boulder: Westview Press.

    1993. *Legislative Leviathan: Party Government in the House.* Berkeley: University of California Press.

    1994. "Bonding, Structure, and the Stability of Political Parties: Party Government in the House." *Legislative Studies Quarterly* 19: 215–31.

    1997. "Toward a Theory of Legislative Rules Changes: Assessing Schickler and Rich's Evidence." *American Journal of Political Science* 4: 1376–86.

    2001. "The Institutional Determinants of Economic Policy Outcomes." In *Presidents, Parliaments and Policy,* eds. Mathew D. McCubbins and Stephan Haggard. New York: Cambridge University Press.

    2002. "Agenda Power in the U.S. House of Representatives, 1877 to 1986." In *Party, Process, and Political Change in Congress: New Perspectives on the History of*

*Congress*, eds. David Brady and Mathew D. McCubbins. Stanford, CA: Stanford University Press.

2004. "Theories of Legislative Organization." *American Political Science Association – Comparative Politics Newsletter* (Winter).

Cox, Gary W., and Keith T. Poole. 2002. "On Measuring Partisanship in Roll-Call Voting: The U.S. House of Representatives, 1877–1999." *American Journal of Political Science* 46: 477–89.

Cox, Gary W., Chris Den Hartog, and Mathew D. McCubbins. 2004. "The Motion to Recommit in the U.S. House of Representatives." Unpublished typescript. University of California, San Diego.

Cox, Gary W., Mikitaka Masuyama, and Mathew D. McCubbins. 2000. "Agenda Power in the Japanese House of Representatives." *Japanese Journal of Political Science* 1: 1–22.

Crook, Sara Brandes, and John R. Hibbing. 1985. "Congressional Reform and Party Discipline: The Effects of Changes in the Seniority System on Party Loyalty in the U.S. House of Representatives." *British Journal of Political Science* 15: 207–26.

Damgaard, Erik. 1995. "How Parties Control Committee Members." In *Parliaments and Majority Rule in Western Europe*. ed. Herbert Döring. Frankfurt: Campus Verlag, pp. 308–325.

Damgaard, Erik, and Palle Svensson. 1989. "Who Governs? Parties and Policies in Denmark." *European Journal of Political Research* 17: 731–45.

Dart, Bob. 2003. "Pryor Clears Judicial Panel; GOP Wins First Round in Bitter Battle." *The Atlanta Journal-Constitution,* July 24.

Davidson, Roger H. 1978. "Breaking Up Those Cozy Triangles: An Impossible Dream." In *Legislative Reform and Public Policy*, eds. S. Welch and J. Petters.

Den Hartog, Christopher F. 2004. *Limited Party Government and the Majority Party Revolution in the Nineteenth-Century House.* Ph.D. dissertation, University of California, San Diego.

Den Hartog, Christopher F., and Craig Goodman. 2003. "Committee Composition in the Absence of a Strong Speaker." Paper presented at the History of Congress conference, December 5–6, San Diego.

Den Hartog, Christopher F., and Nathan W. Monroe. 2004. "The Value of Majority Status: The Effect of Jeffords's Switch on Asset Prices of Republican and Democratic Firms." Paper presented at the annual meeting of the Midwest Political Science Association, April 15–18, Chicago.

Denzau, Arthur T., and Robert J. Mackay. 1983. "Gate-Keeping and Monopoly Power of Committees: An Analysis of Sincere and Sophisticated Behavior." *American Journal of Political Science* 27: 740–61.

Denzau, Arthur, William Riker, and Kenneth A. Shepsle. 1985. "Farquharson and Fenno: Sophisticated Voting and Home Style." *American Political Science Review* 79: 1117–34.

Deschler, Lewis. 1976. *Lewis' Precedents of the House of Representatives of the United States*. Washington, DC: U.S. Government Printing Office.

Dierenfield, Bruce J. 1987. *Keeper of the Rules: Congressman Howard W Smith of Virginia*. Charlottesville: University Press of Virginia.

Diermeier, Daniel, and Timothy J. Feddersen. 1998. "Cohesion in Legislatures and the Vote of Confidence Procedure." *American Political Science Review* 92: 611–21.

Diermeier, Daniel, and Roger Myerson. 1999. "Bicameralism and Its Consequences for the Internal Organization of Legislatures." *American Economic Review* 89: 1182–96.

Dion, Douglas. 1997. *Turning the Legislative Thumbscrew: Minority Rights and Procedural Change in Legislative Politics*. Ann Arbor: University of Michigan Press.

Dion, Douglas, and John Huber. 1996. "Procedural Choice and the House Committee on Rules." *Journal of Politics* 58: 25–53.

1997. "Sense and Sensibility: The Role of Rules." *American Journal of Political Science* 41: 945–57.

Dlouhy, Jennifer A. 2002a. "House Passes Abortion Bill Despite Democrats' Protests Over Health, Constitution." *CQ Weekly*, July 27.

2002b. "Ban on 'Partial Birth' Abortions Nears Vote on House Floor." *CQ Weekly*, July 20.

Dodd, Lawrence C., and Bruce I. Oppenheimer. 1997. *Congress Reconsidered*, 6th ed. Washington DC: CQ Press.

Döring, Herbert, ed. 1995. *Parliaments and Majority Rule in Western Europe*. New York: St. Martin's Press.

2001. "Parliamentary Agenda Control and Legislative Outcomes in Western Europe." *Legislative Studies Quarterly* 26: 145–65.

Douglas, Paul H., and Joseph Hackman. 1938. "The Fair Labor Standards Act of 1938 I." *Political Science Quarterly* 53: 491–515.

1939. "The Fair Labor Standards Act of 1938 II." *Political Science Quarterly* 54: 29–55.

Downs, Anthony. 1957. *An Economic Theory of Democracy*. New York: Harper.

Duggan, John, and Jeff Banks. 2000. "A Bargaining Model of Collective Choice." *American Political Science Review* 94: 73–88.

Edwards, George C. III. 1989. *At the Margins: Presidential Leadership of Congress*. New Haven: Yale University Press.

Engstrom, Erik, and Sam Kernell. 2003. "The Effects of Presidential Elections on Party Control of the Senate Under Indirect and Direct Elections." Paper presented at the History of Congress conference December 5–6, San Diego.

Epstein, David, and Sharyn O'Halloran. 1999. *Delegating Powers: A Transaction Cost Politics Approach to Policy Making Under Separate Powers*. Cambridge: Cambridge University Press.

Evans, C. Lawrence, and Walter J. Oleszek. 2002. "Message Politics and Senate Procedure." In *The Contentious Senate: Partisanship, Ideology, and the Myth of Cool Judgment*, eds. Colton C. Campbell and Nicol C. Rae. New York: Roman and Littlefield, pp. 107–27.

Evans, Diana. 1994. "Policy and Pork: The Use of Pork Barrel Projects to Build Policy Coalitions in the House of Representatives." *American Journal of Political Science* 38: 894–917.

Fagan, Amy. 2002b. "House Panel OK's Abortion Curb; Revised Partial-Birth Ban Goes to Floor." *The Washington Times*, July 18.

2002a. "House Bill Targets Type of Abortion; Partial-Birth Measure Goes to Senate." *The Washington Times*, July 25.

Fenno, Richard F. 1966. *The Power of the Purse*. Boston: Little, Brown.

1973. *Congressmen in Committees*. Boston: Little, Brown.

1978. *Home Style: House Members in Their Districts*. Glenview, IL: Scott, Foresman and Company.

Ferejohn, John. 1974. *Pork Barrel Politics: Rivers and Harbors Legislation, 1947–1968*. Stanford, CA: Stanford University Press.

Finocchiaro, Charles, and David Rohde. 2002. "War for the Floor: Agenda control and the relationship between conditional party government and cartel theory." Unpublished typescript, Michigan State University.

2003. "Puzzles of the Partisan Era of the U.S. House." Paper presented at the History of Congress conference, December 5–6, San Diego.

Fiorina, Morris P. 1974. *Representatives, Roll Calls, and Constituencies*. Lexington, MA: D. C. Heath.

1977a. *Congress: Keystone of the Washington Establishment*. New Haven, CT: Yale University Press.

1977b. "The Case of the Vanishing Marginals: The Bureaucracy Did It." *American Political Science Review* 71: 177–81.

1981. *Retrospective Voting in American National Elections*. New Haven, CT: Yale University Press.

1992. *Divided Government*. New York: Macmillan.

1996. *Divided Government*, 2nd ed. Needham, MA: Allyn and Bacon.

Forgette, Richard. 1997. "Reed's Rules and the Partisan Theory of Legislative Organization." *Polity* 29: 375–96.

Fox, Douglas M., and Charles Clapp. 1970. "The House Rules Committee and the Programs of the Kennedy and Johnson Administrations." *Midwest Journal of Political Science* 14: 667–72.

Fox, Harrison W., Jr., and Susan Webb Hammond. 1977. *Congressional Staffs: The Invisible Force in American Lawmaking*. New York: The Free Press.

Friedman, James. 1971. "A Non-cooperative Equilibrium for Supergames." *Review of Economic Studies* 38: 1–12.

Frohlich, Normal, and Joe A. Oppenheimer. 1978. *Modern Political Economy*. Englewood Cliffs, NJ: Prentice Hall.

1992. *Choosing Justice: An Experimental Approach to Ethical Theory*. Berkeley: University of California Press.

Frohlich, Normal, Joe A. Oppenheimer, and O. Young. 1971. *Political Leadership and Collective Goods*. Princeton, NJ: Princeton University Press.

Froman, Lewis. 1967. *The Congressional Process: Strategies, Rules and Procedures*. New Haven, CT: Little, Brown.

Froman, Lewis A., Jr., and Randall B. Ripley. 1965. "Conditions for Party Leadership: The Case of the House Democrats." *American Political Science Review* 59: 52–63.

Galloway, George B. 1968. *History of the United States House of Representatives*. New York: Crowell.

Galloway, George B., and Sidney Wise. 1976. *History of the House of Representatives*, 2nd ed. New York: Thomas Y. Crowell.

Gamm, Gerald, and Steven S. Smith. 2002. "Policy Leadership and the Development of the Modern Senate." In *Party, Process, and Political Change in Congress: New Perspectives on the History of Congress*, eds. David Brady and Mathew D. McCubbins, Stanford, CA: Stanford University Press, pp. 287–311.

Gerber, Alan, and Donald P. Green. 2000. "The Effects of Canvassing, Telephone Calls, and Direct Mail on Voter Turnout: A Field Experiment." *American Political Science Review* 94: 653–63.

Gilligan, Thomas W., and Keith Krehbiel. 1989. "Asymmetric Information and Legislative Rules with a Heterogeneous Committee." *American Journal of Political Science* 33: 459–90.

1990. "Organization of Informative Committees by a Rational Legislature." *American Journal of Political Science* 34: 531–64.

Gladieux, L. E., and T. R. Wolanin. 1976. *Congress and the Colleges: The National Politics of Higher Education.* Lexington, MA: D. C. Heath.

Goldreich, Samuel. 2003. "Old Becomes New Again As Senate Passes Energy Bill" *CQ Weekly*, August 2.

Goss, Carol F. 1972. "Military Committee Membership and Defense-Related Benefits in the House of Representatives." *Western Political Quarterly* 25: 215–33.

Grenzke, Janet M. 1989. "Candidate Attributes and PAC Contributions." *Western Political Quarterly* 42: 245–64.

Grose, Christian, and Antoine Yoshinaka. 2003. "The Electoral Consequences of Party Switching by Incumbent Members of Congress, Incumbent Legislators Who Switched Parties, 1947–2000." *Legislative Studies Quarterly* 27(1): 55–75.

Groseclose, Tim, and David C. King. 2001. "Committee Theories Reconsidered." In *Congress Reconsidered*, 7th ed., eds. Lawrence C. Dodd and Bruce I. Oppenheimer New York: Praeger Publishers, pp. 191–216.

Groseclose, Timothy, and Nolan McCarty. 2001. "The Politics of Blame: Bargaining Before an Audience." *American Journal of Political Science* 45: 100–19.

Groseclose, Timothy, and James M. Snyder. 1996. "Buying Supermajorities." *American Political Science Review* 90: 303–15.

2003. "Interpreting the Coefficient of Party Influence: Comment on Krehbiel." *Political Analysis* 11: 104–7.

Gryski, Gerard S., Gary Zuk, and Deborah J. Barrow. 1996. *The Federal Judiciary and Institutional Change.* Ann Arbor: University of Michigan Press.

Hager, Gregory L., and Jeffery C. Talbert. 2000. "Look for the Party Label: Party Influences on Voting in the U.S. House." *Legislative Studies Quarterly* 25: 75–99.

Hall, Richard. 1996. *Participation in Congress.* New Haven, CT: Yale University Press.

Hall, Richard, and Frank Wayman. 1990. "Buying Time: Moneyed Interests and the Mobilization of Bias in Congressional Committees." *American Political Science Review* 84: 797–820.

Hamilton, Alexander, James Madison, and John Jay. 1961 [1787]. *The Federalist*, ed. Clinton Rossiter. New York: New American Library.

Hasbrouck, Paul DeWitt. 1927. *Party Government in the House of Representatives.* New York: Macmillan.

Haseman J. K., and L. L. Kupper. 1979. "Analysis of Dichotomous Response Data from Certain Toxicological Experiments." *Biometrics* 35(1, March): 281–93.

Hastert, Dennis. 2004. *Speaker: Lessons from Forty Years in Coaching and Politics.* Washington, DC: Regnery.

Helland, Eric. 1999. "The Waiver Pork Barrel: Committee Membership and the Approval Time of Medicaid Waivers." *Contemporary Economic Policy* 17: 401–11.

Heller, William. 1997. "Bicameralism and Budget Deficits: The Effect of Parliamentary Structure on Government Spending." *Legislative Studies Quarterly* 22: 485–516.

Hennig, Robert. 1997. *Between the Margins: Party Politics and Committee Power in Conference Committees of the U.S. House of Representatives.* Ph.D dissertation, University of California, Berkeley.

Hinds, Asher C. 1907. *Hinds' Precedents of the House of Representatives of the United States.* Washington, DC: U.S. Government Printing Office.

Hojnacki, Marie, and David C. Kimball. 1998. "Organized Interests and the Decision of Whom to Lobby in Congress." *American Political Science Review* 92: 775–90.

Howell, William, Scott Adler, Charles Cameron, and Charles Riemann. 2000. "Divided Government and the Legislative Productivity of Congress, 1945–94." *Legislative Studies Quarterly* 25(2): 285–312.

Huber, John D. 1996. "The Vote of Confidence in Parliamentary Democracies," *The American Political Science Review* 90: 269–82.

Hulse, Carl. 2002. "An Abortion Bill Passes, but to an Uncertain Fate." *The New York Times*, July 24.

   2003. "The Supreme Court: Judicial Vacancies; G.O.P. Pushes Easier Rule On Filibusters." *The New York Times*, June 25.

Humes, Brian D., Elaine K. Swift, Richard M. Valelly, Kenneth Finegold, and Evelyn C. Fink. 2002. "Representation of the Antebellum South in the House of Representatives: Measuring the Impact of the Three-Fifths Clause." In *Party, Process, and Political Change in Congress: New Perspectives on the History of Congress*, eds. David Brady and Mathew D. McCubbins, Stanford, CA: Stanford University Press, pp. 452–66.

Hummel, Jeff, and Barry Weingast. 2004. "The Fugitive Slave Act of 1850: Symbolic Gesture or Rational Guarantee?" Paper presented at the History of Congress conference, April 9–10, Stanford, CA.

Hunter, Marjorie. 1965. "Appalachia Bill, Voted by House, Goes to Johnson." *The New York Times*, March 3.

Jackson, Matthew, and Boaz Moselle. 2002. "Coalition and Party Formation in a Legislative Voting Game." *Journal of Economic Theory* 103(1): 49–87.

Jacobs, John. 1995. *A Rage for Justice*. Berkeley: University of California Press.

Jacobson, Gary C. 1996. "The 1994 House Elections in Perspective." *Political Science Quarterly* 111: 203–23.

   2003. "Explaining the Ideological Polarization of the Congressional Parties in the Postwar Era." Paper presented at the History of Congress conference, December 5–6, San Diego.

Jenkins, Jeff. 2003. "Partisanship and Contested Election Cases in the House of Representatives, 1789–2002." Paper presented at the History of Congress conference, December 5–6, San Diego.

Jenkins, Jeffrey A., and Charles H. Stewart III. 2002. "Order from Chaos: The Transformation of the Committee System in the House, 1816–22." In *Party, Process, and Political Change in Congress: New Perspectives on the History of Congress*, eds. David Brady and Mathew D. McCubbins, Stanford, CA: Stanford University Press, pp. 195–236.

Jones, Charles O. 1968. "Joseph G. Cannon and Howard W. Smith: An Essay on the Limits of Leadership in the House of Representatives." *Journal of Politics* 30: 617–46.

Jones, David R., and Monika L. McDermott. 2004. "The Responsible Party Government Model in House and Senate Elections." *American Journal of Political Science* 48: 1–12.

Kalt, Joseph P., and Mark A. Zupan. 1990. "The Apparent Ideological Behavior of Legislators: Testing for Principal–Agent Slack in Political Institutions." *Journal of Law and Economics* 33: 103–31.

Kernell, Samuel. 1986. "The Early Nationalization of Political News in America." *American Political Development* 1: 255–78.

1997. "The Theory and Practice of Going Public." In *Do the Media Govern?* eds. Shanto Iyengar and Richard Reeves. Thousand Oaks, CA: Sage Publishing, pp. 323–33.

2001. "Rural Free Delivery As A Critical Test of Alternative Models of American Political Development: A Comment." *Studies in American Political Development* 15: 103–12.

Kernell, Samuel, and Michael P. McDonald. 1999. "Congress and America's Political Development: The Transformation of the Post Office from Patronage to Service." *American Journal of Political Science* 43: 792–811.

Key, V. O. 1966. *The Responsible Electorate*. Cambridge, MA: Harvard University Press.

Kiewiet, D. Roderick. 1983. *Macroeconomics and Micropolitics: The Electoral Effects of Economic Issues*. Chicago: University of Chicago Press.

1998. "Restrictions on Floor Amendments in the House of Representatives." Paper presented at the Comparative Legislative Research Conference, April 16–18, 1998. The University of Iowa, Iowa City.

Kiewiet, D. Roderick, and Donald R. Kinder. 1981. "Sociotropic Politics: The American Case." *British Journal of Political Science* 11: 129–61.

Kiewiet, D. Roderick, and Mathew D. McCubbins. 1985. "Congressional Appropriations and the Electoral Connection." *Journal of Politics* 47: 59–82.

1988. "Presidential Influence on Congressional Appropriations Decisions." *American Journal of Political Science* 32: 713–36.

1991. *The Logic of Delegation: Congressional Parties and the Appropriations Process*. Chicago: University of Chicago Press.

Kiewiet, Roderick, and Kevin Roust. 2003. "Legislative End Game: An Historical Analysis of the Motion To Recommit." Paper presented at the History of Congress conference, December 5–6, San Diego.

King, Anthony. 1983. *Both Ends of the Avenue: The Presidency, the Executive Branch, and Congress in the 1980s*. Washington, DC: American Enterprise Institute.

King, David. 1997. *Turf Wars: How Congressional Committees Claim Jurisdiction*. Chicago: University of Chicago Press.

King, David C., and Richard Zeckhauser. 2003. "Congressional Vote Options." *Legislative Studies Quarterly* 28: 387–411.

King, Gary. 1989. *Unifying Political Methodology: The Likelihood Theory of Statistical Inference*. Cambridge, UK and New York: Cambridge University Press. Reprinted Ann Arbor: University of Michigan Press, 1998.

Kingdon, John. 1973. *Congressmen's Voting Decisions*. New York: Harper.

Koger, Greg. 2003. "Why a 2/3 Cloture Rule? Institutional Choice in the U.S. Senate, 1913–1919." Paper presented at the History of Congress conference, December 5–6, San Diego.

Koszczuk, Jackie, and Jonathan Allen. 2003. "Late-Night Medicare Vote Drama Triggers Some Unexpected Alliances." *CQ Weekly*, November 29.

Kramer, Gerald H. 1977. "Dynamic Model of Political Equilibrium." *Journal of Economic Theory* 16: 310–34.

Krehbiel, Keith. 1985. "Obstruction and Representativeness in Legislatures." *American Journal of Political Science* 29: 643–59.

1991. *Information and Legislative Organization*. Ann Arbor: University of Michigan Press.

1993. "Where's the Party?" *British Journal of Political Science* 23: 235–66.

1995. "Cosponsors and Wafflers from A to Z." *American Journal of Political Science* 39: 906–23.

1996. "Committee Power, Leadership, and the Median Voter: Evidence from the Smoking Ban." *Journal of Law, Economics, and Organization* 11: 237–59.

1997. "Restrictive Rules Reconsidered." *American Journal of Political Science* 41: 919–44.

1998. *Pivotal Politics: A Theory of U.S. Lawmaking.* Chicago: University of Chicago Press.

1999. "The Party Effect from A to Z and Beyond." *Journal of Politics* 61: 832–40.

2000. "Party Discipline and Measures of Partisanship." *American Journal of Political Science* 44: 212–27.

2003. "The Coefficient of Party Influence." *Political Analysis* 11: 96–104.

2004. "Partisan RollRates in a Nonpartisan Legislature." Research Paper No. 1870R.

Krehbiel, Keith, and Adam Meirowitz. 2002. "Minority Rights and Majority Power: Theoretical Consequences of the Motion to Recommit." *Legislative Studies Quarterly* 27: 191–218.

Krutz, Glen S. 2001. *Hitching a Ride: Omnibus Legislating in the U.S. Congress.* Columbus: Ohio State University Press.

Kupper L. L., and J. K. Haseman. 1978. "The Use of a Correlated Binomial Model for the Analysis of Certain Toxicological Experiments." *Biometrics* 34(1, March): 69–76.

Labaton, Stephen. 1993. "Clinton Expected to Change Makeup of Federal Courts." *New York Times,* March 8, pp. A1, A9.

Ladha, Krishna. 1991. "A Spatial Model of Legislative Voting with Perceptual Error." *Public Choice* 68: 151–74.

Lakoff, George, and Mark Johnson. 1980. *Metaphors We Live By.* Chicago: The University of Chicago Press.

Lancaster, John. 2001. "Senate Republicans Try to Regroup: GOP Caucus Unites Behind Lott as Leader in the Wake of Jeffords's Defection," *The Washington Post,* May 26, p. A.18

Lapham, Louis J. 1954. *Party Leadership and the House Committee on Rules.* Ph.D. Dissertation, Harvard University.

Lapinski, John. 2004. "Measuring and Evaluating Legislative Performance, 1877–1946." Paper presented at the History of Congress conference, April 9–10, Stanford, CA.

Laver, Michael, and Norman Schofield. 1991. *Multiparty Government: The Politics of Coalition in Europe.* Oxford: Oxford University Press.

Laver, Michael, and Kenneth A. Shepsle. 1996. *Making and Breaking Governments: Cabinets and Legislatures in Parliamentary Democracies.* Cambridge and New York: Cambridge University Press.

Lawrence, Eric D., Forrest Maltzman, and Steven S. Smith. 1999. "Who Wins? Party Effects in Legislative Voting." Paper presented at the annual meeting of the Midwest Political Science Association, April 15–17, Chicago.

In press. "Who Wins? Party Effects in Legislative Voting." *Legislative Studies Quarterly.*

Lawrence, Eric, Forrest Maltzman, and Paul J. Wahlbeck. 2001. "The Politics of Speaker Cannon's Committee Assignments." *American Journal of Political Science* 45(July): 551–62.

Lazarus, Jeff, and Nathan W. Monroe. 2003. "The Speaker's Discretion: Conference Committee Appointments from the 97th–106th Congresses." Paper presented at the annual meeting of the American Political Science Association, August 28–31, Philadelphia.

Letter to Henry Hyde. 1999. Downloaded 11/14/2004 from: *http://www.house.gov/ judiciary_democrats/lettertohydeguns.htm*

Levitt, Steven D., and James M. Poterba. 1999. "Congressional Distributive Politics and State Economic Performance." *Public Choice* 99: 185–216.

Levitt, Steven D., and James M. Snyder. 1995. "Political Parties and the Distribution of Federal Outlays." *American Journal of Political Science* 39: 958–80.

Londregan, John. 2000. "Estimating Legislators' Preferred Points." *Political Analysis* 8: 35–56.

Longley, Lawrence, and Walter Oleszek. 1989. *Bicameral Politics: Conference Committees in Congress.* New Haven, CT: Yale University Press.

Lowi, Theodore J. 1969. *The End of Liberalism: Ideology, Policy, and the Crisis of Public Authority.* New York: Norton.

Lupia, Arthur, and Gisela Sin. 2003. "The Constitutional Theory of Congressional Power: How the Senate and President Affect the Balance of Power in the House." Working paper. Available at *www.personal.Umich.edu/~lupia.*

Lupia, Arthur, and Kaare Strøm. 1995. "Coalition Termination and the Strategic Timing of Parliamentary Elections." *The American Political Science Review* 89(3): 648–65.

MacKaye, William R. 1963. *A New Coalition Takes Control: The House Rules Committee Fight Of 1961.* New York: McGraw-Hill.

MacKuen, Michael Bruce, Robert S. Erikson, and James A. Stimson. 1989. "Macropartisanship." *American Political Science Review* 83: 1125–42.

Maddala, G. S. 1983. *Limited-dependent and Qualitative Variables in Econometrics.* New York: Cambridge University Press.

Magar, Eric. 2001. *Bully Pulpits: Posturing, Bargaining and Polarization in the Legislative Process of the Americas.* Unpublished Ph.D. dissertation, University of California, San Diego.

Maltzman, Forrest. 1997. *Competing Principals: Committees, Parties, and the Organization of Congress.* Ann Arbor: University of Michigan Press.

Maltzman, Forrest, and Steven S. Smith. 1994. "Principals, Goals, Dimensionality, and Congressional Committees." *Legislative Studies Quarterly* 19(4): 457–76.

Manley, John F. 1970. *The Politics of Finance: The House Committee on Ways and Means.* Boston: Little, Brown.

Markey, Edward J. 2004. Testimony on House Floor June 16, 2004. Retrieved on November 19, 2004, from: *www.vote-smart.org.*

Marshall, Bryan W. 2002. "Explaining the Role of Restrictive Rules in the Postreform House." *Legislative Studies Quarterly* 27: 61–85.

Mathews, Donald R., and James A. Stimson. 1975. *Yays and Nays: Normal Decisionmaking in the U.S. House of Representatives.* New York: Wiley.

Matsunaga, Spark M., and Ping Chen. 1976. *Rulemakers of the House.* Urbana: University of Illinois Press.

Mayhew, David R. 1974. *Congress: The Electoral Connection.* New Haven, CT: Yale University Press.

    1991. *Divided We Govern: Party Control, Lawmaking, and Investigations, 1946–1990.* New Haven, CT: Yale University Press.

2000. *America's Congress: Actions in the Public Sphere, James Madison Through Newt Gingrich.* New Haven, CT: Yale University Press.

2002. *Electoral Realignments: A Critique of an American Genre.* New Haven, CT: Yale University Press.

McCarty, Nolan M., Keith T. Poole, and Howard Rosenthal. 1997. *Income Redistribution and the Realignment of American Politics.* Washington, DC: The AEI Press.

2001. "The Hunt for Party Discipline in Congress." *American Political Science Review* 95: 673–87.

2002. "Congress and the Territorial Expansion of the United States." In *Party, Process, and Political Change in Congress: New Perspectives on the History of Congress,* eds. David Brady and Mathew D. McCubbins. Stanford, CA: Stanford University Press, pp. 392–451.

McConachie, Lauros G. 1974 [1898]. *Congressional Committees.* New York: B. Franklin.

McConnell, Grant. 1966. *Private Power and American Democracy.* New York: Knopf.

McCubbins, Mathew D. 1985. "The Legislative Design of Regulatory Structure." *American Journal of Political Science* 29(4, November): 721–48.

1991. "Government on Lay-Away: Federal Spending and Deficits Under Divided Party Control." In *The Politics of Divided Government,* eds. Gary W. Cox and Samuel Kernell. Boulder, CO: Westview Press, pp. 113–53.

McKelvey, Richard. 1976. "Intransitivities in Multidimensional Voting Models, with Some Implications for Agenda Control." *Journal of Economic Theory* 2: 472–82.

McNollgast. 1994. "Legislative Intent: The Use of Positive Political Theory in Statutory Interpretation." *Journal of Law and Contemporary Problems* 57: 3–37.

1995. "Political Control of the Judiciary: A Positive Theory of Judicial Doctrine and the Rule of Law." *The University of Southern California Law Review* 68: 1631–83.

Miller, Warren E., and Donald E. Stokes. 1963. "Constituency Influence in Congress." *American Political Science Review* 57: 45–56.

Monroe, Nathan W. 2004. "The Policy Impact of Unified Government: Evidence from the 2000 Presidential Election." Paper presented at the annual meeting of the American Political Science Association, September 2–5, Chicago.

Munger, Michael C., and William Mitchell. 1991. "Economic Models of Interest Groups: An Introductory Survey," *American Journal of Political Science* 35: 512–46.

Murphy, James T. 1974. "Political Parties and the Porkbarrel: Party Conflict and Cooperation in House Public Works Committee Decision-Making." *American Political Science Review* 68: 169–86.

Nather, David. 2003. "Contrite Chairman Does Not Quell Calls for More GOP Comity." *CQ Weekly,* July 26, 2003.

Nelson, Garrison, and Clark H. Bensen. 1993. *Committees in the U.S. Congress, 1947–1992.* Washington, DC: Congressional Quarterly.

Nokken, Timothy P. 2000. "Dynamics of Congressional Loyalty: Party Defection and Roll Call Behavior, 1947–1997." *Legislative Studies Quarterly* 25: 417–44.

2004. "Roll Call Behavior in the Absence of Electoral Constraints: Shirking in Lame Duck Sessions of the House of Representatives, 1879–1933." Unpublished paper.

Nokken, Timothy, and Craig Goodman. 2003. "Roll Call Behavior and Career Advancement: Analyzing Committee Assignments from Reconstruction to the New Deal." Paper presented at the History of Congress conference, December 5–6, San Diego.

Nokken, Timothy P., and Brian R. Sala. 2002. "Institutional Evolution and the Rise of the Tuesday–Thursday Club in the House of Representatives." In *Party, Process, and Political Change in Congress: New Perspectives on the History of Congress,* eds. David Brady and Mathew D. McCubbins, Stanford, CA: Stanford University Press, pp. 270–86.

Odegard, Peter H., and E. Allen Helms. 1938. *American Politics: A Study in Political Dynamics.* New York: Harper and Brothers.

Oleszek, Walter J. 1984. *Congressional Procedure and the Policy Process,* 2nd ed. Washington, DC: CQ Press.

    1996. *Congressional Procedures and the Policy Process,* 4th ed. Washington, DC: CQ Press.

    1998. "A Pre-Twentieth Century Look at the House Committee on Rules." Report for the Committee on Rules, available from: *http://www.house.gov/rules/pre20th_rules.htm.* Accessed 3/18/05.

    2001. *Congressional Procedures and the Policy Process,* 5th ed. Washington, DC: CQ Press.

    2004. *Congressional Procedure and the Policy Process,* 6th ed. Washington, DC: CQ Press.

Olson, Mancur. 1965. *The Logic of Collective Action.* Cambridge, MA: Harvard University Press.

Oppenheimer, Bruce I. 1977. "The Rules Committee: New Arm of Leadership in a Decentralized House." In *Congress Reconsidered,* eds. Lawrence C. Dodd and Bruce I. Oppenheimer. New York: Praeger Publishers, pp. 96–116.

    1981. "The Changing Relationship Between House Leadership and the Committee on Rules." In *Understanding Congressional Leadership,* ed. Frank Mackaman. Washington, DC: Congressional Quarterly, pp. 207–25.

    1983. *History of the Committee on Rules.* Washington, D.C.: Government Printing Office.

    1994. "The House Traffic Cop: The Rules Committee." In *Encyclopedia of the American Legislative System,* ed. Joel Silbey. New York: Scribners, pp. 1049–66.

Ota, Alan K., Liriel Higa, and Siobhan Hughes. 2003. "Fracas in Ways and Means Overshadows Approval of Pension Overhaul Measure." *CQ Weekly.*

Palmquist, Bradley. 1999. "Analysis of Proportion Data." Paper prepared for the annual meeting of the Political Methodology Society, July 15–19, College Station, Texas.

Parker, Flenn, and Suzanne L. Parker. 1985. *Factions in House Committees.* Knoxville: University of Tennessee Press.

Patterson, Kelly, David B. Magleby, and James A. Thurber. 2002. "Campaign Consultants and Responsible Party Government." In *Responsible Partisanship? The Evolution of American Political Parties Since 1950,* eds. John C. Green and Paul S. Herrnson. Lawrence: University of Kansas Press, pp. 101–20.

Peterson, Mark A. 1994. "Health Care and the Hill: Why Is This Year Different from All Others?" *PS: Political Science and Politics* 27: 202–7.

    2001. "The Geometry of Multidimensional Quadratic Utility in Models of Parliamentary Roll Call Voting." *Political Analysis* 9: 211–26.

    2005. *Spatial Models of Parliamentary Voting.* Cambridge: Cambridge University Press.

Poole, Keith T., and Howard Rosenthal. 1991. "Patterns of Congressional Voting." *American Journal of Political Science* 35: 228–78.

1997. *Congress: A Political–Economic History of Roll Call Voting.* New York: Oxford University Press.

2001. "D-NOMINATE after 10 Years: A Comparative Update to Congress: A Political–Economic History of Roll-Call Voting." *Legislative Studies Quarterly* 26: 5–29.

Pressman, Jeffrey L. 1966. *House vs. Senate: Conflict in the Appropriations Process.* New Haven, CT: Yale University Press.

Ramseyer, J. Mark, and Frances Rosenbluth. 1993. *Japan's Political Marketplace.* Cambridge, MA: Harvard University Press.

Ranney, Austin. 1951. "Toward A More Responsible Two-Party System: A Commentary." *American Political Science Review* 45: 488–99.

Reed, Thomas Brackett. 1887. "Rules of the House of Representatives." *The Century Magazine*, March.

Renka, Russell D., and Daniel E. Ponder. 2001. "Musical Chairs: The Changing Seniority System in Congress." Prepared for delivery at the 97th annual meeting of the American Political Science Association, August 30–September 2, San Francisco.

Riker, William H. 1962. *The Theory of Political Coalitions.* New Haven, CT: Yale University Press.

1980. "Implications from the Disequilibrium of Majority Rule for the Study of Institutions." *American Political Science Review* 74(2, June): 432–46.

Ripley, Randall B. 1964. "The Party Whip Organizations in the United States House of Representatives." *American Political Science Review* 58(3, September): 561–76.

Ripley, Randall B., and Grace A. Franklin. 1980. *Congress, the Bureaucracy, and Public Policy.* Rev. ed. Homewood, IL: Dorsey Press.

Roberts, Jason. 2003. "Minority Rights and Majority Power: Conditional Party Government and the Motion to Recommit in the House, 1909–2000." Working paper.

Roberts, Jason, and Steven S. Smith. 2003. "The Evolution of Agenda-Setting Institutions in the House and Senate." Paper presented at the History of Congress conference, December 5–6, San Diego.

Roberts, Steven V. 1983b. "Democrats Reward Loyalty in Giving Assignments," *New York Times*, January 6, p. A25.

1983a. "The Democrats Get Even." *New York Times*, January 9, p. E1.

Robinson, James A. 1959. "The Role of the Rules Committee in Arranging the Program of the U.S. House of Representatives." *Western Political Quarterly* 12: 653–69.

1963. *The House Rules Committee.* Indianapolis: Bobbs-Merrill.

Rohde, David W. 1991. *Parties and Leaders in the Postreform House.* Chicago: University of Chicago Press.

Rohde, David, and Kenneth Shepsle. 1973. "Democratic Committee Assignments in the House of Representatives: Strategic Aspects of a Social Choice Process." *American Political Science Review* 67: 889–905.

*Roll Call.* 1998. "Solomon Leaves Rules to Drier: Committee Sees Subtle Changes." April 30.

Romer, Thomas, and Howard Rosenthal. 1978. "Political Resource Allocation, Controlled Agendas, and the Status Quo." *Public Choice* 33: 27–43.

Rosenbaum, David E. 1995. "House Approves a Line-Item Veto for the President." *The New York Times*, February 7.

Rosenthal, Howard. 1990. "The Setter Model." In *Advances in the Spatial Theory of Voting*, eds. James M. Enelow and Melvin J. Hinich. New York: Cambridge University Press, pp. 199–234.

Rybicki, Elizabeth. 2003. "Unresolved Differences: Bicameral Negotiations in Congress, 1877–2002." Paper presented at the History of Congress conference, December 5–6, San Diego.

Sala, Brian R. 2002. "Party Loyalty and Committee Leadership in the House, 1921–40." In *Party, Process, and Political Change in Congress: New Perspectives on the History of Congress*, eds. David Brady and Mathew D. McCubbins, Stanford: Stanford University Press, pp. 166–92.

Salisbury, Robert. 1969. "An Exchange Theory of Interest Groups." *Midwest Journal of Political Science* 13: 1–32.

Schattschneider, E. E. 1942. *Party Government*. New York: Holt, Rinehart and Winston. 1960. *The Semisovereign People*. New York: Holt, Rinehart and Winston.

Schickler, Eric. 2000. "Institutional Change in the House of Representatives, 1867–1998: A Test of Partisan and Ideological Power Balance Models." *American Political Science Review* 94: 269–88.

2001. *Disjointed Pluralism: Institutional Innovation and the Development of the U.S. Congress*. Princeton, NJ: Princeton University Press.

Schickler, Eric, and Andrew Rich. 1997. "Controlling the Floor: Politics as Procedural Coalitions in the House." *American Journal of Political Science* 41: 1340–75.

Schickler, Eric, and Greg Wawro. 2004. "Cloture Reform Reconsidered." Paper presented at the History of Congress conference, April 9–10, Stanford, CA.

Schiller, Wendy. 2003. "Climbing and Clawing Their Way to the U.S. Senate: Political Ambition and Career Building 1880–1913." Paper presented at the History of Congress conference, December 5–6, San Diego.

Schwartz, Thomas. 1977. "Collective Choice, Separation of Issues and Vote Trading." *The American Political Science Review* 71: 999–1010.

Seelye, Katharine Q. 1995. "House Approves Easing of Rules on U.S. Searches." *The New York Times*, February 9.

Shelley, Mack C. 1983. *The Permanent Majority: the Conservative Coalition in the United States Congress*, Tuscaloosa: University of Alabama Press.

Shepsle, Kenneth A. 1979. "Institutional Arrangements and Equilibrium in Multidimensional Voting Models." *American Journal of Political Science* 23: 27–59.

1989. "The Changing Textbook Congress." In *Can the Government Govern?* ed. John Chubb and Paul Peterson. Washington, DC: The Brookings Institution.

Shepsle, Kenneth A., and Barry R. Weingast. 1981. "Structure Induced Equilibrium and Legislative Choice." *Public Choice* 37: 509–19.

1984a. "Legislative Politics and Budget Outcomes." In *Federal Budget Policy in the 1980s*, eds. Gregory B. Mills and John L. Palmer, Washington, DC: Urban Institute, pp. 343–68.

1984b. "Uncovered Sets and Sophisticated Voting Outcomes with Implications for Agenda Control." *American Journal of Political Science* 28: 49–74.

1984c. "When Do Rules of Procedure Matter?" *Journal of Politics* 46: 206–221.

1987. "The Institutional Foundations of Committee Power." *American Political Science Review* 81: 85–104.

1994. "Positive Theories of Congressional Institutions." *Legislative Studies Quarterly* 19(2, May): 149–79.

1995. "Positive Theories of Congressional Institutions." In *Positive Theories of Congressional Institutions*, eds. Kenneth A. Shepsle and Barry R. Weingast. Ann Arbor: University of Michigan Press, pp. 5–37.

Sinclair, Barbara. 1983. *Majority Leadership in the U.S. House*. Baltimore: Johns Hopkins University Press.

1995. *Legislators, Leaders, and Lawmaking: The U.S. House of Representatives in the Postreform Era*. Baltimore: Johns Hopkins University Press.

1997. *Unorthodox Lawmaking: New Legislative Process in the U.S. Congress*. Washington, DC: CQ Press.

2002a. "Do Parties Matter?" In *Party, Process, and Political Change: New Perspectives on the History of Congress*, eds. David Brady and Mathew D. McCubbins. Stanford, CA: Stanford University Press, pp. 36–63.

2002b. "The Dream Fulfilled? Party Development in Congress, 1950–2000." In *Responsible Partisanship? The Evolution of American Political Parties Since 1950*, eds. John C. Green and Paul S. Herrnson. Lawrence: University of Kansas Press, pp. 121–40.

Sloss, Judith. 1973. "Stable Outcomes in Majority Voting Games." *Public Choice* 15: 19–48.

Smith, Steven S. 1989. *Call to Order: Floor Politics in the House and Senate*. Washington, DC: The Brookings Institution.

2002. "Positive Theories of Congressional Parties." *Legislative Studies Quarterly* 25: 193–215.

Smith, Steven S., and Christopher J. Deering. 1990. *Committees in Congress*, 2nd ed. Washington, DC: CQ Press.

Smith, Steven S., and Gerald Gamm. 2001. "The Dynamics of Party Government in Congress." In *Congress Reconsidered*, 7th ed., eds. Lawrence C. Dodd and Bruce I. Oppenheimer. Washington, DC: CQ Press, pp. 245–69.

Smith, Vernon L. 2003. "Constructivist and Ecological Rationality in Economics." *American Economic Review* 93: 465–508.

Snyder, James M., and Tim Groseclose. 2000. 'Estimating Party Influence in Congressional Roll Call Voting.' *American Journal of Political Science* 44(2): 193–211.

2001. "Estimating Party Influence on Congressional Roll Call Voting: Regression Coefficients vs. Classification Success." *American Political Science Review* 95(3): 689–98.

Snyder, James M., and Michael M. Ting. 2001. "Party Labels, Roll-Call Votes and Elections." Paper presented at Midwest Political Science Association, April 19–22, Chicago.

2002. "An Informational Rationale for Political Parties." *American Journal of Political Science* 46: 90–110.

Steiner, Gilbery Y. 1951. *The Congressional Conference Committee: Seventieth to Eightieth Congresses*. Urbana: University of Illinois Press.

Stewart, Charles H., III. 1989. *Budget Reform Politics: The Design of the Appropriations Process in the House of Representatives, 1865–1921*. New York: Cambridge University Press.

1991. "Lessons From the Post–Civil War Era." In *The Politics of Divided Government*, eds. Gary Cox and Samuel Kernell. Boulder, CO: Westview Press, pp. 203–38.

2004. "Architect or Tactician? Henry Clay and the Institutional Development of the U.S. House of Representatives." Paper presented at the History of Congress conference, April 9–10, Stanford, CA.

Stigler, George J. 1971. "The Theory of Economic Regulation." *Bell Journal of Economics and Management Science* 2(1): 3–21.

Stolberg, Sheryl Gay. 2005. "Arctic Refuge Oil Drilling Is Near Fact, Backers Say." *New York Times.* New York, N.Y. April 30, 2005. p. A10

Strahan, Randall. 2002. "Leadership and Institutional Change in the Nineteenth-Century House." In *Party, Process, and Political Change in Congress: New Perspectives on the History of Congress*, eds. David Brady and Mathew D. McCubbins, Stanford, CA: Stanford University Press, pp. 237–69.

Stratmann, Thomas. 2000. "Congressional Voting Over Legislative Careers: Shifting Positions and Changing Constraints." *American Political Science Review* 94: 665–76.

Strøm, Kaare. 1990. *Minority Government and Majority Rule.* New York: Cambridge University Press.

Studenski, Paul, and Herman E. Krooss. 1963. *Financial History of the United States: Fiscal, Monetary, Banking, and Tariff, Including Financial Administration and State and Local Finance.* New York: McGraw-Hill.

Sullivan, John L., and Robert E. O'Connor. 1972. "Electoral Choice and Popular Control of Public Policy: The Case of the 1966 House Elections." *The American Political Science Review* 66: 1256–68.

Sundquist, James. L. 1981. *The Decline and Resurgence of Congress.* Washington, DC: The Brookings Institution.

  1983. *Dynamics of the Party System: Alignment and Realignment of Political Parties in the United States.* Washington, DC: The Brookings Institution.

  1988. "Needed: A Political Theory for the New Era of Coalition Government in the United States." *Political Science Quarterly* 103: 613–35.

Theriault, Sean. 2002. "Lawmaking in the U.S. Congress: Where and How Legislation Dies." Paper presented at the Annual Conference for the Southern Political Science Association, November 7–9, Savannah, GA.

Theriault, Sean M., and Barry R. Weingast. 2002. "Agenda Manipulation, Strategic Voting, and Legislative Details in the Compromise of 1850." In *Party, Process, and Political Change in Congress: New Perspectives on the History of Congress*, eds. David Brady and Mathew D. McCubbins. Stanford, CA: Stanford University Press.

Thompson, Joel A. 1986. "Bringing Home the Bacon: The Politics of Pork Barrel in the North Carolina Legislature." *Legislative Studies Quarterly* 11(1): 91–108.

Thorson, Greg, and Tasina Nitzschke. N.D. "Testing the Three Theories of Legislative Organization: An Examination of Rule Assignments during the Postreform Period." Available at *www.morris.umn.edu/~gthorson.*

Tirole, Jean. 1988. *The Theory of Industrial Organization.* MIT, Press: Cambridge, MA.

Tolchin, Martin. 1981. "The Troubles of Tip O'Neill." *New York Times,* August 16.

  2001. *The Research Methods Knowledge Base,* 2nd ed. Cincinnati: Atomic Dog Publishing.

Trochim, William. 2001. The Research Methods Knowledge Base. Atomic Dog Publishing. Cincinnati, OH.

Tsebelis, George. 2002. *Veto Players: How Political Institutions Work.* Princeton, NJ: Princeton University Press.

U.S. House of Representatives, Committee on Rules. 2004. Downloaded 11/14/2004 from: *http://usinfo.org/house/rule/beg.htm.*

Van Houweling, Rob. 2003. "An Evolving End Game: The Partisan Use of Conference Committees in the Post-Reform Congress." Paper presented at the History of Congress conference, December 5–6, San Diego.

Vogler, David J. 1970. "Patterns of One House Dominance in Congressional Conference Committees." *Midwest Journal of Political Science* 14: 303–20.

1971. *The Third House: Conference Committees in the United States Congress.* Evanston, IL: Northwestern University Press.

Volden, Craig, and Brandice Canes-Wrone. 2004. "Who Parties? Responsiveness to Party Pressures in Congress." Paper presented at the History of Congress conference, April 9–10, Stanford, CA.

Wattenberg, Martin P. 1998. *The Decline of American Political Parties, 1952–1996.* Cambridge, MA: Harvard University Press.

Wawro, Gregory. 2000. *Legislative Entrepreneurship in the U.S. House of Representatives.* Ann Arbor: University of Michigan Press.

Weingast, Barry R. 1979. "A Rational Choice Perspective on Congressional Norms." *American Journal of Political Science* 23: 245–62.

1995. "The Economic Role of Political Institutions: Market-Preserving Federalism and Economic Development." *Journal of Law, Economics, & Organization* 11: 1–32.

Weingast, Barry R., and William Marshall. 1988. "The Industrial Organization of Congress." *Journal of Political Economy* 96: 132–63.

Weingast, Barry R., and Mark Moran. 1983. "Bureaucratic Discretion or Congressional Control: Regulatory Policy Making by the Federal Trade Commission." *Journal of Political Economy* 91: 765–800.

Weingast, Barry, Kenneth Shepsle, and Christopher Johnson. 1981. "The Political Economy of Benefits and Costs: A Neoclassical Approach to Distributive Politics." *Journal of Political Economy* 89: 642–64.

White, John Kenneth. 1992. "Responsible Party Government in America." *Perspectives on Political Science* 21: 80–90.

Williams, D. A. 1975. "The Analysis of Binary Responses from Toxicological Experiments Involving Reproduction and Teratogenicity." *Biometrics* 31(4, December), pp. 949–52.

Wilson, Rick K. 1986. "What Was It Worth to Be on a Committee in the US House, 1889–1913?" *Legislative Studies Quarterly* 11: 47–63.

Wilson, Woodrow. 1908. *Constitutional Government in the United States.* New York: Columbia University Press.

1956 [1885]. *Congressional Government.* New York: Meridian Books.

Wolf, Jim. 2004. "Veteran Texas Democrat Switches to Republicans." Washington, DC: Reuters.

Wolfensberger, Donald. 2003. "The Motion to Recommit in the House: The Creation, Evisceration, and Restoration of a Minority Right." Paper presented at the History of Congress conference, December 5–6, San Diego.

Young, Roland Arnold. 1956. *Congressional Politics in the Second World War.* New York: Columbia University Press.

Zuk, Gary, Gerard S. Gryski, and Deborah J. Barrow. 1993. "Partisan Transformation of the Federal Judiciary, 1896–1992." *American Politics Quarterly* 21: 439–57.

# Index

# Author Index

For EU product safety concerns, contact us at Calle de José Abascal, 56–1°,
28003 Madrid, Spain or eugpsr@cambridge.org.

www.ingramcontent.com/pod-product-compliance
Ingram Content Group UK Ltd.
Pitfield, Milton Keynes, MK11 3LW, UK
UKHW020348140625
459647UK00019B/2354